Public Opinion

Public Opinion

Measuring the American Mind

Fourth Edition

Barbara A. Bardes and Robert W. Oldendick

ROWMAN & LITTLEFIELD PUBLISHERS, INC.
Lanham • Boulder • New York • Toronto • Plymouth, UK

Published by Rowman & Littlefield Publishers, Inc.
A wholly owned subsidary of The Rowman & Littlefield Publishing Group, Inc.
4501 Forbes Boulevard, Suite 200, Lanham, Maryland 20706
http://www.rowmanlittlefield.com

10 Thornbury Road, Plymouth PL6 7PP, United Kingdom

British Library Cataloguing in Publication Information Available

Library of Congress Cataloging-in-Publication Data
Bardes, Barbara A.
  Public opinion : measuring the American mind / Barbara A. Bardes and Robert
W. Oldendick. — 4th ed.
      p. cm.
  Includes bibliographical references and index.
  ISBN 978-1-4422-1502-3 (paper : alk. paper) — ISBN 978-1-4422-4150-3 (ebook)
  1. Public opinion—United States. 2. Public opinion polls. I. Oldendick, Robert W.
II. Title.
  HN90.P8B37 2012
  303.3'80973—dc23

                                                                    2012003175

♾™ The paper used in this publication meets the minimum requirements of
American National Standard for Information Sciences—Permanence of Paper
for Printed Library Materials, ANSI/NISO Z39.48-1992.

Printed in the United States of America

Contents

List of Figures, Boxes, and Tables   ix

Preface   xiii

PART I: PUBLIC OPINION AND AMERICAN DEMOCRACY

1 **Public Opinion and American Democracy**   3
   Defining Public Opinion   4
   Does Public Opinion Matter?   9
   Public Opinion versus Public Judgment   12
   Opinions, Attitudes, and Beliefs   14
   The Current Environment   15
   The Plan of the Book   15
   Polls, Polling, and the Internet   16

2 **Measuring American Opinion: The Origins of Polling**   17
   The Origins of Public Opinion Polling   18
   The Development of Survey Research   19
   The Election of 1948: A Temporary Setback   21
   After 1948: Continued Growth   24
   A Surge in Telephone Interviewing: The Development
     of Random-Digit Dialing   25
   The Rise of Internet Polling   26
   Polls, Polling, and the Internet   27

PART II: HOW ARE OPINIONS MEASURED AND USED?

3   How Public Opinion Data Are Used   31
Using Public Opinion in Political Campaigns   31
The Use of Public Opinion Polling by Elected Officeholders   36
The Use of Polling Data by Government Agencies   39
Public Opinion and Interest Groups   44
The Use of Polling by the Media   46
Tracking Presidential Approval Ratings   49
The Call-In Poll   51
The Use of Public Opinion Data in Academic Research   52
Polls, Polling, and the Internet   55

4   How Are Opinions Measured?   57
Modes of Survey Data Collection   58
Populations of Interest   58
Selecting a Sample   59
Random-Digit Dialing   62
Sampling for Electronic Data Collection   64
Sampling Error   65
Sample Size   66
Questionnaire Design   67
Data Analysis   79
Polls, Polling, and the Internet   84

PART III: WHAT DO AMERICANS BELIEVE?

5   The Sources of Opinions   87
The Political Learning of Children and Adolescents   89
The Influence of Formal Education   93
The Curriculum   94
Ritual and Ceremony   95
The Teachers   95
School Behaviors   97
The Influence of Ethnic Identity   99
Religion and Public Opinion   102
Gender and Opinions   105
The Influence of Peers   106
Generational Influences on Opinion   108
The Media's Influence on Opinion   110
Polls, Polling, and the Internet   116

6   What the Public Knows about Politics   117
Early Empirical Investigations   118
The Unchanging American Voter   120

Applying Democratic Principles 123
Group Differences in Knowledge 127
The Consequences of Political Knowledge 129
A Glass-Half-Full Perspective? 129
Polls, Polling, and the Internet 130

7 **Political Orientations** 131
Political Ideology 132
Party Identification 139
Confidence in Institutions 144
Trust in Government 147
Power of the Federal Government 151
Summary 155
Polls, Polling, and the Internet 157

8 **Public Opinion on Social-Welfare Issues** 159
Social-Welfare Issues 160
Social Security 161
Education 165
Health Care 167
Assisting the Needy 173
The Environment 177
The Issue of Global Warming 182
Group Differences in Attitudes 183
Summary 186
Polls, Polling, and the Internet 187

9 **Americans' Views on Racial Issues** 189
Racial Desegregation 190
Fair Employment Practices 193
Affirmative Action 194
Government Aid to Minority Groups 198
Spending on Racial Issues 202
Other Issues of Race: Historical and Contemporary 205
The Increasing Influence of Hispanics 211
Summary 213
Polls, Polling, and the Internet 215

10 **Public Opinion on Highly Controversial Issues** 217
The Politics of Crime and Criminal Justice 218
The Politics of Individual Rights 225
Public Opinion toward Abortion 226
Public Opinion on Gay Issues 232
American Views on Gun Control 234
Thinking about Weapons and Government Controls 236

Immigration: A Mind Divided   238
Summary   241
Polls, Polling, and the Internet   242

11 **How Americans View Foreign and Defense Policies**   245
American Opinion in the Post-9/11 World   246
Public Opinion and Foreign Policy: Which Opinions?   248
Foreign Policy Goals and Priorities   250
Issues of War and Peace   253
Terrorism and the Wars in Afghanistan and Iraq   257
Peacekeeping, Rescue, and Other Uses of Military Force   260
Foreign Aid and Other International Issues   261
How Do Americans Think about Foreign Policy?   264
Summary   268
Polls, Polling, and the Internet   268

PART IV: PUBLIC OPINION: A CRITICAL PERSPECTIVE

12 **Challenges Facing Public Opinion Research:
Issues of Reliability and Trust**   273
Pseudo-Polls   275
Technological Developments   276
Respondent Factors   282
The Cost of Survey Errors   286
The Continuing Case for Polling   288
Conclusion   288

Appendix A: Sources of Public Opinion Data   291

Appendix B: Questions from the American National
Election Studies and General Social Surveys   295

Glossary   309

Notes   317

References   333

Index   361

About the Authors   377

List of Figures, Boxes, and Tables

LIST OF FIGURES

3.1	Presidential approval ratings since 1977.	50
7.1	Ideological identification, 1972–2008.	135
7.2	Party identification, 1952–2008.	141
7.3	Confidence in leaders of governmental institutions, 1966–2010.	146
7.4	Trust in government, 1958–2008.	148
8.1	Government spending on Social Security, 1984–2010.	162
8.2	Government spending on welfare, 1973–2010.	176
9.1	Government help blacks and other minority groups, 1970–2008.	199
9.2	Opinions on voting for a black candidate for president, 1972–2010.	206
9.3	Opinions on the impact of slavery by race, 1972–2008.	208
9.4	Opinions on the speed of the civil rights movement by race, 1964–1992.	209
10.1	Percentage of Americans citing crime as the most important problem, 1985–2008.	219
10.2	Public opinion on the death penalty, 1936–2010.	224

10.3   Support for capital punishment by blacks and whites,
       1974–2010.   225

10.4   Support for increasing or decreasing immigration.   239

LIST OF BOXES

2.1   The First Candidate Poll: Family Ties   21

4.1   Sample Selection for Different Modes: Some Examples   63

4.2   Examples of Different Survey Questions with Various
      Types of Filters   69

4.3   Examples of Tone of Wording Effect   70

4.4   Middle versus No Middle Alternative   73

4.5   Examples of Various Types of Response Formats   74

4.6   Example of Question Context Effects   78

6.1   Americans' Knowledge on Selected Issues, 1943–1962   119

6.2   Political Knowledge: Then and Now   123

8.1   Opinions on Social Security   164

8.2   Public Opinion on Health Care Reform   172

8.3   Opinions on Environmental Issues   179

LIST OF TABLES

2.1   The Accuracy of Gallup Preelection Polls   23

5.1   Parent versus Student Partisanship   92

5.2   National Civics Assessment Test: Percentage of
      Children Scoring Proficient, 2008   98

5.3   Gender and Political Information and Interest   106

6.1   Tolerance of Nonconformists, 1954   125

6.2   Should Groups Be Allowed to Make a Public Speech,
      1954–2010   126

7.1   Ideological Identification, 1972–2008   136

7.2   Political Ideology by Demographic Characteristics, 1972–2008   138

7.3 Party Identification, 1952–2008 140

7.4 Party Identification by Demographic Characteristics, Selected Years, 1952–2008 143

7.5 Confidence in Institutions, 1966–2010 145

7.6 Trends in Confidence in Leaders of Governmental Institutions 147

7.7 "Trust Government to Do What Is Right" by Demographic Characteristics, 1958, 1964, 2000, 2002, and 2008 150

7.8 Power of the Federal Government, 1964–2000 153

8.1 Government Provide More or Fewer Services, 1975–2010 160

8.2 Spending on Improving the Education System, 1973–2010 166

8.3 Federal Spending on Education, 1984–2008 167

8.4 Federal Government Responsibility for Paying for Medical Care, 1975–2010 168

8.5 Spending on Improving and Protecting the Nation's Health, 1973–2010 169

8.6 Support for a Government Insurance Plan, 1970–2008 170

8.7 Opinions on Government Guarantee of Jobs and Living Standards, 1972–2008 174

8.8 Opinions on Government Improving Living Standards for Poor Americans, 1975–2010 175

8.9 Opinions on Improving and Protecting the Environment, 1973–2010 178

8.10 Opinions on Selected Social Welfare Issues by Sociodemographic Characteristics, 2008 184

9.1 Attitudes toward Minority Employment, 1986–2008 193

9.2 Attitudes toward Minority Employment by Race, 1956–2008 194

9.3 Opinions on Affirmative Action (National Election Studies), 1986–2008 197

9.4 Opinions on Affirmative Action (General Social Surveys), 1994–2010 197

9.5 Opinions on Affirmative Action by Race 198

9.6 Government Help Blacks and Other Minority Groups, 1970–2008 199

9.7   Government Help Blacks and Other Minority Groups
       by Race, 1970–2008   200

9.8   Government Improve Living Standards for Blacks,
       1975–2010   201

9.9   Government Improve Living Standards for Blacks
       by Race, 1975–2010   201

9.10   Opinions about Spending and Improving the Conditions
       of Blacks, 1973–2010   203

9.11   Opinions about Spending on Assistance to Blacks,
       1984–2010   204

9.12   Opinions about Spending on Racial Issues by Race,
       1973–2010   205

9.13   Opinions on the Impact of Slavery   207

9.14   Opinions on Interracial Marriage   210

9.15   Opinions on Interracial Marriage by Race   210

9.16   Opinions of Whites, Blacks, and Hispanics on
       Selected Issues, 2008   212

10.1   The Perceived Goals of Prisons   222

10.2   Support for Legal Abortion under Different Conditions,
       1962–2010   228

10.3   Opinions on Abortions under What Circumstances,
       1975–2011   229

10.4   Opinions on Abortion Restrictions   230

10.5   Equal Job Opportunities for Homosexuals   233

10.6   Opinions on the Validity of Gay Marriage   235

10.7   Public Opinion on Stricter Gun Laws   237

11.1   Support for an Active Role in the World, 1947–2011   247

11.2   Most Important Goals for U.S. Foreign Policy, 1974–2010   251

11.3   Comparing Elite and Public Views on American Foreign
       Policy Goals, 2009   252

11.4   Public Views on the Iraq War as a Mistake, 2003–2010   259

11.5   Public Views on the Afghan War as a Mistake, 2001–2010   259

11.6   Elite and Public Support for Economic Aid, 1974–1998   262

Preface

Newspapers, television, cable talk shows, and blogs all seem to report a new poll every day. Today in a presidential election year, hundreds of polls are being generated and reported on which Republican candidate will be nominated and how that person might do in a contest with President Barack Obama. There are polls on every issue facing the U.S. public from anger toward Wall Street to cutting the deficit to the war in Afghanistan. Given the widespread use of polls in this country, our goals for this book are to characterize the "American mind," meaning contemporary public opinion in the United States, but also to describe how public opinion data are collected, how they are used, and the role they play in the U.S. political system.

One objective of this book is to provide information on how survey data are collected and the factors a good consumer of polls should know in order to evaluate public opinion data. Characteristics of a survey, including the way the sample was chosen, the design of the questionnaire, and how the data were collected, are discussed fairly extensively in order to provide questions you should ask when you are presented with poll results.

A second objective is to demonstrate various ways in which public opinion data are used. The federal government conducts thousands of survey interviews each month for various governmental departments, and those data are used for federal, state, and local policy decisions. State and local governments also contract for polls on their own issues. Candidates for public office depend on surveys in deciding how to develop their campaigns. The results of survey research are important to academic researchers in a variety of fields, including political science, sociology, mass communications, and public health. The media make use of surveys in their coverage of elections as well as in their reporting on public policy issues. Our discussion of the use of public opinion data provides an overview of the many ways in which survey data are a part of U.S. political life.

Any text on public opinion must provide information on what the public believes, and this is the focus of much of the text. We discuss how Americans come to hold opinions on issues and politics, then describe the American public's views on a number of social-welfare issues, racial questions, cultural issues, and foreign policy issues. We also look at how the public expresses its political views and attachments to the system. A new chapter in this fourth edition looks at the question of how much the public knows about the political system and how that knowledge base or lack thereof impacts public opinion.

Finally, we consider the role that public opinion plays in the U.S. political system. Does public opinion matter in our democratic system, and how is public opinion translated into public policy? As part of this discussion, we also take a critical look at the way in which public opinion data are collected and used; we then identify several factors that may change the way in which poll results are used.

We present data on a number of different issues, but these represent only a minute fraction of the vast array of current and historical survey data available. Such data are becoming more available through the Internet, so we have included in each chapter a section on "Polls, Polling, and the Internet." These sections identify websites at which data are available or which contain information about polling and the survey industry. The range of topics for which data are available is virtually limitless, and we encourage you to visit these sites and explore your interests concerning the American mind.

An effort such as this is not completed without the assistance of a number of people. We thank the Department of Political Science at the University of Cincinnati and the staff of the University of South Carolina's Institute for Public Service and Policy Research for their support. In particular, we thank Dennis Lambries, Ron Shealy, and Chris Werner at South Carolina for their research assistance. Earlier versions of this book have benefited significantly from the suggestions of our reviewers: Richard Chesteen, University of Tennessee at Martin; Brian Gaines, University of Illinois at Urbana Champaign; Ted Jelen, University of Nevada, Las Vegas; William Jacoby, Michigan State University; Eric Plutzer, Penn State University; and Clyde Wilcox, Georgetown University. We are grateful for the support of Jon Sisk and Darcy Evans of Rowman & Littlefield in making this edition possible. Their assistance has been invaluable.

Part I

PUBLIC OPINION AND AMERICAN DEMOCRACY

1

Public Opinion and American Democracy

In historical perspective, the importance of public opinion in the United States is evident in the origin of the nation. The authors of *The Federalist* refer to "the public voice proclaimed by the representatives of the people," and though the Founding Fathers were wary of the evils resulting from an overbearing majority, they recognized the need to acknowledge the public's voice in developing public policy (*Federalist* No. 10: 81). Although the general notion of "public opinion" was anticipated in the works of Plato and Aristotle as well as by the Romans (Palmer, 1936: 231–232), we can trace the modern concept of public opinion to Rousseau in 1744 (Hubert, 1992: 30). The idea that emerged from the Enlightenment of a mass public competent to exercise its sovereignty was instrumental in shaping the role of the public in the democratic society that developed in the United States.

In addition to a system in which the individual is the focus of the political process, traditional democratic theory assumes that each member of the electorate is interested in public issues, motivated by principle, aware of relevant facts, and capable of making decisions rationally. In a democratic system, the opinions of the public are to be translated into action (Hennessy, 1981: 13–15). As stated succinctly by Achen, the starting point of democratic theory is that "public opinion on policy matters" (1975: 1220). It is the views of adults on policy issues that we refer to as the "American mind."

Elisabeth Noelle-Neumann (1984: 76) has noted that David Hume's basic principle, that it is on opinion only that government is founded, became the doctrine of the Founding Fathers of the United States. The importance of public opinion has been evident throughout this country's history. Abraham Lincoln, for example, wrote that in politics "public

3

sentiment is everything. With public sentiment, nothing can fail. Without it nothing can succeed" (quoted in Minow, Martin, and Mitchell, 1973: 10). Lyndon Johnson's decision not to run for reelection in 1968 was in large part attributable to the erosion of public support for the Vietnam War and, consequently, his presidency (P. Converse, 1987). Similarly, public disapproval of his performance in office, along with myriad other factors, contributed to Richard Nixon's decision to resign the presidency in 1974. Modern political campaigns, not only for the presidency but at all levels, are replete with references to "what the public wants."

The role that public opinion should play in American democracy has also been a topic for debate in contemporary politics. During Congress's consideration of the impeachment and conviction of President Bill Clinton for lying about his relationship with a White House intern, the media and polling organizations supplied almost daily polls regarding what the public thought and what the public wanted Congress to do. As the Senate began to consider conviction of the president in 1999, polls showed public approval of the job he was doing remaining very high, higher than before the scandal began. Polls showed that the public did not want the president ousted from office by conviction in the Senate. As the scandal and the trial dragged on, only public views regarding the president's moral character declined. The Senate, controlled by the Republicans, could not muster the two-thirds vote to convict Clinton, in part, because there was no public sentiment for them to do so.

In describing the place of public opinion in American politics, Philip Converse (1987) recounted the exchange that took place during the Iran-Contra hearings in which Lieutenant Colonel Oliver North chastised the members of Congress for failing to support the Contra resistance in Nicaragua and was, in turn, chastised by Senator Warren Rudman. Senator Rudman indicated that Congress had been appropriately reflecting public sentiment, pointing out that public opinion polls had been running 75–25 against support for the Contras. In Converse's view, what was significant about this event from the standpoint of public opinion was that (1) nobody challenged the accuracy of the public opinion figures, and (2) nobody challenged Rudman's claim of basic authority for the voice of the public. The importance of the public's views is inherent in debates over public policy. Throughout the history of the United States, the important role played by public opinion has evidenced itself in many ways.

DEFINING PUBLIC OPINION

Despite—or perhaps because of—its long history in American political discourse, there is no generally agreed-upon definition of "public opinion."

For example, V. O. Key (1967: 14) defined public opinion as "those opinions held by private persons that governments find it prudent to heed." For Monroe (1975: 6), public opinion "is the distribution of individual preferences within a population. In other words, *public* opinion is simply the sum or aggregation of *private* opinions on any particular issue or set of issues." In Simon's (1974: 7) terms, public opinion "is the aggregate of views people hold regarding matters that (the pollsters decide) affect or interest the community," while for Hennessy (1981: 4) it is "the complex of preferences expressed by a significant number of people on an issue of general importance." Erikson and Tedin (2011: 8) define the concept as "the preferences of the adult population on matters of relevance to government." Cummings and Wise (1974: 168) view it as "the expression of attitudes relevant to government and politics," while Noelle-Neumann (1984: 62–63) holds that it involves "opinions on controversial issues that one *can* express in public without isolating oneself." For Weissberg (1976: 9), public opinion is simply "a preference for a course of action."

Although these definitions have a common element, each differs slightly to reflect the varying points of view and areas of emphasis in the study of this phenomenon. The following definition of public opinion, in our view, best reflects the important elements of the concept and therefore structures the approach taken in this book:

> **Public opinion** is the aggregate of the views of individual adults on matters of public interest.

The first element of this definition, "aggregate of the views of individual adults," was a source of some controversy in the early development of modern public opinion research in the United States. As discussed later, critics of the use of polling techniques to measure public opinion, such as Blumer, argued that the summation of individual opinions in a "one person, one vote" style was exactly what public opinion was *not*. In the critics' view, public opinion was more accurately reflected in the views of the relatively small group of influentials in the community, who paid more attention to and were more knowledgeable about matters of public affairs (Blumer, 1948). Variations of this view held that public opinion in a community was represented by the integration of the views of all its major interest groups, or that it was articulated by certain community leaders, such as a newspaper editor or elected officials, who could claim some heightened sense of the "community interest."

As Philip Converse (1987) has noted, however, the development of the public opinion polling industry has served to homogenize and stabilize the definition of public opinion. In his words, "it is ironic that it is exactly this kind of 'one person, one vote' tally of opinions as reported by polls and surveys which has now become the consensual understanding the world around as to a baseline definition of public opinion." In Blumer's (1948) view, a design that selected unrelated individuals from the whole and as-signed an equal weight to the opinion of each was a travesty in any realistic understanding of public opinion. As Philip Converse (1987: S14) notes, however, "it is now true that just such responses, elicited in just the same way and counted up with equal weights, are in fact brought forcefully to the attention of authorities at all levels of government."

As Converse goes on to recognize, public opinion as measured by sample surveys is not the same as "effective" public opinion. That is, the "public opinion" that is effective in the political arena is not identical to that reported in public opinion polls; although they are often reasonably convergent, they can at times diverge remarkably. This acknowledgment does not suggest, however, that the definition of public opinion offered here needs to be modified. Rather, examining the conditions under which these two types of public opinion converge or are at odds, and the factors underlying these conditions, is an important consideration to investigate as part of the present definition. The aggregate of the views of individuals in a jurisdiction, equally weighted, is central to our approach to the study of public opinion.

The second component of this definition, "of individual adults," stems from our focus on the role of public opinion in the political process. We focus on the opinions of those 18 and older—the voting age population—because it is the opinions of this group to which elected officials and policy makers are more likely to pay attention. Although those under 18 certainly hold opinions—which, as we will show in Chapter 3, can sometimes be important to policy makers—for the most part public officials pay more attention to the views of the potential electorate. Most of the widely known general public opinion polls conducted in the United States (for example, those done by Gallup, Zogby, CBS News/*New York Times*, NBC News/*Wall Street Journal*, ABC News/*Washington Post*, CNN/*USA Today*/Gallup Poll, the *L.A. Times*, and Fox News/Opinion Dynamics) collect data from this voting-age population. There is also a great wealth of data on the opinions of the adult population available for **secondary analysis** (that is, analysis by researchers other than those who originally collected the data). Given these considerations, we have centered much of our attention on the opin-ions "of individual adults." Examining the opinions of subgroups—the "in-formed" public, demographic groups, registered voters—is not excluded by this definition; rather, it is another important consideration to investigate.

In exploring the final component of this definition, "on matters of public interest," we have adopted an extremely broad-based approach. Any issue of interest to the public, whether at the national, state, or local level, and at any point in the political process—during the campaign, prior to the vote on an issue, after a policy has been adopted—falls under the scope of our definition of public opinion. For example, the public's views of a candidate's strengths and weaknesses, the image of his or her opponent, and the most important issues in the campaign are, from this perspective, "matters of public interest." Similarly, citizens' views on national concerns (for example, protecting the environment), state matters (state budget priorities), and local questions (increasing the property tax to fund schools) are included under this definition. The public's evaluation of government programs or services—from the federal food stamp program, to state parks, to the local schools—its approval or disapproval of the way various individuals and institutions are performing their roles, the needs it feels should be addressed by government, as well as its general beliefs about the principles underlying the governmental process are all topics that will be considered under this broad conceptualization of "matters of public interest."

Private sector concerns about what the public thinks, though certainly a part of the larger American mind, will not be addressed in this work. Although market researchers employ many of the same techniques for gathering information as those who study public opinion, their interests are largely outside the realm of "public interest." Our concern is not with what the public thinks is the best video game on the market. Knowing how they feel about government regulations on the content of such games for violence and nudity, however, is a question that falls under our definition of "public opinion."

By adopting this relatively simple and straightforward definition, we leave unanswered a number of questions, including differences in **intensity of opinion** (the strength of an individual's views on an issue), the knowledge that underlies opinions, the division of opinion, the role of multiple publics, and the impact of public opinion on policy. On the question of intensity of opinion, for example, one of the points that critics such as Blumer make of the type of definition we have proposed is that it treats all opinions equally. That is, the views of the individual who had never thought about an issue until asked about it by a survey interviewer are treated the same as those of a person who had a long-standing and passionate view on the matter. In our "one person, one vote" framework, each individual's position on an issue is treated equally. The effect that differences in intensity of opinion might have on other actions a person might take (for example, contacting a legislator, writing a letter to a newspaper, posting a message on Facebook) or how such variations on issues such as gun control may lead to policies that appear to conflict with "majority rule" are fertile subjects for more extensive investigation.

A similar concern can be raised over equal treatment of the opinions of people who have potentially quite different levels of knowledge on an issue. In our "democratic" conceptualization of public opinion, the person whose first thoughts on an issue came in response to the interviewer's question is equivalent to the person who has spent a great deal of time reading about, thinking about, and refining a position. How the views of those with less knowledge may be more unstable and easily shifted by new information and events, and how the more knowledgeable person may be better able to use his or her knowledge to influence the opinions of others, also present interesting avenues for further inquiry.

The term "matters of public interest" implies some form of controversy or division of opinion. In defining the scope of "public opinion," we treat as a separate class those topics on which there is uniform agreement or disagreement, known as **valence issues** (Stokes, 1966). The number of valence issues in U.S. politics is relatively small. Although there is general consensus over the basic principles of democracy in abstract terms (for example, democracy is the best form of government; every citizen should have an equal chance to influence government policy), there is disagreement over even the specific applications of these principles (Prothro and Grigg, 1960). We can view "law and order" as a valence issue; virtually no one opposes law and order (Scammon and Wattenberg, 1970). This topic moves from a valence issue into our sphere of public opinion when the discussion turns to the means for achieving "law and order." Harsher punishment for criminals, more emphasis on rehabilitating offenders, gun control, and the death penalty are examples of issues over which there is considerable disagreement among the American public. Whether in the domain of social-welfare policy, foreign policy, or social issues, and at each level of government, public opinion in the United States is characterized more by conflict than consensus, and virtually all "matters of public interest" involve some degree of controversy. These divisions of opinion and the differences that exist among various groups will be considered extensively in Chapters 7 through 11.

Another consideration in interpreting "public opinion" involves the existence of **multiple publics** for any particular issue. By our definition, all adults in a jurisdiction are members of the general public whose "aggregate of views" are to be considered in determining public opinion. In addition to having their opinions included as part of the general public, citizens can make their views known to policy makers through other means, such as writing letters, contacting their representatives directly, or working through groups of which they are members. Take, for example, a case in which a local gun control ordinance is being considered by the city council. Mr. Jones is a gun enthusiast and a member of the National Rifle Association (NRA) and is active in his neighborhood civic association. If the city council was presented with results of an opinion poll of a representative sample of the public (see Chapter 4), then the views of Mr. Jones, and those who felt as he did, would be appropriately represented as part of the general public. In addition, the NRA might stage a rally, organize a letter-writing campaign, or arrange to have its members contact council members individually. In this way, Mr. Jones's views might be made known as a member of an "interested public." Similarly, if the neighborhood association were to hold a special meeting or make a concerted effort to influence the council's vote on this issue, Mr. Jones's views might be made known as a member of this "concerned public." For any public policy question, there are a number of potential "publics" on both sides of the issue. Although the views of such special publics are an important component in the policy process, they are not what we consider "public opinion." They are important to our treatment of this topic, in that the views of "multiple publics" can affect how public opinion is translated into public policy.[1]

DOES PUBLIC OPINION MATTER?

In our approach to public opinion, we begin with the premise that, in a democratic society, what the public wants is in some way translated into public policy. Given the large number of potential influences on policy, however, establishing a definite linkage between public opinion and public policy is extremely difficult. Even if we found that a legislator's or council member's vote on an issue corresponded with the sentiment of his or her constituency, we don't have proof that public opinion had an effect. Correspondence between public opinion and public policy may result from the fact that lawmakers and their constituents often have similar background characteristics and experiences, so that they share the same views on many issues. It is also possible for congruence between opinion and policy to arise as a result of leadership by policy makers (policy affecting opinion) or from manipulation of public opinion by government officials (Weissberg, 1976: 242). As Page and Shapiro (1983: 176) have noted, "It is hard to tell whether correspondence between opinion and policy arises from democratic responsiveness, from leadership or manipulation of opinion, or from some combination of these."

Much of the research on the "linkage" between public opinion and public policy has centered on the correspondence between the legislators' votes and the views of their constituents. For example, Miller and Stokes (1963) examined the relationship between the views of members of Congress, their nonincumbent opponents, and their constituents and found a modest degree of correspondence between the views of legislators and those of their constituents in the domains of social welfare, foreign involvement, and civil rights. Similarly, Adams and Ferber's (1980) analysis of the roll-call votes of members of the Texas House of Representatives and the votes of their constituents on the same issues demonstrated a fairly high level of consistency between them.

Other approaches have examined public opinion and policy outcomes. Monroe (1979) studied the correspondence between national survey data and federal policy outcomes and found that policy decisions were consistent with public preferences about two-thirds of the time, although his later work in this area (Monroe, 1998, 2001) indicated that such consistency had dropped to about 55% during the period from 1980 to 1999. Similarly, Page and Shapiro's (1983) analysis of changes in preferences and changes in policy in the United States showed a substantial congruence between changes in opinion and policy.[2]

Despite the difficulties in proving that public opinion has a direct impact on policy, various methods of examining this question have shown that opinion–policy congruence does occur. As summarized by Monroe (1979: 8), there is a "definite tendency for public policy to be in accordance with public opinion, though the relationship is decidedly imperfect." This linkage between opinion and policy is imperfect in the sense that there is not a strict correspondence between the public's desires and the government's actions. Rather, opinion is linked to policy in that the public's preferences provide broad guidelines within which policy makers can operate. Public opinion is more effective in preventing totally objectionable policies than in specifying a policy mandate. As Weissberg (1976: 242) has noted, "Linkage mechanisms probably narrow down both public demands and government responses to a point where almost any publicly considered policy will be at least tolerable (though not preferred) for most people."

In their review of this issue, Manza and Cook (2002) reiterated the point that the capacity of a political system to respond to the preferences of its citizens is central to democratic theory and practice. Without some congruence between public policy and the views of the citizenry and responsiveness by the government to the public's wishes, a democratic system would break down. But while public opinion in the United States sets the parameters within which policy makers operate, the boundaries are rather broad. The public's lack of a coherent view on many policy questions, together with the ability of policy makers to help shape public attitudes, provides public officials with substantial room to maneuver in making policy decisions. When the public expresses a coherent view on policy questions that is recognizable by elites, the movement of policy will be in the direction of public opinion.

Evidence from policy makers, while largely unsystematic, also provides an indication that the influence of public opinion is primarily indirect. For example, in a discussion of the impact of polls on the policy environment, the former chair of the Consumer Product Safety Commission (CPSC) observed that the group used polls to alert it to issues that were bothering people and to problems that the commission was not explaining well or that needed more attention. As the chair noted, "The polls suggest *how we* should pursue a given objective and, in a negative sense, how we should *not* attempt to pursue a given objective" (Cantril, 1980: 138).

An example of how policy makers use public opinion data is provided by an assessment of the "Don't Ask, Don't Tell" policy of the U.S. Department of Defense (2010). The review of the issues associated with this policy reported that "in the early 1990s, polls by major national polling organizations consistently indicated that 50–60% of the American public supported allowing gay men and lesbians to serve in the military, and around 40% supported allowing gay men and lesbians to serve openly. In the years since, polls indicated that public opinion has shifted toward greater support of open military service by gay men and lesbians" (U.S. Department of Defense, 2010: 24).

Members of Congress frequently cite public opinion in their consideration of issues. In the congressional debate over the repeal of "Don't Ask, Don't Tell," for example, Representative Laura Richardson (D-California) noted that the change in public opinion on this issue "has been so dramatic that repeal . . . no longer represents a subject of controversy for a large majority of Americans. Indeed, repealing 'Don't Ask Don't Tell' brings public policy in line with informed popular sentiment, which is nearly always a positive good" (Richardson, 2010).

Poll results also are used by officeholders to urge action or inaction on a policy issue. During consideration of legislation to address global warming, Senator James Inhofe (R–Oklahoma) cited public opinion as one of his arguments against passing legislation on this issue. As he stated, "The latest Gallup Poll . . . further reveals the American public has a growing skepticism. A record-high now say [global warming] is exaggerated. This represents the highest public skepticism since the whole issue began" (Inhofe, 2009). Similarly, during consideration of a "public option" as part of the Patient Protection and Affordable Care Act, Senator John Cornyn (R–Texas) noted "Last week, we saw the *Washington Post*-ABC News poll that supposedly said that support for a government-run plan was growing. In fact, support has fallen by 5 points since June. These numbers can be misleading" (Cornyn, 2009). The public's view has also been invoked in the congressional debate over the federal budget and the national debt. Senator Olympia Snowe (R–Maine) remarked that "if you ask the American taxpayer, 'Do you think your Federal dollars are being spent wisely and efficiently?'—the response is a resounding 'no' as reflected in many polls and public opinion surveys" (Snowe, 2011).

In his assessment of the impact of polls, Philip Converse (1987: S22) asserts that "few politicians consult poll data to find out what they should be thinking on the issues . . . but they have very little interest in flouting the will of their constituency in any tendentious, head-on way." He makes an indirect but rather persuasive argument for the impact of polls when he notes that the influence of polls must "occur in very large doses among political practitioners, or it would be extremely hard to explain why such users pay many millions of dollars a year for this expensive class of information." This mounting acceptance of public opinion data was, in his view, best symbolized by the daily polls of the national electorate done for President Ronald Reagan by his pollster, Richard Wirthlin (P. Converse, 1987: S17–S22). In sum, data from polls provide the broad contours within which policy making takes place.

A number of methods have been used to evaluate the impact of public opinion on public policy. The general conclusion from these studies is that even though the public's desires are not perfectly satisfied, the political system produces acceptable outcomes in a majority of the cases. It is not the case that the public makes its desires known through public opinion polls and these desires are then directly translated into policy, nor should we expect it to be. Rather, policy makers at all levels of government are influenced by public opinion as they take account of the public's views not only in their decision making but also in identifying those issues that are important to the public and the broad outlines within which government can operate.

PUBLIC OPINION VERSUS PUBLIC JUDGMENT

In completing the description of the way in which we have chosen to present "public opinion," we should note the distinction between this term and **public judgment**. Yankelovich (1991) believes that the "public opinion" that is reported on the basis of polls is misleading because it reflects people's top-of-the-head views rather than their thoughtful, considered judgments. In his terms, public judgment is a "state of highly developed public opinion that exists once people have engaged an issue, considered it from all sides, understood the choices it leads to, and accepted the consequences of the choices they make" (Yankelovich, 1991: 6). He argues that enhancing the quality of public judgment is necessary to ensure effective self-governance in the United States.

Yankelovich cites capital punishment as an example of an issue on which the citizenry has reached "public judgment." In describing Americans' views on this topic, he notes that prior to the 1970s a majority of the public was not in favor of the death penalty for murder and other serious crimes. Support for the death penalty built slowly over the next two decades and reached an average of 73% during the 1980s. Moreover, interviews with people who took this position show "that most have struggled with the argument that imposing the death penalty means that some innocent people will die" (Yankelovich, 1991: 26). In contrast to the snap judgments reflected in polls, where the views of the public may change significantly when presented with the consequences of a decision, supporters of capital punishment "realize and accept this implication, but they do not change their views even when contemplating these consequences" (Yankelovich, 1991: 26). Of course, recent developments in DNA testing of old evidence have led to the release of some felons who were wrongly convicted. Such events will probably reopen the case for the death penalty in the minds of many Americans.

We do not disagree with Yankelovich over the distinction between public opinion and public judgment; the criticism that respondents to public opinion polls make snap judgments, as opposed to those individuals who have actually considered both sides of an issue, is one that has long been recognized (Gallup, 1947). We do not believe, however, that public opinion, as we have described the term, is a less important consideration than public judgment in the way in which government decisions are made in the United States. From our perspective, examining (1) the reasons some people are more informed about various topics, (2) the factors underlying an individual's position on an issue, and (3) the determinants of varying levels of intensity of opinion are all important components of an overall understanding of public opinion. These various components of public opinion, from how opinions are formed to their ultimate impact on the political process, will be examined in the following chapters. Limiting the scope to "informed" opinion or judgment would unnecessarily preclude a more complete examination of the factors that underlie differences in public opinion in the United States and their consequences for public policy.

A related critique of the approach we have adopted in defining public opinion has been made by Fishkin (1996). Although Fishkin would not snub the distribution of opinion as it is, he does argue that the views of the public are better represented through the results of a **deliberative opinion poll**. A deliberative poll typically involves selecting a random sample of individuals, bringing them together in one location, immersing them in the issue(s), and providing them with carefully balanced briefing materials, with intensive discussions in small groups, and with the chance to question competing experts and politicians. At the end of several days, the participants are polled and the results represent the considered judgments of the public—the views the entire population would come to "if it had the same experience of behaving more like ideal citizens immersed in the issues for an extended period" (Fishkin, 1996: 1).

Such polls have been criticized on a number of grounds, including whether they are truly representative of some population, how the issues for discussion are selected (Mitofsky, 1996), and whether they reflect the process that would occur in a democratic society (Tringali, 1996). While each of these criticisms has some merit—as well as some counterarguments

(Fishkin and Luskin, 1996)—from our perspective the more important factor that limits the utility of deliberative polls is their cost. To identify a representative sample of some group and then to bring them together for a significant amount of time is relatively expensive and requires identifying individuals who are both able and willing to commit to this type of exercise. Although deliberative polls represent another means of deriving some measure of "what the public thinks," the results of this process are generally not what is considered to be "public opinion" and their use for anything more than a limited number of issues would be prohibitively expensive.[3]

OPINIONS, ATTITUDES, AND BELIEFS

Before concluding this description of our definition of public opinion, we need to distinguish among the terms **attitudes**, **opinions**, and **beliefs**. Psychologists often differentiate these terms, and though such distinctions are numerous (Allport, 1935), attitudes are generally defined as relatively enduring orientations toward objects that provide individuals with mental frameworks for making economical sense of the world; opinions are the verbal expression of attitudes; and beliefs are the inclination to accept something as true. In one sense, attitudes may be said to go deeper than opinions and beliefs. As Katz (1960: 163) has described it, the attitudes of individuals are the raw material from which public opinion develops.

Though such distinctions are important in considerations of attitude formation and change, these terms are often indistinguishable in discussions of public opinion. More than 40 years ago, Greenstein (1969: 28) noted that social scientists "sometimes tend to equate the concept 'attitude' with its most prevalent indicator—a discrete response to a question of opinion in a public opinion poll." Similarly, the title of an extensive survey-based study by Free and Cantril (1968)—*The Political Beliefs of Americans: A Study of Public Opinion*—illustrates the interchangeable use of these terms.

For our purposes, the attitudes, opinions, and beliefs of the American public are all important in that they can have an impact on public policy. As such, each of them will be considered in our discussion of public opinion. Americans' attitudes toward war, their opinions about whether the war with Iraq was worth its cost, and their beliefs about the extent to which this country should be involved in the affairs of other nations all could have had an effect on government decisions during that conflict. In this framework, it makes little difference whether these expressions are referred to as attitudes or opinions or beliefs; "the aggregate of the views of individual adults on matters of public interest" is what we shall consider public opinion.

THE CURRENT ENVIRONMENT

Much has been written in recent years about the polarization of the American electorate (Pildes, 2010). Proponents of this polarized view of the American public cite features such as the divide in presidential electoral outcomes between "red" states and "blue" states (Gelman, 2008), the partisan gap in approval ratings of the president, the growing relationship between party identification and ideological identification, the increase in ideological thinking among the American public (Abramowitz and Saunders, 2008), the continued division in opinion over President Barack Obama's health care plan, and the bitter debate over raising the country's debt ceiling as evidence (Pew Center for People and the Press, 2003). As summarized by Pildes (2010: 2), "By almost all measures, Americans have become dramatically more partisanly divided over the last generation."

The contrary view, led by Morris Fiorina and his colleagues (2008, 2010), is that this depiction of a polarized public is largely a myth. While acknowledging some party polarization (or party sorting) has occurred, those who view the polarization of the public as a myth contend that even if the beliefs and positions of voters remain constant, centrist voters can register voting decisions and political evaluations that "will appear more polarized when the positions candidates adopt and the actions elected officials take become more extreme" (Fiorina, Abrams, and Pope, 2008: 556). The increased polarization of the political class appears to make the citizenry appear more polarized when, in fact, the views of the American public are moderate or centrist.

Proponents of each of these views report a considerable amount of survey data in support of their characterization of the public. The shape of the division of the public's opinions on matters of public interest and how this division has changed or remained the same over time is one of the major themes that will be considered throughout the description of the American mind to be presented in the following chapters.

THE PLAN OF THE BOOK

In defining public opinion, we have made reference to a number of topics to be considered in this book. How opinions are formed, the different levels of knowledge that underlie opinion, variations in intensity of opinion, the factors that account for such differences, and the impact of opinion on the political process are all topics to be examined more thoroughly.

Chapter 2 examines the origins of public opinion polling in U.S. history and discusses how the nature of public opinion polling has evolved in the United States. We describe critical events in its development in this chapter.

Part II contains a description of how opinions are measured and put to use. Chapter 3 provides some examples of the ways in which public opinion data are used, including use by candidates, officeholders, policy makers, researchers, and the media. Chapter 4 details the methods used to collect public opinion data and delineates some of the steps involved in the data collection process, including sampling, designing questionnaires, and interviewing.

Part III focuses on what Americans believe. Chapter 5 explores the origins of Americans' opinions, including political socialization, political learning, and the influence of the media on opinions, while the extent to which Americans are knowledgeable about politics and its implications for the political process is the focus of Chapter 6. Partisan and ideological identifications and the sources of these identifications are covered in Chapter 7. Americans' domestic goals, for example, in the areas of social welfare, the economy, and education, are the subject of Chapter 8, and Chapter 9 explores Americans' views on racial issues. Highly controversial topics, including the death penalty and the rights of gays, are investigated in Chapter 10. Opinions on global political issues, such as the U.S. role in the world and foreign aid, are treated in Chapter 11. In Part IV, Chapter 12 takes a critical look at the current state of public opinion and its measurement. The chapter concludes with a brief summary of what we know about the American mind after seven decades of survey research.

POLLS, POLLING, AND THE INTERNET

The results of recent polls from many different survey organizations are available on the Internet at the Polling Report's website. Pick an issue in the news and then consider how different polling organizations ask the questions. Search for your topic at this website: www.pollingreport.com.

More information on deliberative opinion polls can be found at The Center for Deliberative Democracy, Deliberative Polling®, housed at Stanford University, the website for which is: http://cdd.stanford.edu/polls/docs/summary.

2

Measuring American Opinion: The Origins of Polling

The concept of democracy itself, resting as it does on the consent of the governed, implies some means for determining how the public feels about public policy issues. But while public opinion has always had a prominent role, the way in which the public's views have been measured has changed dramatically over time.

This country's Founding Fathers were themselves somewhat mixed in their views about the role of the public in this country's political process. Even though they wanted to create a system in which the ultimate political authority rested in the hands of the people, they were wary of the unbridled will of the citizenry. As Madison wrote in *The Federalist*, "The public good is disregarded in the conflicts of rival parties, and that measures are too often decided, not according to the rules of justice and the rights of the minor party, but by the superior force of an interested and overbearing majority" (*Federalist* No. 10: 54). Similarly, *Federalist* No. 63 noted that "there are particular moments in public affairs when the people, stimulated by some irregular passion, or some illicit advantage, or misled by the artful misrepresentations of interested men, may call for measures which they themselves will afterwards be the most ready to lament and condemn" (*Federalist* No. 63: 410). The U.S. political system, with its representative government, separation of powers, and system of checks and balances, reflects these reservations concerning the power of "the public."

The way in which government officials have come to know what the public thinks has changed significantly over time. At the time of the Constitution's ratification, representatives relied on personal contacts from citizens and leaders of various groups, letters to the editor, and marches and demonstrations as means for determining public opinion. Although these sources are still used today and are important in learning how various segments of society feel about issues, more scientific means have been developed for assessing public opinion.

THE ORIGINS OF PUBLIC OPINION POLLING

We can trace the origins of public opinion research in the United States not to the desire of government officials to determine the public's views on issues, but rather to a fascination with information about the voting intentions of the electorate (Robinson, 1932: 51). Tallies of results from preelection canvasses in 1824 have been cited by George Gallup as "the earliest counterpart of modern opinion surveys" (Gallup and Rae, 1940: 34–35). During this election, counts at regular public meetings, at militia musters, and at special meetings called to assess the public's presidential leanings, as well as tallies from "poll books" left at various public places such as taverns, were used to predict the outcome of the presidential election (Smith, 1990: 25–27). Though there is some debate about whether these methods were really the first "polls," there is little question that they were "a significant development in the assessment and quantification of public opinion and deserve a special place in the history of election polling" (Smith, 1990: 31).

Straw polls of this type served as an important means of assessing public sentiment for the next century. Newspapers such as the *New York Herald*, *Cincinnati Enquirer*, *St. Louis Republic*, and *Boston Globe* conducted such polls not only for presidential elections but also for some statewide and local contests. Other national periodicals, such as the *Farm Journal* and the *Pathfinder*, carried out straw polls during presidential election campaigns. Newspapers and magazines spent a great deal of resources on these polls not only because they thought the voting intentions of the American public had great news value but also because the polls served to promote these publications (Robinson, 1932: 47–51).

The most prominent of these straw polls was conducted by the *Literary Digest*. The *Digest* poll, which Robinson (1932: 49) describes as "almost synonymous with straw polls," began its predictions on presidential contests in 1916 and used straw polls during presidential elections through 1936. In addition to presidential races, the *Digest* used straw polls to assess public opinion on issues such as bonuses for war veterans, prohibition, and tax reduction.

The method typically used by the *Literary Digest* was to mail ballot cards to a very large number of people, identifying them through telephone directories and automobile registration lists. As many as 20 million ballots were sent out during an election campaign. Though there was often substantial deviation between the *Digest*'s predicted percentage of the vote and the actual vote total, the *Digest* poll was fairly well respected, having correctly predicted the presidential elections of 1920, 1924, 1928, and 1932 (Babbie, 1990: 67). Reports of the *Digest*'s poll results were widely publicized in newspapers across the country, with some even featuring them more prominently than their own polls (Squire, 1988: 126).

During the 1936 presidential campaign, the *Digest* mailed out more than 10 million straw vote ballots, using its usual procedure of drawing its sample from automobile registration lists and telephone books. Over 2.3 million ballots were returned. The prediction from these returns was that the Republican candidate, Alfred M. Landon, would receive 55% of the vote, Franklin D. Roosevelt, the Democratic candidate, 41%, and William Lemke, the candidate of the Union Party, 4%. On election day, Roosevelt won 61% of the popular vote compared to Landon's 37%. The large discrepancy between the predicted and actual outcomes resulted from a bias in the sampling frame (that is, the list from which names were selected) and nonresponse, arising from a low response rate (Squire, 1988: 131). The bias in the **sampling frame** resulted from the fact that the names to whom ballots were mailed were taken largely from telephone directories or state automobile registrations. In 1936 such lists had a disproportionate number of upper-income respondents, while lower-income households were less likely to have telephones or cars and were more likely to vote for Roosevelt. **Nonresponse bias** resulted from the failure of everyone to whom ballots were mailed to return them. Even though more than 2.3 million ballots were received, this represented less than one-fourth of the number mailed out. Sample bias and nonresponse are both topics that will be discussed in more detail in Chapter 4. The *"Literary Digest* fiasco," as it has come to be known, is an important event in the history of public opinion research because it demonstrated dramatically the importance of proper survey design.

THE DEVELOPMENT OF SURVEY RESEARCH

During the period that straw polls were prominent in estimating the vote intentions and issue positions of the American public, developments were taking place that would ultimately lead to the scientific study of public opinion. The straw polls of 1824 can be viewed as the earliest counterparts of modern opinion surveys, although such surveys can also trace their roots to the social surveys that evolved in the late 1800s. In England, Charles Booth, among others, developed methods for collecting and analyzing data that became known as the "English social survey." Their procedures included fieldwork, comprehensive coverage of some domain, examination of detailed cases, quantification, and organization of the data by individual records. Examples of the application of these methods in the United States included the Pittsburgh Survey, which was an effort to provide an overview of the state of that city, and the Country Life Movement, which conducted surveys on agricultural conditions and practices (J. Converse, 1987: 21–26).

The first quarter of the 20th century also marked the beginnings of the U.S. government's interest in surveys. As early as 1915, the Department of Agriculture was conducting surveys on the quality of life in rural America. The Department of Agriculture, along with other agencies such as the Works Progress Administration, continued to engage in a range of survey projects during the administration of Franklin D. Roosevelt.

It was during this period that probability sampling methods were developed. The work of statisticians such as Arthur Bowley, Jerzy Neyman, and R. A. Fisher was instrumental in demonstrating the superiority of probability sampling over purposive sampling procedures.[1] During the 1930s, the Department of Agriculture and the Bureau of the Census applied probability theory to the design of national samples of the American public (J. Converse, 1987: 202).

Advances in survey methods were also incorporated into research being conducted in the commercial sector. During the 1936 election campaign, three pollsters who had established themselves as market researchers— Archibald Crossley, George Gallup, and Elmo Roper—used these more scientific procedures in challenging the *Literary Digest*. Gallup was the most aggressive in this regard, selling his newspaper column with a money-back guarantee that his prediction would be better than the *Digest*'s and warning the *Digest* that it would regret its forecast of a Landon victory (J. Converse, 1987: 117). In response, W. J. Funk, editor of the *Digest*, commented, "Our fine statistical friend should be advised that the *Digest* would carry on with those old-fashioned methods that have produced correct forecasts exactly one hundred percent of the time" (*New York Times*, 1936: 21).

Even though their percentage estimates were far from perfect, the polls of Gallup, Crossley, and Roper each predicted a Roosevelt victory. Contrasted with the *Literary Digest*'s faulty estimate, these results were seen as vindication for the "scientific approach" for gauging public opinion (Jensen, 1980: 59).

In the aftermath of this election, government agencies, public opinion researchers, and market researchers carried out their surveys with confidence in their results. Though some warnings were raised about the limitations of the **quota sampling** procedures commonly employed at the time, their use was generally seen as a necessity, because probability sampling did not seem a practical option for national surveys (J. Converse, 1987: 94).

During this period government agencies greatly expanded their use of surveys. The Department of Agriculture was one of the leading users. In 1935 a small interviewing unit was established to tap farmers' attitudes about the efforts of Department of Agriculture farm programs. The utility of this information led to the creation of a Division of Program Surveys in the Bureau of Agricultural Economics, and the agency was instrumental in promoting the use of area probability samples and the development of standardized interviewing techniques (Bradburn and Sudman, 1988: 22–23; J. Converse, 1987: 138–139). Though this program was founded to address farm issues, it fairly quickly expanded its scope to "national and international problems that had meaning in their own right, such as national morale" (J. Converse, 1987: 160). With the advent of World War II, the substance of these surveys further extended to the areas of American defense and involvement in the war, and this unit conducted surveys for other federal agencies that needed survey data, such as the Office of Facts and Figures and the State Department.

Government use of survey research continued to expand during World War II. As part of the wartime effort, agencies such as the research branch of the Division of Morale of the U.S. Army, the surveys division of the Office of War Information, and program surveys of the Department of Agriculture conducted a wide range of surveys (J. Converse, 1987: 163). Though the federal government's involvement was scaled back after the war, it continued to conduct and commission a variety of surveys (Alpert, 1952). The advancements in areas such as sampling, questionnaire design, and data collection made during this period solidified the base upon which modern public opinion research has been built (Box 2.1).

BOX 2.1
The First Candidate Poll: Family Ties

In working on his doctoral dissertation in applied psychology at Iowa State University, George Gallup used survey methods to measure the readership of print media. This experience, together with his interest in public opinion and journalism, combined with the candidacy of his mother-in-law for Iowa's Secretary of State in 1932 to foster his interest in political polling. As a result, Gallup decided to test the utility of quota sampling for forecasting the election outcomes of 1934. This finding led, in part, to his challenge to the *Literary Digest* in 1936.

Sources: J. Converse, 1987: 114; Moore, 1992: 46; Bradburn and Sudman, 1988: 14.

THE ELECTION OF 1948: A TEMPORARY SETBACK

If 1936 represented a breakthrough for advocates of the scientific approach of collecting survey information, the 1948 election provided a sharp reminder of its limitations. The preelection polls of Crossley, Gallup, and Roper each projected a Dewey victory over Truman, by margins ranging from 5.0% to 15.1% (Mosteller et al., 1949: 17). These polls led newspapers to run headlines such as "Poll Taker Finds Presidency Good as Settled" in the *Times-Picayune* and "Dewey Victory in November by Wide Margin Predicted" in the *Wilmington Morning News* (Mosteller et al., 1949: 32) and, based partly on these poll findings, the *Chicago Daily Tribune* predicted a Dewey victory. On election day, Truman received 49.8% of the popular vote to Dewey's 45.4%, causing one commentator to note, "Everyone believes in public opinion polls. Everyone from the man in the street . . . up to President Thomas E. Dewey" (Babbie, 1990: 67). These results are a stark reminder to survey researchers of the need to carry out all aspects of the survey process with great care.

A review of the events of 1948 by the Social Science Research Council (Mosteller et al., 1949) identified a number of limitations of these election polls and led to some questions about the reliability of poll data. Two major limitations identified were (1) errors of sampling and interviewing, and (2) errors of forecasting. Quota sampling, which was used in the design of many of these surveys, is limited; the composition of the population may not be accurately known for the determination of quotas, and the respondents selected by interviewers may produce a **biased sample**. **Errors in forecasting** resulted from stopping data collection too soon, failing to identify likely voters adequately, and not allocating the undecided voters properly.

As a result of these incorrect predictions, major changes were made in the way in which surveys were conducted. One such change—which applied not only to preelection polls but to surveys more generally—was to move from quota samples, in which interviewers were responsible for respondent selection and were found to overrepresent higher- and middle-income respondents, to **modified area samples**. In addition, preelection interviewing is now continued much closer to election day, and polling organizations have developed some rather sophisticated methods for identifying potential voters and allocating the choices of the "undecideds" (Ladd, 1992: 27).[2] As a result, the preelection polls since this time have been more accurate. As shown in Table 2.1, since 1952 the average deviation between the final Gallup Poll and the actual election results has been 1.9%.[3]

Although properly conducted preelection polls are generally accurate, each presidential election cycle seems to generate some controversy or raise questions about their role in the campaign (Ladd, 1996a; Ladd and Ferree, 1981; Moore, 1996b; Pew Center for People and the Press, 2004; Traugott, 2001). The most recent major controversy involved the 2008 Democratic primary in New Hampshire, which has been described as "one of the most significant miscues in modern polling history" (Kohut, 2008). In this election, which centered largely on the contest between Barack Obama and Hillary Rodham Clinton, all the published polls had Senator Obama comfortably ahead, with an average margin of more than 8%; on election day, Senator Clinton received 39% of the vote to 36% for Senator Obama.

Table 2.1. The Accuracy of Gallup Preelection Polls

Year	Final Survey		Election Results		Deviation[a]
2010	58	Republican	54	Republican	+4
2008	55.0	Obama	53.0	Obama	+2.0
2006	54	Democrat	54	Democrat	0
2004	49.0	Bush	50.7	Bush	−1.7
2002	53	Republican	52	Republican	+1
2000	48.0	Bush	47.9	Bush	+0.1
1998	52	Democrat	50	Democrat	+2
1996	52.0	Clinton	49.2	Clinton	+2.8
1994	54	Republican	54	Republican	0
1992[b]	49.0	Clinton	43.3	Clinton	+5.7
1990	54	Democrat	55	Democrat	−1
1988	56.0	Bush	53.0	Bush	+2.0
1984	59.0	Reagan	59.2	Reagan	−0.2
1982	55	Democrat	56	Democrat	−2
1980	47.0	Reagan	50.8	Reagan	−3.8
1978	54	Democrat	54	Democrat	−1
1976	48.0	Carter	50.1	Carter	−2.1
1972	62.0	Nixon	61.8	Nixon	+0.2
1970	53	Democrat	54	Democrat	−1
1968	43.0	Nixon	43.5	Nixon	−0.5
1966	53	Democrat	54	Democrat	−1
1964	64.0	Johnson	61.3	Johnson	+ 2.7
1962	55	Democrat	53	Democrat	+ 2
1960	51.0	Kennedy	50.1	Kennedy	+ 0.9
1958	57	Democrat	56	Democrat	+1
1956	59.5	Eisenhower	57.8	Eisenhower	+1.7
1954	52	Democrat	53	Democrat	−1
1952	51.0	Eisenhower	55.4	Eisenhower	−4.4
1950	51	Democrat	50	Democrat	+ 1
1948	44.5	Truman	49.5	Truman	−5.0
1946	58	Republican	54	Republican	+4
1944	51.5	Roosevelt	53.8	Roosevelt	−2.3
1942	52	Democrat	48	Democrat	+4
1940	52.0	Roosevelt	55.0	Roosevelt	−3.0
1938	54	Democrat	51	Democrat	+3
1936	55.7	Roosevelt	62.5	Roosevelt	−6.8

Note: No congressional poll done in 1986.

[a]Average deviation for 37 national elections: 2.1 percent.

TREND IN DEVIATION

Elections	Average Error
1936–1950	3.6
1952–2010	1.9

[b]The Ross Perot candidacy created an additional source of error in estimating the 1992 presidential vote. There was no historical precedent for Perot, an independent candidate who was accorded equal status to the major party nominees in the presidential debates and had a record advertising budget. Gallup's decision to allocate none of the undecided vote to Perot, based on past performance of third party and independent candidates, resulted in the overestimation of Clinton's vote.

Sources: *The Gallup Poll Monthly*, November, 1992; *Time*, November 21, 1994; *Wall Street Journal*, November 6, 1996; www.gallup.com

These results led to an extensive investigation by the American Association for Public Opinion Research (2009). This study concluded that the following factors likely contributed to the miscall of this election: (1) polling may have ended too early to capture late shifts in the electorate; (2) some groups that supported Senator Clinton were underrepresented; (3) the influx of first-time voters may have had an adverse effect on likely voter models; (4) variations in weighting procedures produced estimation problems; and (5) the relationship between the race of the interviewer and the respondent had some effect.

AFTER 1948: CONTINUED GROWTH

The events of 1948 would prove to be only a temporary setback for survey research, and the period from 1948 to the mid-1960s was one of steady growth. The improvements in survey methods following this election spurred a period of expansion not only in commercial polling and government surveys but also particularly in universities (DeMaio, Marsh, and Turner, 1984: 27). In the period after World War II, there was a dramatic increase in the amount of survey research conducted in university settings, led by the Bureau of Applied Social Research at Columbia University, the National Opinion Research Center (NORC) at the University of Chicago, and the Survey Research Center (SRC) at the University of Michigan (J. Converse, 1987: 239). Each of these organizations contributed uniquely to the development of survey research, and programs originated by them, such as the American National Election Studies and the General Social Survey, continue to serve as important resources for survey researchers. These research programs will be discussed more fully in Chapter 3.

During the period between 1948 and the mid-1960s, there was also rapid expansion in commercial polling and audience research activities, led by organizations such as Gallup, Harris, Roper, Opinion Research Corporation, and Response Analysis. The latter part of this period also witnessed a growth in the use of surveys by the government, as federal agencies such as the U.S. Information Agency and the Departments of Commerce, Labor, Agriculture, and Health, Education, and Welfare realized their need for survey information. A number of the data collection efforts started during this period provided the foundation for programs that continue today (Sudman and Bradburn, 1987: S73). As noted previously, this was also a period of tremendous growth in academic survey work, as many researchers who were employed by the government during the war migrated to university settings with more technical expertise and greater scientific credibility gained through wartime experiences (J. Converse, 1987: 239–244).

Examples of the ways in which academic researchers, commercial firms, and governments utilize survey data are described in the next chapter.

A SURGE IN TELEPHONE INTERVIEWING: THE DEVELOPMENT OF RANDOM-DIGIT DIALING

By necessity, much of the survey research done through the mid-1960s involved face-to-face interviews. Interviewing by telephone was not considered a practical alternative for most probability samples because of non-coverage of the overall population. In 1936, it was estimated that 35% of the households in the United States had landline telephones. By 1960, this percentage had increased to 75%, and by 1986 it had risen to 93% (Massey, 1988: 3). By the 2000 Census, approximately 95% of households in the United States had landline telephones (U.S. Department of Commerce, Bureau of the Census, 2000).

As telephone coverage increased, data collection by telephone became a more practical alternative for obtaining information from a representative sample of a population, and the increasing costs of face-to-face interviewing gave impetus to the search for a viable alternative. There was, however, a reluctance among survey practitioners to adopt telephone methods, because the procedures typically used for sampling from non-specified populations, such as residents of a city, a state, or the voting age population of the United States, generally involved selection from lists such as telephone or city directories. Such listings contain known biases in that they are incomplete, do not include households with unlisted or recently added numbers, and become less accurate as time passes from their date of publication. The problems of sampling for general population telephone surveys were largely eliminated by the development of **random-digit dialing** (RDD), which is a method that randomly selects telephone numbers from a set of exchanges. More information about this technological advance that greatly facilitated an increase in surveying in the United States is provided in Chapter 4.[4]

The development of RDD also facilitated the increase in academic survey research organizations. As noted previously, in 1950 there were three such organizations: the Bureau of Applied Social Research, the NORC, and the SRC. By the start of the 1960s there were 8, and by 1970 there were 20. Currently, there are over 100 academic survey research organizations. Much of the growth in the number of academic survey research centers can be attributed to the increased demand for survey data that followed from increased governmental activities at the national, state, and local levels, as well as the need to evaluate these programs (O'Rourke, Sudman, and Ryan,

1996: 2–4). The development of RDD enabled university survey units to collect high-quality survey information at a relatively low cost.[5]

THE RISE OF INTERNET POLLING

A number of technological innovations such as **computer-assisted telephone interviewing** (CATI), **touchtone data entry** (TDE), and **voice recognition entry** (VRE) increased the flexibility and efficiency with which survey data were collected and contributed to the dominance of telephone interviewing as the primary means for survey data collection. The next major development in survey research began in the late 1990s. At this time, the situation with regard to Americans' access to the Internet was similar to that for telephones in the 1950s. That is, though an increasing number of households had access to the Internet, this percentage was not yet to the point that public opinion researchers could feel confident that a representative sample of the public could be reached through this means, particularly when those households without Internet access were known to have lower incomes and to be comprised of individuals who were older and generally had less formal education.

Some of the concerns that were starting to be raised about telephone interviewing during this time, together with the perceived possibility for significantly reduced data collection costs, led a number of researchers to explore the use of the Internet for collecting survey data. The first use of online surveys in the American political arena was done in conjunction with the 1998 U.S. elections. Since that time, increasing resources have been devoted to **electronic data collection**. As Brown and Johnson (2011) have recently noted, "The application of Web surveys . . . [has grown] . . . considerably in recent years, largely at the expense of telephone methodologies, which continue to confront increasing nonresponse and new technological barriers." The development and increased used of web survey methods has been characterized as "the most significant transition since the development and widespread adoption of probability sampling in 1936" (Goidel, 2011: 11).

Reflecting this interest in the use of the Internet for survey data collection, *Public Opinion Quarterly* devoted a 2008 special issue to "Web Survey Methods." The articles in this issue demonstrate that though a number of electronic data collection efforts have been successful and this method had a number of potential advantages, it faces its own set of challenges in terms of gathering information about the American mind, particularly when the goal is providing information on a representative sample of the country's population (Couper and Miller, 2008). Some of these challenges, as well as the prospects for electronic data collection, will be described more fully in Chapter 4. As will be evident in this discussion, survey research, like society in general, has changed dramatically since the first straw poll of 1824.

POLLS, POLLING, AND THE INTERNET

The national organization of pollsters, people who study polls and media reports of polls, is the American Association for Public Opinion Research. Visit the homepage of this organization at: www.aapor.org.

The original journal of public opinion scholarship is *Public Opinion Quarterly*, published by AAPOR. You can view the contents of the current issue at: http://poq.oxfordjournals.org/content/current.

Part II

HOW ARE OPINIONS MEASURED AND USED?

3

How Public Opinion Data Are Used

In American politics, public opinion data are used for a variety of purposes. Candidates use polling information as part of their effort to win elective office. Once in office, elected officials frequently use surveys to determine how the public feels on a variety of issues. Such monitoring of public opinion is done not only by officeholders but also by the media, who make independent observations of the public's views on a range of issues as well as take the public's pulse on the job performance of elected officials. Government agencies at all levels use surveys to assess their overall performance as well as to evaluate specific programs and to determine the needs of those they serve. Academic researchers use survey information to test hypotheses and to attempt to uncover those factors that account for differences in attitudes and political behavior. This chapter describes each of these uses of public opinion data in more detail.

USING PUBLIC OPINION IN POLITICAL CAMPAIGNS

In describing the role of public opinion data in American politics, an obvious starting point is their use in election campaigns. Polling data are used throughout the campaign cycle, and the polling that is done in a campaign varies considerably according to the resources available. Polling done for a presidential or senatorial campaign will generally be more extensive than that done for local candidates because far greater financial resources are available at the national level.

Benchmark Polls

A campaign that uses polling data effectively will typically conduct an extensive poll early in the process—that is, before a candidate has decided to run for office—that can be used as a benchmark for tracking the campaign's progress. Such a poll is designed not only to determine the candidate's standing (for example, name recognition and standing in trial heats), but also to identify issues and problems that the electorate views as important. It also identifies special groups within the electorate that may be receptive to special appeals (Roll and Cantril, 1980: 17–20).

The results of a **benchmark poll**—particularly for a nonincumbent—may be so negative in terms of lack of name recognition or the extent to which the individual is trailing in a trial heat that a potential candidate may decide against running. However, benchmark poll results are more commonly used to determine those issues the public feels are important, the stance on these issues that a majority of the public supports, the image that the electorate has of the candidate (and that of his or her potential opponents), and the subgroups that may be sources of voting strength or opposition. This information is used by the candidate's advisors or paid political consultants to aid candidates in (1) developing their issue positions and determining which issues should be stressed in the campaign; (2) identifying the characteristics (for example, competence or honesty) that are viewed positively and should be stressed, the areas in which the candidate's image needs improvement, and the characteristics on which opponents may be vulnerable; and (3) discovering groups whose views on a given issue may be distinct from other groups in a way that would make them responsive to a targeted appeal. If, for example, the benchmark poll for a reelection campaign reveals that the incumbent senator is perceived to be too much of a Washington insider, he or she may be advised to spend a great deal more time back in the state, visiting with the locals and "dressing down" to look more like his or her constituents.

Tracking Polls

Depending on resources, a benchmark survey is followed up at various points in the campaign by more polling to monitor a candidate's standing and to see whether the electorate's issue positions are changing or if new issues are emerging. This information is used to either support the strategy the candidate has been following or to suggest areas where changes are needed. Alternatively—or sometimes in addition to these follow-up surveys—a campaign may commission **tracking polls** over the final weeks of a campaign. Such tracking surveys generally consist of a relatively small number (100 to 200) of interviews that are conducted each day. The results of this daily interviewing[1] are then tracked and aggregated to determine if there are significant factors, such as a distinct trend in the preference of previously undecided voters, that would require some last-minute adjustment in campaign tactics, including the production of new television advertisements.[2]

As noted earlier, not all campaigns have the resources to mount repeated surveys or tracking efforts. Though candidates for local offices may desire more extensive polling data, they are forced to use their more limited resources on other aspects of the campaign and may only be able to conduct a single survey that reports their name recognition and identifies some of the issues that may be important in the campaign.

Pseudo-Polls

In the waning days of the campaign, the supporters of a single candidate or the local party organization may organize a telephone campaign that contacts registered voters to ask if they have decided who to vote for and whether they are planning to cast a ballot. Often such telephone get-out-the-vote" campaigns pretend to be a poll and then ask only two questions. The results of these telephone campaigns are used to organize the election-day strategy of the candidate. Such telephone canvasses are a replacement for the old method of having a precinct captain visit each voter before the election.

In recent years, a technique that has been used more frequently is known as the **push poll**. As described by the American Association for Public Opinion Research (AAPOR, 2003), a push poll is "an insidious form of negative campaigning disguised as a political poll that is designed to change opinions, not measure them." As described by Gawiser and Witt (2005: 9), "in a 'push poll,' a large number of people are called by telephone, often by an automated system, and asked to participate in a purported survey. The survey questions are really thinly-veiled accusations against an opponent or repetitions of rumors about a candidate's personal or professional behavior." In their view, a legitimate poll can usually be distinguished from a push poll by the number of calls made and the identity of those making the calls. A push poll "makes thousands and thousands of calls instead of the hundreds for most surveys" and is conducted by a telemarketing house or the campaign itself; a polling firm usually conducts a scientific survey.

Push polls have been condemned by AAPOR, the National Council on Public Polls, and other professional survey organizations because they intentionally lie or mislead respondents, and in so doing, they corrupt the political process. In most cases, there is no research component to a push poll and no data are actually collected. Instead, as many members of the electorate as possible are called without any sampling. The results of such a poll, if released, "give a seriously flawed and biased picture of the political situation" (Gawiser, 1995: 1).

One of the problems in recognizing push polls is their resemblance to *negative message testing*, which is generally considered to be a legitimate use of survey research done as part of a benchmarking or tracking poll. In negative message testing, **push questions** are asked that contain attacks on a candidate to test how vulnerable that candidate might be to such attacks from the opposing party. Push questions, according to Charlie Cook, "test potential arguments against a rival to ascertain how effective those arguments might be" (quoted in Feld, 2001: 38) and help a political campaign plan its strategy. Failure to distinguish between a push poll and push questions has led to confusion among consumers of polls, and some candidates who are confronted with negative poll results claim that it is because they are the target of a push poll.

One of the most well-known examples of such a push poll debate occurred during the 2000 Republican presidential primary in South Carolina. Polls had indicated that George W. Bush and John McCain were running fairly closely in this race, with McCain seeming to have gained some momentum from his 18-point victory in the New Hampshire primary. The Bush campaign conducted polling in which potential Republican primary voters were asked, among other things, if they approved of McCain's "legislation that proposed the largest tax increase in United States history," and whether they would be more likely to vote for or against McCain after learning that his "campaign finance proposals would give labor unions and the media a bigger influence on the outcomes of elections" (Saletan, 2000). McCain complained that the poll pushed respondents toward a negative view of him. The Bush campaign admitted that it asked tough questions, but that these questions were part of a real poll, not a push poll.

The continued use of push polls has led some legislators and political reform groups to call for legislation to regulate political polling. Push polls are not research based at all but simply spread rumors or lies about a candidate using a quasi-interview format. Rules have been proposed in some states that would require all poll takers to identify the sponsor of the poll before asking any questions. Karl G. Feld (2001: 38) argues that such disclosure would immediately bias the respondents' answers: Republican voters, for example, would be biased against any poll sponsored by a Democratic campaign group. In 2007, Representative Thomas E. Petri (R–Wisconsin) introduced the Push Poll Disclosure Act of 2007 (H.R. 1298) requiring that each participant in a federal election poll be told the identity of the survey's sponsor whenever at least 1,200 households are included and that when a survey's results are not released to the public, the cost of the poll and the sources of its funding be reported to the Federal Election Commission, along with a count of the households contacted and a transcript of the questions asked. Although this attempt to pass a federal law has failed to date, New Hampshire passed a law that is being enforced.[3] Inasmuch as New Hampshire traditionally holds the first primary election with its large field of candidates, the impact of this legislation on the polling industry should be well tested there. Polling organizations fear such legislation and commentators such as Feld (2001: 39) recommend that the polling organization and professional associations focus on educating journalists, political officials, and the public to fend off regulation.

The Polling Industry

Polling has become an industry in its own right with its own industry organizations. The American Association for Public Opinion Research includes members from the major survey research firms together with members of the media and academic practitioners. The Council of American Survey Research Organizations (CASRO) is a trade association of over 250 survey research organizations whose purpose is to represent the industry through public communication and education efforts. It focuses on advancing the professionalism of the survey research community. The National Council on Public Polls (NCPP) is an association of polling organizations whose mission is to set professional standards for public opinion pollsters and to advance understanding among politicians, the media, and the general public about how polls are conducted. The Council for Marketing and Opinion Research (CMOR) works on behalf of the survey research industry to promote positive legislation and prevent the passage of laws that could negatively impact the industry.

Given the amount of resources devoted to polling and the ever-increasing attention given to survey results in developing campaign strategies, the political process in the United States is open to charges of paying more attention to the packaging of a candidate rather than to the presentation of policy positions for voters to evaluate in making their choices. Such a critique, however, ignores the fact that polling data are not the sole basis on which candidates develop campaigns. Their own views on issues, the position of their party, the advice of other elected officials and advisors, as well as information from focus groups all play a role in the development of an election strategy. Though polling data do have an impact on how the candidate is marketed, it is also true that election polls attempt to determine the issue positions of the electorate and incorporate these into the campaign. This information can serve as a base for the candidate, once elected, to use in formulating policies that conform to the wishes of his or her constituents.

THE USE OF PUBLIC OPINION POLLING
BY ELECTED OFFICEHOLDERS

Though public opinion data can be used effectively by any elected official, their use is most visible—and probably most frequent—at the presidential level. The first president to have a regular flow of polling information into his office was Franklin D. Roosevelt (Roll and Cantril, 1980: 10). As described by Cantril (1967), Roosevelt reviewed polls on a range of issues, from sending aid to Britain prior to the United States' entry into World War II to providing farm subsidies. In Cantril's view, "Roosevelt never altered his goals because public opinion was against him or was uninformed. Rather he utilized such information to try to bring the public around more quickly or more effectively to the course of action he felt was best for the country" (1967: 41).

The presidents immediately following Roosevelt—Truman and Eisenhower—did not use polls extensively, although they were briefed on public attitudes toward major issues (Bradburn and Sudman, 1988: 40). Though John F. Kennedy did not commission any polls directly, Louis Harris and others reported the findings of many of their polls to him and "the published polls of Gallup and his colleagues were studied with great care" (Sorenson, 1965: 333).

Lyndon Johnson did, in contrast, commission polls, but his use of them was more effective in campaigning than in governing. On two of the more important issues of his presidency—the tax increase of 1966 and the Vietnam War—Johnson either went against the tide of public opinion or seemingly let it play little role in his decision (Bradburn and Sudman, 1988: 43). As reported by Jacobs and Shapiro (1995: 168), Nixon conducted more surveys than Kennedy "by a factor of over ten" and more surveys than Johnson "by nearly a factor of two." The presidency of Jimmy Carter marked the institutionalization of public opinion as an important component of the governing process, together with an increasing role for the president's pollster as a policy advisor.[4] Pat Caddell was Carter's pollster during the 1976 campaign and moved to Washington after the election. Though he was not an official member of the White House staff, Caddell continued to poll on issues for the president and gained influence in the policy process that was unprecedented for a pollster (Moore, 1992: 145). One of the most famous missteps caused by the use of polling data occurred in 1979. As the Carter administration approached the 1980 campaign, the president wanted to improve his popular standing. Although the low approval ratings and general dissatisfaction of the nation could be traced to very poor economic conditions, pollster Caddell argued that they reflected a more basic "crisis of confidence" (Moore, 1992: 149). At Caddell's urging, Carter canceled a major energy speech just 48 hours before he was scheduled to deliver it and delivered, instead, the famous "malaise" speech. Following the themes laid out by Caddell, the president proclaimed that there was a "malaise" affecting the American public and charged the people to restore faith and rebuild confidence in America. The views of the pollster were clearly evident in what has been termed "the most important speech" of the Carter presidency (Moore, 1992: 149). The reaction of the public and most commentators was surprise and disbelief rather than support for the president's view.

Polling data continued to play an important role during the presidency of Ronald Reagan. Reagan's pollster for the 1980 campaign was Richard Wirthlin, who continued his association with Reagan during his two terms, although he never worked directly in the White House. Instead, Wirthlin would meet with the president every three to four weeks and brief him on the public's view of the issues. The *Washington Post* reported that Wirthlin was spending nearly a million dollars a year in polling for the White House and the Republican National Committee, and Moore reported that more polling was done for the Reagan administration than for any of Reagan's predecessors (Moore, 1992: 215). Although George H. W. Bush collected polling information during his presidency, his use of survey data was less extensive than that of his predecessor. As Murray and Howard (2002: 534–535) report, Bush spent much less for survey research during his first three years in office (about $399,000); the Reagan administration "conducted at least 57 national polls during its first three years as compared with 15 by the Bush administration, a ratio of almost 4 to 1. Moreover, Bush was not above deriding the polls, referring late in the 1992 campaign to "those nutty pollsters" (Funk and Wrinn, *Charlotte Observer*, October 22, 1992) who showed him trailing Bill Clinton.

The Clinton administration raised the use of polls in governing to another level. During Clinton's first year in office, his pollster, Stanley Greenberg, was paid almost $2 million to conduct surveys and focus groups. More than any other president, Clinton "relies on polls and focus groups in helping to determine what he needs to be saying and how he should say it" (Perry, 1994: A16). The influence wielded by the president's pollster had grown to the point that this position had been labeled the "Pollster General" (Schneider, 1997b: 7). After the midterm elections of 1994, Clinton switched from Greenberg to the polling firm of Penn and Schoen, but this switch did not lessen the emphasis on polls. Under Penn and Schoen, the White House conducted a poll per night, using this information to shape policy positions in a way that gives governing aspects of a "permanent campaign." Clinton's use of polls was alternately admired and criticized by his rivals, who acknowledged that even though these polls provided the president with an accurate reading of the public's pulse, they enabled Clinton to change issue positions to take advantage of the public's current thinking on an issue.

President George W. Bush entered office eschewing such use of pollsters. In reply to a journalist's question about a front-page poll in June 2001, Bush responded, "I don't even know what polls you're talking about, nor do I care" (Kiefer, 2001). One part of Bush's campaign strategy (and a reaction to criticism of Clinton's "governing by polls") was to convey the message that he governed "based upon principle and not polls and focus groups" as a way of demonstrating his leadership qualities (Green, 2002). However, political analysts noted that the Bush political team did review polling data to plan political strategy. Analysis of disbursement records of the Republican National Committee indicated that the party and the administration probably spent about what other presidents have, $1 million or more, annually.

President Obama's use of polling appears to be closer to that of President George W. Bush than to President Clinton's. While he has eschewed polling in public, saying he would lead "not by polls, but by principle" (Smith, 2009), the White House political organization uses polling data gathered by pollsters Joel Benenson and Paul Harstad. The surveys, which are paid for by the Democratic National Committee, are often used to test words and phrases so the White House can improve the effectiveness of the president's communications with the public and the media. Unlike President Clinton, Obama does not study polling data closely, leaving that activity to David Axelrod and David Plouffe, his political consultants.[5]

Use of polls by other elected officials is done on a much smaller scale. Members of the House and Senate, governors, state legislators, and local elected officials could use public opinion data in the same way as the president, but the resources usually are not available below the level of the chief executive. Members of Congress often must rely on national or statewide polls and use this information together with other sources (letters, contacts from contributors, feedback from staffers in their district) to determine the views of their constituents. Similarly, local elected officials are infrequently in a position to conduct a special-purpose poll and must rely more often on surveys conducted by departments or agencies within their jurisdiction to gain some idea of the public's feeling on specific aspects of the government's performance.

Polling can, however, become an important part of debates on new legislation being considered by the president or Congress. When the Obama administration began its signature policy initiative, the reform of the U.S. health insurance system, the potential changes in this system and their impacts on the American public became the subject of multiple polls commissioned by interest groups such as the American Association of Retired Persons, the American Medical Association, the national parties, and, of course, the media, who were trying to cover the story. As the debate over health care reform stretched throughout 2009, those who supported the measure and those who opposed it quoted polling data. Public responses to these multiple polling efforts were often contradictory because survey questions were worded to obtain support or opposition from the respondents. Some examples of these question wording effects are discussed in Chapter 8. Interest groups made public the data that fit their point of view while using private survey results to shape their lobbying efforts on Capitol Hill and in the media. Not surprisingly, many polls found considerable reluctance among the public to embrace major changes in the system, no matter how faulty it might be.[6]

Controversy over the use of polls by officeholders will continue indefinitely. In one respect, the use of polls can be seen as consonant with democratic theory in that it provides a way for elected officials to find out what their constituents want. Conversely, officeholders who make extensive use of public opinion data are subject to the charge of governing by the polls and of modifying their positions to satisfy public whims. Nonetheless, public opinion data seem to be playing an increasingly important role in the policy process.

THE USE OF POLLING DATA BY GOVERNMENT AGENCIES

In Chapter 2, we described the use of survey research by the federal government before World War II and as part of the wartime effort. Although the government's involvement in surveys was scaled back after the war, it increased greatly in the mid-1960s, and by 1980 government surveys accounted for 5 million of the 20 million interviews that were conducted (Sharp, 1984: 681), and the number of surveys conducted by the federal government has increased dramatically since that time.[7]

Use by Federal Agencies

Though the government uses surveys for a great deal of data collection, the information collected is for the most part not attitudinal data, but rather demographic and behavioral indicators that provide the context in which the American mind develops. A number of the major surveys carried out by the federal government are not of individuals but of institutions.[8] For example, among the many data collection efforts of the Census Bureau are annual surveys of state and local governments to obtain data on revenue, expenditures, debt, and employment, and a monthly sample survey of about 160,000 nonfarm establishments to get data on employment, hours, and earnings by industry. The U.S. Department of Education conducts an annual survey of all institutions of higher education to collect data on total enrollment by gender, level of enrollment, type of program, racial/

ethnic characteristics, and attendance status of students. The Department of Agriculture carries out surveys of farm operators to collect data on planted acreage and livestock inventories as well as total farm production, expenses, and specific commodity costs of production. These surveys are a source of valuable information to decision makers interested in these specific policy areas. They also provide data that may affect how individual citizens view issues related to these areas.

Major federal data collection efforts involving individuals focus largely on demographic characteristics and behavioral indicators. One of the largest studies is the Census Bureau's Current Population Survey (CPS), which involves a nationwide monthly sample survey of the civilian noninstitutionalized population, 16 years or older, to obtain data on unemployment, the labor force, and a number of other characteristics, and it serves as a vehicle for studies on other subjects, such as tobacco use and marital and birth history. This survey uses a sample of approximately 57,000 households. The Survey of Income and Program Participation (SIPP), also done by the Census Bureau, provides estimates of money and in-kind income and participation in government programs. Recurring questions focus on employment, types of income, and noncash benefits.

In addition to the vast amount of demographic information collected by the Census Bureau, information about various behavioral characteristics of the American public comes from other federal agencies. For example, the National Center for Health Statistics conducts the National Health Interview Survey (NHIS), a sample of about 43,000 households including about 106,000 persons. This survey involves continuous data collection covering the civilian noninstitutionalized population to get information on amount, distribution, and effects of illness and disability in the United States and the services rendered for or because of such conditions.

Other surveys conducted by the Department of Health and Human Services supply information on (1) topics such as health utilization, expenditures, and insurance in addition to related information on health status and disability (National Medical Expenditure Survey); (2) the incidence, prevalence, consequences, and patterns of substance use and abuse (National Household Survey on Drug Use and Health); (3) how individuals view their health and what they do about it in terms of seeking health care, the kind of care sought, and their ability to perform normal functions (National Health and Nutrition Examination Survey); and (4) family planning, contraceptive use and efficacy, and other aspects of reproductive health, family formation, and dissolution (National Survey of Family Growth).

Other federal agencies gather information on topics such as crime victimization (U.S. Bureau of Justice Statistics, National Crime Victimization Survey); family balance sheets, the terms of loans, and relationships with financial institutions (Board of Governors of the Federal Reserve System,

Survey of Consumer Finances); and energy-related household characteristics, housing unit characteristics, use of fuels, and energy consumption
and expenditures by fuel type (U.S. Energy Information Administration,
Residential Energy Consumption Survey).

In addition to these ongoing data collection efforts, various federal agencies conduct surveys for a variety of different purposes, such as needs assessments, as part of an evaluation of a project or program, or in addressing
a specific policy issue. Beyond these surveys conducted directly by federal
agencies, there are a number of programs in which the federal government
sponsors surveys in the states. For example, in the Substance Abuse and
Mental Health Services Administration's Center for Substance Abuse Treatment State Demand and Needs Assessment Project, approximately 250,000
interviews were conducted with members of the general population over a
three-year period. In addition, a number of surveys of special populations—
for example, students, arrestees, the homeless, and welfare recipients—were
conducted as part of this effort. Similarly, the Centers for Disease Control
and Prevention sponsors the Behavioral Risk Factor Surveillance System
(BRFSS), in which the states annually collect data on health risk factors
and attitudes. Described as "the world's largest telephone survey," BRFSS
is designed to monitor state-level prevalence of the major behavioral risks
among adults associated with morbidity and mortality. BRFSS was established in 1984, and by 1994 all states, the District of Columbia, and three
territories were participating. Clearly, the federal government is a major
user of the results of survey research.[9]

As these descriptions indicate, most of the information collected through
federal government surveys involves factual or behavioral characteristics,
with only a limited number of subjective items that are of primary interest
in describing the American mind.[10] Although the number of such items
included in government surveys has increased in recent years, they still
tend to be quasi-factual or to involve evaluations of specific programs. In
considering the American mind, the data from government surveys are important because they serve as the analytic base for formulating policy and
monitoring changes in the conditions of the American public that provides
the milieu within which the American mind functions.

One agency that does collect considerable public opinion information
is the Office of Research, Bureau of Intelligence and Research in the Department of State. This agency is responsible for advising the president,
secretary of state, and other foreign affairs policy makers of foreign public
opinion about the United States and its policies. It commissions public
opinion surveys in nearly every country of the world and analyzes polls of
American opinion published by domestic survey research organizations.

It is important to note that although the federal government conducts
many surveys through its agencies, it also contracts with private commercial

research firms and academic centers to collect data. In addition, many of the surveys that we will discuss subsequently, as well as secondary data analyses, are funded through competitive government grants from agencies such as the National Science Foundation and the National Institutes of Health.

Counting Americans: The Census and Polls

The Census Bureau is one of the largest polling agencies in the United States, conducting polls of thousands of individuals each month. However, the actual Census of the United States is not a poll. The Census is required by the Constitution in order to apportion the members in the House of Representatives among the states. The actual wording in Article I is: "The actual Enumeration shall be made within three Years after the first Meeting of the Congress of the United States, and within every subsequent Term of ten Years, in such Manner as they shall by Law direct."

The decennial Census of the United States is, therefore, an enumeration of the population, meaning that it is an actual count of all the people in the country. It is not a poll of a sample of the population, as are public opinion polls. Over the years, however, the Census has become more difficult to conduct. Some groups in the population have been undercounted, such as members of minority groups and immigrants. In some cases, individuals do not wish to be found by the federal government because they have legal problems that might be discovered or they are suspicious of the government. In other cases, living conditions are such that some individuals simply cannot be counted.

Why does this matter? Not only is the Census used to reapportion elected representatives among the states, it is also used to decide how much funding is to be sent to a state or city under certain federal programs. An undercount can cost the state or urban area millions of federal dollars as well as their representation in Congress.

How do we know if there has been an undercount? Survey research by the Census Bureau has exacerbated the problem because surveys conducted with the best technology available predict that the population totals are different from those reported by the count. In planning for the 2000 Census, the Clinton administration proposed that the Census include a component based on survey research in addition to the traditional count. Congressional Republicans opposed this proposal, and eventually the Supreme Court decided that the Census must be based on an "enumeration," not a poll. The results of the 2000 Census, when announced, met controversy, but even scholars could not agree on the right method to correct errors found in the enumeration, although most agreed it was the most accurate Census ever taken in the United States.

Denied the possibility of supplementing the Census "count," the Department of Commerce instituted the American Community Survey (ACS), which provides monthly and annual updates to the information gathered on the "long form" Census document and much more. Each month, the ACS sends out approximately 250,000 surveys to American households. Of those households that do not respond to the survey, a small sample is chosen for follow-up with a high success rate for completions. The ACS seeks demographic, housing, income, and social information that is compiled into annual datasets. Such information, while it cannot be used for the same governmental purposes as the decennial Census, is made available to the public and is widely used by business and government to measure changes in their own states and cities.

State Government

Although states, like the federal government, gather information on institutions, industries, and households as indicators of the state's economic well-being, they also sponsor surveys of public attitudes to guide and evaluate public policies. Individual states conduct a number of ongoing programs that utilize survey information (such as the Alcohol and Other Drug Abuse Treatment Needs Assessment, the Behavioral Risk Factor Surveillance System, and Pregnancy Risk Assessment Monitoring System) with funds from the federal government. Many of these state surveys (as well as those commissioned by local governments) are conducted by survey research organizations affiliated with colleges or universities.

As at the federal level, individual state agencies use surveys for specific needs. In South Carolina, for example, the Institute for Public Service and Policy Research conducts the South Carolina State Survey. Various state departments participate in the twice-yearly survey to gain information about the state's needs and the citizens' perceptions of state programs. Among the agencies that have participated in the survey are the South Carolina Department of Parks, Recreation, and Tourism, the Department of Revenue, the Department of Health and Environmental Control, and Prevent Child Abuse South Carolina.

As these examples illustrate, states use public opinion in a variety of ways to determine how their citizens feel about policy issues; to identify needs they have in areas such as aging, health, recreation, and transportation; to monitor their performance; and to evaluate specific policies or programs.

Local Government

Local governments use public opinion data in many of the same ways as the federal government and the states. One of the primary uses at the local level is services evaluation. The city of Cincinnati, for example, has conducted a number of surveys designed to solicit citizen feedback on the services provided by various city departments, as well as to identify citizen budget priorities (Tuchfarber and Smith, 1995). Individual local government agencies also use surveys for needs assessments, to evaluate individual policies, or to monitor performance. The City of Cincinnati's police department periodically conducts surveys of the public's impressions of the services it provides (Rademacher, 2003), and the city's public transit agency, Queen City Metro, has employed survey data to assess the public's view of a tax increase for transit services (Tuchfarber and Weise, 1982), to evaluate a weekend fare experiment (Oldendick and Tuchfarber, 1984), and to develop a marketing plan (Tuchfarber and Oldendick, 1986).

PUBLIC OPINION AND INTEREST GROUPS

Not all of the public opinion data cited by public officials in policy debates are gathered by political parties or government pollsters. As noted in the discussion of the Obama health care reform plan, policy debates inspire interest groups and, indeed, interested corporations and labor unions, to commission their own polls so that they will have appropriate data to cite during discussions with public officials or to release to the public in an attempt to influence public views. This type of interest group polling can have an impact on policy decisions on the national scene or at the state and local levels. During the buildup to the Persian Gulf War, the Kuwaiti royal family and its supporters commissioned the Wirthlin Group to poll the American people about their support for a military invasion of Kuwait to repel the Iraqi army. The Wirthlin Group implemented weekly tracking polls to measure the opinions of U.S. citizens. One of their findings (which was shared with the George H. W. Bush White House) was that the American people did not support military intervention to preserve access to Kuwaiti oil reserves but did support military action for moral reasons (Wilcox, Ferrara, and Alsop, 1991).

As the debate over federal funding for stem cell research heated up in Congress, the Juvenile Diabetes Research Foundation (JDRF), which supported such research, commissioned a poll that found 65% of Americans supporting federal funding of stem cell research and 26% opposing it. In announcing the results of this poll, Peter Van Etten, president and CEO of JDRF, noted that "this poll is a very significant signal from the American people that federal funding for stem cell research should continue, and we agree." At about the same time, the National Conference of Catholic Bishops (NCCB), which opposed research that destroyed human embryos, commissioned a poll that found Americans opposed federal funding of research that required destroying human embryos, 70% to 24%. "Polls sponsored by groups promoting destructive embryo research claim to show broad support for their agenda," commented Richard Doerflinger of the NCCB Secretariat (NCCB, 2003). They do this, he asserted, by "presenting false and misleading claims as though they are fact, to push the respondent to a favorable answer" (NCCB, 2003). Each of these groups found support for their position and were not hesitant to use poll results to support their stance. The difference in results was produced largely by the questions asked. In the JDRF poll, respondents were read a fairly long description of stem cell research that included the statement "medical researchers believe that human stem cells can be developed into replacement cells to combat diseases such as diabetes, Parkinson's, Alzheimer's, cancer, heart disease, burns, or spinal cord problems," before being asked whether they favored or opposed funding of stem cell research by the National Institutes of Health. The Catholic Bishops question included the wording, "Congress is considering whether to provide federal funding for experiments using stem cells from human embryos. The live embryos would be destroyed in their first week of development to obtain these cells" (Nisbet, 2004: 148).

At the state and local levels, interest groups also commission polls to have an impact on policy debates. Obviously, the sponsoring organizations hope that they will be able to release poll results that back their own position or goals. The Indiana Rural Health Association sponsored a poll in four counties of Indiana that found a majority of rural voters would support a law requiring smoke-free restaurants. The West Virginia branch of the American Federation of Teachers, a union for school teachers, surveyed its members on the desirability of including disabled students in mainstream classrooms. The Tourism and Convention Center of Massachusetts reported that a survey of state voters showed support for a new sports megaplex, and the Columbus, Ohio, based Council for Responsible Waste Solutions showed that Ohioans wanted to take care of disposal problems now rather than wait for some future time. As election day approached in 2011, Florida polls showed conflicting results over whether to bring casinos to south Florida. A poll sponsored by the Genting organization (owner of the casino property) showed that 60% of state residents supported expanding casino gambling in south Florida. A poll sponsored by No Casinos (a Disney-backed group) had different results: it found that 47% of Floridians wanted to "keep things as they are," and 30% believe there is too much gambling already (Klas, 2011). In each of these instances, the respective sponsor of the poll intended to use the poll results to buttress its own position with legislators and with the citizenry of the state. In addition, it hoped to get a good report in the media that would enhance its own reputation as being civic minded.

THE USE OF POLLING BY THE MEDIA

The tracing of the first poll to the straw vote conducted by the *Harrisburg Pennsylvanian* in 1824 illustrates the close connection between polls and the media. In the early years of the 20th century, numerous media outlets, such as the *New York Herald*, the *Cincinnati Enquirer*, the *Boston Globe*, and the *Chicago Examiner*, conducted polls on candidates as well as polls on issues. By 1932, Robinson had identified 85 different media polling operations in the United States, most of which were local or regional. One of the few with a national focus, and one of the largest and most prestigious, was that conducted by the *Literary Digest*.

Part of the intrigue surrounding the preelection polls of 1936 involved Gallup's attempts to increase media subscriptions to his poll. Gallup was convinced that the sampling methods that he had been developing would produce a prediction of the election that was closer than that of the *Literary Digest* and offered newspaper subscribers a money-back guarantee to that effect. Although this gamble was successful, one can only imagine Gallup's anxiety as he awaited the election returns—a wrong prediction of which would have cost him about a quarter of a million dollars (Moore, 1992: 31–32). Following this election, Gallup continued to increase the number of newspapers that carried reports of his polls and also published in the popular press and in advertising trade magazines (J. Converse, 1987: 118).

After 1936, the number of independent polls declined and the media came to rely more on pollsters such as Gallup, Crossley, Roper, and later Harris for their information on the public's views. By the 1960s, reports of the Gallup Poll and the Harris poll represented the major uses of polls by the media (Moore, 1992: 275).

The use of survey data by the media changed dramatically when the major news organizations established their own polling operations. CBS was the first to set up a polling unit in 1967; however, it temporarily halted its polling operations after 1970 (Moore, 1992: 273). After the 1972 election, the major news organizations felt a pressing need to establish a means to conduct their own polls (Moore, 1992: 297). Although the CBS/*New York Times* Poll has maintained its own survey unit, other major news organizations, such as the NBC/*Wall Street Journal* and ABC News/*Washington Post* rely on data from outside polling firms. In charting the rise of poll reporting in the *New York Times*, Brehm (1993: 4) notes that even though only a handful of polls appeared in the early 1950s, by the mid-1960s the number of stories cited jumped to more than 100 per year and by the 1970s, this had reached around 300 citations per year, or nearly one story a day.

Most of these news organizations conduct periodic polls on issues and now emulate the academic surveys by repeating standard questions over time. Foreign policy crises or major policy debates in the domestic arena evoke flurries of polling by the media organizations as they use the polls to cover the developing story and to increase readership. Operation Desert Storm may well have been the most polled-about event in U.S. history, with hundreds of polls commissioned before the combat began. The Iraq War, which has stretched to almost a decade, has generated thousands of polls. However, much of the media's efforts—and resources—is devoted to polling during presidential election years and to monitoring presidential approval in the years between elections.

Trial heats for the succeeding presidential contest begin almost immediately after an election and have become a part of the almost continual campaign for the presidency (one of the first polls for the *2012* election was conducted in February *2009*, less than two weeks after Barack Obama was inaugurated). At a time when the president's approval rating was in the high 60s, the poll tested Republican support for potential candidates Sarah Palin, Mike Huckabee, Mitt Romney, and Bobby Jindal. In the early stages of a campaign, good showings in the polls and the attendant media coverage can be critical factors in determining which potential candidates decide to run and how their showing in the primaries is interpreted (Graber, 1997: 250–253). Though this **horse-race journalism** has been criticized (Wheeler, 1980), the "who's winning" aspect of an election campaign seems to be more interesting to the mass public than in-depth probes of the issue positions of the candidates. Reporting of trial heat results remains an integral part of the media's campaign coverage.

Exit Polling

This focus on trial heats culminates with another type of polling used almost exclusively by the media, the **exit poll**. Exit polling involves the sampling of precincts, with self-administered questionnaires completed by randomly selected respondents as they leave the polling place (Levy, 1983). The first exit polls were used as a check on the election projections made on the basis of key precincts, but over time exit polls have come to play a more prominent role in projecting election outcomes. They also provide a valuable source of information about the factors underlying voter choice. The interviewers who conduct exit polls begin sending their computer-tabulated results to the national office by noon on election day. They are able to have their final exit interviews completed and transmitted within a few moments of the polls closing. By entering these data into sophisticated computer models, the network news organizations are able to project the winners of elections at the state level by the time the polls close.

After facing the huge cost of maintaining separate polling organizations for election day, CBS, ABC, NBC, and CNN combined their exit polling efforts in 1990, creating Voter Research and Surveys, now known as Voter News Service (VNS). On election day 1996, VNS conducted 71,093 interviews. Including the primary election campaign, they did more than 82,371 exit interviews during that year.[11] The consolidated VNS operation provided data to each of the media partners so that they could make independent predictions of the winners and losers.

The role played by VNS in the media's reporting of elections came into sharp focus on election night 2000. VNS provided the results of its exit polling across the country, including Florida, to the networks. The networks did not "call" the presidential race in Florida at 7:00 P.M. when the polls closed in most of the state. Warren Mitofsky, who developed exit polling in the 1960 election and who called the 2000 election for CBS/CNN news networks, explains that they did not call Florida for Al Gore until actual results were received from the sample precincts. At that time, the network and other networks called the state for candidate Gore. Mitofsky believed that in this rare case, a "designed and tested sample yield[ed] an estimate that [was] wide of the mark" (Mitofsky, 2001). As more vote tallies came in, the networks reversed the call and marked Florida as "too close to call." Then, in the middle of the night, basing their projection on reports of precinct vote counts, the networks called the vote for George W. Bush at 2:15 A.M. In that case, networks were working from data that later proved to have been entered into the computer in error. After 2000, the networks declared their intention to keep using VNS for their predictions but also to invest resources into making the VNS data more accurate.

In 2002, problems with the VNS computer system as well as technical problems in collecting information caused VNS to abandon its exit polls, saying it could not guarantee the accuracy of the analysis, and forced the media organizations that were relying on this information for their election night coverage to turn to other sources of information. As a result VNS was disbanded, and in 2004 the firms of Edison Media Research and Mitofsky International were given the responsibility of collecting exit poll information for the National Election Pool (NEP), a consortium of media organizations that include the Associated Press, ABC, CBS, CNN, Fox, and NBC.

Despite efforts to avoid a repeat of the problems that exit polls had encountered in 2000 and 2002, the 2004 elections created their own share of controversy. As characterized by Larry Sabato, director of the University of Virginia Center for Politics, "Let's be honest. They spent four years and a lot of money and were just as bad with their 'exit polls' as they were in 2000. It's disgraceful how bad the information was" (Memmott, 2004a). Although some of the problems with the exit poll data, such as the leaking of data, were out of the control of the NEP, the major criticism of the use of these data was that they significantly overstated the level of support for

John Kerry and led some commentators to hint that Kerry appeared likely to win (Memmott, 2004b).

Following this election, Edison Media Research and Mitofsky International (2005) did an extensive evaluation of their exit poll procedures. Although this report acknowledged that the estimates produced by the exit poll data on November 2, 2004, "were not as accurate as we have produced with previous exit polls," they pointed to one primary reason for the differences between the exit poll estimates and the actual vote count: Kerry voters participated in the exit polls at a higher rate than Bush voters. This evaluation did not find any systematic problems with the way in which the exit poll data were collected and processed, such as with the sample selection of the polling locations. Although they believed that there were motivational factors that made Kerry voters more likely to participate in exit polls than Bush voters, they could not pinpoint precisely the reasons for these differences and concluded that a number of factors, such as distance restrictions placed upon interviewers, weather conditions that lowered completion rates, and interviewer characteristics, contributed to this discrepancy (Edison Media Research and Mitofsky International, 2005: 1–2).[12] Edison Research conducted the exit polls in 2008 and succeeded in keeping the results from being leaked before the polls closed. In general, these polls were more accurate and met the needs of the media sponsors without the controversies of the past.

The technique of exit polling and prime-time predictions has led to some controversy over whether "early calls" of elections discourage voters in western time zones from voting. Critics charge that the exit polls not only may impact final election results in western states but that they are also "an impediment to the citizen's right to privately cast a ballot" (Cantrell, 1992: 414). From time to time, proposals have been made to limit the projection of elections before polls closed in the latest time zone, but any such attempt to limit the media would probably be struck down as violating freedom of the press.

TRACKING PRESIDENTIAL APPROVAL RATINGS

In polls conducted between elections, one of the key measures that is monitored is **presidential approval**, which has been termed "the most closely watched political indicator in the United States" (Erikson and Tedin, 2011: 118). The first general measurement of presidential approval was taken in 1938 when the Gallup Organization asked, "Do you approve or disapprove of the way President Roosevelt is handling his job as President?" Like many other aspects of the polling industry, use of this question has increased dramatically in recent years. It was asked 15 times during Truman's first term in office, 110 times during the four years of the senior Bush's presidency (Ragsdale, 1997: 229), and more than 1,400 times during the eight years of George W. Bush's term.[13]

As shown in Figure 3.1, presidential approval varies significantly over time. Having just been victorious, presidents generally come into office with a relatively high approval rating. As presidents take actions that displease certain groups and are subject to criticism, their approval rating experiences an erosion before stabilizing at a more natural level at the end of their first year. Presidential approval ratings are significantly related to Americans' perceptions of the economy (Kinder and Kiewiet, 1979; MacKuen, Erikson, and Stimson, 1992). When foreign affairs become a salient concern to Americans, the effect is generally to produce at least a short-term increase in presidential approval in a "rally 'round the flag" effect (Mueller, 1973, 1994; Nickelsburg and Norpoth, 2000). As shown in Figure 3.1, public approval of President H. W. Bush soared to 89% in early 1991, signaling strong popular support for the Persian Gulf War and the successful pursuit of that military effort. Within one year, continuing economic difficulties brought a decline in his approval rating to 38%, about the level it had been before Kuwait was invaded (Ragsdale, 1997: 232; see also Parker, 1995). A similar surge and decline was evident in the approval ratings of George W. Bush. In the Gallup Poll conducted immediately before the events of September 11, 2001, 51% approved of the way Bush was doing his job as president. In the immediate aftermath of September 11, this approval rating reached 90%, remained between 85% and 90% through the rest of the year, and continued at relatively high

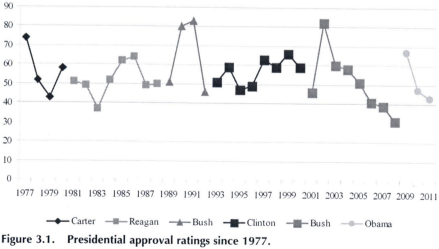

Figure 3.1.   Presidential approval ratings since 1977.
Source: Roper Center Public Opinion Archives.

levels throughout much of 2002. Over time, these high approval ratings eroded, and by August 2005, Bush's approval rating had reached 45%, as Americans expressed increasing concerns about the war in Iraq. His approval ratings continued a slow decline until the end of his presidency in 2008. After an election in which he dominated the contest, President Barack Obama entered office with very high approval ratings. The public seemed to genuinely wish him good fortune in his presidency. From a high of 76% approval (CNN/ORC, February 7–8, 2009), Obama's rating has slowly declined as the economic downturn continues. Six months into his presidency, the same research organization found his approval rating to be 55%, and, by late 2011, 46%. Although historical data suggest that a low approval rating combined with high unemployment make reelection very difficult, President Obama has a deep reserve of popularity with the public and may survive the 2012 campaign successfully.

Presidential approval can sometimes defy scholarly expectations, as in the case of President Clinton during the period of his impeachment and trial. Even though the American public clearly expressed its distaste for his actions in regard to the young woman intern, approval of his job as president climbed to the highest levels of his presidency during 1998 and early 1999, at the same time that the Senate was debating his actions. Clinton's approval ratings remained high through the rest of his presidency, probably due to the strong economy.

THE CALL-IN POLL

Though most polls conducted by the media are done "scientifically"— that is, with probability samples, a well-designed questionnaire, and appropriate attention given to the various aspects of data collection and processing—one type of poll used primarily by the media has caused considerable controversy: the "900 number" call-in poll. As its name implies, call-in polls are ones in which respondents are not randomly selected and contacted by the polling firm but rather ones in which participants select themselves by calling a 900 number.

The obvious problem with such polls from a scientific standpoint is that because respondents are self-selected there is no basis for claiming that the results are representative of some larger population. In fact, such "polls" are biased toward those people with intense opinions on the topic and those with the resources and time to make and pay for the call. At times, interest groups of the right or left or some other special public swamp such numbers, producing the results they want. For the most part, journalists are aware of the nonrepresentative character of such polls; Kathy Frankovic at CBS and ABC's Jeff Alderman have commented on the difficulty of reporting on such polls in a way that presents them accurately (Moore, 1992: 289). To the general public—who may not be aware of these problems—a poll is a poll. The public often weighs the potentially mislead- ing results of a nonscientific poll equally with polls done appropriately. Even worse, the public may see all polls as suspect.

One of the limits of call-in polls is that they are based on a convenience sample; that is, a sample in which respondents are selected not because they represent some larger population, but because of the ease of collecting data from them. In the case of call-in polls, respondents themselves choose to participate. If they are willing to take the time to make the telephone call and to pay the charges that are generally associated with such calls, their opinion is counted.

Two examples demonstrate the distortions that such procedures can pro- duce. A poll conducted in 1990 by *USA Today* showed that Americans loved Donald Trump. A month after the poll results were released, *USA Today* re- ported that 5,640 of the 7,800 calls came from offices owned by Cincinnati financier Carl Lindner, whose employees apparently "admire Mr. Trump" (Crossen, 1991: A1).

As part of its *Nightline* broadcasts, ABC frequently conducts call-in polls. In an effort to deflect some of the criticism of such polls as nonscientific, the network will sometimes conduct a parallel survey of a representative sample of the American public. In a case dealing with the United Nations, 67% of 186,000 calls to the 900 number said that the United Nations headquarters should be moved out of the United States. The results of the representative telephone survey showed exactly the opposite result: 72% of these respon- dents wanted the United Nations to remain (Moore, 1992: 288–289).

THE USE OF PUBLIC OPINION DATA
IN ACADEMIC RESEARCH

Academic researchers use survey research to examine a variety of aspects of human behavior. As noted in Chapter 2, several ongoing programs of survey data collection provide the basis for a significant amount of research in the areas of political science, sociology, social psychology, and mass communications.

The American National Election Studies

One of the most significant of these programs is the American National Election Studies (NES), conducted by the University of Michigan. These surveys are based on representative samples of citizens of voting age, living in private households. Interviewing for this series was first done following the election of 1948 and has been conducted before and after all presidential elections since 1952 as well as after all congressional elections since 1958 except 2006 and 2010. The NES time series encompasses 29 biennial Election Studies spanning five decades. Over time, there have been several variations in the basic design of this study. The 1956–1960 surveys contained a four-year **panel** component in which the same individuals were interviewed in 1956, 1958, and 1960, as did the study conducted in 1972–1976. Some respondents from the 1990 study were reinterviewed in 1992 as part of an examination of the political consequences of the Persian Gulf War. The 1980 study included a panel component that spanned the campaign, and, in 1984, a series of "continuous monitoring" surveys were incorporated into the study in order to examine more extensively the dynamics of the vote decision during the campaign. The 2000 study included an extensive methodological experiment in which much of the data was collected by telephone in order to assess the comparability of the information collected by these modes.

These interviews are rather extensive, and many questions are replicated across studies, facilitating extensive cross-time analysis, that is, comparing results on the same question at different time periods (Miller and Traugott, 1989). The range of topics addressed in the NES includes expectations about the election outcome; perceptions and evaluations of the major parties and their candidates; information about politics; positions on social-welfare, economic, social, and civil rights issues; attention to campaign coverage in the media; and detailed demographic information.

Data from these surveys have also served as the basis for many of the most important investigations of American political behavior, such as *The Voter Decides* (Campbell, Gurin, and Miller, 1954), *The American Voter* (Campbell et al., 1960), and *The Changing American Voter* (Nie, Verba, and Petrocik, 1976). NES data have been used to study topics such as mass belief systems (Converse, 1964), political participation (Bennett and Resnick, 1990; Milbrath, 1965), the effect of the media on mass political behavior (Erbring, Goldenberg, and Miller, 1980), **political efficacy** and trust in government (Miller, 1974), and political socialization (Campbell et al., 1960). Much of the data presented in later chapters is based on these surveys.

The General Social Survey

Another significant source of data concerning the public's views on a range of issues is the General Social Survey (GSS) done by the National Opinion Research Center (NORC). The first GSS was conducted in 1972. Since that time the GSS has been conducted 27 times, and by 2011 a total of 55,087 respondents had been interviewed. The GSS is also an extensive interview; since 1988 there have been over 700 variables in each survey. As described by Smith (1997: 28), the GSS includes major batteries of items on topics such as "civil liberties, confidence in institutions, crime and violence, feminism, governmental spending priorities, psychological well-being, race relations, and work."

The large number of items that are replicated in the GSS surveys facilitates the study of social change and allows for cases to be pooled across surveys to provide sufficient cases for analysis among subgroups, such as blacks or the self-employed. The detailed and extensive set of demographic variables collected in the GSS allows in-depth analysis of the influence of background characteristics on attitudinal differences. The annotated bibliography lists 8,662 uses of the GSS and approximately 300 new uses occur each year (Smith et al., 2004).

Although not as large as the NES or GSS, the economic behavior program at the University of Michigan has since the late 1940s conducted an ongoing survey of the American public designed to measure consumer confidence. Academic economists have long been interested in this measure of consumer behavior, which has only recently become a topic of discussion in the news media. As the American economy fell into recession after the banking crisis of 2008, the Michigan consumer confidence measure became a point of commentary for the media and others who were trying to explain daily stock market fluctuations and variations in employment, and sustained interest in the economy has led to a continued interest in this measure among the media and the general public.

In addition to these major ongoing studies, academic researchers conduct special-purpose surveys (often funded by the federal government through grants or by private foundations) designed to investigate specific topics. Myriad topics have been examined with survey data ranging from attitudes toward health policies to the development of political views in children and their parents (Niemi and Jennings, 1974). It would be virtually impossible to mention a topic of public relevance that has not been suggested for study using survey research. In the chapters that follow, the results of many of these academic studies will be used to illustrate how Americans think about public issues.

Much of the survey-based research done by academic researchers involves analysis not of data that they have collected but rather of secondary analysis of data collected for some other purpose. Much of the research published using the NES or GSS was done not by the principal investigators for these surveys, but by other researchers who were provided the data through the Interuniversity Consortium for Political and Social Research (ICPSR). In addition to the NES and GSS data, many other national, regional, and local surveys are archived by the ICPSR, which provides them to the larger research community. The consortium, which is a partnership of hundreds of colleges and universities, publishes an annual catalog (and online listing) of the datasets available to member institutions for teaching and research purposes. Nonmembers may purchase the datasets as well. The entries include national crime studies, health studies, the election studies, European and other foreign national studies, foreign policy studies, the CBS/*New York Times* datasets, and hundreds of others.

Data from the 2008 National Election Study, or any of the other studies in the **archive**, are available to both undergraduate and graduate students for their research. There are other archives of data, including the Roper Center at the University of Connecticut, which operate in the same fashion. As these examples illustrate, surveys represent an important source of data for academic researchers. The results and analysis of these data, together with information from national, state, and local surveys, the media, and other sources, provide the basis for much of what we know about the American mind.

POLLS, POLLING, AND THE INTERNET

Most of the university survey and research organizations have excellent websites that can be accessed by students as well as researchers. As mentioned in this chapter, two of the most prominent university studies are:

The National Election Study conducted by the Center for Political Studies at the University of Michigan: http://www.umich.edu/~nes/

The General Social Survey conducted by the National Opinion Research Center (NORC) at the University of Chicago: www.norc.org/projects/gensoc.asp

For more information on the 2004 election and the controversies surrounding the exit polling, you can visit the website of the organization that conducted the poll: www.exit-poll.net or the group that charges election irregularities: http://uscountvotes.org or the research group that investigated both the Florida 2000 vote and the 2004 Ohio vote, the Election Science Institute, formerly known as Votewatch: www.votewatch.us.

4

How Are Opinions Measured?

In the previous discussion of public opinion in U.S. history, we described a number of ways by which policy makers are made aware of what "the public" thinks. Attending functions at home in their constituencies, meeting with individuals or groups, talking with other policy makers as well as other influentials, obtaining information from the media, talking with contacts from interest groups, reading correspondence, or scanning the blogosphere all provide some idea of what the public is thinking on an issue. Although policy makers generally take information from each of these sources into account in their decision making, such considerations are not commonly what is meant when we are discussing "public opinion." Recall that public opinion has been defined as the aggregate of the views of individual adults on matters of public interest. Given this approach to public opinion, the methods used to measure such opinion must represent those of some population, whether it is the voting-age population of the United States, women in the state of Illinois, or low-income residents of a U.S. city.

As noted in Chapter 2, the method used to provide public opinion data is survey research, which involves systematic data collection about a sample drawn from some larger population. In a properly designed and executed survey, information collected from a relatively small number of people can be used to represent accurately the views of some larger group. This chapter discusses the ways in which the data used in describing the American mind are collected.[1]

MODES OF SURVEY DATA COLLECTION

Traditionally, there have been three principal ways in which survey data are collected: face-to-face interviews, telephone interviews, and self-administered questionnaires. Over the past 15 years, a fourth mode—collecting data via the Internet or electronic data collection—has emerged as a means of gathering information. There has been a dramatic increase in the development of various types of web surveys used for a variety of purposes, from entertainment to attempting to obtain a **representative sample** of the U.S. population (Brown and Johnson, 2011; Couper, 2000). Although these modes have relative advantages and disadvantages, they each involve certain common characteristics, including identifying a population of interest, selecting a sample, designing a questionnaire, and processing and analyzing the data collected. In describing the major steps involved in the survey process, the following sections present some of the elements that are common to these different approaches and that must be considered in identifying the views of some population. Later we describe some of the advantages and disadvantages of these modes of data collection.

POPULATIONS OF INTEREST

A **population of interest** is an identifiable group of individuals whose opinion on some issue or set of issues is important to a policy maker. From the perspective of public opinion, the number of potential "populations of interest" is almost limitless. For example, the president of the United States might be interested in how "the American public" feels about some issue; in this case, the American public—typically defined as those age 18 and older—would constitute the population of interest. Similarly, a governor may want to know whether the electorate in the state approves of the way he or she is performing in office; in this case, registered voters in that state would compose the population of interest. A council member may wonder how the town's residents feel about building a new sewer line, in which case these residents form the population of interest.

Other subgroups can also constitute populations of interest. On certain issues, policy makers may be particularly interested in the opinions of African Americans, women, or those between the ages of 30 and 45. Political party officials often have an interest in how members of groups such as the AFL-CIO or the Right-to-Life Society feel about particular issues. The opinions and experiences of those who are unemployed and looking for work are important to officials charged with evaluating programs designed to reduce unemployment. How physicians, hospital administrators, insurance company representatives, and members of other groups feel about potential changes in the health care system and their impact on service delivery is an important consideration to both federal and state officials considering changes in the health care system; each of these groups is a population of interest on this issue. In sum, any group whose opinions are of interest to a policy maker is a potential population of interest.

The wide range of potential characteristics of different populations can affect the choice of mode for data collection. As noted in Chapter 2, in the early history of scientific survey data collection, the in-person method was generally considered the only way to gather reliable information. Developments in survey research have made it possible to collect data effectively by telephone, through self-administered surveys, with **paper-and-pencil interviewing**, and by electronic means. In most cases, an in-person survey will cost more to conduct than a comparable telephone, self-administered, or electronic survey, and resource considerations are an important part in the choice of mode of data collection. In addition to resource considerations, the characteristics of the group from which data are being collected, the ease of identifying and contacting individuals in the population, and the types of information being collected will affect the decision on the means of gathering information.

SELECTING A SAMPLE

Once a population of interest has been identified, it is possible to collect information from all members of this group. Although this approach may be appropriate if the population is extremely small, gathering information in this manner for most groups of interest to policy makers would be not only very time consuming, expensive, and inefficient, but also unnecessary. The principles of probability theory allow those interested in public opinion data to collect information from a small but carefully selected subset of the population—known as a **sample**—and to make inferences about the entire population with a high level of confidence.

There are two major types of sampling methods: **probability sampling** and **nonprobability sampling**. In a probability sample, each individual or combination of individuals in the population has some known probability of being selected, while nonprobability samples are based on human judgment. The problems with the *Literary Digest* poll of 1936 and the incorrect forecasts of the election of 1948 were a result—at least in part—of the use of nonprobability samples.

When a sample is selected from a population, the interest is not in the opinions of the sample members, in and of themselves; rather they are of interest because they *represent* the characteristics of the population. In order to be confident that the sample does represent the population, some type of probability sampling must be employed. The key to any type of probability sample is random selection. In a probability sample, each element or individual in the population has some known, nonzero probability of selection.

There are several types of probability samples. The most notable of these—and the one that is assumed by the body of statistics typically used by survey researchers—is **simple random sampling** (SRS). In a SRS, each element in the population is listed and assigned a number, and a sample is drawn using a computer program or a random number table to generate the selected elements. Although a SRS represents the "ideal" probability sample, in practice such samples are seldom used. Unless the population is small, it is not practical to identify all members of a population, much less assign them each a unique identification number for selection.

Systematic random samples are similar to simple random samples in that they are generally drawn from a list of elements. They differ, however, in that while each number in a simple random sample is randomly generated, a systematic sample involves randomly selecting a single number, then taking every *k*th element in the list (for example, every 25th) until the desired number of elements has been selected. For example, if we wanted to select a sample of 80 individuals from a list of 2,400, we would take every 30th person, with the first one randomly selected from the first 30 on the list. If number 27 were initially selected, then numbers 57, 87, 117 . . . 2,397 would be included in the sample.

In a **stratified sample**, the elements of the population of interest are divided into groups (or strata), and independent samples (either simple random or systematic) are selected within each stratum. The advantage of a stratified sample is that it provides a greater degree of accuracy in the sample for those characteristics on which elements have been grouped.

Take as an example a study in which your population of interest is undergraduates at a state university. Of the 20,000 undergraduates, 5,500 are freshmen, 5,200 are sophomores, 4,800 are juniors, and 4,500 are seniors. Selecting a simple random or systematic sample of 1,000 would provide you with close to, but not exactly, 275 freshmen, 260 sophomores, 240 juniors, and 225 seniors. If the list of the population was stratified by class and a systematic sample was chosen, you would select exactly the correct proportion from each class.

A stratified sample ordinarily yields more reliable results than a simple random sample, and because stratification is a relatively simple process, it should be considered in deciding the type of sampling procedures used. To select a stratified sample, however, requires knowing something in advance about the characteristics of the population. Variables such as age, race, gender, or location generally are used as a basis for stratification.

The final type of probability sampling is known as **cluster sampling**. It is often used in surveys in which the population of interest is spread over a wide geographic area or for which compiling a list of elements may be prohibitively expensive. In a cluster sample, the population is divided into groups, or clusters, often on the basis of geography. Cluster sampling is less costly than other types of sampling; unfortunately, from a research perspective, cluster samples have a larger potential for error due to sampling. Cluster sampling is used for most of the major face-to-face surveys conducted in the United States today, including the National Election Studies and the General Social Surveys, which provide much of the data presented in later chapters.

A properly designed and executed cluster sample can be very complex. To give some indication of how cluster sampling works, take an example in which the population of interest is residents of the county in which you live who are 18 years of age or older. Potential lists, such as telephone directories or driver registration records, are likely to be incomplete and somewhat out of date. Attempting to compile a list of all individuals or households in the county would be time consuming and require considerable resources. In situations such as this, cluster sampling provides a cost-effective way of selecting a probability sample.

In this case, the county could be divided into clusters based on **census tracts** and a random sample of census tracts selected. Within each of the selected tracts, a random sample of **census blocks** could be selected, and an interview would be conducted with a selected individual at each household in the selected block. In this process, rather than having to list all households in the county, only those households in the selected tracts and blocks would need to be identified. In addition, the interviews to be conducted would be *clustered* in a relatively small number of blocks rather than spread throughout the county, thus saving interviewer time and travel expense. A cluster sample usually involves several steps in which lists (for example, census tracts, blocks within selected tracts, or households within selected blocks) are compiled and a sample selected. At each of these stages, some type of probability sample must be selected in order for the results to be representative of the population of interest.

You may encounter situations in which nonprobability sampling procedures have been used. In **pilot investigations** or **purposive studies**, such samples are often used for generating hypotheses or for obtaining information about individuals with unique characteristics. The limitation of data collected through nonprobability techniques is that the results cannot be used to make inferences about some larger population of interest. Virtually all of the studies of public opinion in which we are interested are based on some type of probability sample.

RANDOM-DIGIT DIALING

Random-digit dialing (RDD) is a technique for selecting a probability sample in telephone surveys. Because of its importance in the history of public opinion research (see Chapter 2) and its extensive use in current survey practice, we will describe it here in some detail.[2]

In selecting an RDD sample, all of the working telephone exchanges in the area in which the population of interest resides have to be identified.[3] For example, if the population of interest consisted of adults living in the state of Louisiana, then all exchanges in use in the state would have to be determined. Once these exchanges have been identified, one of them is randomly selected, and a second random number between 0000 and 9999 is generated to complete the telephone number. The same process is used to select a second telephone number, and this is repeated until a sufficient quantity of numbers has been generated to produce the desired number of completed interviews.

The telephone numbers produced by these procedures will not all be household residences. The sample will include numbers that are not in service as well as numbers for businesses and institutions, and several refinements to these procedures have been developed (Waksberg, 1978). The result of these refinements has been to increase the efficiency of RDD samples by reducing the number of "unproductive" calls, that is, calls made to businesses and not-in-service or otherwise ineligible numbers; the underlying principles of RDD are the same. It should also be recognized that some type of stratification, particularly by area, is possible with an RDD sample.[4] Ultimately, the means chosen for selecting a sample will depend on the characteristics of the population of interest, the purposes of the study, and the resources available for carrying out the research (Box 4.1).

Factors such as the increasing number of cell phone–only households, declining response rates, call screening devices, and number portability have raised serious concerns about the continued viability of telephone surveys based on RDD samples (Blumenthal, 2009). In response, survey researchers have turned to other methods of sample selection, one of which is address-based sampling (ABS). The foundation for ABS is the delivery sequence file (DSF) used by the U.S. Postal Service, which contains all delivery point addresses serviced by the postal service, with the exception of general delivery, and provides coverage of 97% of U.S. households. A representative sample of addresses is selected from this file and used in conducting a mail survey. An ABS includes cell phone–only households or those that are without telephone service, is geographically identifiable, and produces response rates similar to those for an RDD telephone survey. Given the concerns about RDD telephone surveys, there has been an increase in recent years in the use of ABSs (Link et al., 2006, 2008).

BOX 4.1
Sample Selection for Different Modes: Some Examples

This chapter describes various modes of data collection and different methods of sample selection. The following examples illustrate the use of different types of samples.

Face-to-Face Interviewing, Cluster Sampling: The American National Election Studies are studies of citizens of the United States who live in the 48 contiguous states and are of voting age on or before election day. Data are collected in face-to-face interviews conducted in the households of selected respondents. Selecting a representative sample of this population involves a relatively complex process in which sampling is done of (1) standard metropolitan statistical areas (SMSAs) and counties; (2) area segments within the selected SMSAs and counties; (3) housing units within the sampled area segments; and (4) a single respondent within selected housing units.

Telephone Interviewing, Random-Digit Dialing (RDD): The South Carolina State Survey is a survey of 800 adult residents of South Carolina that is conducted by telephone. The sample for this survey is selected by RDD. In generating this sample, all the working area code and telephone exchanges in the state are identified. A computer program randomly selects one of these exchanges and then adds to it a randomly generated number between 0000 and 9999. This process is repeated until enough telephone numbers have been selected to achieve the desired number of completed interviews. Using this method, individuals who live in households without telephones are excluded from the sample. From 1989 through 2007, only land line telephone exchanges were included in the sampling frame. Beginning in 2008, cell phone exchanges were added in order to reach the increasing proportion of the population living in cell phone–only households.

Mail Survey, Stratified Random Sample: A survey on the uses of alternative and complementary medicine done with physicians in the state of South Carolina provides an example of a mail survey using a stratified random sample. A list of licensed physicians in the state was provided by the South Carolina State Data Center. Physicians on this list were stratified according to their specialty. A random sample within each of these strata was drawn and a questionnaire mailed to the selected physicians.

Self-Administered Questionnaire, Cluster Sampling: The Monitoring the Future Study, which has been conducted each year since 1975, consists of surveys of high school seniors that explores changes in important values, behaviors, and lifestyle orientations of contemporary American youth. Cluster sampling for this study involves three stages: (1) geographic areas; (2) schools (or linked groups of schools) within the geographic areas; and (3) classes within sampled schools. Selected students are then asked to fill out a questionnaire that consists of about 300 questions on a range of topics, including drug use, attitudes toward government, social institutions, race relations, and background characteristics.

Mail Survey, Address-Based Sampling: An address-based sample was used in a mail survey of the U.S. adult population's views on issues related to nanotechnology. The U.S. Postal Service Delivery Sequence File, which covers about 97% of U.S. households, was used to select a simple random sample of households.

(*continued*)

BOX 4.1
(continued)

Electronic Data Collection: In a study of how Americans would deal with the federal budget deficit, Knowledge Networks used an Internet panel for sample selection. To develop this panel, Knowledge Networks begins with a sample of households that are identified and recruited through an address-based sample. If a recruited household does not have access to the web, it is provided with a netbook computer and free Internet service. The households that agree to cooperate form the Knowledge Networks panel, and from this panel a random sample of households was selected to participate (Pineau and Slotwiner, 2003).

SAMPLING FOR ELECTRONIC DATA COLLECTION

Sampling for electronic data collection presents a unique set of challenges. For specialized populations, such as members of an organization, students at a university, or agency clients receiving a particular service, a relatively complete list of e-mail addresses may be available, and in such cases a simple random sample, a systematic sample with a random start, or a stratified sample can be employed, much as for other modes in situations in which listings are available (Couper, Blair, and Triplett, 1999). For surveys of more general populations, such as the adult residents of a county or a state, no list of e-mail addresses is available that includes a sufficient proportion of the population for a researcher to have confidence in the representativeness of the results, and no list of this type is likely to be available in the near future.

Given this, electronic surveys have relied on various options for sample selection, including several convenience sample approaches. One such method is "uncontrolled instrument distribution" (Schonlau, Fricker, and Elliott, 2001: 35). An example of uncontrolled instrument distribution is the posting of a survey on the web for anyone to fill out, and participation in such a survey is completely self-selected. Another convenience sampling method uses systematic sampling of visitors to a website, for example by having a survey "pop up" on the screen for every *n*th visitor to the site. While such a sample would be a probability sample of visitors to this site, the results are not representative of any larger population.

Another method, the volunteer panel, "relies on assembling a group of individuals who have volunteered to participate in future surveys. The individuals are generally recruited into the panel through some form of advertising" (Schonlau, Fricker, and Elliott, 2001: 36). The Harris Poll Online uses a method similar to this for recruiting its online panel respondents. Participants are recruited from a multitude of sources, including "co-registration offers on partners' websites, targeted e-mails sent by online partners to their audiences, graphical and text banner placements on partners' websites . . . tradeshow presentations, targeted postal mail invitations, TV advertisements, and telephone recruitment of targeted populations" (Harris Interactive, 2009). The Harris Poll Online (2002) has a multimillion member global panel, whose members are generally contacted with a new survey invitation no more than once every 7 to 10 days. It uses propensity weighting methods to project from a panel sample to the population of interest.

A fourth type of sample for Internet-based surveys is the prerecruited panel, which involves a group of potential survey respondents who are recruited by some probabilistic method and who are available for repeated surveying (Schonlau, Fricker, and Elliott, 2001: 39). One of the best examples of a prerecruited panel is provided by Knowledge Networks (KN). When established in 1999, KN used RDD to recruit a representative sample of participants. In 2009, it switched to ABS for selecting a representative sample. The KN panel consists of about 50,000 adult members, as well as approximately 3,000 teens, ages 13 to 17. Panel members living in households without Internet service are provided with a netbook computer and free Internet service so that they can participate. KN panelists participate in about two surveys per month, which require generally between 5 to 20 minutes to complete. (For a more complete description of these methods, see Knowledge Networks, 2011.)

SAMPLING ERROR

One of the most important concepts in surveys and public opinion research is **sampling error**. If you have seen or read reports of public opinion polls, you may be familiar with the statement "the error due to sampling could be plus or minus three percentage points for results based on the entire sample." This statement refers to the sampling error. The term "error" does not imply that the data are wrong or that mistakes were made in the way they were collected; rather, all samples are subject to such potential error resulting from the fact that data are not obtained from all members of the population.

As noted earlier, when data are collected from a sample, the interest is not in the characteristics of the members of the sample themselves, but rather the characteristics of some larger population whom they represent. If a properly designed survey conducted close to an election found that Candidate X would receive 52% of the vote, then we would expect that this candidate would receive close to, but not exactly, 52% of the ballots cast. Probability theory provides us with a means for estimating how close the sample estimate is to the true population value, given that we are willing to take a certain risk that the findings of the study are incorrect. The level of risk most commonly used is the 0.05 level (or the 95% **confidence level**). When survey results are reported, this means the researcher is confident that 95% of the intervals reported will contain the correct percentage for the population. So when you hear or read a report from a survey that "Candidate X has the support of 52% of those interviewed" and that "the potential for sampling error for this survey is plus or minus 4%," you can be 95% confident that the true percentage for this candidate is between 48% and 56% (assuming, of course, that there were no other factors such as sampling bias, nonresponse, question wording, or interviewer effects that influenced the results). For surveys in which approximately a thousand people are interviewed, the sampling error would be about ± 3.1%. The larger the number of people interviewed, the smaller the sampling error.[5]

SAMPLE SIZE

In designing any survey, an important consideration is the number of individuals from whom data should be collected. There is no ideal **sample size**, and the number of cases in any survey depends on the study's purpose, the precision needed, and the resources available. As noted previously, the larger the sample size, the smaller the sampling error, and in most instances a survey researcher will attempt to collect data from as many individuals as possible in order to increase the precision of the estimates of the population characteristics. The obvious tradeoff, however, is that each additional individual from whom data are collected requires some added cost, whether it be postage and clerical time in a mail survey, interviewer time and telephone charges in a telephone survey, interviewer time and travel expenses in a face-to-face survey, or sample identification and processing time in an electronic survey.

Another consideration in determining the sample size is the purpose of the study. In some studies, the estimates based on the survey are required to be very precise; in such cases, data must be collected from an extremely large number of people. For example, the Current Population Survey, conducted by the U.S. Census Bureau, is designed to provide estimates of the employment, unemployment, and other characteristics of the general labor force and the U.S. population as a whole. As part of this survey, approximately 60,000 households are contacted each month, with information collected on about 110,000 individuals. As Bradburn and Sudman (1988: 131) note, as a result of this large sample size, "sampling variation between repeated samples is only about one-tenth of one percent; therefore, policy makers are assured that changes of more than one-tenth of one percent up or down reflect real changes in the economy and are not caused by sampling."[6]

A study in which the researcher is interested in examining differences among groups will also generally require a larger sample size than one designed solely to estimate the characteristics of the population. For example, if one were interested in differences in opinions of individuals with varying amounts of education (such as among those with less than a high school education; high school graduates; those with some college; and college graduates), a larger sample size would be required in order to make accurate estimates for each of these groups. In general, the larger the sample, the more detailed the analysis that can be conducted.

In other cases, a very small sample size may be sufficient for the purpose of the study. For example, if one were interested in the opinions of the members of a regional professional association that consisted of 150 members, it would be possible to select a sample of as few as 30 individuals and still be fairly confident in your results. In situations where you are dealing with a very small population of interest, however, it is generally possible to attempt to collect information from each individual.

Many of the more publicized polls, such as those of Gallup, the Pew Center for People and the Press, and the major media polls typically conduct interviews with about 1,000 people. The number of people interviewed in the American National Election Studies has ranged from 662 in 1948 to 2,705 in 1972. Most statewide or regional polls are based on between 500 and 800 interviews, and the average local survey consists of between 200 and 500 cases. The decision about the number of cases for which data will be collected depends largely on the resources available and whether the benefits of greater precision and more detailed analysis justify the increased costs.

QUESTIONNAIRE DESIGN

The basic data collection instrument in survey research is a questionnaire that may include items that ask people about their opinions, experiences, or background characteristics. The form of the questionnaire is essentially the same for each of the four modes of data collection. Questions are presented to respondents in either **closed-ended** (respondents select their answer from a list provided) or **open-ended** (respondents provide their own answers to the question) format, and responses are either recorded by interviewers (face-to-face and telephone surveys) or completed by the respondents (self-administered and electronic).

Survey researchers have long been aware that the way questions are asked can have an effect on the results of a study, and there are a number of considerations involved in developing any question and designing a questionnaire (Payne, 1951; Schuman and Presser, 1981). The following examples illustrate some of the decisions that must be made in crafting a questionnaire.

Type of Question

There are two basic question types, open-ended and closed-ended. In an open-ended question, respondents are asked to provide their own answers to the question, while in a closed-ended question they are provided with a list of alternatives from which to choose. The item "What do you feel is the most important problem facing this country today?" is an example of an open-ended question. "In general, how satisfied are you with the services provided by your city government . . . very satisfied, somewhat satisfied, not too satisfied, or not at all satisfied?" demonstrates a standard closed-ended item.

The advantage of open-ended questions is that they do not restrict respondents to alternatives provided by the researcher, while closed-ended questions are more efficient in terms of data collection, coding, and analysis. Because of these efficiencies, most survey questions are closed-ended. Although the type of question asked should be determined by the purpose of the study, the advantages of closed-ended questions have led survey researchers to use this type predominantly (J. Converse and Presser, 1986).

Filter Questions

Once the type of question has been determined, another consideration is whether to include a **filter question**. That is, is it appropriate for everyone in the sample to be asked the question or is there a reason to exclude some respondents? When some respondents are to be excluded, the question would include a filter.

Filter questions are most frequently used with opinion questions. If you are interested in opinions on an issue, do you want to ask everyone or do you only want answers from those people who are more interested in or have thought about the issue? Those who feel that filter questions should be used argue that asking those who are ill-informed or have not thought much about an issue to give an answer artificially creates opinion and provides a misleading impression of "the aggregate of the views of individual adults on matters of public interest" (Bishop, 2005: 52). Those who believe that filters are not needed contend that "many people act or react on a wide variety of subjects where they have no specific knowledge" (Mitofsky, 1989: 618).

In survey questions that include a filter, respondents are typically read a statement on some issue and then "filtered" on the basis of their knowledge or interest. Commonly used filter questions include: "Do you have an opinion on this issue?" "Have you been interested enough in this issue to favor one side over the other?" "Have you thought much about this issue?" and "Where do you stand on this issue or haven't you thought much about it?" Examples of survey questions with different types of filters are presented in Box 4.2.

BOX 4.2
Examples of Different Survey Questions with Various Types of Filters

No Filter
Some people don't pay much attention to the political campaigns. How about you? Would you say you have been very much interested, somewhat interested, or not much interested in following the political campaigns so far this year?

Filter First
The government ought to help people get doctors and hospital care at low cost. Do you have an opinion on this or not? (IF YES): Do you agree that the government should do this or do you think the government should not do it?

Filter After
Some people feel that if black people are not getting fair treatment in jobs, the government in Washington ought to see to it that they do. Others feel that this is not the federal government's business. Have you had enough interest in this question to favor one side over the other? (IF YES): How do you feel?

Filter After
Some people feel that the government in Washington should see to it that every person has a job and a good standard of living (they would be at point 1). Others think that the government should just let each person get ahead on their own (they would be at point 7). And, of course, other people have opinions somewhere in between. Where would you place yourself on this scale, or haven't you thought much about this?

Source: American National Election Studies 1948–1994 Continuity Guide (Ann Arbor, MI: Interuniversity Consortium for Political and Social Research, 1995).

Another argument for using filter questions in surveys is based on the demonstrated tendency of about one-third of respondents to give opinions on issues that are obscure, such as the Agricultural Trade Act (Schuman and Presser, 1981: 196), or fictitious, such as the 1975 Public Affairs Act (Bishop et al., 1980). If the use of a filter question can deter respondents who do not have an opinion from providing an answer, then the results should be more reliable and provide a more accurate reflection of the public's views. Although the use of filter questions has been shown to increase the percentage of "don't know" or "no opinion" responses compared to asking the same question without a filter, such questions generally have little effect on the division of substantive opinion and have mixed effects on the relationships between items (Schuman and Presser, 1981: 196; see also Bishop, Oldendick, and Tuchfarber, 1983).[7] There is, then, no right or wrong answer to the question of whether survey items should include a filter; the decision should be based on the purpose of the research.

Tone of Wording

It should be obvious that the words used in survey questions can make a difference in the results. The conclusions reached from a question that asks respondents whether they favor "killing babies" are likely to be quite different from those based on a question of support for "a woman's right to choose." Several less extreme examples demonstrate how seemingly minor changes in wording can make a considerable difference in the conclusions one would reach about the public's views.

For instance, Smith (1987) found that the percentage of the public who felt that the government was spending too little on "assistance to the poor" was consistently about 40% greater than the percentage who thought the government was spending too little for "people on welfare." Likewise, Schuman and Presser (1981: 276–285) demonstrated that the percentage of the public who felt that the United States should "not allow" public speeches against democracy was about 15% higher than the percentage who thought that the United States should "forbid" such speeches. Similarly, asking about approval of expenditures of "public funds" produces different results than expenditures of "tax money," and "sending troops" is supported by a smaller number of people than "sending troops to stop a communist takeover" (Box 4.3).

BOX 4.3
Examples of Tone of Wording Effect

Speeches Against Communism

Do you think the United States should forbid public speeches in favor of communism?		Do you think the United States should allow public speeches in favor of communism?	
Yes (forbid)	39.3%	**No (not allow)**	56.3%
No (not forbid)	60.1%	Yes (allow)	43.8%

Sending U.S. Troops

If a situation like Vietnam were to develop in another part of the world, do you think the United States should or should not send troops?		If a situation like Vietnam were to develop in another part of the world, do you think the United States should or should not send troops to stop a communist takeover?	
Send troops	18.3%	**Send troops**	33.2%
Not send troops	81.7%	Not send troops	66.8%

Source: Howard Schuman and Stanley Presser, *Questions and Answers in Attitude Surveys: Experiments on Question Form, Wording, and Context,* pp. 281; 285, © 1981. Reprinted by permission of Sage Publications, Inc.

In examining public opinion on the Holocaust, Moore and Newport (1994: 28) compared the results of the following questions:

(a)   The term "Holocaust" usually refers to the killing of millions of Jews in Nazi death camps during World War II. Does it seem possible or does it seem impossible to you that the Nazi extermination of the Jews *never* happened?

(b)   The term "Holocaust" usually refers to the killing of millions of Jews in Nazi death camps during World War II. Do you doubt that the Holocaust actually happened, or not?

They found that the percentage of Americans who doubted that the Holocaust happened was 26% less (35% to 9%) than the percentage who said it seemed possible (or were unsure) that it never happened. They attributed this difference to the fact that in the first question, the respondent had to choose the double negative response (that it seems *impossible* that this *never* happened) in order to affirm belief in the Holocaust and the use of the term "extermination" (rather than an *attempt* to exterminate).

You should recognize that the words used in a question—the tone of **wording** the question—will have an effect on the results. In constructing a survey question, it is important to be aware of this consideration and not to use words that are emotionally laden or that will tend to lead respondents in one direction or another. For a survey question on an issue to be informative to policy makers, the item must reflect the substance of the issue as well as the choices to be made. In evaluating survey questions, you should consider how the tone of wording of the question may have influenced the results. As Smith (1987: 83) has noted, failure to consider such effects can lead to "the possible policy and scientific misapplication of survey data."

Middle Alternatives

Another consideration in designing survey questions is whether or not to include a **middle alternative**. Although many survey questions ask respondents to choose between two alternatives, there is frequently a logical middle position that people might prefer. Those who feel that such survey questions should be presented without a middle alternative argue that the middle alternative provides an "easy out" for those who do not have a strong position on an issue or who have not thought much about it, and that for many issues a policy maker must make a choice between two "extremes"; presenting a middle choice limits the ability to determine which alternative the public prefers. Arguments for including a middle choice include the points that many people actually prefer a position somewhere between the two extremes and that if results show a large majority with this view, policy makers might be encouraged to compromise or to stake out some middle ground.

As an example, consider a legislator in a state facing a budget crisis. The legislature is faced with the choice of increasing taxes or reducing state services. The legislator is interested in the public's will on this issue: Are people willing to pay increased taxes, or would they prefer a reduction in state services? One way to ask this question, which is taken from the Ohio Poll, is: "Like most states, Ohio faces the problem of not having enough tax money to pay for the various services and programs that the state government provides. One way to solve this problem is to raise taxes. Another way to resolve the problem is to reduce state services and programs. Which do you prefer?" When asked in this way, 52% of those surveyed preferred reducing services, 35% supported raising taxes, and 13% were undecided.

In a later poll, however, the issue was posed somewhat differently, this time with a middle alternative. Respondents were asked, "Suppose the state of Ohio's budget problem is serious. In that situation the state could make major cuts in state funding for elementary and secondary schools, colleges and universities, and most other state services, or it could pass a major tax increase. Would you prefer: (1) major cuts for schools and other services; (2) a major tax increase; or (3) a combination of a tax increase and budget cuts?" The results of this survey found 13% favoring major cuts, 17% supporting a major tax increase, 12% undecided, and 58% favoring a combination of budget cuts and a tax increase.

A legislator would draw different conclusions from the results of these two questions. The question of the right way to ask a question cannot be answered as a purely technical matter, because questions can appropriately be asked either with or without a middle alternative. The decision as to how to ask a question should be guided by the substantive issue for which the public's opinion is being sought. If a middle alternative is a viable option, the question should include this alternative; if the issue is a matter of choice between two extremes, including a middle alternative in the question would be less useful. In this example, the Ohio legislature adopted a combination approach for addressing the state's budget crisis (Tuchfarber, Oldendick, and Bishop, 1984).

A second example of how presenting a middle alternative might affect results is provided by questions on defense spending. A commonly asked survey question involves whether the United States should increase or decrease spending on defense. In this case, the middle alternative, "keep spending about the same as it is now," is a viable option and should be offered as part of the question. As the data in Box 4.4 demonstrate, a policy maker might come to different conclusions about the public's feelings on defense spending as a result of whether or not the question included a specific middle alternative.

BOX 4.4
Middle versus No Middle Alternative

No Middle Alternative		Middle Alternative Offered	
Increase	52%	Increase	23%
Decrease	40%	Decrease	17%
Keep About the Same (Volunteered)	8%	Keep About the Same	60%

In general, the effects of including an explicit middle alternative in a question are to: (1) increase the percentage of respondents choosing the middle alternative; (2) have little effect on the division of substantive opinion; that is, if you take out those people who chose the middle response, the remaining division between those on either side of the issue is generally the same; and (3) have mixed effects on the relationships among items (Bishop, 2005: 57). As with the other decisions that must be made in developing a survey question, the choice of whether or not to include a middle alternative should be guided by the substantive purpose for which the results are to be used.[8]

Response Format

Another element that can affect the results of survey questions is the **response format,** or the way in which choices are presented to respondents. The previous description of middle alternatives illustrated some of the consequences of variations in question forms, and response formats generally can influence respondents. One commonly used response format asks subjects to choose between two alternatives, such as "favor/oppose," "approve/disapprove," or "yes/no." Another form of this **forced-choice format** presents respondents with two sides of an issue and asks them which one comes closer to their point of view (Box 4.5).

Another commonly used question format is the **agree-disagree format,** in which respondents are read a statement and asked whether they agree or disagree with its content. Frequently additional choices of "strongly agree" and "strongly disagree," along with a middle ("neutral") alternative, are included to create a five-point **Likert-type item** (Selltiz et al., 1959: 366). Agree-disagree items suffer from an **acquiescence response set,** which is the tendency of respondents to agree with a statement regardless of its content. Because of this, forced-choice items are generally preferred over agree-disagree questions (J. Converse and Presser, 1986: 38).

One of the limitations of forced-choice items is that presenting only two alternatives (or extreme positions) does not allow for differentiation

BOX 4.5
Examples of Various Types of Response Formats

[YES/NO FORMAT]: Now thinking about health care: Can you (and your family) afford to pay for the health care that you need?
1. YES
2. NO

[AGREE/DISAGREE (2-POINT) FORMAT]: Sometimes politics and government seem so complicated that a person like me can't really understand what's going on. Do you agree or disagree with this statement?
1. AGREE
2. DISAGREE

[AGREE/DISAGREE (5-POINT) FORMAT]: This country would have many fewer problems if there were more emphasis on traditional family ties. Do you agree strongly, agree somewhat, neither agree nor disagree, disagree somewhat, or strongly disagree?
1. AGREE STRONGLY
2. AGREE SOMEWHAT
3. NEITHER AGREE NOR DISAGREE
4. DISAGREE SOMEWHAT
5. STRONGLY DISAGREE

[FORCED CHOICE (2-POINT) FORMAT]: Some people are afraid that the government in Washington is getting too powerful for the good of the country and the individual person. Others feel that the government in Washington is not getting too strong. What is your feeling . . . do you think the government is getting too powerful or do you think the government is not getting too powerful?
1. THE GOVERNMENT IS GETTING TOO POWERFUL
2. THE GOVERNMENT IS NOT GETTING TOO POWERFUL

[FORCED CHOICE (7-POINT) FORMAT]: Some people feel that the government in Washington should see to it that every person has a job and a good standard of living. Others think that the government should just let each person get ahead on his or her own. And, of course, other people have opinions somewhere in between. Suppose people who believe that the government should see to it that every person has a job and good standard of living are at one end of the scale—at point 1. And suppose that the people who believe that the government should let each person get ahead on his or her own are at the other end—at point 7. Where would you place yourself on this scale?
1. GOVERNMENT SEE TO JOB AND GOOD STANDARD OF LIVING
2.
3.
4.
5.
6.
7. GOVERNMENT LET EACH PERSON GET AHEAD ON HIS OR HER OWN

[RATING FORMAT]: Some people don't pay much attention to political campaigns. How about you . . . would you say that you have been extremely interested, very interested, somewhat interested, not too interested, or not at all interested in the political campaigns so far this year?
1. EXTREMELY INTERESTED
2. VERY INTERESTED
3. SOMEWHAT INTERESTED
4. NOT TOO INTERESTED
5. NOT AT ALL INTERESTED

[RANKING FORMAT]: Different types of government services are provided by the federal government, by state government, and by local government. If government is to be reduced, which of these levels of government do you feel should be reduced first . . . the federal government, state government, or local government? And which should be reduced second? And which should be reduced third? (RECORD "1" FOR LEVEL OF GOVERNMENT MENTIONED FIRST, "2" FOR THE LEVEL MENTIONED SECOND, AND "3" FOR THE LEVEL MENTIONED THIRD.)
_____FEDERAL GOVERNMENT
_____STATE GOVERNMENT
_____LOCAL GOVERNMENT

[MULTIPART QUESTION]: Generally speaking, do you usually think of yourself as a Republican, a Democrat, an Independent, or what?
  (IF RESPONDENT CONSIDERS SELF REPUBLICAN): Would you call yourself a strong Republican or a not-very-strong Republican?
  (IF RESPONDENT CONSIDERS SELF DEMOCRAT): Would you call yourself a strong Democrat or a not-very-strong Democrat?
  (IF RESPONDENT CONSIDERS SELF INDEPENDENT, NO PREFERENCE, OTHER): Do you think of yourself as closer to the Republican Party or to the Democratic Party?

1. STRONG DEMOCRAT
2. WEAK DEMOCRAT
3. INDEPENDENT—LEANS TOWARD DEMOCRATS
4. INDEPENDENT—DOES NOT LEAN TOWARD EITHER
5. INDEPENDENT—LEANS TOWARD REPUBLICANS
6. WEAK REPUBLICAN
7. STRONG REPUBLICAN

Source: Adapted from items in the *American National Election Studies 1948–1994 Continuity Guide* (Ann Arbor, MI: Inter-university Consortium for Political and Social Research, 1995).

in opinion or moderation for those whose views lie between the extremes. The **seven-point forced-choice format** attempts to overcome this restriction by placing the alternatives at points "1" and "7" of a scale and leaving the remaining points for respondents who have an opinion that falls between the extremes. This format is used frequently in the American National Election Studies.

   Rating scales are regularly used in public opinion surveys in evaluating performance or citizen satisfaction. In a typical rating question, respondents are asked to make judgments along a scale varying between two extremes, such as from excellent to poor, extremely satisfied to extremely dissatisfied, and the like. The following illustrates a common rating scale question: "How would you rate the job [state the name] is doing as governor? Would you say she is doing an excellent job, a good job, a fair job, a poor job, or a very poor job?"

   In **ranking scales**, respondents are presented with a list of items and are asked to rank them along some dimension, such as importance, desirability, or preference. Ranking scales are more difficult for respondents, particularly if they involve more than four or five items, and are especially unwieldy in telephone interviews. As a result, rating scales are much more commonly used than are rankings.

   Another format with which you should be familiar is the **feeling thermometer**. As its name implies, this format uses the concept of a thermometer, generally ranging from 0 degrees (very negative) to 100 degrees (very positive), in measuring reactions to political figures, countries or groups.

   The formats described here are those commonly used in gauging public opinion. As with each decision made in designing questions, the type of format used should be that which is most appropriate for the substantive question of interest. Question format, like other question attributes, can have an effect on results.[9]

Order of Alternatives

   The order in which alternatives are presented to respondents is another factor that can affect survey results. In some instances, the alternative that is given to the respondent first is selected more often, simply because it is presented first. This is known as a **primacy effect**. In other cases, the choice that is presented last is selected more frequently due to its position in the list. This is known as a **recency effect**.

   An example of such an effect is provided in a series of experiments on response order conducted by the Gallup Organization (Moore and Newport, 1996). Survey respondents were asked the following question about the issue of tax reform:

Thinking about the federal tax system—which of the following would you prefer? The current system in which people with larger incomes pay higher tax rates than people with smaller incomes—and taxpayers can take deductions for charitable contributions, interest paid on home mortgages, and other items, or a different system in which all people would pay a flat tax rate of 17 percent regardless of income and no deductions would be allowed. Families with four or more people and incomes of less than $36,000 per year would pay no income tax.

Half the respondents were read the question with the current tax alternative presented first and the flat tax alternative presented second, while the other half were presented with these alternatives in reverse sequence. When the flat tax alternative was provided last, 56% said that they favored this change. When the flat tax option was presented first, only 43% supported it and a majority (52%) favored the current tax system. Policy makers would reach different conclusions about whether a majority of Americans supported or opposed a flat tax system depending on the order in which the alternatives were presented.

Such effects do not occur in all cases, and survey researchers do not yet know enough about them to be able to specify if they might occur in a particular situation. Research has shown that recency effects occur more frequently than primacy effects and are more likely to appear when questions are more difficult to comprehend, the response options are complete sentences rather than single words or phrases, and among questions that involve options that are not mutually exclusive (Bishop and Smith, 2001; Holbrook et al., 2007). The possibility of primacy and recency effects is another element that must be considered in developing survey questions.

Context Effects

The **context** in which a question is asked can have a significant effect on the results. The preceding questions in a survey provide the setting in which the subject responds to an item, and changing these circumstances can make a large difference in the survey results and in how a policy maker might interpret what "the public thinks" about an issue (Schuman, 2009).

A frequently cited example of such context effects involves public opinion on communist and American reporters. As shown in Box 4.6, when respondents in a 1948 survey were asked a question on whether the United States should let communist newspaper reporters from other countries come in and send back to their papers the news as they saw it, 37% more said "yes" when this question was asked after an item on whether communist countries should let U.S. newspaper reporters go into communist countries and report the news as they saw it than when the question concerning communist reporters was asked first.

A similar example of how the context in which a question is asked can affect survey results is provided by research on Americans' "interest in public affairs" (Bishop, Oldendick, and Tuchfarber, 1984). When survey respondents were asked about "how much you follow what's going on in government and public affairs," 18% more said they followed it "most of the time" when this question was asked as the first question in the survey than when it was asked after questions on whether the person remembered anything special their U.S. representative had done for their district and

BOX 4.6
Example of Question Context Effects

Communist reporter item: Do you think the United States should let communist reporters from other countries come in here and send back to their papers the news as they see it?

American reporter item: Do you think a communist country like Russia should let American newspaper reporters come in and send back to America the news as they see it?

	% "YES" TO COMMUNIST REPORTER ITEM	% "YES" TO AMERICAN REPORTER ITEM
Communist reporter item asked first	36.5%	65.6%
American reporter item asked first	73.1%	89.8%

Source: Howard Schuman and Stanley Presser, *Questions and Answers in Attitude Surveys: Experiments on Questions Form, Wording, and Context,* p. 29, © 1981. Reprinted by permission of Sage Publications, Inc.

how their congressman/congresswoman had voted on any legislative bill. Because most people did not remember anything their representatives had done for their district or how they had voted, they said "don't know" to these items. When they were then asked how often they followed government and public affairs, they were less likely to say "most of the time." The "hard knowledge" questions had provided a different context for what the interviewer meant by "following government and public affairs."

The debate over the issue of abortion has been ongoing in the United States for a fairly extended time, and this is an issue on which many people have strong feelings. Even in such a prominent issue area, question context can have an effect on survey responses. As Schuman and Presser (1981: 37) have demonstrated, a "general" abortion question[10] receives support from 61% of the public when it is asked before a more specific abortion item[11] but is supported by only 48% when it comes after the specific item. If a policy maker were presented with the results from a survey in which the general question had been asked first, he or she would conclude that a solid majority of the public *favored* making it possible for a woman to obtain a legal abortion; if presented with results from a survey in which the same question had been asked after the specific abortion item, the conclusion would be that a majority *opposed* this position. In interpreting survey results, policy makers need to be conscious not only of the way in which questions are worded but also the context in which they are asked.

The ability to provide visual images in web surveys is another potential source of context effects. As Couper and his colleagues (Couper, Conrad, and Tourangeau, 2007; Toepoel and Couper, 2011) have demonstrated, results from web surveys can vary significantly when different visual images are presented in conjunction with the question. For example, web survey respondents who were exposed to a picture of a sick woman in a hospital bed rated their own health condition more positively than did those in which this question was associated with a healthy woman jogging (Couper, Conrad, and Tourangeau, 2007). Although verbal language can reduce the impact of visual cues, the variation in context provided by different images is another factor that must be considered in the design of web surveys.

A number of practical considerations, such as avoiding "double-barreled" items, not framing questions in such a way as to bias respondents, asking relevant questions, and not assuming behavior or knowledge on the part of respondents, need to be kept in mind when developing survey questions. A good list of such specific suggestions is provided in Frey (1989: 178–179).

DATA ANALYSIS

The techniques used in analyzing survey data are also common to the four modes of survey data collection. Typical survey analysis consists of **univariate description**, or the description of one variable at a time; **bivariate analysis**, in which the relationship between two variables is examined, generally by constructing some type of table or correlation; and **multivariate analysis**, which involves examining relationships among three or more variables. Techniques appropriate for analyzing survey data are applicable to information collected by face-to-face interviewing, telephone interviewing, self-administered questionnaires, or by electronic means.

Advantages and Disadvantages of Different Modes

Although the preceding considerations are common to data collection for either face-to-face, telephone, or self-administered surveys, or electronic data collection, each mode has certain advantages and disadvantages. The greatest difference among the four modes is cost. Face-to-face household surveys are generally most expensive, followed by telephone surveys, electronic data collection, then mail and other self-administered surveys.[12] The magnitude of the difference among these modes depends to some extent on the population of interest. In a national face-to-face survey, for example, the personnel (interviewer and supervisor) costs, together with travel costs, are much greater than those for a similar survey conducted by telephone or by mail.[13] As a general rule, the cost of conducting face-to-face interviews is from three to five times more expensive than collecting the same information by telephone, and a properly designed and executed mail survey can be done for approximately half the cost of data collection via telephone. The relative cost of electronic data collection varies considerably depending on factors such as the population of interest and the method of sample selection. For a situation in which data are to be collected from members of a known population and for which e-mail addresses are available, the survey process can be a simple matter of developing the questionnaire, putting it on the web, sending an e-mail to the selected sample with a link to access the survey, and capturing the data as respondents complete the questionnaire. Such a situation is generally the least expensive way of collecting survey information. At the other end of the spectrum, electronic data collection can also be comparatively costly. In a situation where some general population is of interest, selecting a representative sample would first involve using an RDD or ABS sampling frame to identify households, recruiting them to participate by telephone, providing them with a netbook computer for survey administration, then developing the survey, notifying selected households about the survey, and capturing the information as surveys are completed (Huggins and Eyerman, 2001: 2–3). Conducting a survey using these procedures is relatively expensive.[14]

Although face-to-face surveys are more expensive than other forms of data collection, they have a number of advantages over other modes, including **population coverage**, **response rates**, and the types of information that can be collected. The extent to which the population of interest can be reached through these various modes is to some extent dependent on the population. In a survey of adult residents of a state, for example, it is possible to identify virtually all households, and only a small percentage of the population (for example, those institutionalized, the homeless) would be excluded from the sample. In a telephone survey, these same groups would be excluded with the addition of those individuals who live in households without telephones. As noted in Chapter 2, this was once a more serious disadvantage for telephone surveys than it is today, although it must be considered if the population of interest is likely to include a high percentage of individuals without telephones.

Face-to-face surveys also generally have higher response rates—that is, more of those selected in the sample participate in the survey—than do telephone or mail surveys. Traditionally, low response rates were viewed as one of the principal disadvantage of mail surveys, and this approach was generally not employed when a large segment of the general public was the population of interest (Krysan et al., 1994). Given the decline in response rates for telephone surveys and the development of ABS, a low response rate is no longer necessarily a disadvantage for mail surveys (Link et al., 2008).

Another advantage of face-to-face surveys is the amount of information that can be collected. Many face-to-face surveys, such as the General Social

Survey or the American National Election Study, contain several hundred questions and require an hour or more to complete. Telephone survey researchers generally try to limit their questionnaires to about 20 minutes, although there are examples of telephone surveys averaging 45 minutes or more. Mail surveys generally contain fewer questions than either face-to-face or telephone surveys and, in general, the shorter the mail survey, the higher the response rate. The maximum length for a mail survey of a nonspecialized population is about 12 pages if an acceptable response rate is to be achieved. Face-to-face surveys and mail surveys also allow for the presentation of visual materials, which is not feasible in a telephone survey, and web surveys present even greater possibilities, not only for displaying images but also including videos as part of the survey process.[15] Interviewers in face-to-face situations are able to develop greater rapport with the respondent, which is generally considered an advantage in obtaining reliable information. In addition, face-to-face interviewers can use visual cues to detect if a respondent is having difficulty understanding a question and to probe responses more effectively.

As noted in Chapter 2, one of reasons for the development of RDD and the increasing use of telephone surveys was that the percentage of households with landline telephones in the United States approached 100% and response rates to telephone surveys—while not as great as those for face-to-face surveys—were generally high. This situation has changed in recent years and has raised increasing concerns about the representativeness of samples selected through RDD. As Curtin, Presser, and Singer (2005) report in their study of response rates for the Survey of Consumer Attitudes, response rates have declined dramatically over the past quarter century, with the decrease averaging roughly one percentage point a year. Moreover, "The decline has accelerated in the last few years . . . the yearly decline averaged 1.50 percentage points between 1997 and 2003" (Curtin, Presser, and Singer, 2005: 96). Even the most well-designed and executed RDD telephone surveys are now achieving response rates in the 40% range, and response rates in the 20% range are now more typical (Keeter et al., 2006).

The other significant development that has increased concerns about the representativeness of the results of telephone surveys is the substantial rise in the use of wireless telephones. Traditionally, most major survey research organizations did not include wireless telephone numbers when conducting RDD telephone surveys. Given the substantial increase in the percentage of households that have abandoned their landlines and become "cell phone–only" (CPO)—estimated to be 29.7% in 2011 (Blumberg and Luke, 2011)—respondents reached by landline telephones were less representative of the population. Those living in CPO households were more likely to be younger, renters, living with unrelated roommates, and members of minority populations. As a result, a well-designed telephone survey of the general population must now include cell phone numbers. Incorporating cell phone numbers into a telephone sample is more costly and creates new challenges, since a landline phone was a means for reaching a household while a cell phone is generally an individual, personal communication device (Christian et al., 2010). Although factors such as declining response rates and the increasing use of cell phones have made telephone surveys more difficult to execute and have increased their costs, research to this point indicates that this has not produced a bias in the results, and that telephone surveys based on RDD samples remain a viable method for collecting public opinion data (Curtin, Presser, and Singer, 2005; Groves, Presser, and Dipko, 2004; Keeter et al., 2000, 2006).

The principal drawback to web-based surveys for studies of a general population is coverage. Approximately 70% of households have access to the Internet, and older people, households with lower family incomes, and those where residents have less education are less likely to have Internet access. As described previously, Knowledge Networks and the Harris Poll Online have developed different approaches for addressing this issue.

The utility of the web for conducting surveys of the general population has been a source of controversy since the first extensive use of online surveys in the American political arena was done in conjunction with the 1998 U.S. elections. In this election, Harris Online attempted to estimate the outcomes for governor and U.S. Senate races in 14 states, covering 22 races (Taylor and Terhanian, 1999: 20). In this test of Internet survey methods, they correctly projected the winner in 21 of 22 races, had an average "spread" (difference between the projected and actual margins of victory) of 6.8%, and an average "candidate error" (difference between the projected and actual percentages of the vote received by candidates) of 4.4%. Based largely on these results, Humphrey Taylor, chairman of Louis Harris and Associates, and George Terhanian, director of Internet research for Harris Black International, concluded that Internet polling is "an unstoppable train, and it is accelerating. Those who don't get on board run the risk of being left far behind (p. 23)."

Not surprisingly, many traditional survey researchers were skeptical of these methods and pointed out that while these results may have been impressive, the methods for sample selection did not warrant the claim that these results were representative. In Warren Mitofsky's (1999: 24) critique of these methods, he mentioned the *Literary Digest*—which collected data from millions and was perceived to be fairly reputable before 1936—and argued that "people recruited into panels are self-selected, with characteristics that differ from the larger population. People on the Internet do not represent the adult population of the country, and the Internet panelists do not even represent people on the Internet. At best, we end up with a large sample representing nothing but itself."

Election projections from online polls were also relatively accurate in the 2000 election, leading researchers from Harris Online to proclaim that "we

have demonstrated that on-line polls can be designed and executed to measure voting intentions with high accuracy" (Taylor et al., 2001: 38–41), and
since then their record of accuracy has been comparable to those of polls
conducted with other modes. For example, in the 2008 election—in which
President Obama received 6.6% more popular votes than did Senator
McCain—the final Internet polls reported by Harris Interactive and You-
Gov/Polimetrix had Obama's advantage at 8% and 6%, respectively, while
the Gallup telephone poll had Obama's lead at 11% and that of Pew Research had it at 7% (Blumenthal, 2008).[16]

An extensive investigation of this issue by the American Association
for Public Opinion Research concluded that "researchers should avoid
nonprobability online panels when one of the research objectives is to accurately estimate population values" and that "nonprobability samples are
generally less accurate than probability samples" (AAPOR, 2010), and a
Census Bureau report also raises concerns about the ability of online panels
to represent the views of the population accurately (Pasek and Krosnick,
2010). Defenders of Internet-based surveys point to flaws in these criticisms, as well as their track record of accuracy in demonstrating that a well-
designed web survey can effectively represent the views of large populations
(Rivers, 2009). Despite this controversy, web-based surveys have become
an increasingly important mode for measuring the American mind, and
their role is likely to increase.

It is possible, of course, to combine various modes of survey data collection in order to gather information more effectively (Dillman, 1978,
2000). For example, in a mail survey, those individuals who had not
returned a questionnaire after several follow-ups can be contacted by
telephone in an attempt to obtain the information. Similarly, if the basic
design of a survey involves telephone interviews, an attempt can be made
to collect information by mail or face-to-face from those individuals who
do not have phones. As this description of the advantages and disadvantages of these various modes has shown, none of these approaches is
ideal. The significantly higher cost of face-to-face interviews makes this
approach prohibitive for all but a few surveys, such as the National Health
Interview Survey, the Survey of Income and Program Participation, and
the National Crime Survey. Declining response rates and the increasing
use of cell phones have raised concerns about the continued viability of
telephone surveys, mail surveys are plagued with generally low response
rates, and electronically based data collection faces concerns about coverage, particularly when some general population is of interest. Surveys
that take advantage of the strengths on these different approaches—in
Dillman's (2000) terms, the "tailored design method"—provide the most
effective means for measuring the American mind. Methods for collecting
survey information have changed tremendously since the tallies of preelection canvasses in 1824.

POLLS, POLLING, AND THE INTERNET

If you are interested in the scientific basis of polling, a good website to visit is that of the American Statistical Association: www.amstat.org/.

For more information about the programs at the Institute for Social Research at the University of Michigan, look at the website located at: www. isr.umich.edu/src/.

There is information regarding graduate training in survey research methodology at the website of the Joint Program in Survey Methodology at the University of Maryland: www.jpsm.umd.edu/.

Part III

WHAT DO AMERICANS BELIEVE?

5

The Sources of Opinions

When pollsters call to survey opinions, most often people are quite prepared to answer their questions about politics or policies with opinions and perceptions reflecting their views. One of the questions that most intrigues students of public opinion is how individuals come to hold opinions on such a wide range of issues. At what point in a person's life does he or she "learn" the answer to the question "Do you consider yourself to be a Republican, a Democrat, or an Independent?" When do people decide to be liberals or conservatives? An important aspect of that learning process begins, it appears, in childhood.

In 2008, millions of school children, their parents, and teachers participated in a project called Kids Voting USA. Using prepared curricula tailored to each grade level, teachers led children in discussions of the upcoming presidential election and the meaning of voting. According to the sponsors of the project, the intent of the project was "preparing young people to be educated, engaged citizens,"[1] or, in other words, to have children learn to be active voting citizens. Studies have shown that if people vote soon after becoming eligible at the age of 18, they are much more likely to participate in elections for the rest of their lives. On election day, thousands of parents and community members volunteered to conduct mock elections at the same polling places where voters cast their ballots. More than 1.8 million children cast "ballots" for president in 29 states under the auspices of Kids Voting. A similar effort is sponsored by the Nickelodeon network, which allows students to cast votes online. The Kids Voting project was widely acclaimed to be a success in preparing children for their future role as voters. In an unanticipated outcome, research on the impact of earlier Kids Voting projects conducted by Steven Chaffee of Stanford University showed that the project actually had a "trickle up" effect, stimulating the parents of the children to participate in the election. Chaffee found that the Kids Voting curriculum motivated families to discuss politics and provided a "second chance at socialization" for parents at the lower end of the socioeconomic scale (Evans, 1996). Kids Voting tries to involve school children in the political system at an early age as a way to increase participation later. This project raises two issues for us as students of public opinion. First, why is it necessary to teach citizens to participate in the system, and second, how do children learn about politics at such an early age?

The process of learning about the political system is generally called **political socialization**. As defined by Roberta Sigel, political socialization is "the process by which people learn to adopt the norms, values, attitudes, and behaviors accepted and practiced by the ongoing system" (1970: xii). According to this definition, the goal of political socialization is to teach the appropriate behaviors and attitudes to citizens so that they will support the political system. Investigating this process became a very important thrust of research in political science in the late 1960s as part of the drive to discover the processes by which democratic societies could be sustained. Work by a number of authors was based on the assumption that "the operation of the political system is seen as dependent on the political outlooks of the citizenry" (Dawson, Prewitt, and Dawson, 1977: 10; Jaros, 1973). The alternative approach to political socialization focuses on the growth and development of the individual personality of the citizen rather than the needs of the system, defining the process more broadly as "the acquisition of political attitudes, values, and behaviors," regardless of whether they support the current system or not. Scholars who work from this psychological perspective are interested not only in how the citizen acquires values and behaviors that may support the system, but also where the process of learning about politics fits into the development of human personality and ongoing human relationships. (See the work of Greenstein, 1965; Hess and Torney, 1967; Hyman, 1959; and Shapiro, 2004, for the origins of this approach.)

For the purposes of this book, it is helpful to consider political socialization from both perspectives—the needs of the political system and individual development—because the two processes interact continually. Through educational systems and public policy, the larger political system tries continually to influence individuals to exhibit certain attitudes and behaviors, such as being law-abiding and voting. The individual, however, is engaged in a lifelong journey of learning and development. The political socialization of childhood will be affected through the lifespan by a range of influences that are beyond public influence.

As we begin to look at the process of political socialization in children and adults, it is useful to think about why certain groups and institutions such as parents and schools can act as agents of socialization. Paul Allen Beck has suggested that in order for an individual to be influenced, three conditions must be met: exposure, communication, and receptivity (1977: 117). In other words, for the Kids Voting USA project to have an influence over the future opinions and voting habits of school children, the students had to be exposed to the project, receive communications from their teachers and parents about it, and, most important, be motivated by some force to be receptive to the messages about voting. Obviously, the success of the project will only be known many years in the future.

THE POLITICAL LEARNING OF CHILDREN AND ADOLESCENTS

To the surprise of the first researchers who studied the political attitudes of children, kindergarten students were able to identify major political figures such as the current and past president and to express, in many cases, an identification with a political party. Undoubtedly, elementary school children carried such identification into the Kids Voting project. How do small children gain such identifications and attitudes? Clearly, the influence of the family is paramount in the political socialization of young children. To recall Beck's conditions, mothers and fathers have maximum *exposure* with children, *communicate* with the child frequently, and, most important, experience maximum conditions of *receptivity*. Children are extremely dependent on the approval of their parents and other family members for the development of emotional and intellectual maturity and stability. When a child points at the televised image of President Obama and says, "I like his smile," and the parent responds approvingly, whether with a smile or verbal agreement, the child's predisposition to share the parent's opinion is reinforced. Negative attitudes toward individuals or political views are also reinforced by parental actions. Behavior is influential as well: A child who is raised in a family where both parents actively participate in campaigns and elections is likely to participate regularly as an adult. Recent research suggests that as parents converse with each other and with their young children, they are unconsciously constructing a "family identity" that can include partisan identification or approval of a specific political candidate (Gordon, 2004).

In their seminal work on political socialization, David Easton and Jack Dennis proposed four psychological processes that characterize children's views of politics and the political system (1969: 391). In the first stage, **politicization**, children become aware of the existence of authority figures and institutions beyond their parents, adult relatives, and teachers. They seem to be aware that there exists some form of power in terms of government and laws beyond their immediate social circle. When children begin to think about **political authority**, they are likely to think in terms of individuals or persons instead of institutions such as the courts. Easton and Dennis found that children saw both the police officer and the president to be representatives of government. As they put it, "As representatives of political authority for the child—the policeman is seen as working for the government and the president *is* the government—both figures . . . have some psychological importance for the child" (152). This process, which is epitomized by the child's admiration of Abraham Lincoln or Martin Luther King, Jr., is termed **personalization**. The third process is named **idealization**, referring to the child's identification of political authority as generally benevolent and trustworthy. One suspects that children would expect a parallel between the loving relations with the family and relations with these other authority figures. The classic example of political socialization is the visit by the firefighter to the kindergarten class for a discussion of fire safety. Children are seeing an example of authority beyond the family in the person of the firefighter, and they are asked to see this professional as their friend and protector. Indeed, Easton and Dennis's surveys of children showed that younger children saw both the president and the policeman as helpful to their families. Later in the development of children's ability to conceptualize, the process of **institutionalization** takes place, and the firefighter or police officer then can become part of the concept of local government. Not until this process of institutionalization begins are children able to conceptualize such institutions as the Congress or city government.

The earliest studies of political socialization of children found remarkably positive feelings among children toward the political system. As Hess and Torney concluded from their studies in the 1960s, "The young child perceives figures and institutions of government as powerful, competent, benign, and infallible and trusts them to offer him protection and help" (1967: 213). To some extent these feelings may have been generated by the political atmosphere of the 1950s and early 1960s when the children were studied. However, other research showed that the children selected for these studies were enrolled in mostly middle-class schools with largely white populations. The question then became whether the strong positive feelings that children expressed toward government were based on the socioeconomic class of their families or were reflective of all children. (See also the classic work of Greenstein, 1965.)

Several different studies were conducted during the late 1960s in large industrial cities, focusing on the political attitudes of nonwhite children (Dennis, 1969; Rodgers and Taylor, 1971). Some of the studies showed high levels of support for authority figures such as the police officer and the president among very young children but less support for the government among older African American children. Greenberg (1970), among others, reported consistent differences in levels of support for government figures even among younger children. The research of Jaros, Hirsch, and Fleron (1968), who replicated the research in schools that enrolled poorer minority and Appalachian children, demonstrated the possibility of cultural differences in these patterns of socialization. Where the middle-class white children demonstrated positive attitudes toward political figures and institutions and showed considerable trust in the democratic systems, those in the study by Jaros et al. expressed much more negativism in their feelings toward political figures and pessimism about how the system worked. The results of such studies of subgroups suggest that for some children, the idealization phase of development may be replaced by such antipathy toward government that the phase becomes one of **hostilization**. This contrast in outcomes clearly underlines the power of the family as a primary influence in the adoption of political attitudes.

Studies conducted by researchers in the 1970s also demonstrated that the political cynicism of the period was transmitted by parents to the children. For example, the study conducted by Dennis and Webster (1975) in 1974 found that children were less likely to idealize government than those studied in the early 1960s. In 1974, only 25% of sixth-grade children said that the president keeps his promises, compared to almost 71% who answered positively in 1962. Arterton's (1974) study of children's attitudes during the Watergate period showed an increase in general cynicism among third and fifth graders and a startling decline in children's feelings of approval for the president. Such comparisons over time provide strong indications of the parents' influence over their children's basic outlook on government. Of course, it is also important to note that older children may be influenced by sources outside the family, including the media, peers, and other authority figures.

What is clear from the research is that families are most successful at influencing children in their identification with a political party and much less successful at transmitting views on particular political issues. Much of the knowledge about these processes is drawn from a longitudinal study conducted by Jennings and Niemi, who surveyed adolescents and their parents in 1965 and then resurveyed these groups in 1973 and 1982. The first results of the Jennings and Niemi (1968) study underscored the ability of parents to influence their children's political party identification. As shown in Table 5.1, in the 1965 study, 59% of the high school students chose the same political party identification as their parents. Agreement on political issues was much lower, and in a finding that Jennings and Niemi say indicates the positive environment of schools, adults were more cynical about politics than their children. The results of the first Jennings and Niemi survey raised a number of issues for students of public opinion: Why is partisanship transmitted so successfully to children? What other variables intervene to keep political attitudes and preferences from being transmitted as well? What will happen to the partisanship of these students as they age?

Table 5.1.   Parent versus Student Partisanship

	Parents		
Students	Democrat	Independent	Republican
Democrat	66%	29%	13%
Independent	27%	43%	36%
Republican	7%	17%	51%
Number of cases	(914)	(442)	(495)

Source: Jennings and Niemi, 1974: 41.

All of the studies that look at the political socialization of children eventually come to the question of persistence. Will the views and behaviors expressed by children in the fifth or 12th grade persist into adulthood? How long-lasting are the effects of the family or the school system? The Jennings and Niemi survey of high school seniors and their parents was repeated in 1973 and in 1982 to try to ascertain the degree to which attitudes persisted or changed over time. By 1973, the students showed much less agreement with their parents' partisan preference: only 45% of the students and parents agreed (Jennings and Niemi, 1974, 1975). Though a larger percentage of children were declaring themselves to be independent voters, only a modest number expressed an identification with a different party than that endorsed by their parents. What does this tell us about the persistence of childhood political socialization? Jennings and Niemi interpret the results to say that these families certainly show **life cycle effects**, meaning changes in political views that are attributable to stages in life, and perhaps some examples of **generational effects**, which can be attributed to events taking place for a particular generational cohort. They conclude, however, that more forces seem to be bringing the generations together than pushing them apart (1975: 1335).

Although Lewis-Beck et al. (2008) suggest that when parents share partisan identification, up to 75% of children adopt that identity, Wolak (2009) tested that persistence during the midterm elections of 2006 to see whether competitive campaigns and exposure to the media would influence the partisan identification of adolescence. She hypothesized that the child's personality and motivation to become engaged with politics would play a part in whether the child kept the same party identity as their parents or whether his or her choice was affected by a current campaign. Her results upheld the prevailing view that most students maintained their party identity even when exposed to a competitive campaign year. In fact, she finds that students who express the most interest in politics are least likely to change parties (Wolak, 2009: 579). There is, however, a correlation between adolescents who challenge their parents and engage in political talk with them and change in partisan identity. She concludes by seeing adolescents as constructing their own political socialization through their search for political information and willingness to engage in political conversations.

THE INFLUENCE OF FORMAL EDUCATION

Every society, whether primitive or highly structured, has struggled with passing on its cultural values and rules of behavior to its children. Even though the process of political socialization always begins within the child's family, societies have often turned to formal processes of schooling to carry on the socialization process. Primitive societies may rely on gender-segregated processes for educating boys and girls to their adult duties. During the formative years of the American republic, schooling followed the patterns set in Western Europe. Adolescent boys of upper-class families were often sent to formal schools, with only the children of the elite enrolling in what we would now call a postsecondary education. In the late 17th and early 18th centuries, girls (and young boys) were educated only at home, first by their mothers and, if wealthy, by private tutors. The importance of the woman's role in inculcating appropriate democratic values into her sons and daughters was often cited in the years following independence as evidence of women's value to the nation (Kerber, 1980). As the principle of universal suffrage (for men) spread across the American states, it became evident to the political leaders that some provision should be made for increasing the civic education of future citizens. In the 19th century, public education systems were devised at the elementary and secondary levels. With the influx of European immigrants, the public schools became the agents of "acculturation" for the new citizens (Marquette and Mineshima, 2002: 543). Most publicly supported colleges and universities came into being after the Civil War with the establishment of land grant universities through the Morrill Act (1862).

There can be no doubt that public education in the United States was driven first by the need to produce citizens who could support this radical democratic system and second by the need to develop skills for individuals. The question that has challenged scholars, however, is whether the extensive public education system of this country has had its desired impact on the process of political socialization. The data from a number of studies, including the National Civics Test, most recently reported in 2010, are decidedly mixed.

If the goal of the school system is to produce citizens who will participate in the system in an informed way, what tools do the schools have to influence children? Obviously, school systems attempt to socialize children through the curriculum, including the selection of textbooks and the requiring of specific courses for graduation. In some states, courses such as American Government or Texas Government (to name only one state) are mandated in public universities. As noted by Dawson, Prewitt, and Dawson (1977: 144), schools may be engaging in civic education or, in the more extreme case, in political indoctrination. Schools also shape students' attitudes through the activities that Dawson et al. call "classroom ritual life," including the daily salute to the flag and reciting the Pledge of Allegiance, the annual celebration of the Pilgrim feast, and the study of American heroes such as Washington and Lincoln. The third force cited by most scholars is the influence of the classroom teacher. Does the teacher teach his or her own political values to the students, or is the teacher an effective instructor of the school system or community's chosen values and behaviors? The final component of the school's influence is the classroom behavior that is encouraged or discouraged, whether by the individual teacher or by the community in which the school is located. Students may, it has been hypothesized, learn as much from the encouragement of debate and dialogue or a strict code of obedience to authority as from the actual subjects taught in any grade.

THE CURRICULUM

A number of different scholars have looked at the impact of the curriculum on political socialization with fairly negative results. In a pioneering study, Edgar Litt (1963) compared the effects of civics instruction in three school districts, each using a different type of text and having a different socioeconomic makeup. Generally, Litt found that there was some influence on the civic learning of the students when texts were used that tried to influence participative values, but in no case were more than one-quarter of the students affected. Jennings, Langton, and Niemi (1974) reported on a comparison of students who had taken a traditional American government or history course versus those who had enrolled in a more contemporary (and supposedly more engaging) American Problems course. As they summarize the study, "An overview of the results offers strikingly little support for the impact of the curriculum" (Jennings, Langton, and Niemi, 1974: 190). It did not appear to matter which curriculum or course students took in terms of their level of political knowledge or orientation. Indeed, the most important effect seemed to be one of recency: if the students had just completed the course, their recall was better. Jennings, Langton, and Niemi did, however, find quite significant differences between white and African American youth. The civics curriculum did seem to change the orientations of black students on a number of dimensions, increasing their feelings of loyalty to the system while decreasing trust and participation (1974: 202).

As part of their conclusion, Jennings, Langton, and Niemi suggest that the ineffectiveness of the curriculum may result from several factors, including the redundancy of the material presented, the training and pedagogy of the teachers, and the general environment of the class and school. Hess and Torney's (1967) study of the influence of school on younger children comes to much the same conclusions. As they note, "The young child's attitude toward authority or institutions, however, seems not to correspond directly to the amount of emphasis on these topics reported by the teacher. Compliance to rule and authorities is a major focus of civic education in elementary schools" (1967: 217). They suggest that while the school is an important factor in political socialization, it is most effective at teaching obedience and relatively ineffective at teaching the responsibilities of citizenship or the actual political processes of the system.

RITUAL AND CEREMONY

American school systems consciously adopt rituals and practices designed to instill patriotism and loyalty in children. Besides the Pledge of Allegiance and the learning of U.S. history, schools provide avenues for participation through elected student councils. Although these practices may instill a sense of loyalty among students, most researchers who have studied these activities believe that they may instill passivity rather than political knowledge or interest in participation. At the elementary school level, students see elections as important, but, with little knowledge of political parties or election processes, "children wish to minimize conflict" (Hess and Torney, 1967: 216). It is suggested that what might be happening in the elementary grades is the setting up of an idealized view of the citizen, one who is nonpartisan and whose individual vote makes a difference. If this idealization is internalized by children, they may become even more cynical and alienated from the system when they realize the role of conflict and interest groups in the system.

THE TEACHERS

Elementary and secondary school teachers, as well as college professors, are often recalled by their former students as having had a dramatic impact on their lives. In fact, teachers may become the object of community disapproval if their influence appears to be greater than that of the parents or the community. Thus, as Jennings, Ehrman, and Niemi put it, teachers "are criticized both for being too effective and too ineffective" in the area of social science

(1974: 226). Since the curriculum seems to have little impact on students, perhaps it is because of a lack of teacher preparation or interest. On the other hand, if students become activists on a particular topic, teachers or college professors are likely to be blamed. Although it is quite difficult to study the impact of teachers on their classes apart from the curricula and the community's social mix, Jennings and colleagues suggest that the same principles apply to teacher–student–parent relationships as to those of students and their parents. If the teacher is reinforcing the views of parents, the students tend to be pushed toward homogeneity of views. If parents and teachers hold conflicting views, the students tend to adopt a middle position.

After comparing the curriculum, district climate, teacher preparation and attitudes, and other characteristics of two school systems, Richard Merelman (1971: 197) suggests that teachers may not be very influential over children's views because they are themselves "political ingenues." By this he means that teachers are not drawn into the profession by their political views, nor do they have very well-defined ideas about politics. Merelman found that teachers had little reluctance to have discussions about political issues in their classrooms, but they were woefully uninformed about political issues in their own community and had few political predispositions. The exception to this finding involved male social science teachers, who tended to exhibit lower morale and more dissatisfaction than other groups of teachers. They were often the ones to encourage students in discussion but, perhaps because of their own alienation, they did not convey higher support for democratic values to their students.

Work by Rogoff and colleagues (2003: 177) suggests that the kind of teaching a child experiences may have an impact on how active he or she becomes politically. In teaching that can be characterized as the *transmission* model, the teacher (or parent) transmits knowledge about a behavior to children who are essentially passive. Much of what occurs in the civic education of American children could be described in this way. However, if the teacher or other authority figure expects the children to be learning through "intent participation," the learner is already anticipating using the knowledge in the future and, perhaps, participating in real activities such as voting sooner rather than later. Recent research by Campbell (2008) tested the hypothesis that rather than avoiding discussion of political conflict in the classroom, teachers should introduce complex policy issues to students and expose them to the conflicting points of view of different interests. He finds that students who are exposed to an "open classroom" have higher test scores on a civic knowledge test. In fact, such exposure improves performance for students of high and lower socioeconomic status. Campbell suggests that "it is actually the nature of political discussion within the classroom, not simply the frequency of formal social studies instruction, which has the effect" (2008: 450).

SCHOOL BEHAVIORS

The curriculum, the teachers, and the rituals of the playground do not seem to have a great impact on the civic-mindedness of children, so what other kinds of learning take place within the educational institutions? Although it is quite difficult to study, researchers suggest that the climate of the classroom—whether students have significant chances to participate in discussions or decisions—might impact their holding of democratic values. In addition, the diversity of the classroom in terms of the student body seems to have an impact on students. Peer influence, another major agent of socialization, also plays a role within formal schooling. Some studies (Langton, 1969; Newcomb et al., 1958) show that children will tend to conform to the dominant ideology or viewpoints of their classmates.

It is worth noting the work by Talcott Parsons on this subject. Parsons, in his "The School Class as a Social System," reminds us that children adopt social roles within the classroom. Although the gender of students is fixed, children can become leaders or valued teammates within the classroom setting. They may be well rewarded for their efforts by teachers or by their classmates. Parsons believed that "the elementary school class is an embodiment of the fundamental American values of equality of opportunity" (quoted in Dawson, Prewitt, and Dawson, 1977: 155). In addition, students may learn the rules of competition, cooperative behavior, and fairness in the classroom, or they may learn the opposite. Dawson and colleagues remind us that children may become aware of the tension between the democratic values being taught in the curriculum and the emphasis placed on passivity and orderliness by school authorities (1977: 155).

The School as a Sorter Mechanism

It is important to note that schools and the educational system operate both to educate all the children sent to them and to sort children as they move through the educational ladder of success. Given the generally lackluster success of the school system in conveying political knowledge and civic behaviors to students, as documented by many studies, it should not be a surprise to find that those students who come from homes where the parents have college educations or have a higher socioeconomic status are more interested in political events, pay more attention to the news, perform better on tests of civic knowledge, and generally have higher levels of participation in politics. What we may see in terms of the impact of schools on political socialization is a reinforcement of the family's political involvement.

As a part of a congressionally mandated program to test student achievement on a wide range of subjects, the National Civics Awareness Test was administered to a nationally representative sample of students in 1988. A revised version of this test was administered in 1998, 2006, and 2008. The results of this test were reported in *The Nation's Report Card: Civics* (2010) published by the U.S. Department of Education. Although the test showed small increases in the percentages of students who tested at the "basic" level of civics knowledge, the difference between the 2008 results and two previous tests was not significant. Table 5.2 shows the percentage of students in grades 4, 8, and 12 who tested at the "proficient" level of civics knowledge. It is clear that there are vast demographic differences in these outcomes. Girls tend to outscore or match the test results of boys until the 12th grade, when they fall behind. A much larger percentage of white children score at the proficient level than do African American children or Hispanic children, although the Hispanic results were much higher than in previous tests. Two measures of socioeconomic family status are measured: eligibility for the school lunch program for elementary school children, and level of parental education for middle school and high school students. As shown in Table 5.2, children from families whose incomes qualify them for free or reduced-price lunches are much less likely to score at the proficient level, while students who are not eligible for these programs or whose parents have completed some schooling after high school are more likely to score

Table 5.2.   National Civics Assessment Test: Percentage of Children Scoring Proficient, 2008

	Grade 4	Grade 8	Grade 12
Gender			
Male	24	22	25
Female	30	22	22
Race/Ethnicity			
White	37	29	30
Black	12	9	8
Hispanic	10	11	13
Asian/Pacific Islander	37	30	29
Eligible for school lunch[a]			
Free lunch	10	8	
Reduced-price lunch	17	17	
Not eligible	40	31	
Level of parents education[b]			
Did not finish high school		6	8
High school grad		10	13
Some education after high school		22	20
College graduate		32	33

[a]School lunch program information is not available for grade 12.
[b]Data for parents' education is not available for grade 4.

Source: Nation's Report Card, U.S. Department of Education, Institute of Education Sciences, National Center for Education Statistics, Washington, DC, 2010.

at the proficient level of civics knowledge. These demographic differences are striking and are likely due to the multiple influences of family socialization, family interest in politics, family financial resources, and differences in the overall achievement levels of the schools attended by these children. Even with all of the advantages of parental education and economic status, however, only 33% of the children from homes with college-educated parents score at the proficient level of the National Civics Test and scores are not improving over time.

What do all of these studies tell us about the impact of formal education on the political opinions and behaviors of Americans? It appears that even though the school system may be successful at instilling loyalty and patriotism in children, as well as obedience to the law, it has much less impact on the formation of attitudes toward political institutions and processes in this country. The impact of the family and the community in which the child is raised may be reinforced by the civics curriculum for children from upper socioeconomic levels but may have little impact on the political opinions and outlook of children from other backgrounds.

THE INFLUENCE OF ETHNIC IDENTITY

Americans hold widely varying opinions on public issues ranging from abortion to air pollution. However, on many issues, the divisions within public opinion are linked to the ethnic background or ethnic identification of the respondents. How does a person's ethnic origin come to influence his or her views? Obviously, the earliest source of ethnic identification comes from the family. For white Americans, ethnic identity is most likely transmitted to children through the practice of family traditions or the telling of the family history. For children of color, ethnicity and physical characteristics are shared with parents and siblings.

In the case of Hispanic families, the major source of ethnic identity may be the use of Spanish as a primary language in the home or the Spanish surname, rather than their shared physical traits. The family may transmit a clear sense of ethnicity or group membership to the children or that identity may be deemphasized. In most second- or third-generation white families, the ethnic origin of the child may be so mixed as to have little or no meaning. Recent immigrants are, naturally, more closely tied to their native culture and heritage.

The ethnic background of individuals, though first transmitted by the family, is likely to be either reinforced or modified by later socialization processes. As noted in the discussion of formal schooling, African American and Hispanic children demonstrate less positive support for the political system and, after exposure to civics education, may respond by becoming more disaffected with the system. Learning about racial issues seems to increase the cynicism of African American high school students. As they grow older, children absorb messages about how their own ethnic group is perceived by others through personal experiences and through the media. They may become more aware of their own identity and the experiences of their group than they were within the nuclear family. According to Conover (1984), those individuals who have the strongest group identity are more likely to express distinct political views and preferences linked to their group's interests or values.

African Americans

In general, African Americans are much more liberal on domestic policy issues than virtually any white ethnic group, with the exception of Jewish voters. Given the history of slavery and discrimination that effectively barred African Americans from participation in the political life of the country until after the Civil War in the North and until the 1960s in the South, it is not surprising that African Americans express much stronger support for affirmative action programs, for government enforcement of civil rights, for government action to assist poor Americans, and for a strong federal government than do whites. There is also considerable support within the African American community for redistributing income through the tax system and for a national health care system. The support for national social-welfare policies extends throughout the African American community, regardless of income level, education, or social class. Although African Americans mostly identified with the Republican Party as the party of Lincoln after the Civil War, they changed their allegiance to that of the Democrats during Roosevelt's New Deal. Since the 1940s, almost 90% of African American voters regularly cast their ballots for the Democratic candidate for president.

There are other areas where the distribution of opinions within the African American community is somewhat different from that within the white community, but the difference is not as strong as it is on civil rights and social-welfare issues. Since the Vietnam War, which saw a disproportionate number of African Americans serving in the army and suffering casualties, this ethnic group is somewhat less likely to support the use of military force involving American soldiers overseas. African Americans are also less likely to support open access to abortions for women, although African American women are just as likely as white women to undergo the procedure.

Perhaps some of the most striking differences between black and white Americans are found in their extremely disparate perceptions of racism and opportunity for people of color in this country. African Americans are much more likely to perceive society as racist and discriminatory than are whites. Research by Sigelman and Welch (1991) also showed that more than

40% of blacks thought that racism seemed to be getting worse nationally, although only 25% believed that conditions were worsening in their own community. One study (*Time*/CNN poll, 1997) showed that there are generational differences within the public on the question of racism: Both white and African American teenagers are less likely to see racism as responsible for the problems of African Americans than are adult Americans. This generational difference suggests that the views of parents are being modified by their children's experiences in the world in a way that reduces some of the gap in opinions between black and white Americans.

Hispanic, Asian, and Native Americans

Hispanic Americans have also suffered discrimination and lack of opportunity in the United States, especially in the southwestern region of the nation. However, it is much more difficult to define a national pattern of opinions distributed by Hispanic people because of the strength of ties to their respective countries of origin. Cuban Americans, most of whom immigrated after Fidel Castro's rise to power, tend to be middle class and to hold opinions very similar to other groups of white ethnic Americans, except for their views on whether the United States should try to overthrow the Castro regime. In contrast, Mexican Americans and Puerto Ricans, who have been among the poorest groups in the United States, tend to express support for social welfare programs and antidiscrimination measures at levels similar to those seen in the African American community. There are other, smaller communities of Hispanic people scattered throughout the country, including immigrants from all the nations of Central America and South America.

There are some aspects of Hispanic cultures, however, that tend to cross the national origin boundaries. Hispanics are largely Catholic in their religious affiliation and are strongly antiabortion in their views. With a somewhat more traditionalist culture, Hispanic communities strongly value religion, the church, and the family.

The influence of the family is probably strongest in the maintenance of Spanish as the language of the home for many Hispanic families. At least one study has shown that children whose primary language is Spanish demonstrate less attachment to the political system than do children who are bilingual or whose primary language is English (Lamare, 1974). Of course, those children who are facile in English are more likely to come from households with better-educated parents and higher household income. Because those characteristics are also associated with stronger attachment to the institutions of government for all young people, it is not easy to sort out the effects of being raised in a Spanish-speaking family.

Asian Americans make up only 4.2% of the U.S. population. Like Hispanics, there are many countries of origin for Asian Americans and thus many varieties of opinion among the communities. Opinions are more distinct in areas where there is an enclave of similar ethnic peoples, as in some California communities, but there is very little research available on the distribution of opinions among Asian Americans across the nation.

Another ethnic group that undoubtedly conveys its ethnic identity to its children is that of Native Americans. Again, this community is fragmented by tribal identity, but the overall poverty and lack of education among Native Americans has tended to depress interest in politics and public issues among these communities. Another factor that has led to considerable cynicism and distrust of government among Native Americans has been the long history of federal government control of many aspects of these people's lives.

RELIGION AND PUBLIC OPINION

For many Americans the source of religious affiliation is the family of their birth. Just as a little girl does not know that she is Irish or German until someone tells her, small children have no idea of religious affiliation other than what they learn from their parents or other family members. For some of the groups that immigrated to the United States, religious affiliation is closely linked to ethnic identity. Among those groups would be Hispanic Americans, Italians, and many Eastern European and Irish families who are most likely Catholic in affiliation. Other ethnic groups such as the German Americans descended from Protestant, Catholic, or Jewish immigrants.

For some Americans, religious affiliation is more a family characteristic than a source of political attitudes or opinions. For others, the important influence is not as much the affiliation as the basic principles of the faith that guide their lives. These principles may have a great influence on their political and social views. In the course of studying the distribution of opinions among religious denominations, researchers have found that affiliation with a religion is not a very good predictor of opinions for many individuals. It is true that Catholics are, in general, more likely to vote for Democratic candidates than for Republicans and may be more liberal on some social issues than the general public, but the differences are declining. Members of the mainstream Protestant denominations show no pattern different from the majority of Americans in their views. Looking more closely at the way that religion influences an individual and his or her opinions, scholars have looked for other indicators of how religion influences opinions. With the growth in political strength and activity among conservative or fundamentalist Protestant groups, it has become clear that holding a certain set of religious beliefs is linked to a particular set of political views and opinions for this subgroup.

The Evangelicals

Over the past 20 to 30 years, a number of Protestant denominations and independent churches began to take political action and attempt to influence public policy. In fact, one television evangelist, Pat Robertson, became a Republican candidate for the presidency. The adherents of these churches tend to be quite conservative on social issues, including strong opposition to abortions, and to be Republican in partisanship. Because some of the churches taking a more political stand were within mainline Protestant denominations, looking at opinions by denominational affiliation "hid" these groups from analysis. Scholars tried various survey questions to tease out those individuals who held this more evangelical perspective. In general, it has been possible to identify this group by asking a series of questions, including whether they view the Bible as inerrant, whether they consider themselves to be "born again," and whether one can be saved by faith alone. Individuals who answer affirmatively to all three are generally considered to be evangelical Protestants (Jelen, 1989). About 20% of Americans could be considered evangelical or fundamentalist Protestants.

In terms of their beliefs, these conservative Christians are more likely than mainstream Protestants to oppose social-welfare programs and big government programs, to oppose easy access to abortions, to support prayer in the schools, and to oppose the inclusion of gays in the military. They are much more likely to identify themselves as Republicans than as Democrats, and, according to the 2004 exit poll, only 21% of self-declared (white) evangelicals voted for John Kerry, as compared to 49% of the national electorate.

The Catholics

As pointed out by Leege and Welch (1989), there are also evangelical groups within the Catholic church who may hold some similar religious beliefs. They differ considerably from the Protestant evangelicals because their views are considerably more liberal, especially on social welfare issues. Leege and Welch's work confirmed the general trend for Catholics to be more liberal than the general public, but looked more closely at the beliefs that are deeply held by individuals to see if these predicted political views. Specifically, Leege and Welch focused on the degree to which Catholics held individualistic or communitarian beliefs, that is, the degree to which they were closely tied to parish and community life. They found evidence that communitarian indicators were linked to certain more traditional views, including the importance of the male breadwinner, opposition to abortion, and concerns about changes in society. Religious individualism is associated with more liberal social views. What Leege and Welch make clear is that the American Catholic community includes individuals with different beliefs and that those differences will be reflected in different political views. In addition, they note that the more assimilated the individual is into mainstream society and the higher the income and educational attainment, the less likely it is that the person will be strongly Democratic and liberal.

Jewish Opinions

Like Catholics, Jewish Americans have long been considered to be very liberal in their views on social and political issues. They have been highly identified with the Democratic Party and its more liberal candidates. In a study of Jewish voters, Cohen and Liebman (1997) examined a number of possible explanations for the liberal record of these Americans. They tested explanations ranging from a theology that specifies charity and good works, to the independent and relatively secular lifestyle of most American Jews, to their history as an oppressed minority. Though the results of this study showed that Jews are, in general, more liberal on a range of positions than are non-Jews, when the data are controlled for equal levels of educational attainment, it appears that Jews are only more liberal than non-Jews on a particular subset of issues. Specifically, Jews are far more likely to identify with the Democratic Party (72%) than are non-Jews. They are also strongly supportive of civil liberties, of the separation of church and state, of permissive social norms including abortion, and of spending on some domestic programs. Cohen and Liebman conclude from their research that Jews are liberal and highly identified with the Democratic Party because they have been a minority group needing the protections of the government and that their liberalism on this set of issues is probably not related very clearly to religious beliefs or practices.

Religiosity as an Explanation

In addition to the specific belief questions that are now used in surveys to identify evangelical Christians, individuals of all denominations including Protestants, Catholics, and Jews are often asked about the habits of religious practice. Research has shown that individuals who most frequently attend religious services are most likely to express more conservative views than others of their faith. This is known as a measure of **religiosity**. It is not understood whether these individuals are simply less willing to tolerate a wide range of beliefs different from their own or whether they are driven by their own personal needs to engage in a greater degree of religious practice.

GENDER AND OPINIONS

Over the past three decades, there has been growing evidence of a **gender gap** in voting for the presidency. By the 1992 election, Bill Clinton received 46% of the women's vote but only 41% of the men's vote. The gender gap first appeared in a significant way during the 1980 election when a majority of women cast their votes against Ronald Reagan (Frankovic, 1982). Since that time, much attention has been focused on the distribution of opinions within gender groups and on testing various explanations for the gender differences that are found.

Some of the early students of political socialization did notice that there were differences between boys and girls at the elementary school level, particularly with respect to their interest in politics and political issues (Greenstein in Dennis, 1973). Girls were less interested in political issues and the topic of government than were boys, and the margin of disinterest stayed about the same across age groups. Thinking about other work on gender differences in achievement in school, it might be hypothesized that girls become less interested in politics because they are not encouraged to do so, in much the same way that adolescent girls are now known to lose interest in science and mathematics because they are not expected to be interested in those topics and future careers. Another hypothesis would suggest that with relatively few role models of women holding high political office, girls, like young people of color, see little reason to pursue an interest in politics, because the likelihood of holding political office is perceived to be slim.

Although there is not enough evidence to validate either of those hypotheses, it is clear that women continue to exhibit less interest in politics and to possess less information about political topics than do their male counterparts (Delli Carpini and Keeter, 1992, 1996: Chap. 4). A study by Verba, Burns, and Schlozman (1997) examined the gender gap between men and women in political knowledge, political efficacy, and political interest. As indicated in Table 5.3, it appears that women are less likely than men to know the answers to a number of political questions and to care much less for discussion about politics. Both genders are equally likely to know about local politics, to pay attention to local politics, and to pay attention to the news.

According to Verba, Burns, and Schlozman (1997), the difference in interest and engagement in politics and political issues, especially beyond the local level, remains even among men and women of equal education, equal occupations, and equal access to extensive personal resources that might support political activity. They also found, however, that in some states, having a female governor or U.S. senator seemed to greatly increase

**Table 5.3. Gender and Political Information and Interest
(percentage giving the correct answer)**

Measures of Political Information	Women	Men
Name of one U.S. Senator	51	67
Name of second U.S. Senator	30	43
Name of U.S. Representative	32	42
Name of state representative	18	22
Name, head of local school system	30	27
Meaning of civil liberties	77	84
Measures of Political Interest		
Very interested in politics (screen question)	24	29
Very interested in national politics	29	38
Very interested in local politics	21	22
Discuss national politics nearly every day	20	31
Discuss local politics nearly every day	16	22
Enjoy political discussion	26	36

Source: Adapted from Verba, Burns, and Schlozman, 1997: 1055.

the sense of engagement among women. Thus, they question whether the relative lack of women in positions of political power might discourage women from following politics more closely.

Regardless of the gender gap in interest and engagement, there are issues on which women seem to take different positions from those of their male counterparts. Within the past 30 years, as noted previously, women are more likely to vote Democratic for president than are men. There also is a tendency for women to be more opposed to the use of force in foreign policy situations: Women were less supportive than men of U.S. intervention, even in the Gulf War, which commanded extremely high levels of support in the populace. Some scholars have suggested that women are, in general, more risk averse than men, leading to their increased opposition to nuclear power, to environmental pollution, and, similarly, to foreign policy stances that may lead to war. There has been no clear explanation of why the genders differ on these issues, although evidence has been presented that traces the gender gap on the use of force back over more than 40 years of survey research (Shapiro and Mahajan, 1986). There are some theories about why women take different positions on these issues, but none provides a complete explanation.

THE INFLUENCE OF PEERS

If the conditions for political socialization for children include *exposure, communication,* and *receptivity,* then it seems highly likely that an individual's opinions can be influenced by friends, neighbors, and, as an adult, by colleagues or co-workers in the workplace. There is, surprisingly, very little research to confirm the degree of influence that might be exercised between friends or colleagues, but if the expression of opinions might increase an individual's acceptance within the group, peer influence must exist. Some students of behavior have suggested that the expression of opinions actually works as a mechanism of social adjustment for individuals, that is, to ease their relations with others. In addition, it is thought that individuals who aspire to join a particular group begin to model the behavior of their future career, including expressing the opinions appropriate to the new role, long before they actually achieve this new status. For example, a young woman who aspires to become a business executive might begin dressing in business attire and discussing the stock market and economic conditions early in her college career, long before she begins the process of job interviews for her intended position.

Some of those scholars who looked at childhood socialization did examine the relationships between elementary and high school friends in terms of political opinions. The Niemi and Jennings (1974) study of parents and high school students also included the students' best friends of the same gender for some questions on party identification and issues. Considering the early age at which partisanship is transmitted by parents, it is not surprising that there was little agreement among peers on party identification. There was some evidence of peer agreement on political issues, most notably on those that affect younger people. A study by Langton (1969), however, produced stronger results. After studying children in the Caribbean, he found that when children of middle-class families were attending school with mostly working-class children, their views moderated toward those of their peers. The converse was also true. In European nations such as Italy, where the political party structure is much more ideological, students are likely to have friends from the same social and political background. Settle, Bond, and Levitt (2011: 250) take a larger view, looking at whether students who are well integrated into a social network are more likely to adopt civic norms and to view civic participation positively. Investigating students' own perceptions of being socially integrated, they found that students who had a strong social network and had friends who expressed the same feelings were more likely to trust government, to want to participate in the system, and to volunteer in the community.

These results confirm our common-sense knowledge of adolescent behavior. Except during an election year, when there may be some activity that includes youth, specific political issues are not very important to young people. However, peer groups are extremely powerful in transmitting the correct and accepted social norms and behaviors to their members, so one would expect that if peer groups were more actively involved in civic life, they would be agents of political socialization. Remember that in 1992,

MTV for the first time took an active role in the political campaign, launching its "Rock the Vote" series to increase participation in the elections among young people. The campaign was generally evaluated as effective in increasing voting turnout in the 18- to 21-year-old age group.

The influence of peers among adults is theorized and sometimes assumed, but there is very little research to report. There is some work that shows that husbands and wives tend to hold similar opinions, especially relative to their socioeconomic class and educational levels. Similarly, in the case of beliefs shared by colleagues and co-workers, it is very difficult to ascertain whether working journalists or individual members of labor unions or stockbrokers share political viewpoints because of their self-selection into a particular career or because of their contact with peers who influence their opinions. What we know about political socialization and how it relates to the need for social approval by children might suggests that adult peer socialization is a more powerful effect than we recognize. One reason we have so little evidence about the impact of peers is that it is difficult to measure through survey research. Most people are reluctant to admit that they hold certain opinions to please others, and, in most cases, they may have internalized a viewpoint so firmly that it is now their own opinion. Finally, individuals who live in the same neighborhood, belong to the same church, or work in the same company may share opinions because of a recognition of the best interest of the neighborhood or company. Recent research suggests, in fact, that families may choose to live in communities that are more homogeneous in political viewpoints, therefore exposing themselves to less diversity of opinion (Bishop, 2008; Levendusky, 2009).

GENERATIONAL INFLUENCES ON OPINION

Common sense and personal life experience lead us to expect differences in opinions between different generations of Americans. Grandparents rarely seem to approve of grandchildren piercing body parts, living together without the benefit of marriage, or choosing a career in rock music. Yet these are mostly personal lifestyle decisions. Do the generations hold different views on current public issues? Does growing older tend to create a generation of conservative voters? There is evidence in the presidential vote patterns over time that older Americans are somewhat more likely to be Republican in their voting habits and, perhaps, more conservative on some issues. The rate of participation in elections rises steeply as cohorts age, with more than 70% of registered voters over the age of 45 turning out to vote, as compared to less than 40% for those 18 to 20 years old.

The tendency for older Americans to classify themselves more as conservatives than do the younger groups is a generational difference that we attribute to life cycle effects. As individuals age, they are more aware than ever of their own interests and will express opinions that support those interests, and they are probably more aware of changes in society that they do not approve or share. The oldest generation of Americans is less comfortable with change and unlikely to wish to participate in some of the changes taking place in society. Younger Americans, who are likely to vote and participate in politics at a very low level, are more interested in establishing their lives, pursuing a career, and finding companionship than in discussing political issues. Interest in and engagement with politics definitely shows an increase for individuals after they turn 30, probably stemming from their interest in their communities, their economic prospects, and their families' well-being. So there are life cycle changes both in participation and in interest in certain public issues.

There are other types of differences between members of different age groups that can be identified as true generational effects. What is meant by that term is that a cohort of people who were born at a certain time demonstrates a similarity of political views or political attachment that is related to events that took place during the years in which they formed a political identity. Theories of psychological development suggest that political views are most influenced by events during the adolescent years. Davis (2004) shows that individuals who were adolescents during the turbulent 1960s do show a greater increase in liberal attitudes than seen in earlier and later cohorts. As will be discussed in Chapter 7, research demonstrates that Americans who came of political age, that is, became engaged with politics, during the years of the Great Depression are likely to still be strong Democratic voters. Similarly, it appears that Americans who came of age during the years of the Reagan presidency may become identified with the Republican Party in greater numbers than other generations. Baby Boomers show much less proclivity toward one party or another, perhaps because one party did not dominate during their formative years. Some evidence suggests that Americans who became adults during the period of the 1960s protest movements demonstrate less attachment in general to the political parties as a result of their disagreement with the political system in their youth.[2] Evidence provided by Erikson and Stoker (2011) suggests that an even more unique group—men who received low draft numbers in 1969 and were likely to be drafted into the military—were more likely to be antiwar in their views, more liberal, and more likely to change their partisan identity. These results persisted for three decades.

The generational effect that brought so many Americans to the Democratic Party during the presidency of Franklin Roosevelt occurred during the same period in which many African American voters were persuaded to move from a Republican affiliation to a Democratic one. One of the questions that remains unanswered for students of this phenomenon is whether any political event of the past 50 years has had such an enduring effect. Partisan identity, once fixed either by childhood socialization or a generational event, tends to persist for the rest of the individual's life if the attachment is strong enough. Independent voters tend to stay independent voters as well. As will be discussed in Chapter 7, the increase in independent voters may signal a general weakening of partisan identification unless a major political event places its imprint on a new generation of voters.

THE MEDIA'S INFLUENCE ON OPINION

The impact of the news media on public opinion is a vast topic, one that has its own extensive literature (Bennett, 1996; Davis, 1996; Graber, 1997; Iyengar and Kinder, 1987; Neuman, Just, and Crigler, 1992) and one that is constantly changing as the mechanisms for delivering news and information undergo rapid change. At one point in this nation's history, the only medium for the transmission of news and political debate to the people was local newspapers. In 2010, people turn to a multitude of sources for their news, moving from one technology to another during a single day. A recent Pew Center news consumption survey (2010) found that their respondents had increased the amount of minutes per day spent getting the news by adding online news sources to the 57 minutes spent with television, radio, or print news. Although the percentage of Americans who read a newspaper continues to decline, exposure to news online continues to increase. For Americans in their 30s, a majority reports getting their news from one or more digital sources including the Internet, Twitter, podcasts, or e-mail. However, more than 40% of people in their 40s and 50s also report getting news online or from other digital sources. Before the advent of cable television and, more recently, satellite television, many commentators feared that the news was becoming too homogenized: All Americans would receive a sanitized and, perhaps, biased version of the news from the three networks. The electronic revolution has certainly displaced that fear. Today, Americans choose between major networks including the Fox network, CNN and other cable news sources, and thousands of sources of information available over the Internet. Instead of centralized news, political information today is fragmented and, in the case of the Internet, may be fraudulent or totally politicized, depending on the source. In addition to there being more news outlets, there is more news being reported. With the advent of cable television, the "news cycle" became 24/7, meaning that news is reported 24 hours a day, seven days a week. This explosion of news coverage forces individual citizens to decide how to narrow their search for relevant information or be cognitively buried by too much news.

In terms of influencing the opinions of Americans of all ages, the media performs three functions: supplying information about issues and candidates through broadcasting the news; setting the agenda for public debate through editorial decisions; and conveying a vast array of messages from the government, politicians, and major interests to the public in the form of news and advertising. Early research on the influence of the media on public opinion looked at the direct effects of the media on individuals, assuming that the political elites send direct messages to the citizens and expect citizens to alter their behaviors in turn. One might think of the direct messages sent to Americans during World War II to buy war bonds and conserve resources. Although many direct messages are intended to improve the safety of individuals (be prepared for hurricanes, for example), others may be considered government-sponsored propaganda.

For the past several decades, scholars of political communication have been more interested in what are termed indirect effects of media exposure. These include shaping the public's view of the most important issues of the day or **agenda setting**, influencing how citizens regard certain issues (**framing**), and giving media consumers criteria by which to choose their own positions on the issues (**priming**) (Iyengar and McGrady, 2007: 12).

Supplying Information

Americans readily admit their dependence on the media, and television in particular, for news about their community, the nation, and the world. In terms of how much influence it has on their opinions about public issues, it is important to ask what kinds of information the news is supplying and how people actually process the news they receive. The question of whether the news is biased has occupied the attention of both liberal and conservative commentators for decades. Liberals claim that the editorial bias of media is conservative because all forms of the media, with the exception of public radio and public television, are actually part of corporate America, with a bias toward capitalism. Studies over time have consistently shown that journalists themselves are more left of center than the general public, although the most recent survey conducted by the Pew Center for Excellence in Journalism found a moderating trend. Surveying more than 1,100 journalists, the American Journalist study found that only 31% of the journalists said that they were "a little to the left" and 9% reported being "pretty far to the left," for a total of 40%. This is a decline of 7% from the prior survey. More journalists identified themselves as moderates than in the past, and there was a slight increase in the number who identified themselves as "leaning to the right," up from 22% to 25%. The Pew Center does note, however, that "journalists are still more than twice as likely to lean leftward then the population overall" (Pew Research Center for the People and the Press, 2006). In every election year, the media are studied to identify any such biases, especially in their coverage of the candidates and campaigns with, most often, inconclusive results. There is, however, a school of thought that charges the media with a form of **establishment bias**. Work by Graber (1997), Exoo (1994), and others finds that the question of which stories to cover and which sources to use is definitely slanted toward the government and known establishment sources. Bennett (1996) argues that what the media do is *index* the degree of interest and conflict in the establishment and then, if there is debate within the elites, cover that story. What this means is that many issues that may confront ordinary Americans or the issues that truly impact minority or severely disadvantaged groups receive little or no news attention.

The other charge leveled against the media, both print and electronic, is that a premium is put on sensationalism and high-interest stories. In the case of newspapers, the coverage of campaigns has become focused on the question of who is winning the "horse race" rather than on the policy positions and character of the candidates. Increased polling by the media provides data for these stories. In the past few elections, the major national papers and network news organizations have attempted to provide more substantive information about the candidates, but there is still more headline news in the polls. Television news is particularly subject to the charge of putting entertainment first. Primetime news programs compete by changing anchors to attract new viewers or by changing formats to appear "lighter." In part, the actual physical characteristics of television news push it into a show business format. Time is limited, and viewer interest is stimulated by short, tight stories with great video shots. The effect is that the news is sometimes dominated by available footage rather than complicated news stories.

What do people learn from the news that has an impact on their opinions?[3] People watch the news in great numbers, but they actually pay attention to a subset of stories. The Pew Research Center tracks interest in the news on a weekly and annual basis: according to their findings, the stories that generated the most interest among Americans in the first decade of the century were the terrorist attacks of 9/11/01 (with 78% following the news very closely) and the damage from Hurricanes Katrina and Rita (with 73% following the news closely). Other top stories of the decade included the crash of the economy in September 2008, the Iraq War, and the 2008 presidential election (Pew Research Center, 2010a). Graber's year-long work with a panel of Chicagoans showed that people scan the news both on television and in newspapers but remember only about half of the important news stories of a year. They paid close attention to less than one-quarter of all the major news stories, although they discussed many more with friends. The stories that people found most interesting were those with personal relevance, those with human interest, and those with societal importance. People also admitted to rejecting some stories because they were of no interest to them or because the issue was beyond their control (Graber, 1984: 86–87). Given the relative lack of new information presented on television news, Graber finds that people's learning from the news is quite sensible. As she concludes, "The findings indicate that people know how to cope with information overload, that they balance a healthy respect for their own pleasures with moderate willingness to perform their civic duties, and that they have learned to extract essential kernels of information from news stories while discarding much of the chaff" (97).

Setting the Agenda

Another function of the media for shaping public opinions is to shape the agenda of what is news. Part of that agenda-setting function is the identification of the important stories and debates to be covered, as just discussed. Not only do the media identify the issues that will become "headline news," but their treatment of those issues may also have an effect on public opinion. Iyengar and Kinder (1987) suggested that media priming, the choosing of which issues to emphasize as important, shapes the political choices that citizens might make. For example, an emphasis on the loss of jobs and the slowdown of the economy in conjunction with stories about the president could "prime" citizens to think of the economic downturn as the president's fault. As mentioned above, the news media's attention to the competitive nature of political campaigns, or "horse-race" journalism, primes voters, especially in the primary campaign, to evaluate candidates in terms of their likelihood of winning the election rather than in terms of their platforms or past performance.

Yet another aspect of agenda setting is the media's ability to "frame" an issue. As defined by Iyengar and McGrady (2007: 219), "framing . . . refers to the way in which opinions about an issue can be altered by emphasizing or de-emphasizing particular facets of that issue." The media could choose to tell a story about the decline in the housing market and the number of mortgages in default by emphasizing the role of Wall Street bankers in the crisis or by looking at the individuals who invested in homes that were clearly beyond their means. The "frame" of the story could lead the news consumer to view the bankers as responsible for the crisis or the individual borrowers. When the individual responds to a survey question about the mortgage crisis, the news frame is likely to influence his or her answer to the interviewer.

The media also shape the agenda for the public through their choice of coverage for political campaigns and issues. Patterson (1980) has examined the media's blind emphasis on the daily events of the campaign and its treatment of campaigning as a type of national game over several election cycles. He suggests that the ordinary citizen is poorly served by the media during campaigns because the coverage actually leads the public away from thinking about the real issues that divide parties and candidates. It is not, he points out, the fault of the media, but a result of letting the media set the agenda for public discussion.

The media have actually formalized the process of setting the agenda for the public through their focus on the "most important problem" question that is asked by Gallup in its national poll and is repeated by polls sponsored by the media. A study by MacKuen (1981) compared the content of news stories with the responses to the most-important-problem question over a period of 15 years. He found that the most important problem identified by survey respondents tended to follow an increased number of reports on that problem. For example, the "drug problem" rose to number one on the most-important-problem list following two months of national stories about drug usage. Other stories have shown that media coverage of problems actually tends to peak after the problem itself has peaked in intensity. There is no question that people do tend to follow the lead of the media in determining which issues are most important to discuss. As noted earlier, however, this means that some problems do not make it to national prominence because of a lack of coverage, either because the political leadership does not want to address these problems or because the problem is too complex to cover.

Conveying Messages

Finally, the media conveys the messages of candidates, political leaders, and political interests to the people as part of the attempt by these message senders to influence public opinion. This *manipulation* of the news media has reached new proportions in U.S. political campaigns, with the sending of huge advance teams to the site of candidate speeches to ensure that the most flattering and patriotic camera shots will be released to the news. The same kind of planning also takes place for presidential visits at home and abroad. The use of the media to send messages was probably perfected by Franklin Delano Roosevelt, who used his "fireside" chats on radio to reassure the nation during the Great Depression and World War II. Since that time, presidents and other political leaders have learned to use television to grab the attention of the people. The practice of "creating" news events has reached such a level in every White House that it has been called the "permanent campaign" (Cook, 2002). Politicians at every level have also learned to try to control news reporting through the practice of "spin control," which means that the politician explains on camera how an event or speech is to be regarded, thus preempting the comments of the journalists and editors. The practice of spin control then becomes a topic for journalists, who report on the efforts of the politicians and their representatives to shape public opinion.

Politicians are not the only practitioners who use the media for messages. Corporate America, interest groups, foreign leaders, nonprofit groups, and consumer advocates all try to get news coverage of their messages to try to influence public opinion. And as the degree of sophistication increases, all of these players are more conscious of the public relations strategies necessary to convey a message via the media. During the United Parcel Service strike of 1997, the Teamsters Union was widely regarded as the public relations victor through its constant focus on the needs of the workers, the overuse of part-time employees, and the fairness of its demands. The success of the union in sending those messages to the public improved the image of that individual union and the labor movement as a whole.

To what extent are individuals influenced by these attempts at media manipulation? Research conducted by McClure and Patterson (1976) during a presidential election suggests that most people view campaign advertisements with considerable selectivity (Patterson, 1980; also the early work of Lazarsfeld, Berelson, and Gaudet, 1944). They watch the ads of the candidates they like and generally reject or ignore messages sent by candidates they have rejected. For all of the money spent on advertising for candidates, there is very little evidence that a voter will change his or her mind in response to the information in ads. The truly independent voters, and those voters with the least information about politics and the system, are those most likely to be influenced by the information received through the media. The impact of the media on noncampaign issues is also not as great as the message senders think. Graber and others suggest that most people use the media as a supplement to information they gain in other ways—from experience, from friends and colleagues, and from their own perceptions and memories.

As we have seen, certain influences act on the individual earlier in life. That is, the ethnicity of an individual and, possibly, his or her religious background are part and parcel of the family environment in which the child is raised. The formal educational system influences the child or, at minimum, mediates some of the family effects of socialization, as does the interaction with peers and the media during childhood. When the child becomes an adult, socialization continues through peers, spouse, and family, generational effects, and the impact of the media. In the chapters that follow, we will look at how these influences impact public opinion about the issues that have confronted the American electorate in recent years.

POLLS, POLLING, AND THE INTERNET

There are myriad Internet sites that focus on the media. Liberal commentators blog about conservatives and vice versa. Almost all newspapers and television stations have their own websites. There are also many websites that study and analyze the media's performance of its functions.

For an example of a media website that caters to young Americans and encourages participation, go to Rock the Vote: www.rockthevote.org.

If you are interested in more of the data and conclusions from the National Civics Test, you can find the entire report at: nationsreportcard.gov/civics_2010.

The Pew Research Center is the portal to two excellent websites: Excellence in Journalism and the Pew Center for the People and the Press. Go to: www.pewresearch.org and enter your search terms. The site will direct you to one of their suborganizations as appropriate.

6

What the Public Knows about Politics

As described in Chapter 1, traditional democratic theory assumes that each member of the electorate is interested in public issues, motivated by principle, aware of relevant facts, and capable of making decisions rationally. This chapter focuses on the "aware of relevant facts" component of this description. How do Americans measure up in terms of meeting this standard? Are Americans interested in public issues? How aware are they of the facts underlying policy debates?

One of the most extensive reviews of what the American public knows about politics was done by Delli Carpini and Keeter (1996). In this work, they examined the argument that democracy functions best when its citizens are politically informed. They contend that "although it is true that citizens cannot be experts on all aspects of politics, a general familiarity with (1) the rules of the game . . . (2) the substance of politics . . . and (3) people and parties . . . is critical to the maintenance of a healthy democracy" (1996: 14).

There is little consensus as to what Americans should know about their country. How many of the nine Supreme Court justices should "good citizens" be able to name? Should they know the current unemployment rate? The federal poverty level? The rights included in the First Amendment? The name of the prime minister of Canada? As Delli Carpini and Keeter (1996: 13) note, "Any attempt to assemble a list of critical facts is sure to fail." Yet if citizens are to engage effectively in the policy process, to understand the consequences of political decisions, to communicate their positions to the appropriate officials, and to vote for candidates who best represent their views, then some knowledge of how the system works, what the issues are, who the decision makers are, and what their positions are on the issues is important.

In describing the "paradox of modern democracy" Delli Carpini and Keeter (1996: 22) note that in theory a democracy requires knowledge, yet democracy in this country has thrived for more than 200 years despite evidence that a large percentage of the public is uninformed about fundamental aspects of the political system and specific policy issues. Some researchers who have observed the public's low level of political knowledge have argued that the country's political system is in crisis. The contrary view is that "real democracy functions through some combination of control by elites, the availability of attentive publics, resourceful use of heuristics and information shortcuts by citizens, and the beneficent effects of collective rationality wherein the whole of citizen awareness is greater than the sum of its parts" (Delli Carpini and Keeter, 1996: 23). Despite the relatively low levels of knowledge that have frequently been observed, the practice of democracy in the United States has flourished for more than two centuries.

EARLY EMPIRICAL INVESTIGATIONS

Assessing the public's level of political knowledge has been an interest of researchers since the first empirical survey-based studies of the electorate. Hyman and Sheatsley (1947: 414) found that the "generally uninformed group, therefore, is of considerable magnitude" and argued that a number of psychological barriers made it difficult to increase the general public's level of information. Berelson, Lazarsfeld, and McPhee (1954: 312) concluded that "individual voters seem unable to satisfy the requirements for a democratic system outlined by political theorists." In *The American Voter*, Campbell and his colleagues (1960: 174) reported that on average about one respondent of every three either had no opinion or could not correctly identify what the federal government was doing on the important issues of the time. Philip Converse (1964: 212) noted that the public's knowledge on many subjects "could virtually be measured as a few 'bits' in the technical sense" and has concluded that "popular levels of information about politics are, from the point of view of the informed observer, astonishingly low" (Converse, 1975: 79).

In a series of reports appearing in *Public Opinion Quarterly*, Erskine (1962, 1963a, 1963b, 1963c) described various aspects of Americans' political knowledge during the period from the late 1940s through the early 1960s. Selected items from these reports are presented in Box 6.1. These examples demonstrate that there is some information about what the government is and does, substantive issues, and political leaders and groups for which the public demonstrates a fairly highly level of awareness, but others for which only a small percentage of the electorate is knowledgeable. In 1947, 98% could identify President Harry Truman and 97% recognized General Douglas MacArthur, but only 11% knew the United States' chief delegate to the United Nations (Warren Austin), and in 1948 just 11% could name

BOX 6.1
Americans' Knowledge on Selected Issues, 1943–1962 (percent)

	Reasonably Correct	Incorrect, Don't Know
Rules of the Game		
How many Senators are there in Washington from the state (1945)	55	45
What the term "filibuster" means (1949)	54	46
What is meant by the electoral college (1955)	35	65
Know anything it says in the Bill of Rights (1945)	21	79
How many states will elect members of the U.S. House of Representatives this fall (1954)	11	89
Awareness of Issues		
Heard or read about the Taft-Harley Law (1947)	61	39
Heard or read about the Egyptian-Israeli struggle (1955)	61	39
Heard or read about the Marshall Plan (1947)	49	51
Heard or read about the Kennedy administration's plan to increase our trade with other nations (1962)	46	54
Read about the Republican Party platform (1952)	22	78
People and Institutions		
Know who Harry Truman is (1947)	98	2
Know who Douglas MacArthur is (1947)	97	3
What the initials "FBI" stand for (1949)	78	22
What the initials "GOP" stand for (1952)	47	53
Know the names of two U.S. Senators from the state (1945)	35	65
Know the presidential candidate for the States' Rights Party (1948)	11	89
Know the U.S. chief delegate to the United Nations (1947)	11	89

Sources: Hazel Erskine Gaudet, *Public Opinion Quarterly*, 1962, 1963a, 1963b, 1963c.

Strom Thurmond as the presidential candidate of the States' Rights Party. In terms of the basic structure of government, 55% knew how many U.S. senators their state had (in 1945), 54% could reasonably describe a filibuster (in 1949), and 35% knew what the electoral college was (in 1955). In 1945, only 21% knew anything contained in the Bill of Rights, and in 1954 only 11% knew how many states would elect members to the House of Representatives that fall. On political issues, 61% in 1947 had heard or read about the Taft-Hartley Law and the same percentage was aware of the

Egyptian-Israeli struggle in 1955, but only 22% had read about the Republican Party platform in 1952.

As noted previously, it is unrealistic to attempt to assemble any list of critical facts about the political system that a citizen should be expected to know. Yet many analysts looked at results such as those presented by Erskine—particularly those related to the "rules of the game," such as the content of the Bill of Rights or the number of senators a state has—and raised concerns about the performance of American democracy (Entman, 1989).

THE UNCHANGING AMERICAN VOTER

It has been argued that after 1964 the major empirical indicators of mass political sophistication, such as attitudinal consistency and issue voting, rose sharply due to the increased salience of political issues in the 1960s and the electorate's increasing educational attainment (Nie, Verba, and Petrocik, 1976). As America moved out of the politically quiescent period of the 1950s, did the electorate's level of political knowledge increase?

A series of analyses conducted by Bennett (1988, 1989, 1995a, 1995b, 1996) led to the conclusion that there was not much change in the political knowledge of the American electorate after 1964. In one study, Bennett updated Hyman and Sheatsley's (1947) work on "know-nothings" and found that "29 percent of adult Americans constitute the know-nothings among the contemporary American public, almost the same percentage so classified by Hyman and Sheatsley. Given the different instruments used and the changes in America since 1947, to find virtually no change in the percentage of know-nothings is remarkable" (1988: 433). In examining trends in political knowledge between 1967 and 1987, Bennett used questions on knowledge of the state's governor, U.S. representative, and head of the local school district.[1] In both 1967 and 1987, "between 19–24% knew all three officials, and 45–53% either missed all three or got only one correct." Given these results, he concluded that "in neither year could the public be said to be particularly well acquainted with key public figures. More important, the public was slightly better informed in 1967," despite increases in education during this period (1989: 426).

Extending this research into the 1990s, in comparing data from 1988 and 1992, Bennett concluded that "the blunt truth is that Americans are largely ignorant of public affairs in both years" (1995a: 523). Similarly, in revisiting the research on "know-nothings," he found "the 1994 data show that 32.9% of the American public missed all five items. In short, sizable portions of the American public—probably about a third—were 'know-nothings' in 1946 and 1994" (1996: 224). Echoing Converse's (1990) observations about the intractability of political ignorance, Bennett concluded that "unless the 'costs' of acquiring knowledge substantially change, or people's motivation to learn information alters, we should not expect levels of information to vary significantly" (1995a: 529).

Delli Carpini and Keeter's (1991, 1992, 1996; Delli Carpini, 1993) wide-ranging investigation of the public's knowledge of politics reached conclusions similar to those of Bennett. In this research, they collected information on "over 2000 survey questions tapping factual knowledge of politics that were asked over the past 50 years. These questions covered a range of topics that one might expect an informed citizen to know, including knowledge of institutions and processes . . . of substantive issues and indicators of the day . . . and of public figures and political organizations" (Delli Carpini, 1999).[2] These researchers present a vast amount of information on Americans' knowledge of institutions and processes, people and players, and the substance of politics (1996: 69–86). Similar to the results reported by Erskine, they found that the public's level of knowledge on specific items varied widely.

Among their findings in the area of institutions and processes, for example, was that 94% of Americans (in 1986) knew that warrants allow police searches and that 93% knew the length of a president's term (in 1952). The percentage of awareness dropped to 76% of those who knew that the Constitution can be amended (in 1986), to 69% who knew that popular votes do not determine who will be president (in 1986), to 58% who recognized that the Supreme Court determines a law's constitutionality (in 1992), and to 41% who could define the Bill of Rights (in 1986). Even lower levels of knowledge were found for items on defining the electoral college (35% in 1955), the length of the term for the U.S. House of Representatives (30% in 1978), and naming all three branches of government (19% in 1952).[3]

A similar pattern of variation was found for knowledge of public figures and political organizations. In 1996, 99% of adults could name the U.S. president, and awareness of a figure like FBI director J. Edgar Hoover was also relatively high (75% in 1960). But the public's ability to identify "political players" declines when the subject is someone who is not frequently in the media. In 1985, 59% knew whether their governor was a Democrat or a Republican and in 1984 only 51% correctly identified Warren Burger as the chief justice of the Supreme Court. The percentage of the public who could name both their U.S. senators was 35% (in 1985), who could correctly identify Eugene McCarthy (in 1967) was 19%, and who could name the prime minister of Norway was 1% (in 1986).

Public awareness of the substance of politics also varied over a wide range for both domestic and foreign policy issues. In 1952, for example, 96% knew what the steel dispute was about, but in 1973 only 54% knew what Watergate was about. In foreign affairs, while 93% could name one country with nuclear weapons (in 1988), 49% knew that the United States was the only nation to use nuclear weapons (in 1986), and only 4% knew the percentage of U.S. real estate that was foreign owned (in 1989). As summarized by Delli Carpini and Keeter (1996: 82–86), "more than 60% of the items tapping knowledge of domestic politics could not be answered by as many as half of those asked" and "more than half of the 553 foreign affairs items could be answered by less than half the general public."

As part of their research, Delli Carpini and Keeter also examined changes in the public's level of political knowledge over time. Although the public in 1989 was slightly more knowledgeable than in the 1940s and 1950s, "more striking than the differences is the overall similarity. . . . Over 40 years, the level of political knowledge of some basic facts about the political system has remained remarkably stable" (1991: 590). In summarizing trends in knowledge over time, they noted that "in spite of an unprecedented expansion in public education, a communications revolution that has shattered national and international boundaries, and the increasing relevance of national and international events and policies to the daily lives of Americans, citizens appear no more informed about politics" (1996: 133).

Recent research conducted by the Pew Center for the People and the Press provides another perspective on what Americans know and how levels of political knowledge have changed over time. In comparing political knowledge between 1989 and 2007, Kohut, Morin, and Keeter (2007) found that "on average, today's citizens are about as able to name their leaders, and are about as aware of major news events as was the public nearly 20 years ago" (Box 6.2). But a deeper analysis revealed that "Americans didn't do as well in 2007 compared with how similarly-educated Americans performed in 1989. Across the board, scores declined significantly among college graduates, those with some college as well as for those with a high school education or less."

As part of its monitoring of public opinion on political issues, the Pew Research Center frequently includes a series of political knowledge items in its polls. The results of these surveys typically show the same type of pattern exhibited in the studies of Erskine and Delli Carpini and Keeter: There are some items for which a high percentage of the public is knowledgeable and others for which a relatively small percentage are aware. In a Pew Center for the People and the Press (2011c) survey, for example, 80% were able to identify that the No Child Left Behind legislation dealt with education, 43% could correctly identify John Boehner as Speaker of the House, and 29% knew the U.S. government spends more on Medicare than on education, scientific research, or interest on the national debt. The great increase in the sources from which Americans can get their news and the changes in the way in which the electorate uses various media to get information have not led to an increase in the public's level of political knowledge.

Another resource for data on Americans knowledge of the political arena is the Intercollegiate Studies Institute American Civic Literacy Program. Its 2008 survey of 2,508 U.S. adults conducted for this program contained 33

BOX 6.2
Political Knowledge: Then and Now

	1989	2007	Diff.
Percent who could name			
The current vice president	74	69	−5
The state's governor	74	66	−8
The president of Russia[1]	47	36	−11
Percent who know			
America has a trade deficit	81	68	−13
The party controlling the House	68	76	+8
The chief justice is conservative	30	37	+7
Percent who could identify			
Tom Foley/Nancy Pelosi	14	49	+35
Richard Cheney/Robert Gates	13	21	+8
John Poindexter/Scooter Libby[2]	60	29	−31

[1]President of Russia trend from February 1994.
[2]John Poindexter trend from April 1990 at the conclusion of this trial for involvement
in the Iran-Contra affair while in the Reagan administration from 1985–1986.

Source: Pew Center for People and the Press, www.people-press.org/files/legacy-pdf/319.pdf

civics questions. Among the findings from this survey were that less than half of the respondents could name all three branches of government; 55% knew that the power to declare war belongs to Congress, with almost 40% incorrectly believing it belongs to the president; and only 21% knew that the Bill of Rights expressly prohibits the establishment of an official religion in the United States. Overall, 71% "failed" this test, with an average score of 49%. The report of this survey concluded that "the results reveal that Americans are alarmingly uninformed about our Constitution, the basic functions of our government, the key text of our national history, and economic principles (Cribb, 2008)."[4]

More than 60 years of empirical research on Americans' knowledge of politics leads to the conclusion, as summarized by Delli Carpini (1999: 6), that "the 'average' citizen is woefully uninformed about political institutions and processes, substantive policies and socioeconomic conditions, and important political actors such as elected officials and political parties."

APPLYING DEMOCRATIC PRINCIPLES

In describing the political knowledge of the public, it is not only the awareness of various facts that is important in characterizing the American mind, but also the application of the general principles of which Americans are aware to specific situations. One of the first empirical investigations of this topic was reported by Prothro and Grigg (1960). They interviewed samples of citizens in two cities and found virtual unanimity (from 95% to 98%) on questions of fundamental principles such as: (1) democracy is the best form of government; (2) public officials should be chosen by majority rule; (3) every citizen should have an equal chance to influence governmental policy; (4) the majority should be free to criticize majority decisions; and (5) people in the minority should be able to try to win majority support for their opinions (1960: 282–284). When they moved from these fundamental principles to more specific applications—for example, should only the informed be allowed to vote, should a socialist be allowed to speak, or should a communist be barred from running for office—"consensus breaks down completely . . . respondents in both communities are closer to perfect discord than to perfect consensus on over half the statements."

McClosky (1964) reported similar results from his investigation of the electorate's division on fundamental democratic values and its understanding of politics and political ideas. He examined the public's responses to items concerning the democratic "rules of the game" and applications of free speech and procedural rights and concluded that "a large proportion of the electorate has failed to grasp certain of the underlying ideas and principles on which the American political system rests." Moreover, "the principles of freedom and democracy are less widely and enthusiastically favored when they are confronted in their specific, or applied, forms" (365–366).

In his seminal work on attitudes on civil liberties, Stouffer (1955: 13) investigated the reactions of the American public to two dangers: "One, from the Communist conspiracy outside and inside the country. Two from those who in thwarting the conspiracy would sacrifice some of the very liberties which the enemy would destroy." In this work, Stouffer analyzed data from two surveys conducted in 1954 to gauge Americans' tolerance for nonconformists as measured in responses to three groups: communists, a person who was against churches and religion (atheists), and those favoring government ownership of railroads and big industries (socialists). Among other items, respondents were asked whether a member of these groups should be allowed to make a speech in the community, keep a book they published in the public library, or teach at a college or university.

The data in Table 6.1 show that, in general, the American public exhibited a relatively low level of tolerance in 1954, and that it was more willing to grant civil liberties to those advocating government ownership than to those who were against churches and religion or to communists. Almost 60% were willing to allow a socialist to give a speech in the community, while only 37% supported an atheist's right to do so, and just 27% would allow a communist to speak. There was even less support for

Table 6.1. Tolerance of Nonconformists, 1954 (percentage giving "tolerant" response)

	Communists	Socialists	Atheists
Allow public speech	27	58	37
Allow book in library	27	52	35
Allow to teach in college or university	6	33	12

Source: Stouffer (1955: 30–45).

allowing an individual from one of these groups to teach at a college or university; the percentages who said that a person who expressed these beliefs should be allowed to teach was 33% for socialists, 12% for atheists, and 6% for communists.

When several of the items used in the Stouffer study were repeated in the early 1970s, the public exhibited a marked increase in tolerance. As described by Mueller (1988: 3), "Between 1954 and 1972 or 1973, there was an increase of between 24 and 33 percentage points in tolerance as measured by these two questions and a decrease of between 23 and 34 percentage points in intolerance." Similar increases in tolerance were reported by Davis (1975), who found a 22% increase in tolerance between 1954 and 1971, and by Nunn, Crockett, and Williams (1978), who reported that tolerance for communists and atheists increased significantly between 1954 and 1977, with increases ranging from 25% to 35%, depending on the question.

The data in Table 6.2 provide the cross-time trends for questions on Americans' willingness to allow members of various groups to make a speech in the community advocating their point of view. The dramatic increase in tolerance for communists, socialists, and atheists between 1954 and 1972 noted previously is shown in these data. Since 1974, the percentage who would allow a communist or an atheist to give a public speech in their community has been relatively stable. The percentage who would permit a communist to give a speech was 62% in 1974, and since that time has varied only between 56% in 1976 and 72% in 1993, with about two-thirds of the public supporting this position throughout this period. The percentage who would allow an atheist to speak was 63% in 1974 and has not fallen below this percentage since, reaching a high of 78% in 2006. Since 1987 the percentage who would allow an atheist to speak has consistently been more than 70%.

The data for racists and militarists, introduced in the General Social Survey (GSS) in 1976, show that a majority in each year would allow these groups to give a speech in the community claiming that blacks were inferior or doing away with elections and letting the military run the country. The percentage who would allow racists to speak has ranged only between 58% and 65%, while the percentage who would support this right for

Table 6.2.   Should Groups Be Allowed to Make a Public Speech, 1954–2010 (percent)

Year	Communist	Atheist	Socialist	Racist	Militarist	Homosexual	Muslim
1954	27	37	57	—	—	—	—
1972	55	68	82	—	—	—	—
1973	62	67	81	—	—	64	—
1974	60	63	78	—	—	66	—
1976	56	66	—	63	55	65	—
1977	57	64	—	60	52	64	—
1980	56	66	—	63	58	68	—
1982	56	63	—	58	54	67	—
1984	61	69	—	58	57	70	—
1985	59	66	—	58	56	69	—
1987	60	69	—	60	55	69	—
1988	63	72	—	62	59	73	—
1989	66	73	—	62	62	79	—
1990	67	74	—	65	60	78	—
1991	69	74	—	63	63	78	—
1993	72	72	—	63	67	81	—
1994	69	74	—	63	66	82	—
1996	66	75	—	62	64	82	—
1998	68	76	—	64	68	84	—
2000	68	76	—	61	65	83	—
2002	70	77	—	63	70	84	—
2004	70	77	—	62	67	83	—
2006	69	78	—	63	67	83	—
2008	67	77	—	59	67	83	42
2010	66	77	—	59	70	87	41

Sources: For 1954: Stouffer (1955). Data for all other years are from the General Social Survey.

militarists has varied from 52% in 1977 to 70% (in 2002, 2010) and has been close to 70% in recent years.

These data also show the increasing tolerance for homosexuals. In 1973, 64% would allow a homosexual to give a speech in the community. This percentage has increased to 79% by 1989 and to 87% by 2010.

These results also show that there are groups for which Americans express less tolerance. In 2008 the GSS introduced a question on whether a Muslim clergyman preaching hatred of the United States should be allowed to speak. In 2008, 42% would allow such speech, and in 2010 this percentage was 41%.

The findings on tolerance of outgroups, such as those shown in Table 6.2, particularly the substantial rise in tolerance between 1954 and 1973, raised questions as to whether the observed changes represented increased levels of tolerance among the American public or a decrease in the salience of the perceived threat from groups such as communists (Gibson, 2006). Sullivan, Pierson, and Marcus (1979) attempted to address this

concern. They contended that earlier studies of tolerance "were not con-
tent-free, since the questions asked invariably referred to specific groups,
generally of the leftist persuasion. The items used in Stouffer's study and
in subsequent attempts to monitor changing levels of tolerance, referred
to communists, atheists, and socialists" (785). The public's level of tolerance, therefore, may have been confounded with the particular groups
about which questions were asked. To account for this, Sullivan and his
colleagues developed a content-controlled measure of tolerance in which
respondents were asked tolerance questions about the group they *liked
least*. They found that "these content-controlled items reveal more intolerance than the Stouffer items because they allow respondents to select
from a much wider range of groups," and concluded that "intolerance has
not necessarily declined much over the past 25 years, but merely has been
turned to new targets" (787–792).

The data on trends in tolerance of the groups that were the focus of
the Stouffer study show substantial increases in tolerance over time. The
results reported by Sullivan, Piereson, and Marcus demonstrate that there
are groups in society for which a large majority of the public is willing to
restrict civil liberties. The data from the 2008 and 2010 GSSs on the public's
willingness to allow a Muslim clergyman preaching hatred of the United
States to speak in the community reflect this distinction (see Table 6.2). In
the 2010 GSS, the lowest percentage who would allow members of other
"outgroups" to give a public speech in the community was 59% for racists, and this percentage was as high as 87% for homosexuals; for Muslim
preachers, less than a majority (41%) expressed the view that they should
be allowed to make a speech.[5]

Although the American public's knowledge of specific aspects of how the
political system works is frequently not at the level prescribed in classical
democratic theory, there are certain fundamental principles of democracy
for which a high percentage of the public is aware and on which there is a
high level of agreement. Clearly, there is less awareness among the public of
the implications of applying these principles in specific situations.

GROUP DIFFERENCES IN KNOWLEDGE

In Delli Carpini and Keeter's study of political knowledge, they make
the case that as a product of historical factors that have limited their engagement in the political process, individuals from lower social classes,
blacks, women, and younger people would be less politically informed
(1996: 156). Their analysis of 68 knowledge items largely confirmed their
hypotheses: (1) in no case was the percentage for low-income citizens as
high as that for upper income ones; (2) in no case was the percentage

for blacks as high as for whites; (3) the correct percentage for women was as high or higher than that for men in only five cases; and (4) 55 of the 68 questions were answered by a greater percentage of older people than younger people (157).

Although these group differences are significant and in many cases substantial, the effect of these background characteristics on knowledge is less important than that for education, which is "the most powerful predictor of political knowledge" (Delli Carpini and Keeter, 1996: 188). Delli Carpini and Keeter (1991: 594) identified vast differences in knowledge levels among those with a college degree relative to high school graduates or those who did not finish high school, and these differences have been maintained over time.

Other research on political knowledge has demonstrated the importance of education on level of political knowledge. Erskine's (1963a, 1963b, 1963c) data from the 1940s through the early 1960s show substantial difference across levels of education on questions such as how many senators there are from each state, the line of succession for the president, the use of fluoride in drinking water, and awareness of the Marshall Plan. Similarly, Bennett (1988: 484) found education to be the "most important predictor" of political information, accounting for 58% of the variance. The Pew Center study of political knowledge over time (Kohut, Morin, and Keeter, 2007: 6) reported that "More than six-in-ten college graduates (63%) fall into the high knowledge group, compared to 20% of those with less than a high school education—among the largest disparities observed in the survey." In the March 2011 Pew Center for the People and the Press survey, 62% of college graduates could name John Boehner as the Speaker of the House, compared to 41% of those with some college education, and 32% of those with a high school education or less. Similarly, 55% of college graduates knew that the Republicans had a majority in the House of Representatives; 42% of those with some college education were aware of this, as were 26% of those with a high school education or less. Overall, the effect of education is consistently evident across an array of domains of political knowledge, and the differences in awareness between those with a college education and those with a high school education or less are often quite large.

The significant impact of education is also evident in the application of democratic principles in specific situations and in political tolerance. Prothro and Grigg found that the percentage of "democratic" responses to basic principles was greater in each case for those with more than 12 years of schooling than for those with 12 years of education or less, and in some cases the differences were substantial. For example, among those with more education, 62% disagreed that only the informed should vote, compared to 35% of the low education group. Similarly, 56% of the high education group disagreed with the statement that a communist should be barred from office; only 34% of those with less education shared this view (Prothro and Grigg, 1960: 285). Stouffer (1955: 91) found that "the better educated tend to be more tolerant than the less educated," and Davis (1975: 507) also reported that "the better educated are more tolerant." In the 2010 GSS, the percentage who would permit a Muslim clergyman preaching hatred of the United States to give a public speech was 14% among those who had not completed high school, 30% among those with a high school diploma, 43% for those with some college education, and increased to 65% among those with a college degree or more education.

THE CONSEQUENCES OF POLITICAL KNOWLEDGE

Group distinctions in political knowledge are important not only because they demonstrate that different groups have advantages in terms of their awareness of the political process, but also because such differences are related to political participation. Individuals with high levels of political knowledge are more likely to vote. The percentage of the most knowledgeable that votes in presidential elections is close to 90%, compared to less than 20% among the least knowledgeable. The more knowledgeable are also more likely to engage in other forms of participation such as contributing money to a campaign, attending a campaign rally, or trying to influence another person's vote.

In addition to increasing participation, Delli Carpini and Keeter (1996) argue that greater political knowledge helps citizens construct stable, consistent opinions on a broad array of topics. This greater store of knowledge helps citizens to identify their true interests, connect these with their political attitudes, and vote for candidates who are most likely to represent their interests. In sum, "For citizens who are informed, the political system does operate as intended, while for those who are not the system is far less democratic" (17).

A GLASS-HALF-FULL PERSPECTIVE?

The perspective we have adopted in describing political knowledge has been based in traditional democratic theory. In this view, "An informed citizenry armed with the knowledge to appreciate their own interests and to make intelligent judgments is a key element of democracy" (Bennett, 1988: 477). From this standpoint, the level of knowledge demonstrated by the American public about the political process, public policies, and the actors involved is generally found to be lacking.

There is an alternative perspective that holds that low levels of political knowledge are not a threat to democratic politics. In this view, citizens compensate for their lack of wide-ranging political knowledge by using cognitive shortcuts. In taking their cues from political parties, interest groups, political leaders, or a trusted information source, individuals are able to adopt a position on an issue or candidate without the need for an extensive store of political knowledge. Moreover, since there is some segment of the population—the attentive public—that is paying more attention and has more information on a particular topic, the views of this group can help to create a condition in which "the aggregate views of individual adults on matters of public interest" are accurately represented through a process in which "the whole is greater than the sum of its parts" (Delli Carpini and Keeter, 1996: 23).

For people who are knowledgeable about politics, the system works as intended. From the point of view of classical democratic theory, one would expect—or hope for—higher levels of political knowledge among the citizenry. Although democracy may function best when its citizens are politically informed, "For the last 200 years the United States has survived as a stable democracy, despite continued evidence of an uninformed public. This is the paradox of modern democracy" (Delli Carpini and Keeter, 1996: 22).

POLLS, POLLING, AND THE INTERNET

Would you like to test your level of political knowledge? If so, take the civic knowledge quiz at: http://www.americancivicliteracy.org.

The Pew Center for the People and the Press frequently includes a set of knowledge items as part of its periodic polls on public policy issues. An example of the results of one such poll can be found at www.people-press.org/2011/03/31/well-known-clinton-and-gadhafi-little-known-who-controls-congress/. For the most recent politics quiz visit this website and search for "News IQ Quiz."

7

Political Orientations

In the previous chapters we have outlined some of the ways in which public opinion is formed, how it is measured, and how such data are used. With this chapter we turn to the distribution of public opinion on a variety of topics, and we begin with some broad orientations that are of particular import in American politics: political ideology, party identification, trust in government and political institutions, and the power of the federal government.

Political ideology is central to any discussion of public opinion. As Bennett (1995a: 259) has noted, ideology among the American public "has been a staple of public opinion research over the past 30 years." In Jacoby's terms, "Virtually all political stimuli (candidates, parties, issue stands, etc.) can be described in ideological terms" (1991: 202). Therefore, ideological thinking is likely to have multiple effects on public opinion. As Neuman (1986: 18) argues, "The terms *liberalism* and *conservatism* have served for the last century as the fundamental yardsticks for measuring political life . . . political life is incomprehensible without some sense of its central continuum."

Similarly, party identification has consistently been shown to be "an important source of policy orientations in the American electorate" (Jacoby, 1988: 643) and to be strongly associated with positions on policy issues (Abramowitz and Saunders, 1998). The authors of *The American Voter* (Campbell et al., 1960) attributed a central role to party identification in influencing attitudes toward candidates and issues, and this role has been demonstrated to be more or less enduring over time (Miller, 1991: 566). As individuals develop a personal attachment to one of the parties, the party's position on a specific issue supplies a useful guide for the person's attitude on that issue. Party identification and political ideology are rated as overriding orientations in American politics because "previous research has shown that they have the strongest, most pervasive effects across a variety of issues" (Jacoby, 1991: 183). These orientations help determine individuals' positions on policy issues.

Although ideology and party identification have generally been viewed as independent variables[1] and are significant for their role in shaping positions on other issues, orientations such as confidence in institutions and trust in government are important in that they provide the context within which political opinions are shaped. As stated by Miller (1974: 951), "A democratic society cannot survive for long without the support of a majority of its citizens." When confidence in political institutions and trust in government are low, the potential for change in the political and social system is enhanced. Diminished confidence in institutions raises questions about the legitimacy of government, making it more difficult for the government to remain effective without the leeway provided by diffuse support (Hetherington, 1998: 791). Without public support for institutions and the sense by the public that they are able to have some effect on the political process, "problems will begin, will become more acute, and if not resolved will provide the foundation for renewed discontent" (Hetherington, 1998: 804).

Finally, the issue of the power of the federal government is included as a "fundamental orientation" because divisions on this question run to the core of this country's history. Many of the key battles between the Federalists and the anti-Federalists during the ratification of the Constitution were over the amount of power that should rest with the central government. The question of the power of the federal government has been a source of conflict through such landmark events as the Supreme Court's ruling in the case of *Gibbons v. Ogden*, the Civil War and Reconstruction, the New Deal, World War II, and the Great Society programs developed in the 1960s. The passage of the Patient Protection and Affordable Care Act, frequently referred to as "Obamacare," in March 2010 provides a stark example of the continuing conflict between liberals and conservatives on the proper role for the government, with liberals favoring this act's expansion of the role of the central government in the country's health care system and conservatives expressing considerable concern. The division on this basic issue of the federal government's role has an impact on the public's views on more specific policy issues.

POLITICAL IDEOLOGY

In the study of the American mind, there has been considerable controversy over the extent to which the American public engages in ideological thinking about politics. A public that perceives political debate and policy issues in ideological terms would measure issues against a fairly strict philosophical standard, whether that is liberal, Marxist, conservative, or libertarian. If voters are highly ideological, they are unlikely to vote against increased environmental protection in the same election in which they elect a very liberal senator who supports this policy. The authors of *The American Voter* (Campbell et al., 1960: 250) argue that only a small segment of the public thinks about politics in ideological terms. As portrayed by Converse (1964), the typical American voter possessed low levels of information about public affairs, did not exhibit meaningful beliefs on policy issues, and voted more on the basis of social characteristics and party identification than because of any well-reasoned consideration of the parties and candidates.

In the more than 50 years since these findings were presented, there has been a great deal of debate over the extent to which Americans engage in ideological thinking. Some have argued that the low levels of such thinking found among the mass public are more a result of measurement error in the survey questions used in examining this topic than a lack of sophistication among the public (see, for example, Achen, 1975; Erikson, 1979). Others, such as Norman Nie and his colleagues (Nie with Anderson, 1974; Nie, Verba, and Petrocik, 1976), maintain that the rather unflattering portrait of the mass public provided by *The American Voter* authors was largely a product of the time in which the research was conducted, and that the increased salience of politics in the 1960s and 1970s led to more ideological thinking among the public. Critics of this research (for example, Bishop et al., 1978; Bishop, Tuchfarber, and Oldendick, 1978; Sullivan, Piereson, and Marcus, 1979) contend that this perceived increase in political sophistication was not a true change in the way the public thinks about politics, but rather an artifact resulting from the way in which these attitudes were measured. Another argument advanced in this debate is that while the public does not demonstrate the broad, overarching connectedness of opinion generally associated with ideological thinking, there are subgroups of individuals—issue publics—who are well informed and exhibit consistent opinions across a more narrow range of issues (Carmines and Stimson, 1980; Kirkpatrick and Jones, 1974; Natchez and Bupp, 1968).

Despite the differing perspectives and conclusions of these studies, one common element is their use of the **liberal-conservative continuum** as the primary dimension underlying political thinking in the United States. Viewing issues in terms of this "left–right" political spectrum allows individuals to make sense of a broad range of events, and this dimension has proven to be a useful organizing principle for studying the beliefs of the American public.

As with the term "public opinion," there are a wide variety of definitions and uses of the term "ideology." Common to many of these uses—and central to our definition of this term—is the notion of *a closely linked set of beliefs about the goal of politics and the most desirable political order* that enables individuals to interpret political events and provides a guide to decision making. Two relatively moderate ideological positions—liberalism and conservatism—have dominated the U.S. political system. Although there are numerous distinctions between liberals and conservatives, their basic split is over the role of government: Liberals believe that government should take strong, positive action to solve the nation's social and economic problems; in contrast, conservatives hold that individuals are primarily responsible for their own well-being. Conservatives are less supportive of government initiatives to redistribute income or to craft programs that will change the status of individuals (Mayer, 1992: 11–13).

To a large extent, the American public does not think about politics in an ideological manner. In their examination of this topic the authors of *The American Voter* found that less than 5% of the public could be classified as ideologues, with another 9% being "near ideologues." Forty-two percent thought about politics in terms of "group benefits," 24% conceptualized it in terms of the "nature of the times," and 22% exhibited "no issue content" in their political thinking (Campbell et al., 1960: 249). In their replication of this study, Lewis-Beck and his colleagues (2008: 279) found that there had not been a substantial change in the American electorate over a 40-year period. They classified 11% of the public as ideologues, 9% as near ideologues, 28% as group benefits, 28% as nature of the times, and 24% as having no issue content in their conceptualization of the political process.

Similarly, when the ideological character of the public's thinking is measured in terms of **constraint** or consistency among idea elements, "there is virtually nothing in the way of organization to be discovered" (Converse, 1964: 230). Although variations in the ideological character of the American mind have been reported (for example, Field and Anderson, 1969; Nie with Anderson, 1974; Nie, Verba, and Petrocik, 1976; Pierce and Hagner, 1980), the proportion of the citizens who exhibit consistent, well-integrated attitudes across a range of policy issues is rather small (Smith, 1989).

Despite these limitations, the liberal-conservative continuum has proven to be a valuable tool in the study of public opinion, and there is a general tendency for individuals to be fairly consistently "left," "right," or centrist in their political views (Zaller, 1992: 26). Although only a small segment of the public engages in the higher-order political thinking marked by an active use of ideological dimensions of judgment or high levels of constraint among idea elements, a large majority of American citizens classify themselves as liberal, moderate, or conservative. Though this ideological identification is distinct from ideological thinking, it has been shown to have an impact on issue attitudes (Jacoby, 1991: 202). One way to measure the ideological stance of the American public, which has been used in the

American National Election Studies since 1972, is to ask: "We hear a lot of talk these days about liberals and conservatives. Here is a seven-point scale (extremely liberal; liberal; slightly liberal; moderate, middle-of-the-road; slightly conservative; conservative; extremely conservative) on which the political views that people hold are arranged from extremely liberal to extremely conservative. Where would you place yourself on this scale, or haven't you thought much about this?"

Responses to this question are shown in Table 7.1 and Figure 7.1.[2] These data show that, despite some minor fluctuations, the ideological composition of the American electorate has remained fairly constant during this period, with liberals comprising about one-fourth of the public, one-third classifying themselves as moderates, and roughly 40% identifying themselves as conservatives. During this time, the percentage of conservatives has consistently been greater than that of liberals, and the difference has increased slightly over time. In 1972, for example, 26% identified themselves as liberals, while 37% held conservative views; in 2008 the corresponding percentages were 29% and 43%.[3] Although there has been a slight decline in the percentage who call themselves middle-of-the-road, there is little evidence of a dramatic increase in the polarization of the American public on this measure.

Fluctuations in the percentage expressing liberal or conservative views also varied with the fortunes of the two major parties. In 1980, when Ronald Reagan was elected to his first term, the percentage of conservatives jumped by 7% from that found in 1978. Similarly, the year 1994, when Republicans gained control of the House of Representatives for the first time in 50 years, saw the highest percentage of self-identified conservatives,

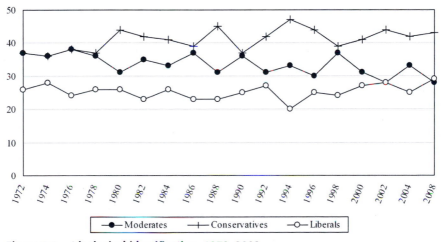

Figure 7.1. Ideological identification, 1972–2008.
Source: American National Election Studies.

Table 7.1. Ideological Identification, 1972–2008 (percent)

Ideology	Extremely Liberal	Liberal	Slightly Liberal	Middle-of-the-Road	Slightly Conservative	Conservative	Extremely Conservative
1972	2	10	14	37	21	14	2
1974	2	15	11	36	17	16	3
1976	2	10	12	38	19	16	3
1978	2	11	13	36	19	16	3
1980	2	9	14	31	21	30	3
1982	2	9	12	35	20	19	3
1984	2	10	13	33	20	19	3
1986	2	8	14	37	20	19	2
1988	2	8	13	31	22	17	2
1990	2	11	12	36	21	20	4
1992	3	12	13	31	21	15	3
1994	2	8	10	33	21	17	4
1996	2	9	14	30	19	24	4
1998	3	9	12	37	20	21	4
2000	2	12	12	32	20	16	3
2002	2	15	11	28	16	21	5
2004	3	12	10	33	13	26	5
2008	4	13	12	28	16	22	4

Source: American National Election Studies.

47%. The lowest percentage of respondents identifying themselves as liberals, 20%, also occurred in this year, although this percentage was somewhat higher in 1992 (27%) and 1996 (25%) when Bill Clinton won the contest for the presidency.[4]

Table 7.2 shows the breakdown of ideological identification among various subgroups for selected years. These data indicate that the relationship between ideological identification and certain background characteristics has changed somewhat over time. At the beginning of this period, the largest differences in ideology were between blacks and whites. In 1972, a much higher percentage of blacks than whites identified themselves as liberals, 54% to 23%. This 30% gap in the percentage of blacks and whites identifying themselves as liberals dropped to 16% by 1980 and was less than 10% in 1990 and 2008. A much smaller percentage of blacks than whites identified themselves as conservative. In 1972, 14% of blacks said their political views were conservative, compared to 39% of whites; in 2008, these percentages were 26% among blacks and 46% among whites, with a higher percentage of blacks classifying themselves as middle-of-the-road.[5]

Although citizens under 45 years old are generally more likely to consider themselves liberals, the strength of this relationship has varied over time. In 1972, people under 30 were much more likely to call themselves liberals, with an 18% difference (39% to 21%) in the percentage of this youngest age group who identified themselves as liberals compared to those age 65 or older. In the 1980s and 1990s, the differences across age groups narrowed somewhat, but since 2000 those under 30 have again been much more likely to consider themselves liberal. In 2008, 38% of those under 30 thought of themselves as liberal compared to 18% of those 65 and older, and older citizens were much more likely to think of themselves as conservative, with 56% of those age 65 or older putting themselves in this group.

Although the differences in ideological identification between men and women are not large, the distinctions between them have increased over time and parallel the differences in presidential choice described in Chapter 5. In 1972, there was no difference in the percentages of men and women who thought of themselves either as conservatives, moderates, or liberals. By 1990, a higher percentage of men than women described themselves as conservatives, and in 2008, about 10% more women than men described themselves as liberals.

The relationship between education and political ideology is not as distinct and also varies somewhat over time. There is a tendency for those with less education to think of themselves as middle-of-the-road and for a higher percentage of those with more education, particularly college graduates, to describe themselves as either liberal or conservative. In 2008, for example, 41% of those with a high school education considered themselves middle-of-the-road, compared to 19% of those with a college degree, while

Table 7.2. Political Ideology by Demographic Characteristics, 1972–2008 (percent)

	1972			1980			1990			2008		
	Lib.	Mid.	Con.	Lib.	Mid.	Con.	Lib.	Mid.	Con.	Lib.	Mid.	Con.
Age												
18–29	39	35	27	31	28	41	26	38	35	38	29	33
30–44	23	37	40	25	30	45	31	31	38	29	32	39
45–64	17	41	42	22	31	47	19	37	43	28	29	44
65 and older	21	37	42	22	35	43	19	44	37	18	26	56
Race												
Black	54	31	14	40	30	30	33	40	27	34	40	26
White	23	38	39	24	31	46	24	36	40	26	27	46
Gender												
Male	26	36	38	26	26	48	26	32	42	24	31	44
Female	26	38	36	25	35	40	24	41	35	32	27	41
Education												
Less than high school	19	46	35	21	35	44	18	52	30	20	41	39
High school graduate	20	43	37	20	38	42	17	45	38	22	36	42
Some college	33	32	35	31	25	44	26	31	42	29	30	41
College graduate	39	19	41	31	20	48	38	22	40	35	19	46
Income												
Lowest quartile	33	37	30	27	35	38	29	31	40	31	36	32
Second quartile	26	40	34	26	33	42	24	31	45	24	36	32
Third quartile	23	37	40	28	30	42	23	36	41	30	27	42
Highest quartile	25	37	38	21	24	55	19	29	52	22	17	61

Source: American National Election Studies.

a higher percentage of those with a college degree thought of themselves as liberal (35% to 20%) or conservative (46% to 39%). Across income levels, those with higher family incomes are more likely to be conservatives. This distinction across income groups was particularly large in 2008, with a much larger percentage of those in the highest income group classifying themselves as conservative.

Political activists tend to be more ideological in their beliefs. Polls of political convention delegates have consistently shown them to be more extreme in their ideology than average party members. In 2004, 22% of Democratic Convention delegates (and only 1% of Republican delegates) classified themselves as "very liberal," whereas 33% of Republican delegates (and no Democrats) considered themselves "very conservative" (Seelye and Connelly, 2004: 15-1), and in 2008 a higher percentage of Democratic delegates than Democratic voters classified themselves as liberals, while a larger percentage of Republican delegates than Republican voters thought of themselves as conservatives. In later chapters, in which differences in opinion on policy positions among ideological groups are reported, this variable will be shown to be a significant discriminator across a range of issues.

PARTY IDENTIFICATION

Party identification is one of the most important elements in the American political mind. Compared to other political attitudes, it is relatively stable over time (Converse and Markus, 1979: 38) and has been shown to be highly correlated with other indicators of political behavior, political attitudes, and the vote decision (Weisberg, 1980: 33; see also Bartels, 2000). As defined by Campbell et al. (1960: 121), party identification is a "standing decision," perhaps made in childhood, to support one party or the other. It is "generally a psychological identification, which can persist without legal recognition or evidence of formal membership and even without a consistent record of party support." The measure of party identification used in the National Election Studies (NES) first asks respondents, "Generally speaking, do you think of yourself as a Republican, a Democrat, an Independent, or what?" Those who classify themselves as Republicans or Democrats are then asked, "Would you call yourself a strong (Republican, Democrat) or a not very strong (Republican, Democrat)?" Those who classify themselves as Independents are asked, "Do you think of yourself as closer to the Republican or Democratic Party?" The result is a seven-point classification scheme ranging from Strong Republican to Strong Democrat. The distribution of these responses from the NES data is shown in Table 7.3 and summarized in Figure 7.2.[6]

Table 7.3. Party Identification, 1952–2008 (percent)

Party Identification	Strong Democrat	Weak Democrat	Leaning Democrat	Independent	Leaning Republican	Weak Republican	Strong Republican
1952	23	26	10	6	7	14	14
1956	21	24	7	9	9	15	15
1958	28	23	7	8	5	17	12
1960	21	26	6	10	7	14	16
1962	24	24	8	8	6	17	13
1964	27	25	9	8	6	14	11
1966	18	28	9	12	7	15	10
1968	20	26	10	11	9	15	10
1970	20	24	10	14	8	15	9
1972	15	26	11	13	11	13	11
1974	18	22	14	15	9	14	8
1976	15	25	12	15	10	14	9
1978	15	25	14	14	10	13	8
1980	18	24	13	13	10	14	9
1982	20	25	11	11	8	15	10
1984	17	20	11	11	13	15	13
1986	18	23	11	12	11	15	11
1988	18	18	12	11	13	14	14
1990	20	19	13	11	12	15	10
1992	17	18	14	12	13	15	11
1994	15	19	13	10	12	15	16
1996	18	20	14	8	11	16	13
1998	20	18	14	11	11	16	10
2000	19	15	16	12	13	12	12
2002	17	17	15	8	13	16	14
2004	16	16	17	10	12	12	17
2008	18	15	17	11	12	13	14

Source: American National Election Studies.

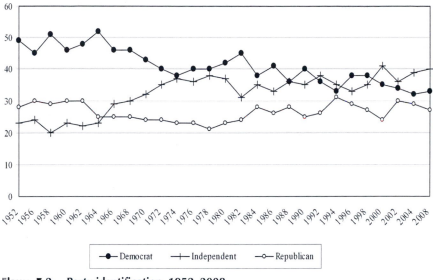

Figure 7.0. Party identification 1952–2008.
Source: American National Election Studies.

These data show a decline in identification with the Democratic Party during this period. Prior to 1966, approximately half of the public called themselves Democrats. Since then, this percentage has declined, and today about one-third of Americans identify with the Democratic Party. There has been less variation during this era in the percentage of the electorate identifying themselves as Republican. This percentage has hovered around 25%, ranging from a low of 21% in 1978 to a high of 31% in 1994. Corresponding to the decline in the proportion of self-identified Democrats has been the rise in the proportion of Independents. In 1952, fewer than one in four respondents considered themselves an "Independent"; over the past 10 years, this proportion has consistently been more than one-third and since 2000 has been at about 40%.[7]

Data from the Gallup Poll, going back to 1940, indicate that the increase in political Independents has been even more striking than that portrayed in the NES data, and that there has been more distinct movement by adherents of the two major parties. In 1940, 42% of the electorate considered themselves Democrats, 35% were Republicans, and 18% thought of themselves as Independents. After 1940, the percentage of Democrats increased, reaching its highest level—55%—in 1964, while the proportion of Republicans declined fairly steadily, reaching its low point in 1979. During this time, the percentage of Independents continuously increased, and more recent Gallup Poll data show the public to be fairly evenly divided among Democrats, Independents, and Republicans.[8]

Group differences in party identification are more consistent over time than those reported for ideology. As evidenced in Table 7.4, the largest and most consistent of these differences have been between blacks and whites. In 1952, 64% of blacks indicated they were Democrats, compared to 47% of whites. Over time, the percentage of blacks who are Democrats first increased, reaching 81% in 1964. Over the past two decades, approximately two-thirds of blacks have identified with the Democratic Party. Among whites, the percentage identifying themselves as Democrats has declined during this period, while the number of Independents has increased.[9]

Education and family income show similar and consistent relationships with party identification over time. Identification with the Democratic Party is greatest among those with less than a high school education and generally decreases as the level of education increases, while the highest percentage of Republicans is found among college graduates and declines as educational attainment decreases. Similarly, individuals with lower family incomes are more likely to be affiliated with the Democratic Party, with the percentage of Democrats decreasing across income levels, and the highest proportion of Republicans is consistently evident among the highest income group.

There is also a significant relationship between age and party identification, although the nature of this relationship changes somewhat during this time. Throughout this period, there is a tendency for a lower percentage of younger people to identify with the Republican Party (Converse, 1976: 10), although the strength of this tendency has decreased over time. In the 1950s a slightly higher percentage of younger people identified themselves as Democrats. As the percentage of Independents has risen over time, the increase has been particularly evident in the youngest age group. Since 1976, close to half of those ages 18 to 29 describe themselves as Independents, and this percentage is higher than that in any other age group. Comparing the 1952 and 2008 data demonstrates the relationship between age and the rise of Independents. While the percentage of Independents increases in all age groups over time, it moves from 20% to 30% among those 65 and older but increases from 29% to 53% for those under 30. In current American politics, older people are more likely to identify themselves as either Democrats or Republicans, while younger people tend to have weaker partisan ties and are more likely to view themselves as Independents.

Some evidence of the gender gap found for presidential vote choice is also apparent in the partisan views of men and women. Though there was little difference in partisanship between men and women until about 1980, over the past 30 years a slightly higher percentage of women than men call themselves Democrats, while men are more likely to be Independents. In 2008, 38% of women were Democrats, compared to 29% of men, while a higher percentage of men than women (44% to 36%) considered themselves to be Independents.

Table 7.4. Party Identification by Demographic Characteristics, Selected Years, 1952–2008 (percent)

	1952			1964			1976			1988			2000			2008		
	Dem.	Ind.	Rep.	Dem.	Ind.	Rep.	Dem.	Ind.	Rep.	Dem.	Ind.	Rep.	Dem.	Ind.	Rep.	Dem.	Ind.	Rep.
Age																		
18–29	51	29	20	50	31	19	35	48	16	28	45	28	28	56	16	30	53	17
30–44	53	23	24	51	27	21	35	42	22	34	40	26	31	42	28	33	41	26
45–64	44	22	34	57	18	24	46	28	26	40	31	29	40	34	26	36	36	28
65 and Older	45	20	35	46	14	40	45	24	31	43	25	32	43	32	26	37	30	34
Race																		
Black	64	21	16	81	13	6	71	24	4	64	30	6	69	27	4	70	27	3
White	47	23	29	50	24	27	36	38	26	31	38	32	29	42	29	27	41	32
Gender																		
Male	48	26	26	51	25	24	37	42	20	30	42	29	30	42	28	29	44	27
Female	49	21	30	54	21	26	42	32	26	40	32	28	38	40	22	38	36	26
Education																		
Less than high school	54	22	24	63	20	18	52	28	20	46	34	21	44	39	17	44	40	16
High school graduate	45	23	32	48	24	28	40	39	21	36	40	24	35	46	19	34	43	23
Some college	41	23	36	40	30	30	33	42	25	32	32	35	34	40	26	30	44	26
College graduate	24	36	40	38	25	37	30	38	32	28	37	35	31	36	34	34	32	35
Income																		
Lowest quartile	56	17	27	62	18	20	52	28	20	42	35	23	40	40	20	40	41	19
Second quartile	52	23	25	56	21	23	45	35	21	40	32	28	38	42	20	36	42	22
Third quartile	48	27	25	51	25	24	35	46	19	33	42	26	30	50	21	29	42	29
Highest quartile	10	25	35	40	27	34	28	37	34	27	36	37	32	37	31	25	28	49
Ideology																		
Liberals	—	—	—	—	—	—	48	45	7	52	35	13	54	38	7	62	33	5
Moderates	—	—	—	—	—	—	41	42	17	37	42	21	32	50	18	32	53	29
Conservatives	—	—	—	—	—	—	26	34	41	21	31	48	18	34	48	12	29	59

Source: American National Election Studies.

These data also demonstrate the consistent relationship between ideology and partisanship. In 1976, almost half of those who considered themselves liberals also identified with the Democratic Party and less than 10% identified themselves as Republicans, while 41% of conservatives said they were Republicans and 26% were Democrats. This relationship had strengthened somewhat by 2008, with 62% of self-identified liberals also identifying with the Democratic Party and 59% of conservatives saying they were Republicans. In this year, only 5% of liberals identified with the Republican Party, while only 12% of conservatives identified with the Democrats. Following the 2004 election, many commentators suggested that Americans were becoming increasingly polarized on lines of ideology and party, and it has been argued that this polarization increased through the course of the 2008 election (Pildes, 2010). The data suggest that although there is some increase in consistency between party and ideological position, a plurality of Americans still consider themselves moderates and, though they may differ on issue positions, there is little evidence of increasing polarization (Fiorina, Abrams, and Pope, 2004).

CONFIDENCE IN INSTITUTIONS

In addition to political ideology and party identification, the public's general feelings toward government, its institutions, and the political process are significant components of the American mind. As Arthur Miller (1974: 951) has noted, "A democratic political system cannot survive for long without the support of a majority of its citizens. When such support wanes, underlying discontent is the necessary result, and the potential for revolutionary alteration of the political and social system is enhanced." If a country experiences a prolonged loss of confidence in its institutions, it can lead to a significant loss of legitimacy that reduces the country's chances of withstanding a crisis of effectiveness (Lipset and Schneider, 1983). Orientations such as confidence in institutions, trust in government, and views on the power of the federal government are each important elements in the public's general estimation of government and the political process.

The confidence Americans place in their institutions provides a backdrop against which positions on more specific policy issues can be viewed. The data reported in Table 7.5 show the percentage of the public who reported having "a great deal of confidence" in the people running various institutions. In their analysis of similar data, Lipset and Schneider (1983: 42) noted that in 1966 a majority of the public had a great deal of confidence in the people running "medicine," "the military," "education," "major companies," and "the U.S. Supreme Court," and more than 40% had confidence in "the Congress," "organized religion," and the "executive branch

Table 7.5. Confidence in Institutions, 1966–2010 (percentage saying "great deal of confidence")

	Mil.	Bus.	Rel.	Edu.	Exec.	Fin.	S.C	Lab.	Con.	Med.	Pres.	Sci.	TV
1966	62	55	41	61	41	—	50	22	42	72	29	—	—
1971	27	27	27	37	23	—	25	14	19	61	18	—	—
1973	33	31	36	37	29	—	34	16	24	54	23	41	18
1974	40	32	45	50	14	32	34	19	18	62	26	50	23
1975	36	20	26	32	13	32	35	10	14	52	24	42	18
1976	42	22	32	38	13	40	36	12	14	55	29	48	18
1977	37	28	41	14	28	43	37	15	20	54	25	45	18
1978	30	22	32	28	13	32	38	12	13	46	20	39	15
1980	29	28	36	30	12	33	25	16	9	54	23	45	15
1982	30	24	33	34	20	27	32	14	13	46	19	43	14
1983	31	25	30	29	14	24	28	9	10	53	18	47	13
1984	38	32	32	28	19	31	35	9	13	51	18	47	13
1986	32	26	26	28	22	21	41	9	17	47	19	42	15
1987	37	32	30	35	19	28	39	11	17	53	18	48	11
1988	36	26	21	30	17	28	37	11	16	53	20	42	14
1989	34	26	22	30	22	19	36	10	18	48	17	45	14
1990	34	26	24	27	25	17	36	11	16	46	15	41	14
1991	62	21	26	30	27	12	39	12	18	48	16	43	15
1993	42	22	23	23	12	15	31	8	7	41	11	41	21
1994	38	27	26	26	12	18	32	11	8	43	10	41	10
1996	38	24	26	23	10	25	30	12	8	45	11	43	10
1998	37	28	28	27	14	26	33	12	11	45	9	43	10
2000	41	30	29	28	14	30	34	14	13	45	10	45	10
2002	57	18	19	26	28	23	37	12	14	37	10	40	10
2004	58	19	24	29	22	30	32	14	15	38	9	42	10
2006	48	18	25	28	16	30	34	12	12	40	10	43	9
2008	52	16	20	30	11	19	32	13	10	39	9	40	9
2010	54	13	20	28	17	11	31	12	10	42	11	42	13

Key: Mil.: the military; Edu.: education; S.C.: Supreme Court; Med.: medicine TV: television; Bus.: major companies; Exec.: executive branch; Lab.: organized labor; Pres.: press; Rel.: organized religion; Fin.: financial institutions; Con.: Congress; Sci.: scientific community.

Sources: 1966, 1971: Louis Harris and Associates; 1966–2010: NORC General Social Survey.

of the federal government." Between 1966 and 1971, however, "confidence had declined in the leadership of every institution named in the surveys." The generality of these trends, they conclude, indicates that this "was not a period of declining confidence in just business or government or labor, but a loss of faith in institutional leadership generally: a trend of public alienation, in varying degrees from the leaders of all major institutions" (Lipset and Schneider, 1983: 43).

With the exception of "organized religion" in 1974, the level of confidence in the leaders of any of these institutions never reaches the level of the 1966 survey. Although there have been brief periods of modestly increasing or decreasing confidence in the leaders of these various institutions since 1971, they do not compare to the stark and consistent drop found between 1966 and 1971 (Lipset and Schneider, 1987).

The trends for the governmental institutions—Congress, the executive branch, the Supreme Court, and the military—are displayed in Figure 7.3 and summarized in Table 7.6. As shown in Table 7.5, all four of these institutions experienced a substantial drop in confidence between 1966 and 1971. Since that time, overall evaluations of the Supreme Court and the executive branch have remained fairly constant, while those for Congress have declined slightly. Although the evaluations of the military have declined since 1966, there has been considerable fluctuation in these ratings over time. The public's confidence in the military showed a decline similar to that for other institutions between 1966 and 1990, but confidence in the military showed a large increase in 1991, as a response to the military

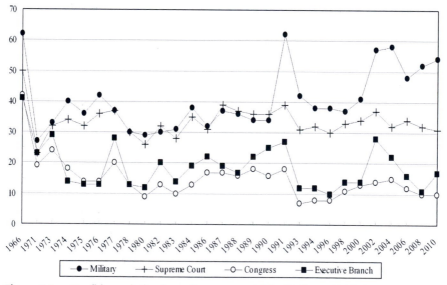

Figure 7.3.   Confidence in leaders of governmental institutions, 1966–2010.
Source: General Social Surveys.

Table 7.6. Trends in Confidence in Leaders of Governmental Institutions (percent)

	Congress	Executive Branch	Supreme Court	Military
1966	42	41	50	62
1970s	21	19	32	35
1980s	14	18	33	32
1990s	11	17	34	42
2000s	13	18	34	52

Source: Summarized from Table 7.5. American National Election Studies.

success achieved in Operation Desert Storm, and such confidence is also relatively high in 2002 and 2004, a reaction to the military's involvement in the war on terror following the events on September 11, 2001. The relative stability in confidence in the executive branch since the 1970s shown in these summary data masks some fluctuation that occurred in 2002, as public support for the president increased in the wake of 9/11. The percentage expressing a great deal of confidence in the executive branch doubled from 14% in 2000 to 28% in 2002, but has declined since that time.

As a whole, these data indicate that Americans have become increasingly distrustful of all major institutions in society. Although in recent years the public has expressed increased confidence in the military, this is an exception to the overall decline in trust in institutions expressed by the American public. Almost 20 years ago, Patterson and Magelby (1992: 539) noted that such data raise concerns about the health and vigor of the institutions of democratic governance, and the data from recent years are even more disconcerting.

TRUST IN GOVERNMENT

Closely related to confidence in institutions is the concept of **trust in government**. As described by Arthur Miller (1974: 952), the dimension of trust in government "runs from high trust to high distrust or **political cynicism**. Cynicism thus refers to the degree of negative affect toward the government and is a statement of the belief that the government is not functioning and producing outputs in accord with individual expectations." As such, we would expect trust in government to be related to confidence in institutions.

In the NES, there are five questions that are regularly used to measure trust. Trends for these items are shown in Figure 7.4.[10] In examining the data from the early part of this period, Miller (1974: 952) concluded that "the data reveal a strong trend of increasing political cynicism for the general population between 1964 and 1970," a trend that he attributed to dissatisfaction with the policy alternatives that the major parties offered as solutions to contemporary problems. Similarly, Lipset and Schneider

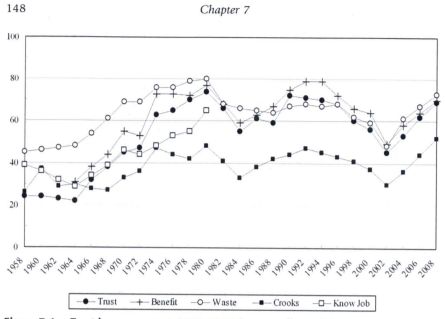

| —●— Trust | —+— Benefit | —O— Waste | —■— Crooks | —□— Know Job |

Figure 7.4.   Trust in government, 1958–2008 (percent distrustful).
Source: American National Election Studies.

(1983: 16) noted "a virtual explosion in antigovernment feeling" between 1964 and 1970, with mistrust increasing an average of 8% between 1964 and 1968 and another 9% from 1968 to 1970.

The dramatic impact of Watergate is evident in the 1974 data. The percentage of distrustful responses on each of these items rose between 1972 and 1974, with the increase ranging from 4% on the question of whether government employees "know their jobs" to 20% on the question of whether the government is "run for the benefit of a few big interests." This relatively high level of cynicism toward government continued through 1980, and it was data of this type that led President Jimmy Carter's pollster Patrick Caddell (1979: 2) to declare a "crisis of confidence" that resulted in Carter's "malaise" speech of 1979 (see Chapter 3).[11]

These indicators of trust in government rebounded slightly during the presidency of Ronald Reagan. The percentage who believed that the government can be trusted only some of the time, for example, decreased from 74% in 1980 to 59% in 1988. Similarly, the percentage who felt that the government wastes a lot of tax money declined from 80% in 1980 to 64% in 1988, and the percentage who thought the government is run for the benefit of a few big interests dropped from 77% to 67% during this period, reflecting an increase in trust resulting from an improving economy and the absence of a crisis atmosphere during much of this time (Lipset and Schneider, 1987).

The rebound in trust during the Reagan years, however, did not approach nearly the magnitude of the decline of the preceding two decades. In the years immediately after Reagan left office, the percentage of "distrustful" responses on three of the four items asked during this period—trust in government, whether government is run for the benefit of all people, and the extent to which government wastes tax money—increased slightly before declining back to Reagan-era levels in 1998 and 2000, while the percentage of such responses for the item on the number of people running the government who are crooks was relatively stable during this time.

The data from 2002 show the impact that dramatic events, such as those that occurred on 9/11, can have on indicators of the public's trust in government. The percentage of "distrustful" responses on each of these four items declined substantially between 2000 and 2002. For example, on the item of "how much of the time you can trust the government to do what is right," the percentage of "only some of the time" responses dropped from 56% in 2000 to 45% in 2002. Results from the Gallup Poll show similar changes. In a July 2000 survey, Gallup found that 58% gave a "distrustful" response to the "trust in government" item. In a poll conducted shortly after 9/11, this percentage had declined to 39%. As Newport (2001) reported, "One effect of the terrorist attacks of September 11 has been an extraordinary increase in the faith and confidence that Americans have in their federal government."

The 2004 and 2008 National Election Study data indicate that the increase in trust evident in the wake of 9/11 has not been sustained, and that the percentage of distrustful responses has increased significantly in the past several years. This change is also reflected in the Gallup Poll. By June 2002, the percentage of "distrustful" responses to the "trust in government" item had risen back to 54%, and by June 2005 this figure had reached 70%. As Moore (2003) concludes, the unusually high levels of trust and confidence found in the aftermath of the 9/11 terrorist attacks has faded, and the public's trust in government "has now fallen below the levels measured just before 9/11." The rate of decline in trust in government increased after 2005, and by January 2010 the percentage of "distrustful" responses had reached 81% (Gallup Report, 2011b).

Despite some short-term fluctuations over these 50 years, the overall conclusion must be that for more than four decades, the American mind has exhibited a distrustful disposition toward government. It appears that the significant events of this period—Vietnam, Watergate, the energy crisis, recession, hyperinflation, campaign fundraising scandals, the housing and financial institution crisis—have produced increasingly cynical public attitudes.

As might be expected given the magnitude of these changes, this decline in trust has been evident across all subgroups. To demonstrate these changes, Table 7.7 presents data from the early part of this period, when trust was relatively high, to compare with those from 2000 in illustrating the variation that has taken place among subgroups. The data from 2002

Table 7.7. "Trust Government to Do What Is Right": by Demographic
Characteristics, 1958, 1964, 2000, 2002, and 2008 (percentage saying
"Only Some of the Time")

	1958	*1964*	*2000*	*2002*	*2008*
Total Sample	24%	22	56	45	70
Age					
18–29	21	17	60	48	66
30–44	21	20	58	48	73
45–64	27	26	56	41	68
65 and Older	32	27	46	40	70
Race					
Black	33	25	67	60	72
White	24	22	54	42	70
Sex					
Male	23	20	56	43	71
Female	25	24	55	46	86
Education					
Less than High School	31	27	55	38	69
High School Graduate	20	18	58	45	71
Some College	16	19	57	46	68
College Graduate	16	20	52	47	70
Income					
Lowest Quartile	36	27	56	48	71
Second Quartile	22	25	54	45	73
Third Quartile	18	19	58	43	68
Highest Quartile	19	18	57	42	72
Party Identification					
Democrats	27	20	52	48	66
Independents	24	24	58	48	72
Republicans	18	27	56	38	69
Ideology					
Liberals	--	--	52	48	65
Moderates	--	--	47	38	66
Conservatives	--	--	58	42	73

The question asked was, How much of the time do you think you can trust the government to
  do what is right—Just about always, most of the time, or only some of the time.

Source: American National Election Studies.

and 2008 have been included to show the short-term impact that 9/11 had
across subgroups and the consequent large increase in distrust among all
groups since that time. Between 1958 and 2000, the change in the percentage who felt that the government could be trusted "only some of the time"
was 32% among all respondents and ranged from 14% among those age 65

or older to 41% among those with some college education. In 1958, it was those with lower family incomes, less education, Democrats, blacks, and older people who were least trustful of government. In 2000, blacks were still more distrustful of government than whites, but it was the youngest age group rather than the oldest that was least trustful, and there were few differences in level of trust in government among other groups.

The increase in trust in 2002 was evident in all subgroups, with the largest decline in distrustful responses found among Republicans (from 56% to 38%) and the smallest drop—from 52% to 48%—among Democrats and among liberals. Between 2002 and 2008, the percentage of distrustful responses increased in all groups, with the largest increases found among those with less than a high school education, Republicans, and conservatives. Given these fluctuations, by 2008 a high percentage of *all* groups was distrustful of government, and there are virtually no differences in trust across respondent characteristics. In 2008, the percentage of distrustful responses across all groups ranges only from 65% among liberals to 73% among those ages 30 to 44, those in the second income quartile, and conservatives. The events of 9/11 provided a brief respite from the decline in trust in government that Americans had been experiencing. This level of distrust has increased substantially among all groups since 2004 to the point where two-thirds or more of all groups express a lack of trust in government. These data reinforce the view that the American mind has experienced a declining faith in governmental institutions.

POWER OF THE FEDERAL GOVERNMENT

As noted in the description of ideology, beliefs about the power of the federal government are a major feature distinguishing liberals and conservatives. Fearing the rise of an all-powerful leviathan on the Potomac, conservatives have traditionally opposed almost any proposal that would enlarge the role of the central government in U.S. society. Liberals, on the other hand, are inclined to see government as a vehicle for promoting what they feel to be social justice; hence, they advocate programs that expand Washington's power (Bennett and Oldendick, 1977).

As described by Bennett and Bennett (1990), the public's view on the power of the federal government can be traced to this country's origins and has changed in response to social and economic conditions. The battle over the ratification of the Constitution was, in large measure, one over the role the central government should play, with the Federalists desiring more federal power and the anti-Federalists wary of an increasing role of the central authority. Some of the earliest public opinion polls on this issue showed Americans to be slightly in favor of the growth in the power of the central government that occurred during the New Deal and suggested that this country's involvement in World War II solidified this judgment (Bennett and Bennett, 1990: 21–24). Although the issue of Washington's power was not a significant factor in the 1950s and early 1960s, it increased in salience in 1964 with the candidacy of Barry Goldwater, who had declared the federal government to be "out of touch with the people, and out of their control" (Goldwater, 1960: 20).

It was in 1964 that the NES began asking the following question to assess public sentiment on the power of the federal government:

> Some people are afraid the government in Washington is getting too powerful for the good of the country and the individual person. Others feel the government has not gotten too strong for the good of the country. Have you been interested enough in this to favor one side over the other? [IF YES]: What is your feeling, do you think the government is getting too strong or the government has not gotten too strong?

Responses to this question are displayed in Table 7.8.

In 1964, the public was about evenly divided between those who thought the government had gotten too powerful and those who thought it had not.[12] The balance moved slightly to the side of those who thought the government was getting too powerful in 1966 and 1968, returned to equilibrium in 1970, and moved back to a 60–40 split in favor of those who thought the government was becoming too strong in 1972. Between 1972 and 1976 there was a significant increase in the perception that the government had gotten too powerful, and this increase continued through 1980. Citing this and other survey results, Bennett and Bennett (1990: 31) conclude that "the early 1980s may have marked the height of a quarter-century-long shift away from support of a powerful central government."

President Reagan's first term in office appeared to calm some of the public's fears about increasing federal power. Between 1980 and 1984, the percentage who felt the government had gotten too powerful declined from 76% to 59%, and this increased only slightly (to 63%) in 1988. By 1992, however, the proportion of those with an opinion on this item who believed that the government had gotten too strong returned to 7 of 10, and it remained at this level in 2000. Although the pattern of responses to this item is not as stark as some of the others examined in this chapter, the overall picture is one in which a large and increasing percentage of Americans believe that the federal government is getting too powerful. Such a finding is consistent with beliefs about the government that are less trusting and a system in which Americans feel a diminished sense of their ability to influence the political process.[13]

Opinions about the power of the federal government among subgroups and how these opinions changed between 1964 and 2000 provide some

Table 7.8. Power of the Federal Government, 1964–2000 (percent)

	1964	1966	1968	1970	1972	1976	1978	1980	1984	1988	1992	2000
Getting too powerful	46	59	57	48	61	72	76	76	59	63	71	69
Not gotten too strong	54	41	43	52	39	28	24	24	41	37	29	31

Source: American National Election Studies.

insight into the dynamics of the American mind on this issue. In 1964 there was a division of opinion along race, class, and party lines and, to a lesser extent, among age groups. An overwhelming majority of blacks felt that the government had not gotten too powerful, and those with more education or with higher family incomes were more likely to say the government had gotten too strong. More than twice as many Republicans as Democrats were wary of the federal government's power, and those under 30 years of age were least concerned that the government was getting too strong. As noted by Bennett and Oldendick (1977: 9), by 1972 "differences that had been substantial, and in some cases huge, had shrunk into insignificance." Differences across education levels and income groups as well as among age groups were no longer significant, and the gap between black and white attitudes had shrunk from 43% in 1964 to 13% by 1972, reflecting a large increase in the percentage of blacks who were skeptical of the government's power. Similarly, party identification, which had been a solid predictor of views on the power of the federal government in 1964, had become a less reliable divider of opinion by 1972. In 2000, a majority of all groups examined felt the government was getting too powerful. There is some evidence that in 1964 the public's views on this question reflected policy positions and the fundamental liberal-conservative division over the proper role of the government. Over time, however, this question of federal power has come to reflect the public's trust in government, and the changes in opinion on this item provide another indicator of the increasing distrust of government that has developed in the American mind (Bennett and Oldendick, 1977: 23).

Although the NES has not asked the question on the power of the federal government since 2000, other organizations such as Gallup and the Pew Research Center have continued to track this issue using similar indicators. The passage of a federal economic stimulus plan in 2009 and the Patient Protection and Affordable Care Act of 2010 seemed to have sparked a public reaction against "big government" that has fueled the rise of the Tea Party movement and contributed to the Republicans gaining control of the U.S. House of Representatives in the 2010 midterm elections (Karpowitz et al., 2011).

Although the polls have shown some increase in concern about government becoming too big, they do not reflect a massive upswing in the sentiment that the government has gotten too powerful. For example, on the Gallup Poll question that asks, "Some people think the government is trying to do too many things that should be left to individuals and businesses. Others think that the government should do more to solve our country's problems. Which comes closer to your view?," the percentage who said the government was doing too much increased from 53% the last time the question was asked (September 2008) before President Obama's election

to 58% in September 2010. This percentage is similar to those reported between 1995 and 1998 when between 58% and 60% of Americans felt that
the government was trying to do too many things. Similarly, in response to
the question, "Do you the federal government today has too much power,
has about the right amount of power, or has too little power?," the percentage choosing the "too much" option increased from 52% in September
2008 to 59% in March 2011 (Gallup Report, 2011a).

Findings from the Pew Research Center also reflect a slight shift in the
public's views of federal government power. In a series of surveys conducted in 2010, Pew researchers found that about half of the respondents
consistently indicated that they would rather have a smaller government
with fewer services, while about 40% have consistently preferred a bigger
government providing more services. Shortly before President Obama's
election, the public was evenly divided on this issue, with 42% favoring
smaller government and 43% supporting bigger government. The percentage who believes that federal government programs should be cut back as
opposed to being maintained has shown a similar increase (Pew Research
Center, 2010a)

Despite the public's concern over the size of the federal government,
its desire for cuts in federal government spending on specific programs
remains limited. In a Pew Research poll conducted in February 2011, more
people wanted to see spending increased than decreased on 15 of 18 issues
tested, ranging from education to agriculture. As noted in the report on
this study, "the only area where a plurality favors decreased spending is on
economic assistance to needy people around the world; even here, just under half (45%) support spending cuts, while 21% say spending should be
increased and 29% want to keep spending the same" (Pew Research Center,
2011a). Although a majority of Americans believes that the federal government has gotten too powerful, when the focus is on specific programs
such as Social Security, education, or combating terrorism rather than "the
government" in general, there remains a sense among the public that the
federal government has an important role to play.

SUMMARY

This chapter has examined the more significant general orientations toward
government that comprise the American mind. Although there is some debate over the extent to which Americans engage in ideological thinking, the
ideological composition of the American electorate—at least as measured
by the number of people identifying themselves as "liberals," "moderates,"
or "conservatives"—has remained fairly constant over the past 40 years.
About one-fourth of the public view themselves as liberals, approximately

4 in 10 consider themselves conservatives, and a third classify themselves as middle-of-the-road.

Party identification is one of the most important and more stable attitudes in American politics. There has, however, been significant change in the partisan composition of the American electorate over the period during which polls have measured this phenomenon. In 1940, 42% of the electorate considered themselves Democrats, 35% were Republicans, and 18% thought of themselves as Independents. The percentage of Democrats increased between 1940 and 1964, while the proportion of Republicans declined fairly steadily until about 1980. This period also saw the rise of political independents, and each of these three groups currently comprises about one-third of the national electorate.

Since the late 1960s, there has been a major decline in trust in government and in the institutions of society. Recent surveys have indicated that only slightly more than 10% of the public have a great deal of confidence in Congress, and while confidence in other institutions such as the military or the executive branch have experienced some short-term increases in public confidence in response to events, Americans' confidence in their institutions overall has declined over time. Similarly, the extent to which the public exhibits trust in government has dipped sharply during this period, and this stark decline has been evident across all subgroups of the population. Although the public's trust in government rose in response to the events of 9/11, the increases that were evident immediately following this event have not been sustained over time.

Americans have also become increasingly concerned about the power of the federal government. Although a majority of those with an opinion on this issue in 1964 believed that the government had not gotten too strong, in 2000, 69% felt that the government in Washington had become too powerful. This increase in the sense that the government was becoming too strong was also evident across all subgroups of the population. Despite this, the public voices a good deal of support for a continued and, in some cases, even increased role for the federal government in specific areas, such as education.

The way in which the American mind views government and its institutions is vastly different from that of a generation ago. Americans today exhibit less psychological attachment to either of the two major parties, are less trustful of government and its institutions, fear the federal government's power, and are less certain they can have an impact on the political process. The data presented in this chapter may not demonstrate unequivocally that a "crisis in confidence" exists in the United States, but the patterns presented here certainly should raise concerns about the stability and long-term health of the political system.

POLLS, POLLING, AND THE INTERNET

As you have noted from the data presented in this chapter, the foremost source of information about political partisanship and ideology are the National Election Studies, conducted by the Institute for Political and Social Research at the University of Michigan. To find information about the questions asked in each of the election year surveys, go to their website at: www.electionstudies.org.

For similar information from the General Social Survey, go to: www3 .norc.org/GSS+Website/.

8

Public Opinion on
Social-Welfare Issues

In each era of U.S. history, certain issues have dominated political debate and, by so doing, have structured political campaigns and party platforms. The debate began with the struggle over ratification of the Constitution between the Federalists and anti-Federalists and evolved to the battle between eastern commercial interests and western and southern agricultural interests, to the North–South battle over slavery, and to the sectional politics that characterized the era between the Civil War and 1920. American political culture has limited the success of left-wing political movements, and the fundamental belief in the separation of church and state has constrained the role of religion as a major dividing force in this country. In the era of modern polling, the major division in American politics has been socioeconomic (McSweeney and Zvesper, 1991).

Since 1932, the issues that have dominated discussion at the national level have involved the government's role in the economic sphere and in providing for the welfare of its citizens. Issues such as Social Security, welfare, government guarantee of jobs, civil rights, and protection of the environment reflect various components of this dimension.

Polls conducted during the early years of the New Deal showed that Americans were divided over President Roosevelt's policies during the 1930s and 1940s, favoring programs such as Social Security and wages-and-hours legislation but opposing the National Recovery Administration and the Agricultural Adjustment Administration (Bennett and Bennett, 1990: 21). Since these early polls, surveys of the public's views on questions concerning the welfare state have reflected the central role that such issues play in American politics. In this chapter we examine a number of socioeconomic issues, including recent trends in opinion and differences in views across subgroups.[1]

SOCIAL-WELFARE ISSUES

In general terms, the public is divided on the question of the government's role in the area of social welfare. An item first included in the General Social Survey (GSS) in 1975 asked respondents whether "the government in Washington is trying to do too many things that should be left to individuals and private businesses" or whether "the government should do even more to solve our country's problems." The data in Table 8.1 show the division in opinion on this issue. In analyzing these data, responses 1 and 2 are treated as representing the "government should do more" position, while points 4 and 5 represent the view that "government does too much." In 1975, about one-third of respondents took a middle position, and the percentage who felt the government should do more was about 10% larger than that for the view that "the government does too much." Beginning in 1983 and

Table 8.1. Government Provide More or Fewer Services, 1975–2010 (percent)[a]

Response Category	1. Government Should Do More	2.	3. Agree with Both	4.	5. Government Does Too Much
1975	27	12	31	12	18
1983	13	12	39	19	17
1984	15	13	39	18	15
1986	13	13	44	16	14
1987	19	15	38	14	13
1988	14	15	42	15	14
1989	14	15	41	16	14
1990	14	16	43	16	11
1991	15	16	42	16	12
1993	14	15	40	16	15
1994	12	14	37	19	17
1996	13	13	40	18	17
1998	11	13	42	19	16
2000	12	13	40	18	18
2002	15	10	49	14	12
2004	16	10	45	14	15
2006	17	10	44	16	13
2008	17	14	41	13	15
2010	16	12	37	15	20

[a]The wording of the question was: "Some people think that the government in Washington is trying to do too many things that should be left in individuals and private businesses. Others disagree and think that the government should do even more to solve our country's problems. Still others have opinions somewhere in between. Where would you place yourself on this scale, or haven't you made up your mind on this?"

Source: General Social Surveys.

continuing throughout this period, the percentage who took the middle position on this issue has been about 40%. Also, between 1975 and 1983, the balance between "government should do more" and "government does too much" responses switched, with the percentage of "government does too much" being about 10% greater than that for the "government should do more" position. During the 1984 to 1993 period, the gap between these two alternatives narrowed, and the public was fairly evenly divided on the question of whether the federal government should do more or less. The largest percentage difference in these positions during this decade was in 1987, when 34% felt that the government should do more compared with 27% who thought it was already doing too much. Between 1994 and 2000, the percentage of the public who believed that the government does too much outnumbered the percentage who felt the government should do more. In the four surveys conducted during this period, approximately 35% expressed the view that the government does too much, while one-fourth of the public believed the government should do more. Between 2000 and 2008, the percentages who believe that the government does too much or that it should do more are about equal, with a slight increase in the percentage of "the government does too much" appearing in 2010. The American mind, then, is divided on the issue of whether the government should provide more or fewer services. In the following sections we shall see that this division can vary substantially by the specific type of service considered as well as by subgroups of the population.

SOCIAL SECURITY

One topic that has been of great interest to the American public in the area of social welfare is Social Security, and this issue has received even more attention in recent years as the federal budget deficit has increased. In his February 2005 State of the Union address, President George W. Bush promoted his proposals to change the current Social Security system. The president noted that "one of America's most important institutions— a symbol of the trust between generations—is also in need of wise and effective reform. . . . The system, however, on its current path, is headed toward bankruptcy. And so we must join together to strengthen and save Social Security." The president proposed a number of reforms to the system, the centerpiece of which was generally considered to be establishing private accounts that would allow workers to place some of their payroll contributions in private investments (Kohut and Doherty, 2005). President Barack Obama also recognized the issues facing the Social Security system, and in his January 2011 State of the Union address, he noted that, "To put us on solid ground, we should also find a bipartisan solution to strengthen Social Security for future generations. We must do it without putting at risk current retirees, the most vulnerable, or people with disabilities; without slashing benefits for future generations; and without subjecting Americans' guaranteed retirement income to the whims of the stock market." As a candidate, President Obama opposed privatization, raising the retirement age, or cutting benefits.

This program has changed considerably since the passage of the Social Security Act of 1935, expanding from a single compulsory program, Old-Age and Survivors Insurance, to include Disability Insurance and Hospital Insurance (Part A Medicare), together with increases in benefits for its recipients (Penner, 1982: 17; Weaver and Max, 1995: 16). From its inception, Social Security has been popular. As Page and Shapiro (1992: 118) report, in "1935, 89% of the public told Gallup interviewers that they favored 'old age pensions for needy persons'; 90%–94% favored such pensions according to Gallup questions asked in 1938, 1939, and 1941." Even though a number of questions were asked about this issue in the 1930s and 1940s, the early consensus that emerged made it of less interest to poll-takers, and there is a relative lack of appropriate cross-time data for tracking the American mind on this issue (Shapiro and Smith, 1985: 561).

The data in Figure 8.1 provide a description of the public's view over time on the question of whether the government is spending too much, too little, or about the right amount on Social Security, an item that has been asked in the GSS since 1984. These data show continuing high levels of support for Social Security. Between 1984 and 1991, a majority of the American public felt that the government was spending "too little" on Social Security. This percentage dipped slightly in the mid-1990s but has increased since then, reaching more than 60% in the three surveys between 2000 and 2008 before declining slightly—to 57%—in 2010. Throughout

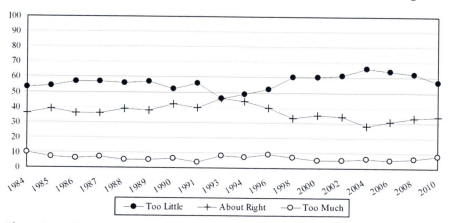

Figure 8.1.   Government spending on Social Security, 1984–2010.
Source: General Social Surveys.

this period, little evidence has surfaced of any sentiment that too much spending is being devoted to Social Security. Since 1985, consistently fewer than one in ten Americans have felt that too much is spent on this program. Other polls demonstrate similar levels of support, with large majorities opposed to cuts in Social Security and majorities believing that the government should do more to improve the program's benefits. The perceptions that Social Security is designed to benefit large numbers of people, that its targets are individuals in circumstances over which they have little or no control, and that workers put aside some of their wages for future benefits have contributed to the immense popularity of this program (Page and Shapiro, 1992: 120–121).

The concern over the need for reform of the Social Security system has been building for some time. In 1999, Roscho noted that increased concern over the question of the long-term viability of the Social Security system and proposals for various methods to "reform" this system had generated "a deluge of polls by news media, policy advocates, and public service organizations" (25) that go beyond the question of general support for the system and attempt to gauge the public's reactions to potential changes. Polls conducted in the late 1990s concluded that even though a majority of Americans supported various changes in the Social Security system, such as allowing individuals to put a portion of Social Security taxes into an individual retirement account, the public would prefer to see Social Security remain essentially as it has been, and it would not support major changes in this program (Blendon et al., 2000: 43).

Polling on this issue that has taken place during the public debate over proposed reforms has demonstrated the cross-currents in the public's views on this issue (Kohut and Doherty, 2005).[2] Results from several questions that were included in a March 2005 ABC News/*Washington Post* poll and repeated in March 2011 are presented in Box 8.1. These figures demonstrate that the public recognizes that the Social Security system faces problems. In 2005, 71% thought that the Social Security system was heading for a crisis if changes were not made, and this figure had increased to 81% by 2011.

Despite the fact that the American public feels that the Social Security system is heading toward a crisis, there is a lack of support for various proposals to change this system. Of the six proposed changes in the system asked about in these surveys, the only one that received majority (53%) support in 2011 was for collecting Social Security taxes on all the money a worker earns. Slight majorities are opposed to changing the way Social Security benefits are calculated and further reducing the benefits paid to people who retire early. Raising the retirement age from 67 to 68 is opposed by 57% of the public, and there is even less support for increasing the Social Security tax rate (61% opposed) or for reducing guaranteed benefits for future retirees (66% opposed). Although a majority of the public is not ready to

BOX 8.1
Opinions on Social Security (percent)

A. Now thinking about the Social Security system that mainly provides retirement income for senior citizens. If changes are not made, do you think the Social Security system is heading for a crisis down the road or not?

	Yes	No	Already in Crisis (vol.)	Unsure
March 2011	81	15	1	3
March 2005	71	23	1	5

B. I'm going to mention changes some leaders have proposed for Social Security. Please let me know if you support or oppose each one . . . increasing the Social Security tax rate.

	Support	Oppose	Unsure
March 2011	35	61	4
March 2005	31	64	4

C. Collecting Social Security taxes on all the money a worker earns, rather than taxing only up to about $107,000 (2005: first $90,000) of annual income.

	Support	Oppose	Unsure
March 2011	53	43	4
March 2005	56	40	4

D. Raising the retirement age to receive full Social Security benefits to 68, instead of the current 67.

	Support	Oppose	Unsure
March 2011	42	57	1
March 2005	33	66	2

E. Further reducing the benefits paid to people who retire early. For instance, people who retire at age 62 would get 63% of their full benefits, rather than the current 70%.

	Support	Oppose	Unsure
March 2011	46	52	2
March 2005	36	62	2

F. Changing the way Social Security benefits are calculated so that benefits increase at a slower rate than they would under the current formula.

	Support	Oppose	Unsure
March 2011	45	48	6
March 2005	37	57	6

G. Reducing guaranteed benefits for future retirees.

	Support	*Oppose*	*Unsure*
March 2011	32	66	2
March 2005	20	75	5

Source: ABC News/*Washington Post* Poll, March 2005 and March 2011.

embrace many of the proposed changes in the Social Security system, there is some evidence in these data of the need to take some action to reform the system. In addition to the increase in the percentage of the public who believe that the system is headed toward crisis, support for these various proposals generally increased between 2005 and 2011, typically by about 10%. For example, the percentage of the public who supported raising the retirement age to receive full benefits was 33% in 2005 but had increased to 42% in 2011.

Overall, Americans are supportive of the Social Security system and feel that the government is not spending enough in this area. The public also recognizes that there are some serious problems facing the system but is divided on the best approach for dealing with them. How the issue of Social Security is addressed, and the role the American mind plays in shaping these changes, is one of the key topics in contemporary American politics.

EDUCATION

Another area in which the public is largely supportive of government activity is education. Data from the National Election Studies (NES) conducted during the 1950s and early 1960s show that 60–70% of the public agreed that the government in Washington ought to help cities and towns around the country if they needed help to build more schools, and Gallup Polls during this period showed substantial majorities in favor of "federal aid to help build new public schools" (Page and Shapiro, 1992: 132).[3]

Moreover, as the figures in Table 8.2 demonstrate, over the past 40 years a majority of Americans has thought that the government is spending too little on education, and this percentage is increasing. In the GSS of the 1970s, about 50% of the public felt too little was being spent on education. This percentage increased to around 60% in the 1980s, was approximately 70% throughout the 1990s, and has been above 70% in each of the surveys conducted since 2000. At no point in this period did more than one in eight Americans believe that too much was being spent on education, and in more recent surveys this percentage has been about 5%. The results from

Table 8.2. Spending on Improving the Education System, 1973–2010 (percent)[a]

Response Category	Too Little	About the Right Amount	Too Much
1973	51	39	9
1974	54	38	8
1975	52	36	12
1976	53	38	9
1977	50	40	10
1978	53	35	12
1980	56	34	10
1982	57	34	9
1983	62	32	6
1984	64	33	3
1985	63	32	5
1986	61	34	5
1987	62	31	7
1988	66	30	3
1989	69	28	3
1990	74	23	3
1991	71	24	5
1993	70	24	6
1994	72	22	6
1996	70	24	6
1998	71	23	6
2000	72	23	5
2002	74	21	5
2004	74	22	5
2006	74	22	5
2008	71	23	6
2010	72	23	5

[a]The wording of the questions was: "Are we spending too much, too little, or about the right amount on improving the nation's education system?"

Source: General Social Surveys.

the NES, using a slightly different question, are consistent with these data (Table 8.3). When asked whether federal spending on public schools should be increased, kept the same, or decreased, slightly more than half of those surveyed in 1984 said it should be increased, with another 40% believing it should remain at the same level. The percentage who felt that spending on public schools should be increased rose to about 65% from 1988 through 1996 and grew to more than three-fourths of those responding in the 2000, 2002, and 2004 surveys. Though this percentage declined to 53% in 2008, a majority of the public supported increased federal spending, and there was relatively little support for decreasing spending on education. Mayer (1992: 86) noted that throughout the 1980s the state of public opinion toward

Table 8.3. Federal Spending on Education, 1984–2008 (percent)[a]

Response Category	Increased	Same	Decreased
1984	54	40	6
1988	65	30	4
1990	64	32	4
1992	66	30	4
1996	68	26	7
2000	76	18	5
2002	78	19	3
2004	76	20	5
2008	53	33	14

[a]The wording of the question was: "Should federal spending on public schools be increased, decreased, or kept about the same?"

Source: American National Election Studies.

funding education was substantially more liberal than it has been in earlier years, and this trend has continued since that time.

Although there is a public consensus favoring education, Americans do have some serious concerns about the performance of the country's public schools. For example, a 2010 Gallup Poll found that 54% of those surveyed thought that children today get a worse education than they did, and in a 2009 CBS News poll 70% gave the public schools in the nation as a whole a grade of C, D, or F. Similarly, a 2011 Gallup Poll found that a majority of Americans is dissatisfied with the quality of education students receive in kindergarten through grade 12, and other reports have indicated that close to a majority believes that the country's K–12 education system is in need of major changes or a complete overhaul. President Bush's concern over education was reflected in the No Child Left Behind Act, which he announced three days after taking office in 2001 and he described as "the cornerstone of my Administration." By 2011, 16% of the public felt this law should be eliminated and another 41% believed it needed major revisions. Despite such concerns, the American public is, as Ladd (1995: 22–25) has noted, "deeply committed to education. [They] say so every time asked, no matter how they are asked," and this support cuts across group lines.

HEALTH CARE

Although the public is largely supportive of Social Security and education, it has more mixed views on the issue of health care, and the debate on this issue has become increasingly contentious surrounding the passage of the 2010 Patient Protection and Affordable Care Act and calls for its repeal.

Historically, when the question involves government spending on health care, public support for medical care rivals that for Social Security (Page and Shapiro, 1992: 129). Data from the 1950s and 1960s indicate that a majority of Americans believed that the government ought to "help people to get doctors and hospital care at low cost." Similarly, more people felt that the government in Washington should be responsible for seeing to it that people have help in paying for doctors and hospital bills than those who believed people should take care of these things themselves (Table 8.4). Since 1973, the GSS has included a question on whether this country is spending too much, too little, or about the right amount on improving and protecting the nation's health (Table 8.5). From 1973 through 1986, 60% of the public thought we were spending too little. From the mid-1980s through 1998, this percentage hovered around 70%. In the surveys conducted from 2000 to 2008, more than 70% of the public thought the country was spending too little on improving and protecting the nation's health; this percentage dropped to 60% in 2010, the first measurement taken after the passage of the Affordable Care Act.

Table 8.4. Federal Government Responsibility for Paying for Medical Care, 1975–2010 (percent)[a]

Response Category	1. Government Responsibility	2.	3. Agree with Both	4.	5. People Care for Themselves
1975	37	13	30	7	14
1983	27	20	32	11	10
1984	24	20	35	13	8
1986	29	20	33	12	6
1987	26	21	35	9	8
1988	26	22	37	9	7
1989	32	23	30	8	7
1990	32	26	30	8	4
1991	33	24	27	10	6
1993	29	24	32	9	6
1994	26	21	32	12	9
1996	28	22	33	11	7
1998	26	23	33	10	8
2000	30	22	32	11	6
2002	32	20	34	7	7
2004	32	21	31	8	8
2006	33	19	32	9	7
2008	35	19	30	9	7
2010	30	16	32	11	10

[a]The question asked was: "In general, some people think that it is the responsibility of the government in Washington to see to it that people have help in paying for doctors and hospital bills. Others think that these matters are not the responsibility of the federal government and that people should take care of these things themselves. Where do you put yourself on this scale, or haven't you made up your mind on this?"

Source: General Social Surveys.

Table 8.5. Spending on Improving and Protecting the Nation's Health, 1973–2010 (percent)[a]

Response Category	Too Little	About the Right Amount	Too Much
1973	63	32	5
1974	67	29	4
1975	66	29	5
1976	63	32	5
1977	59	34	7
1978	57	36	7
1980	58	34	8
1982	59	34	7
1983	59	35	6
1984	61	32	7
1985	60	34	6
1986	60	36	4
1987	69	26	5
1988	70	27	3
1989	70	27	3
1990	74	23	3
1991	71	26	3
1993	74	18	8
1994	67	24	9
1996	68	24	8
1998	69	26	9
2000	73	23	4
2002	75	21	4
2004	79	17	4
2006	74	21	5
2008	77	18	5
2010	60	24	16

[a]The question asked was: "Are we spending too much, too little, or about the right amount on improving and protecting the nation's health?"

Source: General Social Surveys.

When the question shifts to whether there should be a government insurance plan that would cover medical and hospital expenses or whether medical expenses should be paid by individuals and through private insurance, the public is more evenly divided. Treating responses 1, 2, and 3 in Table 8.6 as representing the "government insurance plan" side of the issue and points 5, 6, and 7 as the "private insurance" side, the split in public opinion on this issue was relatively even from 1970 to 1988, shifted to a majority support for a government plan during the first two years of the Bill Clinton presidency, and moved back to balance in 1996. In the 2000, 2004, and 2008 NES surveys, a higher percentage of Americans preferred a government insurance plan than favored medical

Table 8.6.   Support for a Government Insurance Plan, 1970–2008 (percent)[a]

Response Category	1. Government Insurance Plan	2.	3.	4.	5.	6.	7. Individuals/ Private Insurance
1970	28	9	8	15	6	9	24
1972	31	7	8	14	7	6	28
1976	28	9	7	12	9	10	25
1978	29	9	8	13	9	10	22
1984	16	10	11	21	16	14	12
1988	20	11	12	19	14	11	13
1992	23	15	14	20	12	9	8
1994	21	14	16	18	12	9	10
1996	14	10	13	21	16	14	11
2000	18	11	16	21	14	10	11
2004	21	12	13	19	15	11	8
2008	20	14	13	19	13	10	11

[a] The question asked was: "There is much concern about the rapid rise in medical and hospital costs. Some people feel there should be a government insurance plan that would cover all medical and hospital expenses. Others feel that medical expenses should be paid by individuals and through private insurance such a Blue Cross. Where would you place yourself on this scale, or haven't you thought much about this?"

Source: American National Election Studies.

expenses being paid by private insurance, though a government insurance plan was supported by less than a majority.[4]

The more mixed views concerning the health care system are evident in more extensive studies of this issue conducted in the 1990s. A number of analysts traced an upsurge in the salience of health care as an issue to a special senatorial election in Pennsylvania in 1991. Blendon and his colleagues (1992a: 3371) assert that in this race "voter interest in reform of the American health care system played a central role in the come-from-behind victory of Democratic Senator Harrison Wofford over Republican candidate Richard Thornburgh." Driven by factors such as spiraling health care costs, the number of uninsured Americans, and lack of access to adequate health care services, the U.S. health care system in the early 1990s was viewed as one "in crisis" (Blendon and Edwards, 1991).

A great deal of public opinion data supports the idea that Americans perceived a crisis in the health care system. For example, a 1991 Harris survey found that 52% of the public thought that fundamental changes to the health care system were needed to make it work better, and another 35% felt that the system had so much wrong with it that it needed to be rebuilt (Blendon et al., 1992b: 19). Moreover, virtually any proposal to change the health care system was supported by a majority of the public: 90% of the public favored a proposal that would make private insurance more affordable and available; 82% supported setting up a new public program to provide coverage for anyone who doesn't get health insurance through their employer; 71% favored requiring all employers, including small employers, to provide health care benefits for their employees; and 69% approved of expanding the Medicare system to cover all Americans (Jajich-Toth and Roper, 1990: 152). A 1991 *Los Angeles Times*/Gallup Poll found that 91% of the American public thought there was a health care crisis in the United States (Blendon and Edwards, 1991: 2).

Public perception of the crisis in health care was one of the factors that led President Clinton to propose wide-reaching health care reform as one of the key initiatives of his first term. When this plan was first introduced, it seemed to enjoy the support of the American public. As this plan was debated in Congress, however, its critics' claims that this plan "went too far" and would create too much bureaucracy raised concerns among the public. As Americans became concerned that Clinton's health care plan would create too much government involvement in the nation's health care system and would create a large and inefficient government bureaucracy, public support for this plan eroded (*Public Perspective*, 1994: 23–28), and the Clinton administration was forced to settle for only minor adjustments in health insurance coverage.

As the cost of health care continued to increase over the following 15 years, the public remained concerned about the issue, but attention moved from a large-scale overhaul of the system to more specific aspects, such as accountability of managed care organizations and a patients' bill of rights. This changed with the election of President Obama and his decision to make reforming the health care system his top fiscal priority, contending that "reining in skyrocketing medical costs is critical to saving the nation from bankruptcy" (quoted in Montgomery and Goldstein, 2009). At the time of Obama's election a Gallup Poll (Saad, 2008) found that 14% of the public thought that the U.S. health care system was in a state of crisis, 59% thought it had major problems, and 26% felt it had minor problems; only 1% said the health care system did not have any problems.

An extensive amount of polling was conducted on the issue of health care during the course of the debate over the Affordable Care Act. Mark Blumenthal's website (pollster.com) listed 177 different polls conducted between March 2009 and the passage of the act that asked the public if they favored or opposed the health care plan, and an additional 60 polls tracking public support on this issue were identified through August 2011. In his review on the polls on this issue after its passage by Congress, Gary Langer (2011) noted that "it's been a simple matter for just about anyone to mischaracterize public opinion on the health care reform measure the president's about to sign. Polling results on it have depended to a large extent on what's asked—a reasonable outcome given conflicted views on the subject." Langer also pointed out that each side in the health care reform debate attempted to lay claim to the high ground in public opinion and could point to individual data points supporting its case. Nonetheless, from the data available, Langer stated "It seems best to describe public attitudes on health care reform as divided."

A February 2010 *Newsweek* poll provides a stark example of the division on the issue (as well as a striking example of a context effect). At the beginning of this survey, participants were asked, "As you know Barack Obama has proposed a plan to change this country's health care system. From what you have seen or heard about what he has proposed, what is your *overall* opinion of Obama's health care reform plan—do you favor or oppose it?" Forty percent of respondents favored this plan, 49% were opposed, and 11% were unsure. They were then asked a series of questions, about specific aspects of this plan, the results for which are shown in Box 8.2.

These data show that a majority of Americans was largely supportive of provisions of a health care reform plan creating a health insurance exchange

---

BOX 8.2
Public Opinion on Health Care Reform (percent)

Do you favor or oppose . . .	Favor	Oppose	Unsure
Creating a new insurance marketplace—the Exchange—that allows people without health insurance to compare plans and buy insurance at competitive rates	81	13	6
Requiring health insurance companies to cover anyone who applies, even if they have a pre-existing medical condition	76	19	5
Requiring most businesses to offer health insurance to their employees, with tax incentives to small business owners to do so	75	20	5
Requiring that all Americans have health insurance, with the government providing financial help to those who cannot afford it	59	36	5
Preventing insurance companies from dropping coverage when people are sick	59	38	3
Creating a government-administered public health insurance option to compete with private plans	50	42	8
Imposing a tax on insurers who offer the most expensive plans, the so-called Cadillac plans, to help pay for health care reform	34	55	11
If health care coverage is required for everyone, imposing fines on individuals who don't obtain coverage and on larger businesses that don't offer it	28	62	10

Source: Newsweek, February 18, 2010.

marketplace, requiring health insurers to cover everyone who applies, and requiring most businesses to offer health insurance to their employees; more evenly divided, but still supportive, of requiring that all Americans have health insurance, preventing insurance companies from dropping coverage when people are sick, and creating a government-administered public health insurance option to compete with private plans; and opposed to imposing a tax on insurers who offer the most expensive plans and to imposing fines on individuals who don't obtain coverage and on larger businesses that don't offer it. After answering these questions about specific provisions of the plan, respondents were asked, "Now please think about the proposals I just described to you. ALL of these proposals are included in Barack Obama's health care reform plan. Having heard these details, what is your *overall* opinion of Obama's plan—do you favor or oppose it?" Opinions on this issue switched, with 48% in favor, 43% opposed, and 9% unsure. Public opinion on health care reform was indeed divided at the time the Affordable Care Act was passed.

Since its passage, the public has remained largely divided on this issue. The Kaiser Family Foundation tracking poll on this issue reported in August 2011 that 39% of the public had a favorable view of the health care reform law, 44% were unfavorable, and 17% were unsure. Between May 2010 and August 2011, the percentage who had a favorable view of this legislation varied only between 39% and 50%, while the percentage with an unfavorable view ranged from 35% to 50%, and the percentage who were unsure was consistently about 15%. Similarly, Americans were divided over the impact of this law. In the August 2011 poll, 24% thought they and their family would be better off under this law, 33% said worse off, and 37% felt it would not make much difference, while 33% thought the country as a whole would be better off, 37% believed it would be worse off, and 21% felt it would not make much difference.

ASSISTING THE NEEDY

When the public's attention turns from those social-welfare programs that potentially benefit large numbers of people to a more specific focus on assisting those in need, its views become even more mixed. This is also an area in which the specific aspect of the issue addressed, as well as the way in which the question is posed, can make a significant difference in responses.

In discussing this issue, Shapiro and his colleagues (1987a: 120) have characterized programs for the poor as the most controversial social-welfare issue because "many Americans associate these policies with 'welfare' fraud and tangled bureaucracies and feel these programs provide disincentives for employment." Page and Shapiro (1992: 124) argue that, in principle, Americans favor government support for the needy, pointing to polls from the 1930s through the 1980s that show large majorities of the public favoring government action to "provide for all people who have no other means of making a living," or "who have no other means of subsistence" and "helping people who are unable to support themselves."

One specific aspect of government involvement in the economic arena concerns government's role in guaranteeing jobs. NES results show that the public is divided on this issue and that question wording can have an effect on opinions. In NES data from 1956 to 1960, close to 65% of respondents agreed with the idea that the government in Washington ought to see to it that everyone who wants to work can find a job. In 1964 and 1968, when seeing to "a good standard of living" was added to the government's role and "letting each person get ahead on his own" was posed as the alternative, the public was not as supportive, with slightly more than one-third feeling this should be the government's role and a majority believing that "the government should just let each person get ahead on his own."

As shown in Table 8.7, from 1972 to 2008 the NES used a seven-point version of this question. Throughout the period the percentage on the "let each person get ahead on his own" side of the scale has been greater than that for

Table 8.7. Opinions on Government Guarantee of Jobs and Living Standards, 1972–2008 (percent)[a]

Response Category	1. Government See to Jobs	2.	3.	4.	5.	6.	7. Let Each Person Get Ahead
1972	16	7	9	23	14	8	22
1974	14	6	10	25	15	10	20
1976	14	6	10	22	13	13	22
1978	9	4	9	24	19	14	21
1980	11	8	11	21	16	19	14
1982	11	7	10	23	18	15	14
1984	12	8	13	23	19	15	10
1986	11	7	9	23	17	15	18
1988	11	7	11	21	18	16	16
1990	13	10	13	21	16	14	13
1992	10	8	12	23	20	14	13
1994	10	7	12	21	20	16	14
1996	8	8	10	21	21	20	13
1998	14	10	12	24	16	11	14
2000	9	6	10	19	21	20	15
2004	13	9	13	20	17	16	13
2008	17	10	12	20	17	13	12

[a] The question asked was: "Some people feel that the government in Washington should see to it that every person has a job and a good standard of living. Others think the government should just let each person get ahead on his/their own. [(1972–78: And, of course, other people have opinions somewhere in between.)/(1998–2000: And, of course, other people have opinions somewhere in between, at points 2, 3, 4, 5, or 6)]. Where would you place yourself on this scale, or haven't you thought much about this?"

Source: American National Election Studies.

the "government should see to it" position. In 2000 a majority supported letting individuals get ahead on their own (responses 5, 6, and 7), though this percentage declined slightly in 2004 and 2008. The GSS measure of this question used during the same period asked not about jobs, but whether the government in Washington should do everything possible to improve the standard of living for all poor Americans as opposed to letting each person take care of him- or herself. In 1975, the balance on this question was on the "government responsibility" side, with 40% saying this was the government's role, 24% feeling that people should help themselves, and 36% agreeing with aspects of both sides or otherwise adopting a middle position (Table 8.8). Opinions shifted slightly in the 1980s, with the largest percentage holding a middle position and slightly more people believing this should be the government's role than asserting that people should help themselves. From 1993 through the 2010 survey, the middle position was still held most frequently, with a roughly equal number of proponents on either side.

Another GSS measure in this area asked respondents whether or not it should be the government's responsibility to provide a job for everyone

Table 8.8. Opinions on Government Improving Living Standards for Poor Americans, 1975–2010 (percent)[a]

Response Category	1. Government Responsibility	2.	3. Agree with Both	4.	5. People Help Themselves
1975	30	10	36	11	13
1983	17	16	41	15	11
1984	17	11	48	16	9
1986	19	13	46	12	10
1987	17	12	46	14	10
1988	17	12	46	13	12
1989	17	15	44	14	9
1990	20	15	44	13	8
1991	17	17	44	13	9
1993	12	15	49	14	10
1994	13	14	45	16	11
1996	13	13	47	16	11
1998	13	13	44	17	12
2000	14	13	43	17	12
2002	17	11	47	13	12
2004	17	10	47	15	11
2006	18	11	48	14	10
2008	20	13	41	15	11
2010	16	12	44	15	13

[a] The question asked was, "Some people think that the government in Washington should do everything possible to improve the standard of living of all poor Americans, they are at Point 1 on this card. Other people think it is not the government's responsibility, and that each person should take care of himself; they are at Point 5. Where would you place yourself on this scale, or haven't you made up your mind on this?"

Source: General Social Surveys.

who wants one. In the years between 1985 and 2006 when this question was asked, a majority held that this should not be the government's responsibility. These findings echo those of Shapiro and his colleagues (1987b: 269), who concluded that "employment is much less thought of as an entitlement than Social Security or medical care." The public clearly has mixed feelings about the government's role in providing a job and good standard of living for all Americans.

The issue of providing assistance to the needy is even more controversial in the American public's mind. In each year since 1973, with the exception of 2000, in which the GSS has asked whether too much, too little, or about the right amount was being spent on welfare, the most frequent response has been "too much" (Figure 8.2). The extent to which public sentiment slanted in the "too much" direction has varied somewhat during this period, starting from a majority in 1973, falling somewhat in the mid-1970s, increasing to more than 60% in the late 1970s, then falling back again through 1991. Between 1991 and 1993, the percentage who felt that too much was being spent on welfare jumped from 39% to 57% and remained at around 60% in the 1994 and 1996 surveys. The public's concern over welfare spending expressed in this question was in part responsible for the passage of the Personal Responsibility and Reconciliation Act of 1996, an act that was intended to produce a radical transformation in the nation's welfare system. Under this act, the states gained more responsibility for establishing welfare rules and managing the welfare program, and the states could experiment with different methods of delivering welfare assistance. The major thrust of this legislation was to transform welfare into a work-based system by, among other things, requiring parents to work after a maximum of two years on aid and limiting able-bodied adults to three months on food stamps in a 36-month period if they did not participate in a work or training program.

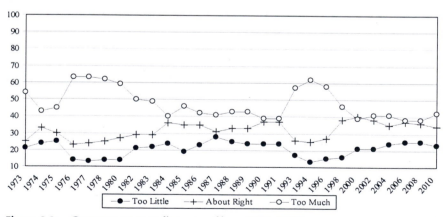

Figure 8.2.   Government spending on welfare, 1973–2010.
Source: General Social Surveys

The public's response to these changes appears to have been positive. In the 1998 GSS the percentage saying "too much" was being spent on welfare declined to 45%, and in 2000 this percentage dipped to 39% and has ranged between 38% and 42% since that time. Although there is little sense that "too little" is being spent on welfare, the impact of the 1996 welfare reform act has been that fewer people believe that too much is being spent on this program and a large percentage feel that welfare spending is now "about right."

Again, choice of words in sampling opinions can change the results. As Smith (1987: 78–79) has shown, in GSS surveys that asked about spending on *assistance to the poor*, the number of Americans who felt that too little was being spent was about 40% greater than the percentage who felt too little was being spent on *welfare*. As he concluded, "The term 'welfare' obviously carries more negative connotations than does 'poor,'" with welfare more likely to conjure up images of "loafers and bums" and the poor more likely to be thought of as the "truly needy."

In analyzing data similar to these, Page and Shapiro (1992: 126) reported that the attitudes that the public expresses, though somewhat ambivalent, are not inconsistent. Instead, they argue that the variations in opinion provided in the answers to these differently worded questions reflect exactly the distinctions the public wants to make on this issue. In their view, the public doesn't "like the idea of welfare programs that give cash payments to people, some of whom may not be truly helpless and may thereby be discouraged from helping themselves." Overall, they conclude that "these views are consistent with one another, form a coherent pattern, reflect the information made available to the public, and fit with Americans' underlying values—which combine generosity with individualism" (127).

THE ENVIRONMENT

Over the past 40 years, the environment has emerged as an increasingly important issue in the American mind. Since the initial peak of the environmental movement in the early 1970s, this issue "has been a persistent concern, prominent in the media and magnified by worldwide environmental groups" (Gilroy and Shapiro, 1986: 270). As awareness of environmental issues increased, the American public has come to expect such things as cleaner air, cleaner water, more parklands, and the preservation of wildlife (Ladd, 1990: 11).

The public's commitment to the environment has been characterized as "genuine and substantial," and polling data have shown that Americans are willing to pay for cleaner air and water; they are not, however, willing to pay *any* price for greater environmental protection (Ladd, 1990: 11). The information displayed in Table 8.9 and Box 8.3 supports this conclusion.

Table 8.9.   Opinions on Improving and Protecting the
Environment, 1973–2010 (percent)[a]

Response Category	Too Little	About the Right Amount	Too Much
1973	65	28	8
1974	64	28	8
1975	58	32	10
1976	59	32	9
1977	52	36	12
1978	55	35	10
1980	52	32	16
1982	54	33	12
1983	58	33	9
1984	63	33	4
1985	59	33	8
1986	64	31	5
1987	68	26	5
1988	68	28	4
1989	76	20	4
1990	76	20	4
1991	71	24	5
1993	59	31	9
1994	61	30	9
1996	61	28	11
1998	63	29	8
2000	63	28	8
2002	60	33	7
2004	64	29	6
2006	69	25	6
2008	68	24	8
2010	58	30	13

[a] The question asked was: "Are we spending too much money, too little money,
or about the right amount on improving and protecting the environment?"

Source: General Social Surveys.

The GSS question on spending for "improving and protecting the environment" shows that since 1973, a majority of the public has felt that too little is spent on the environment.[5] Public support for environmental spending reached its peak at the beginning of the 1990s, when about three-fourths of those surveyed said that too little was being spent in this area. This percentage dropped slightly to the low 60% range from 1993 through 2004, increased to 69% in 2006 and 68% in 2008, before declining to 58% in 2010, its lowest level since 1983. In 2010, 30% of the public thought that about the right amount was being spent on improving and protecting the environment and 13% felt we were spending too much.[6]

BOX 8.3
Opinions on Environmental Issues (percent)

"If you had to choose, which one of the following comes closest to your views? Government should let businesses decide for themselves how to protect the environment, even if it means they don't always do the right thing, or government should pass laws to make businesses protect the environment, even if it interferes with businesses' right to make their own decisions."

Response Category	1993	1994	2000	2010
Government Let Businesses Decide	9	11	12	13
Government Should Pass Laws	91	89	88	87

"If you had to choose, which one of the following comes closest to your views? Government should let ordinary people decide for themselves how to protect the environment, even if it means they don't always do the right thing, or government should pass laws to make ordinary people protect the environment, even if it interferes with people's right to make their own decisions."

Response Category	1993	1994	2000	2010
Government Let People Decide	21	27	34	37
Government Should Pass Laws	79	73	66	63

"In order to protect the environment, America needs economic growth."

Response Category	1993	1994	2000	2010
Strongly Agree	5	6	9	10
Agree	45	39	39	52
Neither Agree nor Disagree	23	26	28	18
Disagree	24	26	21	18
Strongly Disagree	3	3	3	2

"Economic growth always harms the environment."

Response Category	1993	1994	2000	2010
Strongly Agree	2	3	3	2
Agree	18	18	17	16
Neither Agree nor Disagree	26	27	32	22
Disagree	47	47	43	54
Strongly Disagree	6	5	5	6

(continued)

BOX 8.3
(*continued*)

"People worry too much about human progress harming the environment."

Response Category	1993	1994	2000	2010
Strongly Agree	5	5	5	4
Agree	28	32	25	36
Neither Agree nor Disagree	18	15	23	19
Disagree	40	41	38	36
Strongly Disagree	8	7	9	5

"We worry too much about the future of the environment, and not enough about prices and jobs today."

Response Category	1993	1994	2000	2010
Strongly Agree	10	11	11	10
Agree	30	31	27	32
Neither Agree nor Disagree	16	14	18	18
Disagree	34	33	33	32
Strongly Disagree	10	10	10	8

"How willing would you be to pay much higher prices in order to protect the environment?"

Response Category	1993	1994	2000	2010
Very Willing	11	8	10	8
Fairly Willing	40	40	36	38
Neither Willing nor Unwilling	23	25	28	22
Not Very Willing	19	18	15	18
Not at All Willing	7	10	11	15

"How willing would you be to pay much higher taxes in order to protect the environment?"

Response Category	1993	1994	2000	2010
Very Willing	8	6	6	6
Fairly Willing	32	29	26	27
Neither Willing nor Unwilling	21	22	27	22
Not Very Willing	26	27	19	21
Not at All Willing	14	16	22	24

"How willing would you be to accept cuts in your standard of living in order to protect the environment?"

Response Category	1993	1994	2000	2010
Very Willing	6	4	6	6
Fairly Willing	28	28	24	30
Neither Willing nor Unwilling	24	24	26	22
Not Very Willing	26	29	20	20
Not at All Willing	16	15	24	21

Source: General Social Surveys.

The GSS surveys in 1993, 1994, 2000, and 2010 contained a set of items specifically related to environmental issues. Although the length of time between surveys does not permit us to monitor short-term fluctuations on these items, the data for these four years indicate that the public believes it is the government's role to protect the environment. About 90% of those surveyed in each year felt the government should pass laws to make business protect the environment, even if this interfered with a business's right to make its own decisions. Similarly, a large majority of the public believed that government should make laws to protect the environment, even if this interferes with people's right to make their own decisions, although this percentage has declined over time, from 79% in 1993, to 73% in 1994, 66% in 2000, and 63% in 2010.

The public does not believe that protection of the environment necessarily involves a tradeoff with the economy and is less steadfastly pro-environment when the issue is presented in this way. In 1993, 1994, and 2000, about half the public felt that this country needs economic growth in order to protect the environment; this percentage increased to 62% in 2010. Similarly, about half of those surveyed in 1993, 1994, and 2000 disagreed with the idea that economic growth always harms the environment, a percentage that increased to 60% in 2010; approximately one-fourth of the public neither agrees nor disagrees with this notion. In the first three surveys, a higher percentage of people disagreed than agreed with the statement that people worry too much about human progress hurting the environment; by 2010, the percentages agreeing or disagreeing were virtually the same, and the public is fairly evenly divided on the issue of whether we worry too much about the future of the environment and not enough about prices and jobs.

The extent to which Americans say they are willing to make sacrifices to protect the environment also varies by the extent of the sacrifice requested.

About half of those responding said they would be very willing or fairly willing to pay much higher prices to protect the environment. This percentage falls to less than 40% when the sacrifice involves paying much higher taxes and to about one-third if protecting the environment means accepting cuts in their standard of living.[7]

Overall, although Americans are generally willing to support protection of the environment, they do not believe that this goal must come at the price of economic well-being, and there are limits to the public's willingness to pay for an attractive environment (Ladd, 1990: 11). Though Americans remain protective of the environment, over the past decade there has been a shift in favor of economic growth over the environment when these values are seen as competing.

THE ISSUE OF GLOBAL WARMING

One environmentally related issue that has been the source of controversy in recent years is the issue of global warming. Although 97% of climate scientists agree that it is very likely that climate change is caused by human activity (Anderegg et al., 2010), there is not this level of consensus among the public. Comments made by 2012 Republican presidential contender Governor Rick Perry illustrate the divide over this issue. As Governor Perry remarked, "I believe there are a significant range of scientists who have manipulated data so that they will have dollars rolling into their projects . . . we're seeing it practically weekly or even every day, scientists who are coming forward and questioning the original concept that man-made international warming is what is causing the climate to change. Yes, our climates change. They've been changing ever since the earth was formed. But I do not purchase into, that a group of scientists, who in some cases were identified to be manipulating this data" (O'Sullivan, 2011).

Polling on this issue indicates that the public is less convinced that global warming is occurring and less concerned about it. Findings from the Pew Research Center for the People and the Press (2011a) show that in 2006 almost 80% believed that there was solid evidence the earth is warming, but that by 2010 this percentage had declined to 59%, with the percentage saying there was no evidence for the earth's warming rising from 17% to 32% during this period. The percentage who felt that global warming was a very serious problem stood at 43% in 2006 and dropped to 32% by 2010, while the percentage who believed this was not a problem doubled from 9% to 18%. Moreover, in 2006, 59% believed that scientists agreed that the earth was getting warmer because of human activity, a percentage that fell to 44% in 2010.

Gallup Poll data on this issue show a similar trend. One question that Gallup asks is, "Which of the following statements reflects your view of when the effects of global warming will begin to happen—they have already begun to happen, they will start happening within a few years, they will start happening within your lifetime, they will not happen within your lifetime, but they will affect future generations, or they will never happen?" The highest percentage of the public reporting that the effects of global warming have already begun was 61% in 2008, and in that survey another 4% felt that the effects of global warming would be felt within a few years, and 10% said they would occur in their lifetime. The percentage who believed that such effects had already begun declined to 53% in 2009, 50% in 2010, and 49% in 2011, while the percentage who believed that such effects will never happen increased from 11% to 18% during this period. Similarly, the percentage of people who believe that the seriousness of global warming is generally exaggerated in the news moved from a low of 30% in 2006 to 48% in 2010 and dropped only slightly, to 43%, in 2011 (Gallup Report, 2011c).[8] A majority of Americans believe that global warming is occurring, but the percentage who share this belief has been declining in recent years, along with the public's perceptions of the seriousness of this problem.

GROUP DIFFERENCES IN ATTITUDES

To this point, our discussion of the American mind on social-welfare issues has centered on the views of the entire adult population. You should recognize, however, that these overall attitudes may not be shared by all subgroups, and that individuals with different background characteristics and political orientations may differ in their opinions on these issues.

The data in Table 8.10 are from four spending questions on the 2008 GSS, whether we are spending too much money, too little money, or about the right amount on (1) Social Security; (2) improving and protecting the nation's health; (3) welfare; and (4) improving and protecting the environment, and from two questions on the 2008 NES, (1) whether federal spending on public schools should be increased, decreased, or kept about the same, and (2) whether government should guarantee jobs and a good standard of living. These figures provide a breakdown on the questions by subgroups.

As these data demonstrate, there are some fairly substantial and consistent differences across groups in their views on social-welfare issues. The largest of these differences are between blacks and whites, with African Americans consistently more likely to adopt the liberal position on these issues. On the issue of Social Security, for example, 83% of blacks thought we were spending too little, compared to 59% of whites. Similarly, 62%

Table 8.10. Opinions on Selected Social Welfare Issues by Sociodemographic Characteristics, 2008 (percentage giving "liberal" response)

	Social Security	School	Health	Jobs	Welfare	Environment
Total Sample	62	53	77	31	25	67
Age						
18–29	60	56	76	43	29	74
30–44	63	53	76	31	25	71
45–64	66	53	81	28	24	68
65 and Older	49	51	76	24	25	52
Race						
Black	83	62	86	59	42	71
White	59	52	76	24	21	67
Gender						
Male	59	54	75	26	25	66
Female	64	53	79	35	26	69
Education						
Less than high school	57	56	66	52	27	62
High school graduate	71	54	74	30	22	62
Some college	64	53	84	33	28	68
College graduate	53	52	81	23	25	76
Income						
Lowest quartile	68	59	77	45	36	67
Second quartile	66	50	82	27	27	66
Third quartile	64	51	82	25	20	72
Highest quartile	56	50	74	16	21	68
Party Identification						
Democrats	71	58	88	50	34	75
Independents	58	53	73	28	25	67
Republicans	54	48	68	11	15	59
Ideology						
Liberals	64	58	80	48	34	80
Moderates	67	53	84	29	26	72
Conservatives	53	48	68	16	17	54

Sources: 2008 American National Election Study and 2008 General Social Survey.

of blacks, compared to 52% of whites, felt that federal spending on public schools should be increased, and a majority of blacks (59%), compared to only 24% of whites, believed that the government in Washington should see to it that every person has a job and a good standard of living. Blacks were also significantly more likely than whites—42% to 21%—to believe that too little was being spent on welfare.

Differences in opinion across levels of family income were not as large nor as consistent as those between blacks and whites, but family income did have an effect on several of these issues. Across income groups, the general pattern was that a smaller percentage of respondents from higher-income families took a liberal position on these issues. On the issue of spending for Social Security, for example, the percentage that said "too little" was being spent was 68% in the lowest income group, 66% in the second quartile of respondents, and 64% in the third quartile, but dropped to 56% in the highest income group. The questions on whether the government should provide a job and good standard of living and on welfare spending had the largest differences across incomes levels. On the issue of whether the government should provide a job and good standard of living, the percentage giving the liberal response declined from 45% among the lowest income group to 16% in the highest; on welfare spending, the percentage who felt "too little" was being spent ranged from 36% in the lowest income group to 21% in the highest.

There were only minor variations in opinions on these items by education level. The largest differences were on the question of whether the government should provide a job and good standard of living, with the percentage of liberal responses highest (52%), among those with less than a high school education, and lowest (23%) among college graduates. Conversely, those with some college education or more were more likely to say that we are spending too little on improving and protecting the nation's health. On the question of spending on Social Security, the smallest percentages of liberal ("too little") responses were found in the highest and lowest education groups.

Where there are differences in opinion across age groups, the pattern is for a higher percentage of younger people to give a liberal response. This pattern is most evident on the issues of spending to improve and protect the environment and on whether the government should provide a job and good standard of living. For the question on the environment, 74% of those under 30 thought that we were spending too little on the environment; this percentage declined to 71% among those 30–44, 68% among those 45–64, and 52% for those age 65 or older. Similarly, the percentage who felt that the government should provide a job and good standard of living ranged from 43% among the youngest age group to 24% among those 65 or older. The opinions of those age 65 or older are distinct from those of other age groups on the issue of Social Security spending. A lower percentage of those age 65 or older than those in the younger age groups felt that too little was being spent on Social Security.

The differences between men and women on these issues, while generally not large, show a consistent pattern, with women more likely than men to take a liberal position. For instance, a higher percentage of women than men (64% to 59%) felt that too little was being spent on Social Security; on protecting and improving the environment (69% to 66%); and on improving and protecting the nation's health (79% to 75%). Women were also more likely than men to feel that government should guarantee jobs and living standards (35% to 26%).

As noted in the previous chapter, the basic split between liberals and conservatives is over the role of government, with liberals believing in more government action and conservatives feeling that individuals are primarily responsible for their own well-being. Given this, we would expect significant differences in opinion on these social-welfare issues among those who identify themselves as liberals, moderates, or conservatives. The data in Table 8.10 show this to be the case. For each of these six items, a higher percentage of those who classify themselves as liberals than conservatives take the liberal side of the issue, and for four of these six issues, the percentage of moderates falls between the two. The extent to which the percentage of self-identified liberals exceeds the percentage of conservatives who adopt the liberal position on these issues is 32% on government guarantee of jobs and living standards; 26% on spending to improve and protect the environment; 17% for welfare spending; 12% for the item on spending to improve and protect the nation's health; 11% on Social Security spending; and 10% for federal spending on public schools. The positions of the public on these social-welfare issues clearly reflect its general political orientation.

Differences in opinion by party identification are also relatively large and demonstrate the more liberal views of Democrats and conservative attitudes of Republicans. For each of these items, the percentage giving the liberal response was higher among Democrats than among Republicans, and the percentage of Independents voicing the liberal position falls between the two. The difference in the percentage taking the liberal stance on the items ranged from 39% (50% to 11%) on the question of whether the government should guarantee jobs and a good standard of living to 10% on the issue of federal spending on public schools (58% to 48%). Overall, these data illustrate some fairly substantial differences in the social-welfare views of various subgroups of the population. People's general political orientations are related to their views on these issues, with self-identified liberals and Democrats more likely to take a liberal position on these issues than conservatives or supporters of the Republican Party. Blacks, those respondents with lower family incomes, younger people, and women also tended to have more liberal views on these social-welfare questions.

SUMMARY

The views of the American public on social-welfare issues generally reflect the division in the American mind on the role of government in providing for the welfare of its citizens. The public is fairly evenly split on the general question of whether the government should provide more services or fewer, and support for government action varies significantly according to the nature of the program. Public support for a program like Social Security has been high since its inception and remains relatively strong. Americans also support spending for schools and feel that the government should help people get doctors and hospital care. The public is more divided, however, on the question of whether this country should have a government health insurance plan.

Americans have shown themselves to be supportive of protecting and improving the environment. A consistent majority of the public believes that too little is being spent on the environment, and the public generally supports actions, such as government regulation of businesses or individuals, that are perceived as promoting environmental quality. The recent trend, however, is for public support for the environment to have waned slightly, particularly when it is seen as competing with economic growth.

Programs that find less support among the American public are welfare programs and those in which the government attempts to ensure that everyone has a good standard of living. Although Americans are not opposed to helping people in need, they also believe in individual responsibility. They are, therefore, less supportive of government guarantees of living standards and of programs that they feel might discourage people from helping themselves.

Opinions on social-welfare issues vary significantly across subgroups of the population. Individuals who identify themselves as liberals or who support the Democratic Party are more likely to support an active role for the government in the social-welfare arena than are conservatives or Republicans. Whites are more likely to take a conservative position on these issues than are blacks, and those with more education or higher family incomes, older people, and men are also more likely to take a conservative position on questions involving the government's role in providing for the welfare of its citizens.

POLLS, POLLING, AND THE INTERNET

One place in the United States that has gathered polling data and results from a multitude of academic and media sources is the Roper Center at the University of Connecticut. By accessing their website, you can find cross-time trends for many of the social issues discussed in this chapter. To gain access to all of their data, your institution must be a subscriber. Take a look at the website at: www.ropercenter.uconn.edu.

9

Americans' Views on Racial Issues

The place of race in the history of the United States makes it almost inevitable that race and racism will be issues in American society. Race has been a continual source of social and political division from the origins of the Constitution and the "three-fifths" compromise through the Civil War and Reconstruction, significant Supreme Court cases such as *Dred Scott v. Sanford*, *Plessy v. Ferguson*, and *Brown v. Board of Education*, the civil rights movement, Black Power, affirmative action and the backlash against policies that provide preferences to members of minority groups, and the 2008 candidacy of President Barack Obama.

In examining public opinion on racial issues, we should recognize that the period for which we have reliable survey information is also one during which there have been a number of significant upheavals in race relations in the United States. As noted by Mayer (1992: 22), "In little more than two decades, a racial caste system that had prevailed for more than three centuries was stripped of every vestige of legal and moral support." It is important, therefore, to consider the historical context within which public opinion has developed in describing the current state of the American mind on racial issues.

In their examination of racial attitudes in America, Schuman and his colleagues (1997: 2–29) traced the history of such attitudes in this country, from Thomas Jefferson's inability to conceive of a harmonious biracial society through the development of "biological racism," the shift to racial equalitarianism in American ideas, and the civil rights movement. As part of this research, they identified six aspects of recent history that are important to an understanding of trends in racial attitudes: (1) a period of prelude to civil rights politics, that involved the discrediting of theories of biological racism; (2) the growing importance of "black ballots" in American politics; (3) the establishment of effective civil rights organizations; (4) crucial Supreme Court rulings; (5) the passage of landmark legislation, such as the 1964 Civil Rights Act; and (6) disputes over the unfinished civil rights agenda (1997: 8). Consideration of these factors is essential to understanding trends in public opinion on racial matters.

Although considerable data on racial attitudes are available from recent years, there are few data on this topic from the early period of survey research. As Sheatsley has noted, the leading polling organizations had little interest in the study of racial attitudes during the 1930s. In his view, "The polls, for obvious reasons, tend to ask questions about issues that are hot, and it is clear that during the decade preceding World War II, race relations did not qualify on that basis, at least not for the elites who devised polls" (1966: 217).

Data on public attitudes on racial issues that are available indicate that "the expressed attitudes of white Americans toward black Americans have undergone a great transformation over the last forty or fifty years, a change greater than on any other issue" (Page and Shapiro, 1992: 68). Though most Americans today believe in desegregation and are in favor of government action to enforce legal equality, this was not the case 50 years ago. As Page and Shapiro note, "In the early and middle 1940s, then, large majorities of whites took for granted that blacks should be consigned to separate public accommodations, separate schools, and separate neighborhoods" (68–69). Examining public opinion on racial issues provides a unique opportunity to track substantial changes in the American mind that correspond with a rather turbulent period in race relations in this country.

RACIAL DESEGREGATION

The nature of the questions that are included in surveys such as the National Election Studies (NES) and the General Social Survey (GSS) also reflect the changing character of racial issues in the United States. The issue of racial desegregation is one that, in Carmines and Stimson's (1989: 14) terms, has had great long-term impact on the political system since the formation of the New Deal. Schuman and his colleagues' (1997: 77) discussion of the issue of school desegregation reports that in 1942 the percentage of white respondents who felt that white students and black students should go to the same schools was 32%, which rose to 50% in 1956, 84% by 1972, and 90% in 1982. Page and Shapiro's analysis (1992: 69) found that the overall change on this issue "of more than sixty percentage points was the largest for any policy preference of any kind among the thousands we have examined." Data from the GSS show that by 1985, 93% of the public believed white and black students should go to the same schools. Given the large change in attitudes that occurred on this issue between 1942 and 1985, responses to this item "can no longer show substantial overall change for the simple reason that part of the sample is already close to unanimity in choosing the positive response" (Schuman et al., 1997: 104). In sum, this issue went from one in which there was a deep division in the American mind to one on which there is a **consensus** (Frankenberg and Jacobsen, 2011).[1]

Even as the public reached agreement that white and black children should go to the same schools, there was considerable disagreement as to how school desegregation should be achieved and the government's role in this effort. In the early 1970s, **busing** public school students from areas where they lived to schools in other areas was a method used by school districts to reduce segregation. In 1971, the U.S. Supreme Court, in the case of *Swann v. Charlotte-Mecklenburg School District* (1971) held that lower federal courts could order busing as an appropriate remedy to end dual school systems. School busing plans were implemented in a number of American cities during the early 1970s, but court rulings gradually moved away from forced busing as a means of achieving school integration. In September 2001, a federal appeals court ruled that court-ordered desegregation in the Charlotte-Mecklenburg schools should end. The school board voted unanimously not to appeal this ruling, bringing to a close this landmark case that served as the basis for the use of busing to address the issue of segregated schools.

Data from both the NES and the GSS show that public sentiment on this issue was overwhelmingly opposed to busing as a means to achieve racial integration in schools. In the NES question on busing asked between 1972 and 1984, the percentage of "anti-busing" responses varied between 83% and 86%. This conclusion is supported by the results from the GSS question, asked between 1972 and 1996, for which the percentage opposed to busing ranged from 84% (1976) to 62% (1996). Opposition to busing appeared to be strongest during the period when the courts were ordering more school busing plans to be implemented (1972–1977) and declined somewhat as the courts moved away from this position.

As might be expected, there were significant differences in the opinions of blacks and whites on the question of busing. On the NES question close to 90% of whites took a "keep in neighborhood schools" position, and in each year this question was asked the percentage of whites who held this view was significantly higher than the percentage of blacks. The GSS data also show large racial differences, reaching as high as 48% (85% versus 37%) in 1974, with a difference of 25% (66% versus 41%) in 1996. Moreover, these data indicate that during the height of the busing period a majority of blacks were opposed to busing black and white school children from one school district to another. In examining similar questions, Page and Shapiro (1992: 73) concluded that a substantial proportion of blacks have opposed busing, "presumably because the hassle and disruption (if only as a result of white opposition) are seen to outweigh the benefits." Overall, a solid majority of about two-thirds of the American public was opposed to busing throughout the period from 1972 to 1996. As Sears, Hensler, and Speer (1979: 371) have noted, busing is an issue that "the mass white public has been strongly opposed to . . . ever since it has become a visible public issue." As busing faded as a policy for achieving racial integration in schools, the NES and GSS have discontinued asking questions on this issue, with the most recent measure available in the 1996 GSS.

Public opinion on residential integration has followed a path similar to that for school desegregation. An NES question on whether "white people have a right to keep black people out of their neighborhood if they want to, or black people have a right to live wherever they can afford to, just like anybody else" demonstrates that opinions on residential integration have moved in a liberal direction. In 1964, 32% of respondents felt that white people had the right to keep black people out of their neighborhood if they wanted to; by 1976, only 9% expressed this view.

A parallel question asked by the National Opinion Research Center (NORC)[2] covers a longer time period but shows the same pattern. When NORC asked the question in 1963, 60% of white respondents agreed that white people had a right to keep black people out of their neighborhood if they wanted to; in 1968, 56% agreed and in 1970, 47% agreed (Schuman et al. 1997: 106). When asked in the GSS beginning in 1972, close to 40% of white respondents agreed that white people had a right to keep black people out of their neighborhoods. After 1977, this percentage slowly declined until by 1996 only 13% agreed with this statement. In little more than 30 years, the percentage of whites who believed that white people have a right to keep blacks out of their neighborhood had declined by about 45%.

As was the case for school desegregation, there were significant differences in the opinions of blacks and whites on this issue. On the NES question, blacks were virtually unanimous throughout the period in their view that blacks have a right to live wherever they can afford. However, among whites, the percentage expressing this sentiment increased from 65% in 1964 to 90% in 1976. On the GSS question, a higher percentage of blacks than whites in each year disagreed that whites have a right to keep blacks out of their neighborhood, with the trend showing the gap between the races tending to narrow over time. By 1996, 96% of blacks and 87% of whites disagreed with the idea that whites had the right to keep black people out of their neighborhood if they wanted to.

By the end of the 20th century, Americans had reached a consensus on the issue of racial segregation. The American mind has shifted from a widespread acceptance of segregation in the 1940s to a new and equally widespread commitment to racial equality and integration (Schuman et al., 1997).

FAIR EMPLOYMENT PRACTICES

Although the American public has reached a consensus on the question of desegregation, there are much greater divisions of opinion on other issues, such as jobs, affirmative action, and federal spending to aid minority groups as well as over the role the government should play in addressing these issues. One such issue involves the treatment of minorities in terms of job opportunities. Unfortunately the NES and GSS do not include a "pure" measure of this issue that asks simply "whether minorities should receive fair treatment in jobs"; instead, the items that deal with this question all include some measure of whether ensuring fair treatment should be the "government's business," so that responses to these questions tap not only views on minority opportunities but also the government's role in this issue.

The NES item asked in strongly-agree/strongly-disagree format from 1956 to 1960 found that about 70% of the American public agreed that if minorities were not getting fair treatment in jobs and housing, the government should see to it that they do. In the forced-choice version of this item asked in 1964, 1968, and 1972, the public was more divided on this issue, with 45% saying that the government should see to it that blacks get fair treatment in jobs, 47% believing that this was not the government's business, and 8% giving a middle response. There is a gap between 1972 and 1986 in which a question like this was not asked; a slightly different version of this item introduced in the NES in 1986 showed that from the late 1980s through 2008, roughly 53% of the public believed that the government should see to it that minorities get fair treatment in jobs (Table 9.1).

Table 9.1. Attitudes toward Minority Employment, 1986–2008 (percent)[a]

Year	Government Should See to It	Other; Depends	Not Government's Business
1986	56	4	40
1988	54	5	41
1992	55	3	41
1996	48	4	47
2000	53	4	43
2004	54	3	43
2008	52	4	43

[a]The question asked was, "Should the government in Washington see to it that Negroes (colored people/black people) get fair treatment in jobs, or is this not the federal government's business?"

Source: American National Election Studies.

Table 9.2.   Attitudes toward Minority Employment by Race, 1956–2008 (percentage saying that government should see to fair treatment)[a]

Year	Whites	Blacks	Year	Whites	Blacks
1956	68	97	1988	48	90
1958	70	97	1992	49	89
1960	69	98	1996	42	92
1964	39	94	2000	46	90
1968	38	89	2004	42	87
1972	45	91	2008	43	88
1986	47	90			

[a]The questions asked were, (1952–1960): "If Negroes are not getting fair treatment in jobs and housing, the government should see to it that they do." (1964–1972): "Should the government in Washington see to it that Negroes (colored people/black people) get fair treatment in jobs or leave these matters to the states and local communities?" (1968–2008): "Should the government in Washington see to it that Negroes (colored people/black people) get fair treatment in jobs, or is this not the federal government's business?"

Source: American National Election Studies.

There is a stark contrast in the opinions of blacks and whites on this issue (Table 9.2). From 1956 to 1960, blacks were virtually unanimous in their view that if minorities were not getting fair treatment in jobs and housing, the government should see to it that they do. In contrast, the percentage of whites who expressed this sentiment hovered around 70%. On the forced-choice versions of this item (1964–1972 and 1986–2008), the percentage of black respondents who said that the government in Washington should see to it that minorities get fair treatment in jobs was consistently around 90%, while the percentage of whites who shared this view ranged between 38% (1968) and 49% (1992). In 2008, 88% of blacks and 43% of whites felt the government in Washington should see to it that minorities get fair treatment in jobs. In this year, the opinion of Hispanics was between that of blacks and whites, with 60% of this group believing that Washington should see to fair treatment for minorities.

AFFIRMATIVE ACTION

The earlier discussion of school desegregation described the sharp contrast between Americans' support for the general principle of integrated schools and their opposition to a specific approach to achieving this goal, school busing. A similar contrast exists in the public's views on the general principle of fair treatment in jobs for minorities and achieving this end through affirmative action.

In an attempt to put teeth into the 1964 Civil Rights Act, in 1965, President Lyndon Johnson first applied the concept of **affirmative action**—which is a policy that gives special consideration or compensatory treatment to traditionally disadvantaged groups in an effort to overcome the effects of past discrimination. By the early 1970s, regulations imposing numerous employment goals and timetables had been applied to every company that did more than $10,000 worth of business of any sort with the national government (Schmidt, Shelley, and Bardes, 2005: 172).

Affirmative action programs have always been controversial, because they sometimes result in discriminatory acts against majority groups. An early Supreme Court case dealing with this issue was *Regents of the University of California v. Bakke* (1978), which involved a white student, Alan Bakke, who had been denied admission to medical school at the Davis campus of the University of California, even though his academic record was better than those of some minority applicants who got into the program. In this case, the Supreme Court ruled that race could be one of many criteria for admission, but not the only one. In so doing, they held that affirmative action programs, but not specific quota systems, were constitutional. Later Supreme Court rulings, such as in the case of *Adarand Constructors, Inc. v. Pena* (1995), have further limited the principle of affirmative action. The Court's current position is that any program that uses racial or ethnic classifications must be narrowly tailored to meet a compelling government interest.

In the years following the *Adarand* decision the U.S. Supreme Court chose not to confront the issue of affirmative action and left to the lower courts the responsibility for determining if government programs designed to aid disadvantaged minority-owned businesses met the strict scrutiny and compelling government interest criteria it had established (*Adarand Constructors., Inc. v. Mineta*, 2001). In two of its more recent decisions in the area the court has found support for affirmative action programs in one and ruled against them in another.

In the case of *Grutter v. Bollinger et al.* (2003), the Supreme Court held that the use of race as an admissions criteria by the University of Michigan law school was constitutional, in that this use was narrowly tailored to further a compelling interest in obtaining the educational benefits that flow from a diverse student body. This ruling shifted the rationale for the use of a race as a criterion from providing opportunities for traditionally disadvantaged minorities to ensuring student body diversity as "a compelling state interest in the context of university admissions." On the other hand, the case of *Ricci v. DeStefano* (2009) is one in which the Supreme Court limited affirmative action remedies. This case involved white and Hispanic firefighters in New Haven, Connecticut, whose promotions were denied because the results of the exams on which the promotions were based were racially biased and produced a negative disparate impact on racial minorities. The Court ruled in this case that disparately poor performance by members of minority groups was not a sufficient condition for not implementing the results of the exams.

Other events have also sought to limit affirmative action programs. In November 1996, for example, voters in California were asked to consider Proposition 209, also known as the California Civil Rights Initiative, which stated: "The state shall not discriminate against, or grant preferential treatment to, any individual or group on the basis of race, sex, color, ethnicity, or national origin in the operation of public employment, public education, or public contracting." This initiative passed by a margin of 55% to 45%. After a court challenge that delayed its implementation, the U.S. Circuit Court held Proposition 209 to be constitutional. Similar attempts to limit affirmative action were successful in other states, such as Washington (1998) and Michigan (2006), although the Michigan ban on the consideration of race and gender when enrolling students at public colleges and universities was later declared unconstitutional. In 2008, five states were targeted for ballot initiatives that would limit affirmative action, but these efforts were unsuccessful in four of them (Larson et al., 2008).

Surveys on this topic demonstrate that the American public has consistently been opposed to affirmative action. This issue was first addressed in the National Election Studies in 1978 when respondents were asked whether "minorities and women should be given preferential treatment in jobs and admissions" or if "only an individual's experience and ability should count." The opposition to affirmative action was clearly evident on this question, with 11% supporting preferential treatment and 78% believing that only ability or experience should be considered.

This form of the question appeared only in the 1978 NES, and when the issue was next addressed in 1986 the NES asked whether blacks should be given preference in hiring and promotion because of past discrimination or whether such practices were wrong because they gave blacks advantages they haven't earned. As the data in Table 9.3 indicate, public opinion as measured by this question was decidedly opposed to preferential treatment, with between 75% and 86% of respondents during this period saying they opposed preferential treatment. Results from the GSS question asked since 1994 reinforce this conclusion, with 80% or more of respondents in each year opposing preferences in the hiring and promotion of blacks (Table 9.4). As Citrin (1996: 40) has noted, "[W]here specific policies are concerned, it is clear the 'soft' opportunity-enhancing approaches are accepted, while 'hard' preference-giving programs are widely unpopular."

The expected racial differences on this question are evident in Table 9.5. Both the NES and GSS questions indicate that more than four-fifths of white respondents in each year opposed preferences in the hiring and promotion of African Americans, with the greatest opposition (91%) occurring in 1994. Although blacks were much less likely to oppose preferential treatment, their opinion on this issue varies more than that of whites. The largest percentage of blacks in favor of preferences (74%) was found in the 1990

Table 9.3. Opinions on Affirmative Action (National Election Studies), 1986–2008 (percent)[a]

Year	Strongly For	For—Not Strongly	Against—Not Strongly	Strongly Against
1986	12	12	20	56
1988	12	8	17	63
1990	15	9	20	55
1992	11	8	18	63
1994	8	6	22	64
1996	11	6	17	66
1998	13	6	22	59
2000	11	6	22	61
2004	11	8	24	57
2008	10	7	21	62

[a]The question asked was, "Should blacks be given preference in hiring and promotion because of past discrimination, or is such preference in hiring and promotion of blacks wrong because it gives blacks advantages they haven't earned?" In 1988, the second option read, "wrong because it discriminates against whites" rather than "wrong because it gives blacks advantages they haven't earned."

Source: American National Election Studies.

NES survey. Although the NES data for 2008 still indicate that less than a majority of blacks is opposed to preferences in hiring and promotion, the GSS data for this year, as well those going back to 1996, show a majority of blacks opposed to such preferences.[3] In 2010, the view of Hispanics on the issue of affirmative action fell between those of blacks and whites, although somewhat closer to the position of blacks; 68% of Hispanics in the GSS said they were opposed to preferences in hiring and promotion.[4]

Table 9.4. Opinions on Affirmative Action (General Social Surveys), 1994–2010 (percent)[a]

Year	Strongly Support Preferences	Support Preferences	Oppose Preferences	Strongly Oppose Preferences
1994	10	7	26	57
1996	10	7	27	56
1998	8	7	25	60
2000	12	8	28	54
2002	10	7	28	56
2004	10	7	28	55
2006	9	6	27	57
2008	10	7	27	56
2010	11	8	28	53

[a]The question asked was, "Some people say that because of past discrimination, blacks should be given preference in hiring and promotion. Others say that such preference in hiring and promotion of blacks is wrong because it discriminates against whites. What is your opinion—are you for or against preferential hiring and promotion of blacks?"

Source: General Social Surveys.

Table 9.5.   Opinions on Affirmative Action by Race (percentage opposed to preferences in hiring and promotion)

Year	Whites	Blacks	Year	Whites	Blacks
NES			**GSS**		
1986	85	31	1994	89	44
1988	87	35	1996	89	50
1990	82	26	1998	89	61
1992	87	44	2000	87	56
1994	91	50	2002	90	56
1996	88	38	2004	89	53
1998	87	38	2006	90	60
2000	90	36	2008	88	54
2004	88	47	2010	88	56
2008	89	47			

Sources: American National Election Studies (NES) and General Social Surveys (GSS).

GOVERNMENT AID TO MINORITY GROUPS

Another race-related item that has been asked of the American public in the NES since 1970 involves not a specific aspect of discrimination, such as school integration or jobs, but rather the general question of government aid to minority groups. Beginning in 1970, and in almost every NES since, respondents have been asked, "Should the government help blacks and other minority groups or should minority groups help themselves?" Responses to this seven-point scale item are provided in Table 9.6 and summarized in Figure 9.1.

If we treat responses 1, 2, and 3 as representing the liberal side of this issue and 5, 6, and 7 as the conservative stance, these results indicate that more Americans consistently place themselves on the "minorities help themselves" end of the spectrum. Moreover, the proportion adopting this position has tended to increase during this period. In 1970, about one-third of the public was on the "government help minority groups" side of this issue, while about 40% thought that minority groups should help themselves. With slight variations, this pattern was evident through the mid-1980s. In the late 1980s, there was a shift in the conservative direction, with a majority falling on the "minorities help themselves" side of the issue in 1988, 1992, 1994, and 1996. The highest percentage on the conservative side of this issue (59%) was found in 1996. This percentage declined to 44% in 1998, then rose to more than a majority in 2000, 2004, and 2008.

In what should be becoming a familiar pattern by this point, there were significant differences in black and white opinion on this issue throughout this period (Table 9.7). The views of blacks and whites on this question were substantially different when this question was first asked. In 1970, 84% of blacks were on the "government should aid minority groups" side

Table 9.6. Government Help Blacks and Other Minority Groups, 1970–2008 (percent)[a]

Year	1. Government Help Minorities	2.	3.	4.	5.	6.	7. Minorities Help Themselves
1970	15	8	8	25	12	11	21
1972	13	7	13	24	11	12	19
1974	14	7	12	24	12	9	22
1976	13	9	13	22	12	10	21
1978	12	6	10	25	16	12	19
1980	5	5	12	30	21	13	14
1982	8	6	11	30	16	17	12
1984	9	8	15	31	18	10	9
1986	9	7	13	31	19	12	9
1988	8	5	9	24	16	15	22
1990	8	7	11	26	15	15	17
1992	6	5	11	26	16	15	21
1994	5	5	10	26	17	17	20
1996	4	4	10	23	20	19	20
1998	10	8	11	28	15	13	16
2000	6	4	8	27	16	17	20
2004	9	6	9	25	17	17	18
2008	7	6	9	23	14	16	26

[a]The question asked was, "Some people feel that the government in Washington should make every effort to improve the social and economic position of blacks. Others feel that the government should not make any special effort to help blacks because they should help themselves. Where would you place yourself on this scale, or haven't you thought much about this?"

Source: American National Election Studies.

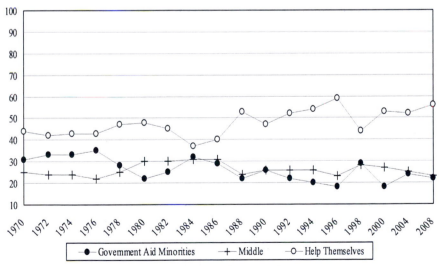

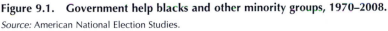

Figure 9.1. Government help blacks and other minority groups, 1970–2008.

Source: American National Election Studies.

Table 9.7.   Government Help Blacks and Other Minority Groups by Race, 1970–2008 (percentage saying that government should help minorities)

Year	Whites	Blacks	Year	Whites	Blacks
1970	25	84	1988	18	44
1972	29	78	1990	22	52
1974	27	79	1992	19	43
1976	30	72	1994	17	43
1978	23	65	1996	16	40
1980	18	51	1998	24	52
1982	21	58	2000	16	37
1984	28	59	2004	18	47
1986	26	47	2008	16	51

Source: American National Election Studies.

of this question compared to 25% of whites, and in 1972 78% of blacks and 29% of whites gave a liberal response. The gap between black and white opinion tended to narrow during this period, and by 2000 there was only a 21% difference (37% to 16%) in the percentage of blacks and whites who gave this response. This gap widened again in 2004 and 2008, and in 2008 the difference between the races stood at 35% (51% to 16%). Even though the percentage of whites who felt that government should aid minority groups declined between 1970 and 2008, the gap in opinion between the races has narrowed during this period due to a steeper decline in the percentage of blacks who thought that government should help minority groups. Although the percentage of blacks who believed that government should aid minorities approached a consensus in 1970, this percentage has generally been slightly below 50% since 1986. In 2008, blacks remain significantly more likely than whites to feel that government should aid minority groups, but over the past 35 years, there has been an increasing sentiment among blacks that minority groups should be more responsible for helping themselves.

The GSS data on this topic over the past 35 years lead to a similar conclusion, although these data show less fluctuation than those for the NES item (Table 9.8). Throughout this period, the percentage who held that there should be no special treatment of blacks was substantially greater than the percentage who felt that the government had a special obligation to help improve living standards for blacks. The percentage on the "no special treatment" side of this question ranged from a low of 44% in 1987 to 55% in 1983, while the percentage on the "government should help blacks" side ranged from 15% (2004) to 28% (1987). The percentage holding a middle position on this issue has consistently been around 30%.

A significantly higher percentage of blacks than whites hold opinions on the "government help blacks" side of the issue (Table 9.9). Although this

Table 9.8. Government Improve Living Standards for Blacks, 1975–2010 (percent)[a]

Year	1. Government Should Help Blacks	2.	3. Agree with Both	4.	5. No Special Treatment
1975	12	9	32	12	41
1983	8	10	27	21	34
1984	10	10	31	18	31
1986	8	10	29	18	34
1987	16	12	29	16	28
1988	8	10	30	18	35
1989	9	10	28	19	34
1990	10	10	34	17	28
1991	11	12	32	19	27
1993	7	10	33	21	28
1994	8	8	30	24	30
1996	8	9	30	24	29
1998	7	11	32	22	29
2000	10	10	33	20	27
2002	8	8	32	20	32
2004	8	7	32	20	34
2006	9	7	34	19	30
2008	9	7	35	20	30
2010	9	9	30	20	32

[a] The question asked was, "Some people think that (Blacks/Negroes) have been discriminated against for so long that the government has a special obligation to help improve their living standards. Others believe that the government should not be giving special treatment to (Blacks/Negroes). Where would you place yourself on this scale, or haven't you made up your mind?"

Source: General Social Surveys.

Table 9.9. Government Improve Living Standards for Blacks by Race, 1975–2010 (percentage saying that government should help blacks)

Year	Whites	Blacks	Year	Whites	Blacks
1975	20	68	1994	10	51
1983	13	57	1996	12	47
1984	15	54	1998	14	39
1986	13	56	2000	13	51
1987	15	55	2002	12	44
1988	12	58	2004	10	39
1989	14	54	2006	12	44
1990	16	54	2008	11	42
1991	16	61	2010	13	40
1993	12	53			

Source: General Social Surveys.

difference in opinion between the races has fluctuated slightly over time, the average difference across these 19 surveys has been approximately 40%, with the difference between black and white opinions on this item narrowing some in recent years.

The views of Hispanics on these two questions in the most recent NES and GSS surveys again fell between those of blacks and whites. On the NES (2008) question, 27% of Hispanics felt that the government should help minorities (compared to 51% of blacks and 16% of whites), while on the GSS (2010) question the percentage who said the government should help blacks was 29% for Hispanic respondents, 40% for blacks, and 13% for whites.

SPENDING ON RACIAL ISSUES

In the GSS, opinions on the general question of race have been tapped by two items on spending. Between 1973 and 2010, the GSS has included an item on whether we are spending too much, too little, or about the right amount on improving the condition of blacks, while from 1984 to 2010 these surveys have contained an item on spending for "assistance to blacks." The data for these items are presented in Tables 9.10 and 9.11.

One of the most striking features of these results is the remarkable consistency in the percentage of people who said "about the right amount" to each of these items. On the question of "improving the condition of blacks," the percentage who gave the middle response only varied between 42% and 50% over the 27 times this item has been asked, while the "about the right amount" response to the assistance to blacks item varied only between 41% and 52% across 18 surveys.

There is slightly more variation in the percentage giving either the "too much" or "too little" responses. For the "improving the condition of blacks" item, 35% said that we were spending "too little" in 1973. This percentage declined slightly during the 1970s, then began to increase through the 1980s, reaching a peak of 41% in 1990, then declining again slightly through the 2010 survey. In 1973 and 1974 the percentage that responded "too little" to this question was about 10% greater than the percentage saying "too much." During the period from 1975 to 1983 the percentage voicing these alternatives was relatively equal. From 1984 to the present, the percentage of "too little" responses has—with minor variation—been about 20% higher than that for the "too much" position. In 2010, the difference in the percentage choosing these two alternatives was 15% (32% to 17%).

For the question on spending on assistance to blacks, there has been a relative balance over this period in the number of "too little" and "too much" responses, with the plurality of respondents choosing the "about the

Table 9.10. Opinions about Spending and Improving the Conditions of Blacks, 1973–2010 (percent)[a]

Year	Too Little	About the Right Amount	Too Much
1973	35	42	23
1974	33	45	22
1975	29	44	26
1976	30	43	28
1977	28	46	26
1978	26	47	27
1980	27	48	25
1982	30	48	22
1983	32	47	21
1984	38	46	16
1985	32	46	22
1986	37	46	16
1987	37	46	16
1988	38	45	17
1989	37	46	17
1990	41	43	16
1991	39	45	16
1993	39	44	22
1994	34	44	22
1996	35	43	21
1998	38	44	18
2000	38	46	16
2002	33	49	18
2004	35	50	16
2006	37	47	16
2008	38	48	14
2010	32	50	17

[a]The question asked was, "Are we spending too much money, too little money, or about the right amount on improving the conditions of Blacks?"

Source: General Social Surveys.

right amount" option. The largest differences in the percentages choosing the extreme options occur in 1991 (15%) and in 2000 (12%), with a larger percentage believing that too little is being spent. Although there is a slight tendency for the American public to believe that too little rather than too much is being spent in these areas, a large plurality of the public feels that about the right amount is being spent on improving the condition of blacks and on assistance to blacks.[5]

The data on racial differences in attitudes on these spending items, presented in Table 9.12, extend the pattern of substantial distinctions in the views of blacks and whites. Throughout this period the average percentage

Table 9.11.　Opinions about Spending on Assistance to Blacks, 1984–2010 (percent)[a]

Year	Too Little	About the Right Amount	Too Much
1984	26	46	28
1985	29	45	26
1986	23	48	29
1987	28	48	24
1988	29	46	25
1989	31	45	24
1990	31	46	23
1991	35	45	20
1993	27	45	28
1994	27	44	29
1996	27	45	28
1998	30	45	25
2000	35	42	23
2002	27	47	26
2004	30	50	20
2006	28	46	26
2008	31	47	22
2010	28	49	22

[a]The question asked was, "Are we spending too much money, too little money, or about the right amount on assistance to Blacks?"

Source: General Social Surveys.

of black respondents who thought that "too little" was being spent on improving the condition of blacks was 80%, with the percentage ranging from a high of 89% in 1982 to 69% in 2002. Conversely, the percentage of whites who thought too little was being spent on this activity averaged 27% over this span, and ranged from 19% in 1978 to 34% in 1990.

The breakdowns by race of the data for spending on assistance to blacks show a similar pattern. The average percentage of blacks saying "too little" was 76% and varied between 62% and 82%, while the average percentage for whites was 21% and ranged between 16% and 27%. Throughout this period, blacks were much more likely than whites to express the view that too little was being spent on programs designed to benefit minorities.

The views of Hispanics on the issue of spending for assistance to blacks again fall between those of blacks and whites, although they are much closer to those of whites. On the 2010 item on spending to improve the condition of blacks, 35% of Hispanics said that too little was being spent, compared to 71% of blacks and 24% of whites. On the 2010 assistance to blacks item the percentage of "too little" responses was 29% among Hispanics, 62% among blacks, and 20% for whites.

Table 9.12.   Opinions about Spending on Racial Issues by Race,
1973–2010 (percentage saying spending "too little")

	Improving		Assistance	
Year	Whites	Blacks	Whites	Blacks
1973	28	83	—	—
1974	26	82	—	—
1975	22	84	—	—
1976	24	83	—	—
1977	20	80	—	—
1978	19	83	—	—
1980	20	80	—	—
1982	23	89	—	—
1983	27	80	—	—
1984	32	71	20	77
1985	28	70	22	81
1986	29	75	17	78
1987	32	80	21	82
1988	30	81	21	79
1989	30	83	24	79
1990	34	82	22	80
1991	29	82	27	73
1993	32	84	20	74
1994	25	81	18	77
1996	26	85	19	72
1998	31	75	21	71
2000	30	78	24	78
2002	25	69	16	73
2004	27	80	20	74
2006	29	80	19	74
2008	31	81	21	78
2010	24	71	20	62

Source: General Social Surveys.

OTHER ISSUES OF RACE: HISTORICAL AND CONTEMPORARY

There are many other issues that could be examined to describe the American mind on the issue of race. The questions that have been included in the NES and GSS over time provide a measure not only of citizen perceptions of important race-related historical events such as slavery and the civil rights movement, but also demonstrate how the public's views have evolved and how changes in opinion have differed for blacks and whites.

Black Candidate for President

A question that reflects the interest in racial issues and changes in the public's attitudes is an item on voting for a minority candidate for president. Beginning in 1958 the Gallup Poll asked people whether or not they would vote for a black candidate for president if one were nominated by their party and he were qualified for the job. In the late 1950s, approximately 40% of white respondents said that they would vote for a minority candidate for president, a percentage that rose to 60% by 1965, and to 75% when the question was first asked in the GSS in 1972. Between 1972 and 1996 the GSS included the item, "If your party nominated a (Negro/Black/African-American) for president, would you vote for him if he were qualified for the job?" Given the results for this item, the GSS dropped this item after 1996 but began asking it again in 2008 with the candidacy of Barack Obama.

Results for the GSS question for the complete sample and by race are presented in Figure 9.2.[6] In 1974, 84% of those interviewed indicated that they would vote for a qualified minority candidate for president. This already high percentage increased slightly over time and remained at about 90% throughout the 1990s. This virtual consensus led the GSS to drop this item as a "non-issue"; when it became salient with President Obama's candidacy in 2008, 94% indicated they would vote for a qualified minority candidate and 97% expressed this view in 2010.

In 1972, three-fourths of white respondents said they would be willing to vote for their party's nominee if he were black. This percentage slowly increased, and by 1996 92% expressed this view. In a 1999 Gallup Poll this percentage had risen to 95%, and in 2003 this percentage was 93%. In the 2008 GSS 94% of whites said they would vote for a minority candidate, and by 2010 this percentage had reached 97%. Not surprisingly, throughout

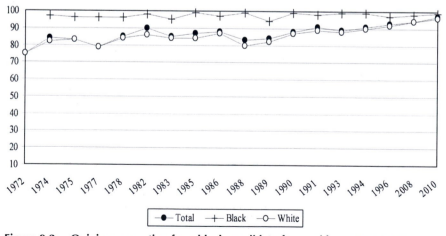

Figure 9.2.   Opinions on voting for a black candidate for president, 1972–2010.
Source: General Social Surveys.

this period blacks have been almost unanimous in their willingness to support a candidate of their race. Over the past 50 years public sentiment has changed from a point at which less than a majority indicated a willingness to vote for a black person for president to a virtual consensus on this issue.

Slavery

In describing the role of slavery on racial issues, Carmines and Stimson (1989: 62) note that the "only time that seems a reasonably certain origin for racial controversy in America would be the date the first black slave was brought ashore. . . . we ought not to look for the origin of racial issues in American politics because racial issues predate American politics." The shape of the American mind on the question of the effect of slavery shows that the public generally feels that generations of slavery and discrimination have created conditions that make it difficult for African Americans to work their way up (Table 9.13). When this question was first asked in the NES in 1972, a clear majority of those surveyed agreed that previous discrimination made it difficult for blacks.[7] In 1986, 61% agreed with this statement, 30% disagreed, and 9% neither agreed nor disagreed. The percentage agreeing dropped to about 50% in 1988 and remained at about that level through 1994. The change in question wording (from "for blacks to work their way up" to "for blacks to work their way out of the lower class") also brought a change in the distribution of opinion. In the two years in which this version of the question was asked, the percentage who agreed that generations of slavery have made conditions difficult dropped to about 40%, and a higher percentage disagreed with this statement.[8]

Table 9.13. Opinions on the Impact of Slavery (percent)[a]

Year[b]	Agree a Great Deal (Strongly)	Agree Somewhat	Neither Agree nor Disagree	Disagree Somewhat	Disagree a Great Deal (Strongly)
1972	30%	42	—	16	12
1986	21	40	9	18	12
1988	16	34	12	24	14
1990	19	35	12	22	12
1992	19	34	10	23	14
1994	14	33	11	24	18
2000	11	28	12	25	24
2008	12	29	14	24	20

[a]The questions asked were (1972–1994): "Generations of slavery and discrimination have created conditions that make it difficult for blacks to work their way up." (2000, 2008): "Generations of slavery and discrimination have created conditions that make it difficult for blacks to work their way out of the lower class."
[b]In 2000 and 2008, the response choice "Agree a Great Deal" was changed to "Agree Strongly" and the choice "Disagree a Great Deal" was changed to "Disagree Strongly."

Source: American National Election Studies.

Although the differences in opinion between blacks and whites on this issue are significant, they are not as large as those for many of the issues examined previously in this chapter. Since 1986, an average of 46% of whites and 67% of blacks have agreed that a history of slavery and discrimination have made it difficult for blacks. Although there have been some slight fluctuations in this trend over time, the tendency is in the direction of fewer people agreeing with this item, and the change in this direction is evident among both blacks and whites (Figure 9.3).

Civil Rights

The civil rights movement has played a central role in shaping contemporary attitudes on racial issues. In 1964, the NES instituted a question on whether respondents thought that civil rights leaders were trying to push too fast, going too slowly, or moving at about the right speed. At the height of the civil rights movement in the mid-1960s, close to two-thirds of the public felt that civil rights leaders were trying to push too fast. As the civil rights movement made gains, this percentage declined to about 50% in 1970 and 1972, with around 40% in these two years saying the speed of the civil rights movement was about right and the remaining 10% feeling that it was not moving fast enough. The percentage who felt that civil rights leaders were trying to move too fast continued to decline until 1986, when it reached about 25%, and it remained at about this level through 1992. Between 1976 and 1992 (the last year in which the NES asked this question), a majority of respondents felt that civil rights leaders were moving at about the right speed, while about one-sixth of those surveyed felt the civil rights movement was going too slowly.

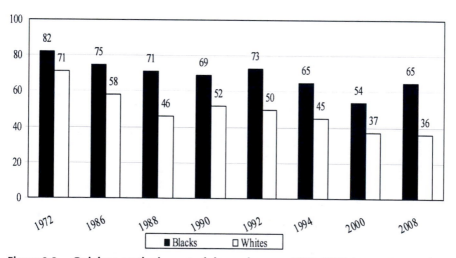

Figure 9.3. Opinions on the impact of slavery by race, 1972–2008 (percentage saying "made it difficult").

Source: American National Election Studies.

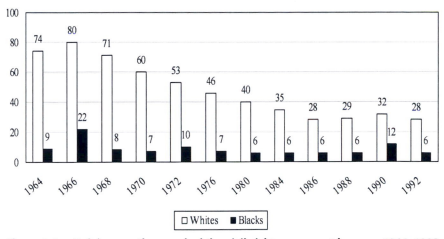

Figure 9.4. Opinions on the speed of the civil rights movement by race, 1964–1992 (percentage saying "going too fast").

Source: American National Election Studies.

Throughout this era of the civil rights movement, the opinions of blacks and whites on this question showed significant differences in outlook, with the decrease in the distinction over time resulting largely from changes in the opinions of whites (Figure 9.4). During this period, about one in ten or fewer black respondents has held the view that civil rights leaders are pushing too fast.[9] On the other hand, the percentage of whites who held this view declined significantly during the period this question was included in the NES. Close to three-fourths of white respondents in 1964, 1966, and 1968 said that civil rights leaders were trying to push too fast. This proportion declined until 1986, when it reached about 30%, where it remained in succeeding years. As was the case with the questions on spending to solve racial problems, blacks are more likely than whites to view the results of the civil rights movement as beneficial to them. It is not surprising, therefore, to find that fewer black respondents felt that civil rights leaders were pushing too fast to achieve their goals.

Interracial Marriage

The final issue examined in this chapter, opinions on interracial marriage, illustrates how opinions on racial matters have changed over time and the enduring differences between black and white opinion. Tables 9.14 and 9.15 provide the results for the question, "Do you think there should be laws against marriage between (Negroes/Blacks/African Americans) and whites?" for the complete sample and by race. Since the GSS did not ask this question of black respondents until 1980, cross-time comparisons for the general public cannot be made before this year. These data show that

Table 9.14. Opinions on Interracial Marriage (percent)[a]

Year[b]	Yes	No	Year[b]	Yes	No
1972	39	61	1988	22	78
1973	38	62	1989	21	79
1974	35	66	1990	19	81
1975	39	61	1991	19	81
1976	33	67	1993	17	83
1977	28	72	1994	14	86
1980	30	70	1996	11	89
1982	26	74	1998	11	89
1984	25	75	2000	10	90
1985	26	74	2002	10	90
1987	21	79			

[a]The question asked was, "Do you think there should be laws against marriage between (Negroes/Blacks/African-Americans) and whites?"
[b]From 1972 through 1977 this question was asked of white respondents only.

Source: General Social Surveys.

between 1980 and 2002 the percentage of the public that favored a law against interracial marriage declined steadily from 30% in 1980 to 10% in 2002. Moreover, there is evidence from the results for whites that this decline was even steeper, since in 1970 39% of whites favored such a law, a percentage which generally declined throughout the 1970s.

The percentage of blacks who have favored a law against interracial marriage has been less than the percentage of whites who favored such a law in each year that this question was asked, with the largest difference in support—33% of whites and 7% of blacks—occurring in 1982. After

Table 9.15. Opinions on Interracial Marriage by Race (percentage favoring a law against interracial marriage)

Year	Whites	Blacks	Year	Whites	Blacks
1972	39	—	1988	26	5
1973	38	—	1989	23	8
1974	35	—	1990	21	7
1975	39	—	1991	20	6
1976	33	—	1993	19	6
1977	28	—	1994	16	3
1980	31	18	1996	13	4
1982	33	7	1998	13	4
1984	27	7	2000	12	4
1985	28	7	2002	10	5
1987	27	8			

Source: General Social Surveys.

this year, the difference between blacks and whites narrowed as the percentage of whites who favored such a law has declined and the percentage of blacks remained at a very low level. By 2002, the American mind had reached consensus on this question, and it has since not been included as an issue in the GSS.

THE INCREASING INFLUENCE OF HISPANICS

The number of Hispanics is growing rapidly in this country. According to the 2010 Census, the Hispanic population outnumbered the black population by more than 10 million persons. The Hispanic population grew 43%—from 35.3 million to 50.5 million—between 2000 and 2010 and accounted for 56% of the nation's growth during this period. As Hispanics have become more visible across the country, this growth has become increasingly controversial in some places (Suro, Fry, and Passel, 2005). Moreover, attention has been given in recent years to the public's views on issues important to this group as well as its views compared to those of blacks and whites on topics that are part of the American mind. It is important to note, however, that Hispanics represent many different nations of origin and that their opinions on some issues may vary depending on their ethnic origin—whether their family came from Puerto Rico, Mexico, or Peru, for example. In 2001, the Pew Hispanic Center was established "to improve understanding of the U.S. Hispanic population and to chronicle Latinos' growing impact on the entire nation." The center regularly conducts public opinion surveys that aim to illuminate Latino views on a range of social matters and public policy issues.[10]

One issue that is considered to be of importance to Hispanics is immigration, a topic that will be covered more extensively in Chapter 10. A June 2011 Gallup Poll found that 43% of Americans say they want the level of immigration into the country decreased. About a third (35%) say they want immigration kept at its present level and 18% want it increased. The views of Hispanics on immigration are more positive than those of blacks and whites. Hispanics are consistently less likely to feel that the level of immigration into the country should be decreased and more likely to believe that immigration is a good thing for the country.

The distinct views of Hispanics on this issue are illustrated by reactions to a controversial immigration law passed in Arizona in April 2010, which would require police to verify the legal status of someone stopped or arrested, if the police suspect that person is in the country illegally. A February 2011 poll conducted by the Pew Research Center for the People and the Press (2011b) found that while a solid majority of Americans (61%) approves of this law, there are significant differences among whites, blacks, and Hispanics. The Arizona law was "supported by 72% of whites, but only 42% of blacks and just 27% of Hispanics."

For several issues examined in this chapter we have compared the views of Hispanics in recent years to those of blacks and whites, and the general pattern for these issues has been for the opinions of Hispanics to fall between those of blacks and whites. Table 9.16 shows the views of these groups for selected issues in 2008.

One exception to the general pattern of the views of Hispanics falling between those of blacks and whites is on the issue of trust in government. Although Hispanics are slightly more trusting than blacks or whites, they still exhibit a fairly low level of trust, a condition that was found among all subgroups, as reported in Chapter 7. Hispanics (56%) are also much more likely than whites (28%)—and very similar to blacks (54%)—to oppose the death penalty for murder. Hispanics were also similar to blacks in the percentage who call themselves liberals, somewhat more likely to self-define as conservatives, and less likely than blacks to identify themselves as middle-of-the-road.

In terms of party identification, a higher percentage of Hispanics identify with the Democratic Party than with the Republicans, and the percentage of Hispanics identifying with the two major parties falls between the percentages of blacks and whites. For the items on whether the government should do more things, government's seeing to fair employment, and whether government should help blacks, the percentage of Hispanics

Table 9.16.　Opinions of Whites, Blacks, and Hispanics on Selected Issues, 2008 (percent)

	Whites	Blacks	Hispanics
Ideological Identification			
Liberal	26	34	36
Middle-of-the-road	27	40	33
Conservative	46	26	31
Party Identification			
Democrat	27	70	44
Independent	41	27	39
Republican	32	3	17
Trust government only some of the time	70	72	65
Government should do more things	44	71	54
Government should see to fair employment	42	89	62
Opposed to preferences in hiring and promotion	89	47	77
Government should help blacks	15	51	29
Too little spending on assistance to the poor	66	93	73
Oppose death penalty for murder	28	54	56

Sources: American National Election Study and General Social Survey.

taking a particular position falls about halfway between those of blacks and whites, while the percentage of Hispanics is still in the middle, but closer to whites, for the items on affirmative action and government spending on assistance to the poor.

Though there is some evidence that the views of Hispanics fall between those of blacks and whites, there are issues such as immigration where the views of the Latino/a population are distinct from the other two groups and others for which the views of Hispanics are quite similar to those of either blacks or whites. Characterizing the views of this group relative to those of blacks and whites is largely dependent on the particular issue. As the proportion of Hispanics in the population continues to rise, their opinions will become an increasingly important component of the American mind.

SUMMARY

Overall, the data on race-related issues examined in this chapter demonstrate that there is a consensus in the American mind on the general idea of racial equality. Overwhelming majorities of the public believe that minorities have the right to live wherever they can afford, that white and black students should attend the same schools, and that minorities should receive fair treatment in jobs and housing. Similarly, there is a consensus on the question of willingness to vote for a qualified minority candidate for president.

The agreement on the general principle of racial equality in the American mind ebbs somewhat when the question of the government's role in ensuring equality is considered and diminishes even more when specific approaches for achieving this goal are evaluated. For example, the public is about evenly divided on the question of whether government should see to it that black people get fair treatment in jobs, but it has shown relatively strong opposition to specific solutions to this problem, such as affirmative action programs.

The findings discussed here are consistent with those of Lipset and Schneider (1978: 44), who reported that "on every issue we have analyzed, the public opinion data show a 'positive' pro-civil rights consensus when only egalitarian considerations are at stake, but a 'negative' anti-civil rights consensus when the issue also pushes up against basic notions of individualism." Most Americans favor equal rights and equal opportunity, but this consensus breaks down "when *compulsory integration* is involved" (44).

Other analyses of trends in racial attitudes have examined data similar to those displayed here and reached the conclusion that there has been a great deal of change in a "pro-integrationist" direction in white racial attitudes in the past 50 years (for example, Mayer, 1992; Page and Shapiro, 1992; Schuman, Steeh, Bobo, and Krysan, 1997). As summarized by Schuman and his colleagues (1997: 288), there have been "fundamental changes in the values of white Americans. . . . The data indicate that there is no longer any attempt . . . to justify segregation in principle, and that this evolution has occurred steadily not only through the 1970s but indeed to the present day."

This does not mean, however, that analysts are agreed upon the interpretation of these data. Some researchers have looked at the difference between opinions on support for the general principles of equality and racial integration and for implementation of specific policies, such as busing or affirmative action, and concluded that this distinction represents a new form of racism. Their argument is that racism lies at the heart of whites' opposition to policies that would benefit minorities.

This "new racism" has been given a number of different labels, including symbolic racism, covert racism, modern racism, subtle racism, and racial resentment (Sears, Hensler, and Speer, 1979). Whatever its label, the core premise is that white attitudes "are based not on self-interest (for example, having one's own children involved in court-ordered busing), but rather on a more general sense that blacks are violating American values of individualism through their persistent demands for special treatment like affirmative action" (Schuman et al., 1997: 293). Individuals who dislike blacks and other minorities need only declare that they opposed government assistance to them not because of dislike, but because they believe in self-reliance (Sniderman et al., 1991: 424). Symbolic stances, therefore, are seen as "a way of expressing general anti-black attitudes in terms that seem culturally appropriate" (Link and Oldendick, 1996: 150).

Although elements of racism remain in American society, there is little question that whites' racial attitudes have changed dramatically during the period in which they have been tracked by survey researchers. The "old-fashioned racism" that incorporated both a biologically based theory of African racial inferiority and support for racial discrimination has been supplanted, and the principle of equal treatment now enjoys majority support (Sears et al., 1997). It is the gap between support for this general principle and the specific application of this principle that has become the defining feature of contemporary research on racial attitudes.

The data presented here have also shown systematic and fairly substantial differences between the views of blacks and whites. There is a vast amount of additional data to which we could point to demonstrate the distinct views of the races (see, for example, Blendon et al., 1998; Ladd, 1998a), such as the much higher percentage of blacks who believe that improving race relations is one of the most important things we need to do for the future of the country or the larger proportion who believe that racial minorities are routinely discriminated against in the United States. As the proportion of Hispanics has grown, the views of this group have become increasingly important in considering the shape of public opinion in this country. Although their views tend to fall between those of blacks and whites, there are issues such as immigration, the most important problem facing the country, and discrimination on which the opinions of the Hispanic population are distinct (Lopez, 2010).

To a large extent, Americans of all races generally agree on the broad issue of racial equality and such general questions as whether blacks and whites have the same rights to live wherever they can afford, whether black and white children should be allowed to go to the same schools, and whether they would vote for a black candidate for president. The questions that now divide the races are more focused on specific means for achieving these goals, such as affirmative action. As issues such as the perceived unequal treatment of blacks in the criminal justice system, police brutality, racial profiling, and reparations for slavery become more prominent, the sharp divisions between blacks and whites that exist on these questions, as well as the increasing importance of the views of Hispanics, will ensure the prominent role of race as an issue on the American political scene.

The election of America's first black president in 2008 led some to believe that the country may have reached a breakthrough in terms of racially divided opinions (Valentino and Brader, 2011). Although this story is not completely written, the early indications are that whatever impact this election may have had was only temporary. In 1964, the Gallup Poll first asked the question, "Do you think that relations between blacks and whites will always be a problem for the United States, or that a solution will eventually be worked out?" The percentage "hopeful" for a solution has stood at about 55%. In a one-night poll taken the day after President Obama's victory over John McCain, this percentage increased to 67%. But as Gallup's report on this topic notes, "About a year after Obama's election, optimism that a solution to the country's race problems will eventually be worked out has settled back down to 56%. This certainly remains higher than in a number of previous years, particularly at points in the 1990s. But the current reading is not significantly improved from the sentiment that prevailed in more recent years prior to Obama's election" (Newport, 2009a). Although opinions on many racial issues have become less divisive over time, there remain large differences between blacks and whites on many of the political and social issues that comprise the American mind.

POLLS, POLLING, AND THE INTERNET

If you are interested in whether and how members of the public in one state might differ from citizens of another state on topics such as school integration and civil rights, you might want to look at a number of state polls that are archived at the Institute for Research in Social Science at the University of North Carolina. The data from the National Network of State Polls (NNSP) can be found at: http://odum/jsp/content_node.jsp?nodeid=463.

10

Public Opinion on Highly Controversial Issues

Some issues simply seem to be more inflammatory than others when it comes to public policy. Whenever Congress, or the president, or, for that matter, politicians at any level begin to discuss laws affecting certain issues such as abortion or the death penalty, emotions flare. Proponents and opponents use public opinion data to demonstrate their respective positions. Candidates for office often feel it necessary to state their own personal views on these issues early in a campaign to attract certain types of support and to get the issue out of the way for other voters. It is worth noting that in recent years there seems to be far more protests and acts of civil disobedience in regard to immigration policy and abortion issues than about civil rights or social-welfare policies.

Is public opinion on these issues—crime, the death penalty, abortion, immigration policy, gun control, and the status of gays—structured differently from other domestic issues? As will be discussed in this chapter, the answer is both yes and no. For most of these issues, partisanship is a poor guide to public opinion. Though the Republican Party has, since 1980, moved to espouse a tough position on capital punishment and an antiabortion stance, these issues do not define that party for its identifiers. Political ideology is, on some issues but not others, correlated to the distribution of opinion. In fact, Stimson (1991) examined these issues and others over time and found that the distribution of views within the American public moved from liberal to conservative and then back toward the center, parallel to the movement away from liberal identification during the 1980s. However, some issues show very stable distributions of opinion over 20 or 30 years, demonstrating unusual consistency within the public. In these cases especially, the roots of the opinion preferences may be in specific values or religious orientations and attitudes that are more deeply rooted than party or ideology.

Such highly controversial issues are particularly interesting to students of American politics because of the impact of public opinion on the policy process. These "hot topics" have the capacity to generate special interest groups that are dedicated to a single cause and to motivate supporters to give their personal time and resources to protect their viewpoints. Thus, politicians may be unwilling to vote against such a vocal minority for fear of being defeated by the group's efforts. Sometimes the vehemence of the opinions expressed actually brings the political system to stalemate, as it has in the case of abortion policies since *Roe v. Wade*. On other issues, such as euthanasia and gun control, individual states have been able to adopt policies that are too controversial to be acted on at the national level and that will serve as social experiments for the public to observe.

In the sections that follow, we will look at the trends in public opinion on issues concerning crime and criminal justice, including the death penalty; issues pertaining to individual rights, including abortions, the rights of gays, the right to own and carry a gun; and the controversial issues surrounding illegal immigration.

THE POLITICS OF CRIME AND CRIMINAL JUSTICE

Public views on the causes of crime and the treatment of criminals have moved through several cycles since the end of World War II. The public moved toward more liberal views on the treatment of criminals, including a decline in support for the death penalty, through the 1950s and early 1960s, but in the years since the mid-1960s, the majority opinion has steadily moved to more conservative positions on the need for punishment, on the death penalty, and on the need for strict law enforcement. In Stimson's (1991) view, the public's positions on these societal issues are part of the long-term swing from liberalism to conservatism and back. Page and Shapiro take a different approach to understanding the public's views on these issues, asserting that "the public has exhibited rational opinions, differentiating clearly among alternative policies and reacting to changing realities" (1992: 90).

What were the changing realities that might have moved public opinion from a more liberal stance to more conservative opinions? Following a period of economic strength and relative domestic peace, the 1960s saw the beginning of the protests against the Vietnam conflict and, by the late 1960s, urban unrest and riots in many of America's major cities. Civil unrest continued until the end of the Vietnam conflict, which was followed by the Watergate scandal and the trials of the figures involved in it. During this period, the use of illicit drugs spread to new segments of the population, and public awareness of the drug problem and the crimes it engendered rose to a new high. By the election of Ronald Reagan in 1980, the tide of public sentiment had turned on a number of issues, with the majority of the public seeking stricter enforcement of laws and stiffer penalties for criminals.

Perceptions of Crime

Fear of crime is a frequent topic in the media and public life in the United States, as is any increase or decrease in violent crime rates. However, it has been very difficult to measure public fear about crime because it is an issue that has both national and personal dimensions. If we look at the question that the Gallup organization has asked for several decades, "What is the most important problem facing the nation?," crime and violence were only named most important in 1994 and 1995. In most of the years the question was asked, economic issues—unemployment, inflation, or the budget deficit—gained the highest percentage of choices. In fact, from 1984 through 1993, only 5% of those surveyed said that crime was the most important problem (Roberts and Stalens, 1997: 54). However, the number increased to 9% in 1993, and in 1994 to 37% of those surveyed. In 1995, the percentage of Americans citing crime as the most important problem declined to 27%, and that reduction in concern continued throughout the 1990s. As shown in Figure 10.1, crime and violence were the most important concerns of less than 1% of Americans in 2008, with only small fluctuations since 2000. What accounts for this fluctuation in concern for crime? It may be that media attention to the increase in crime rates in the early 1990s increased public anxiety about crime and violence. In the same way, the

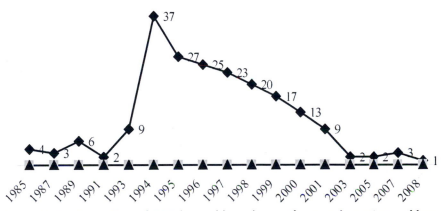

Figure 10.1.   Percentage of Americans citing crime as the most important problem, 1985–2008.

Source: The Gallup Poll, reported in the Sourcebook of Criminal Justice Statistics Online, 2011. Washington, D.C.: U.S. Department of Justice, Bureau of Justice Statistics provided by the State University of New York, Albany at www.albany.edu/sourcebook

reporting on the decline in crime rates in the past decade may be reflected in the decline in the proportion of Americans who see crime as the most important problem facing the nation.

However, crime is not only a national problem, it is also a neighborhood problem and, most important, a personal fear. The intensity of opinion about crime and criminal acts is much stronger when individuals answer questions about their personal perceptions of crime. In attempting to measure the personal dimension of fear, for several decades polling organizations have been asking Americans about their feelings of personal safety and the crimes that they fear most. The results are intriguing. Although an overwhelming number of Americans have said that crime is increasing in the United States—and indeed, for several decades, crime rates did increase—the measurement of personal fear demonstrates amazing stability. Polls conducted since 1965 by the Gallup Organization and the National Opinion Research Center (NORC) have asked the question, "Is there any area around here—that is, within a mile—where you would be afraid to walk alone at night?" In 1965, only 34% of Americans answered yes to that question; by 1982, 48% answered in the affirmative. However, since that time, the proportion expressing fear of walking near home declined to 42% in 1996 (*Public Perspective*, 1997: 11) and to 30% by 2001 (Gallup Poll, 2004). In 2010, the percentage of Americans who expressed fear of walking near home rose to 37% (Gallup Poll, 2010) and overall perceptions of crime have been on the rise, even though crime statistics show an overall decline in violent crime in the United States.

In looking further at the fear of crime expressed by individuals in society, a number of studies have asked Americans about their fear of specific types of crimes. Not surprisingly, the level of fear expressed does vary with the crime described. For example, when asked if they fear their home being burglarized when they are away, 46% of Americans admit that they are worried. Although only 17% of those polled say that they worry about getting murdered and 19% express fear of sexual assault, 66% of respondents indicated that they feared identity theft (Gallup Poll, 2009). Although there are few demographic differences between groups on the general perceptions of crime as an issue and the fear of walking in the neighborhood, there are significant demographic differences relative to these different types of crime.[1]

As Americans age, they are less afraid of sexual assault but are much more fearful of being mugged. Given their physical frailty, this fear makes considerable sense. As you might expect, women are far more afraid of sexual assault and being mugged than are men. The differences in fear expressed by whites, African Americans, and Hispanics are very telling, both in terms of cultural differences and, possibly, in terms of the areas where people of different ethnic backgrounds live. On the question of sexual assault, black

Americans express less fear than whites, but Hispanic Americans are twice as fearful as African Americans. Hispanic respondents also express the greatest fear of being mugged and of burglary. African Americans are more afraid of being murdered than are members of any other group. Though Hispanics may be victimized at a higher rate for some crimes, that rate is not proportional with the fear expressed. Similarly, females in American society have a relatively low rate of victimization from sexual assault, but they express great fear about this possibility. Criminal justice experts have suggested that this "vulnerability" expressed by women reflects their awareness of the inability to defend themselves (Haghighi and Sorensen, 1996: 29). Another factor that speaks to cultural issues or, perhaps, community perceptions within an ethnic group, is that household income seems to have very little influence on fear of these crimes. People who live in poorer households are slightly more fearful of being mugged or murdered than are others. Wealthier individuals have less fear of murder, no doubt because they live in neighborhoods where murder seems rarely to occur.

Perceptions of Punishment

Although the number of Americans who see crime and violence as the most important issue in the nation has declined to less than 10%, Americans do fear specific crimes and, in general, support harsh sentences for criminals. As the prison population has soared in the United States, the question arises: What is the purpose of incarceration as punishment for crime? There have been many studies of this question over the past two decades, and their results suggest that people have conflicting views about the causes of crime and the purpose of punishment.

Two decades ago, Americans expressed much more liberal views about the causes of crime and the goals of the criminal justice system than they do today. Surveys conducted by various groups, including the Gallup Organization, ABC News, and NBC News/*Wall Street Journal*, have asked questions about the reasons for increasing crime rates since 1981. In that year, 37% of those polled said that unemployment and social conditions accounted for the increase in crime rates, 33% blamed the rise on failures of the criminal justice system, and 13% said that drugs were a cause. By 1994, the survey asked which factor was most responsible for crime. The public answered social conditions/unemployment, 8%; failure of the criminal justice system, 20%; crisis of personal values, 30%; and drugs, 20% (*Public Perspective*, 1997: 14). In other years, surveys have found as much as 59% of the public placing the blame on drugs.

Given these changes in the public's view of the causes of crime, it is not as surprising that the American public has also changed its understanding of the goals of the criminal justice system. This change is documented in

Table 10.1. As you will note, in the earliest poll cited, conducted by Louis Harris in 1966, 77% of those polled believed that prisons should be mainly corrective. By 1981, belief in rehabilitation was expressed by only 49%, and by 1994, only 16% of those surveyed by ABC News believed that the main purpose of prisons was to rehabilitate prisoners. Fifty-three percent believed prisons were meant to keep criminals out of society, and 29% felt that they were meant to punish criminals. Data from a 2001 survey that asked the question in terms of the prisoner showed a very different set of responses: 40% said the purpose of sending someone to prison is rehabilitation, while only 21% said the purpose is punishment.

On the question of the purpose of prisons, the American public does begin to show some differences related to demographics and, in a small way, to political views. The study conducted by the Public Policy Institute at Texas A&M and Sam Houston State University in 1995 asked respondents to indicate what *should* be the most important purpose in sentencing adults: deterrence (stopping others from committing crimes); incapacitation (keeping criminals away from society); rehabilitation; or retribution (punishing criminals). Generally, rehabilitation is more likely to be seen as the purpose of sentencing among younger Americans, Hispanic and black respondents, college graduates, and liberals. Conservatives are the most

Table 10.1   The Perceived Goals of Prisons

Question	Percentage Agreeing with the Goals				
	1966	1970	1981	1994	2001
Should Prisons be:[a]					
Mainly corrective	77				
Mainly punitive	11				
Main emphasis of prisons should be[a]					
Punishing		8	17		
Rehabilitating		73	49		
Protecting society		12	31		
Main purpose of prisons is[b]					
Punish criminals				29	
Rehabilitate criminals				16	
Keep criminals out of society				53	
Main purpose of sending a person[c] to prison is:					
To punish					21
To rehabilitate					40
To protect society					21
To deter others					12

[a]Survey by Louis Harris and Associates: June 1966; October 1970; January 1981.
[b]Survey by ABC News, November 17, 1994.
[c]Survey by Belden Russonello & Stewart, January 2001.

Source: Table adapted from *Public Perspective*, June/July 1997, p. 20.

likely to see punishment or retribution as the main purpose, but so are Democrats. There are few, if any, differences between men and women in their views of the purpose of prison.

The data in Table 10.1 suggest that the American people generally wish to see punishment emphasized in the treatment of criminals. However, in other studies, Americans have also supported early release for good behavior, more community-oriented programs for minor offenders, and a wide range of training and educational programs that might help prisoners become productive citizens (Krisberg and Marchionna, 2006). In light of the opinions expressed about retribution, how can support for more rehabilitative measures be explained? After considering all of these seemingly inconsistent points of view, some scholars have suggested that what the public wants are effective, well-run prisons that are also humane and can help offenders who are capable to better themselves (Flanagan, 1996: 92).

The Death Penalty

As we have seen, the public's views on the purposes of incarceration have changed over the past two decades, from correction and rehabilitation to punishment and the segregation of criminals from society. This shift in the views of the public is also found in the pattern of public opinion about the use of the death penalty. In the 1930s, when polling data were first available, the Gallup Poll found that 61% of Americans favored capital punishment for those convicted of murder. The level of support for this penalty remained stable until the mid-1950s (Figure 10.2), when it began to decline, finally reaching 38% in favor of the death penalty in 1966. Page and Shapiro suggest that this trend reflects the general liberalization of societal attitudes during the 1960s; they further suggest that the subsequent rise in support for capital punishment was associated with fear of crime after the urban riots of the 1960s (1992: 94).

During the same period of time that the public reconsidered its views on capital punishment, the Supreme Court of the United States handed down several very important rulings on the issue. After ruling in 1958 (*Trop v. Dulles*) that the constitutional prohibition against "cruel and unusual punishment" could be interpreted according to "evolving standards of decency" in a society, the court moved, in 1972, to outlaw the death penalty altogether (*Furman v. Georgia*). This case provoked a national outcry among law enforcement officials and encouraged public debates in virtually every state because the Court, while finding the Georgia death penalty statute arbitrary and capricious, suggested that states could write death penalty laws that would meet a constitutional standard. In the four years following the *Furman* decision, 35 states wrote new death penalty statutes that specified the crimes for which the penalty could be sought and established specific

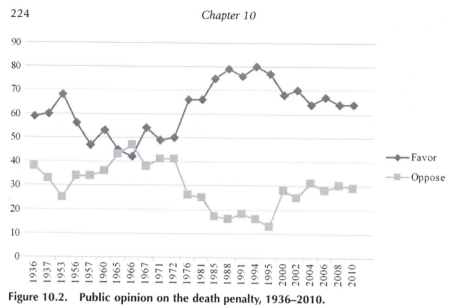

Figure 10.2.   Public opinion on the death penalty, 1936–2010.

Source: The Gallup Organization, 1936–1972; Gallup and General Social Survey, 1973–2010.

procedures for recommending such a punishment (Roberts and Stalans, 1997: 226). The new Georgia statute was ruled constitutional by the Supreme Court in 1976 (*Gregg v. Georgia*).

By the time the Supreme Court struck down the first Georgia law in 1972, more than 60% of the public supported capital punishment for certain crimes. Since that time, as Figure 10.2 shows, support for capital punishment for persons convicted of murder rose to near 80% in the 1990s and dropped to around 70% for a few years and is now closer to 65%.

There are some differences in the level of support by demographic groups that are not very surprising. Women are less likely to see the death penalty as morally acceptable (61%) than men (79%), and Republicans are more supportive (77%) than Democrats (59%) or Independent voters (68%). As you would expect, conservatives are more supportive (75%) than liberals (59%), but that difference is not as great as one might have anticipated (Gallup Poll, 2005). The strongest difference of opinion on the death penalty is found between the races, and it has, as seen in Figure 10.3, been a consistent trend for the past 20 years. African Americans are far less likely to support the death penalty than are white Americans. Given the fact that a much higher proportion of those convicted persons who are on death row are black, this opposition among African Americans is understandable, as is the view that recommendations for capital punishment may involve some elements of racial bias by juries or communities. Recently, the use of DNA testing to prove the innocence of some prisoners on death row has undoubtedly raised concerns about the use of capital punishment.[2] Indeed, a 2009 Gallup Poll found that 59% of respondents believed that someone

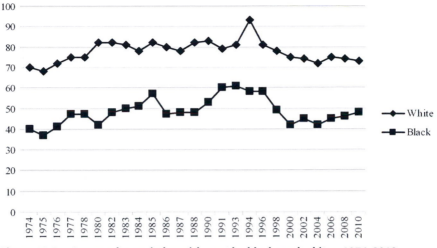

Figure 10.3. Support for capital punishment by blacks and whites, 1974–2010.

Source: General Social Survey.

who was innocent of the crime with which he or she was charged was executed within the past five years.

As noted in Chapter 1, the public's views on capital punishment and the appropriate use of this penalty for convicted murderers may be considered one of those issues on which public judgment has occurred. Following Yankelovich's (1991) definition of public judgment, the data about the public's support for capital punishment show considerable change over time, a certain lengthy dialogue inspired by the Supreme Court's rulings, debates and legislation in most of the states, and, by the late 1990s, stability in the public's support for capital punishment as well as a fairly stable differentiation of opinion between black and white Americans.

THE POLITICS OF INDIVIDUAL RIGHTS

Although the media frequently show the candlelight vigils held outside of prisons when a convicted criminal is about to be put to death, those protesting capital punishment are, for the most part, peaceful in their means and quite aware they are expressing a minority view. In contrast, the opponents and proponents of two other issues of individual choice—abortion and gay rights—are much more intense in their views. The emotions and energy invested in debates about these issues reflect both the degree to which opinions are rooted in deeply held values and the fact that the legal status of the abortion issue and that of the rights of gays to marry, serve in the military, and to adopt children are in contention nationally and at the state level.

PUBLIC OPINION TOWARD ABORTION

Until the Supreme Court decision in 1973, the regulation of birth control information and devices and of abortion were matters for state law. Abortions were for the most part illegal across the United States, although the penalties and laws differed by state. As Page and Shapiro (1992: 104–106) note, however, the debate over the regulation of private decisions about sexual activity and pregnancy first became public with the introduction of the birth control pill in the 1960s. Following the *Griswold v. Connecticut* case, decided by the Supreme Court in 1965, states could no longer bar physicians from distributing information about birth control or devices, including the new pill. In fact, surveys about whether birth control information should be available showed wide public support from the mid-1930s; the Connecticut law and the *Griswold* decision were seen by many as anachronistic. That the debate would move on to the topic of abortion, which also deals with the ability of women to control their bodies, should not be surprising.

Although *Roe v. Wade* brought the topic of abortion to the forefront of public debate (and generated hundreds of poll questions), it is worth noting that NORC had been asking about whether abortion should be legal in specific circumstances since the early 1960s. In 1962, for example, 77% of the public felt that abortion should be legal if the mother's health was seriously endangered by the pregnancy; 55% supported abortion if the baby had a serious birth defect; but only 15% approved of an abortion if the family had a very low income and could not afford the child (Stanley and Niemi, 1995: 36). Between 1962 and 1973, the proportion of Americans who believed that abortion should be legal in cases where the mother's health was endangered had risen to 91%. Support for an abortion in the case of rape was 81%; in case of a birth defect, 82%; and because of low income, 52%. Page and Shapiro assert that, in their view, the changes in American views on abortion and women's control of their own bodies actually occurred before the *Roe* decision in 1973.

Since that galvanizing decision, there have been hundreds of polls on the topic of abortion, the development of several different standard sets of items by the various survey research organizations, many books on the politics of abortion, and many state laws written that have reregulated abortions within the limits of the *Roe* decision. The Supreme Court has, in fact, supported state laws that placed more barriers between women and abortion providers, including mandatory counseling; consent forms for the father of the baby or, in the case of minor women, their parents/ guardians; and waiting periods. However, the essence of the *Roe* decision, which allows (1) abortions by physicians in the first trimester of pregnancy, (2) more state regulation of abortions in the second trimester, and (3) the banning of abortions in the third trimester by the states, still structures the debate.

To begin to understand public opinion about the legality of abortions, survey organizations have, rightly, asked people about their support for abortion under different conditions. Generally, pollsters have asked respondents if they believe it should be legal or possible for a woman to obtain an abortion under the following six conditions:

- if the woman's health is seriously endangered by the pregnancy
- if she is pregnant as the result of rape
- if there is a chance of a serious birth defect in the infant
- if she is married and does not want any more children
- if the family is too poor to support any more children
- if the woman is single and will not be marrying the father of the baby.

To analyze how the individual respondent thinks about these different conditions, Cook, Jelen, and Wilcox (1992: 32–33) have suggested that we look at opinions toward *traumatic abortions* (mother's health, birth defect, rape) and *elective abortions* (poverty, lack of desire for children, single parenthood). Their research suggests that "there is a societal consensus that abortion should be legal in each of the traumatic circumstances" (35).

If we look at the data on these "conditional" questions since 1961, which are displayed in Table 10.2, we can see the evidence that brings Cook and her colleagues to this conclusion. The set of three conditions that they consider to be elective abortions do not, at any time, gather nearly the level of public support as the more traumatic conditions do. Support for making abortions available to women for the elective reasons reached a high in the decade following the *Roe* decision; since that time support for abortions in these situations has declined to more modest levels, as has support for abortion under any condition.

As with the conditions under which the public supports legal abortions, it is also possible to categorize individuals according to their position on these questions and others that ask about the degree of regulation of abortion. Cook, Jelen, and Wilcox (1992) suggest three categories of respondents: pro-life respondents who generally oppose abortion under any condition; pro-choice respondents who believe abortion should be legal under any condition; and *situationalists* who support abortions in some circumstances but not others. There are several ways to determine how many people or what proportion of Americans fall into each of these categories. Cook, Jelen, and Wilcox based their distinction on the number and type of conditions that a respondent finds acceptable for abortion, thus bringing the percentage of absolute pro-life Americans to about 8% in the period 1987–1991 (140). Likewise, pure pro-choice Americans (who believe in no

Table 10.2. Support for Legal Abortion under Different Conditions, 1962–2010[a]

	Percentage Saying Abortion Should be Legal under These Circumstances					
Year	Mother's Health	Rape	Birth Defect	Poor Mother	Single Mother	No More Babies
1962	77	55	15			
1965	70	56	55	21	17	15
1969	80	63	23			
1972	83	75	75	46	41	38
1973	91	81	82	52	47	38
1974	90	83	83	52	47	46
1975	88	80	80	51	46	44
1976	89	81	82	51	48	45
1977	89	81	83	52	48	45
1978	88	81	80	46	40	39
1980	88	80	80	50	46	45
1982	90	83	81	50	47	46
1983	87	80	76	42	38	38
1984	88	77	78	46	43	41
1985	87	78	76	42	40	39
1987	86	78	77	44	40	38
1988	86	77	76	41	38	39
1989	88	80	79	46	43	43
1990	89	81	78	46	43	43
1993	86	79	79	48	46	45
1994	88	81	80	49	46	47
1996	89	81	79	45	43	45
1998	88	80	79	44	42	42
2000	88	81	79	42	39	41
2002	92	80	79	44	42	45
2004	86	76	73	41	41	42
2006	87	77	73	42	40	41
2008	89	76	74	42	42	44
2010	86	79	74	45	44	48

[a]Question wording: "Please tell me whether or not you think it should be possible for a pregnant woman to obtain a legal abortion if there is a strong chance of serious defect in the baby? If she is married and does not want any more children? If the woman's own health is seriously endangered by the pregnancy? If the family has a very low income and cannot afford any more children? If she became pregnant as a result of rape? If she is not married and does not want to marry the man?" (Results are given from strongest support to least rather than in the order of the question.)

Source: National Opinion Research Center.

restrictions on the procedure) number less than 10% of Americans. Thus, more than 80% of Americans might be judged to be situationalists, approving of an abortion under some conditions but not others.

Although the categories suggested by Cook, Jelen, and Wilcox are very useful for their analysis, there are other series of poll questions that allow us to look at the broader contours of American opinion on the legality of abortion. A Gallup Poll question asks, "Do you think abortions should be legal under any circumstances, legal only under certain circumstances, or illegal in all circumstances?" A CBS/*New York Times* poll question asks, "Which comes closest to your view? (1) Abortion should be generally available to those who want it, (2) Abortion should be available but under stricter limits than it is now, or (3) Abortion should not be permitted." Looking at Table 10.3 and the Gallup Poll results, we see that the percentage of Americans who believe that abortion should always be illegal declined from 22% in 1975 to a low of about 12% in the mid-1990s and then rose to 22%. The percentage of those who believe that it depends on the circumstances remained in the mid-50% range for some time but has declined to 50% in 2011. The pro-choice proportion peaked at 33% in 1994 but has declined

Table 10.3.   Opinions on Abortions under What Circumstances, 1975–2011

	Percentage Saying Abortions Should Be Legal		
Year	*Any Circumstances*	*Only under Certain Circumstances*	*Illegal in All Circumstances*
1975	21	54	22
1977	22	55	19
1979	22	54	19
1981	23	52	22
1983	23	58	16
1988	24	57	17
1990	31	53	12
1992	31	53	14
1994	33	52	13
1996	25	58	15
1997	26	58	16
1998	23	59	17
1999	27	55	16
2000	27	53	17
2001	26	58	15
2002	26	53	20
2003	24	56	18
2004	23	54	21
2005	23	54	21
2006	30	53	15
2007	26	55	18
2008	28	54	17
2009	22	53	23
2010	24	54	19
2011	27	50	22

[a]Question wording: "Do you think abortions should be legal under any circumstances, legal only under certain circumstances, or illegal in all circumstances?"

Source: The Gallup Organization.

in recent years. The CBS News/*New York Times* poll question, presented in Table 10.4, finds that between 35% and 40% of Americans believe abortion should be generally available; about 40% prefer stricter limits; and more than 20% would not permit abortions at all. How do we account for the difference in proportions between these two polls? The proportion of Americans who truly oppose legal abortions is between 15% and 20%. At least 40% of Americans (more likely 60% to 70% of Americans) believe that it depends on the circumstances (or are "situationalists"), and about 20% to 35% are pro-choice most of the time. The CBS/*New York Times* question allows the respondent to formulate his or her own definition of "generally available" and "stricter limits," while the Gallup question refers directly to circumstances. This question-wording difference prompts the respondents to answer differently, although the response patterns for both survey organizations have been surprisingly stable over the years.

Because the debate over abortion is often based on differing religious views, with the Catholic Church and others taking official positions op-

Table 10.4. Opinions on Abortion Restrictions[a]

	Percentage Saying:		
Year	Generally Available	Stricter Limits	Not Available
1989	41	42	15
1990	39	40	18
1991	37	38	22
1992	40	39	19
1993	42	36	20
1994	40	37	21
1995	40	37	21
1996	40	41	18
1997	32	45	22
1998	32	45	22
1999	34	41	22
2000	33	43	21
2001	33	43	23
2003	37	38	23
2004	35	41	23
2005	36	37	25
2006	38	39	20
2007	37	39	22
2008	36	41	22
2009	37	39	22
2010	36	39	23

[a]Question wording: "Which comes closest to your view? (1) Abortions should be generally available to those who want it; or (2) Abortion should be available but under stricter limits than it is now; or (3) Abortion should not be permitted."

Source: CBS News Poll.

posing abortion, it is not surprising to find that religious affiliation or belief is a major determinant of abortion opinion, although religion is not as dominant a predictor of individual attitudes as one might think. According to the work of Cook, Jelen, and Wilcox (1992: 104), the intensity and involvement of individuals with their church is the factor that differentiates pro-choice from pro-life members of the same denomination. They find, for example, that only 3% of Catholics who are involved at a low level with their church are pro-life in their attitudes, as compared to 25% of those who are highly involved. In the evangelical Protestant denominations, the patterns are similar. Members of any Protestant denomination or the Catholic Church who believe that the Bible is inerrant are also more likely to be pro-life.

Groups that are likely to be pro-choice are younger people, especially those who identify with the Democratic Party, and the most highly educated segments of the society. In general, polls show women to be more supportive of legal abortions in all situations than men (about a 6% gap); Jewish respondents are much more supportive than are other religious groups; and black Americans are marginally more favorable than whites, although that distinction has varied over time.

Given the fact that the issue of abortion rights is central to the feminist political agenda, it seems natural that pro-feminist attitudes would predict opinions on abortion. The work of Cook, Jelen, and Wilcox (1992: 76–80) demonstrates that those who hold feminist views are more likely to be pro-choice in their views on abortion. They note that those respondents who can be classified as favoring "private feminism," namely, those who are supportive of a woman's right to work full time and have a family, are the most likely to be pro-choice. However, when these authors compared holding feminist attitudes with conservative views on sexual morality and the belief that abortion is "a matter of life and death," they found that opinions on sexual morality are the strongest predictors of attitudes toward elective abortions (1992: 87).

The polls of the late 1990s showed a decline in support for abortion in all situations across all demographic groups. In a 1998 article, Lydia K. Saad reported on a trend in the Gallup Polls that found the proportion of Americans who said that abortion should be legal in all circumstances dropping from the stable one-third in prior years to 25% (1998: 7). It is possible that the change in opinion toward more limits on abortion was a result of the widespread debate over "partial-birth abortions" that was carried on in Congress during 1997. The bill outlawing this procedure was, in fact, vetoed by President Bill Clinton because he said that the procedure was rarely used, and then only in cases of medical necessity. Pro-life forces promised to pursue legislation to outlaw the procedure, obtaining success in 2003 when President George W. Bush signed a bill passed by the

Republican-controlled Congress. Recent work by Wilcox and Norrander (2002: 135) suggested that there has been a strong increase in the number of men and women who believe that life does begin at conception. They speculate that new technologies, especially ultrasound imaging of fetuses, might contribute to a change in beliefs and, subsequently, to more opposition to abortion in general.

When the data on public attitudes toward abortion are looked at from a larger point of view, it seems pretty clear that the majority of Americans support legal abortions under some circumstances, while small, intense minorities are totally pro-life or pro-choice. On this issue, the public has not come to a common view on the topic nor, given the minorities' strength of belief and their willingness to engage in political and legal action, is the debate likely to be resolved in the near future.

PUBLIC OPINION ON GAY ISSUES

The issue of gay and lesbian rights in American society became a national issue after the Stonewall riots of 1969, when police raided a bar in New York that catered to homosexual patrons. Since that time, gay men and lesbians have formed political organizations and sought to ensure their rights to equal treatment in the United States. During the decades that followed the Stonewall incident, most laws outlawing homosexual relations were either repealed or rejected by the courts.

In many states, laws have been passed to guarantee homosexual citizens freedom from discrimination in employment and housing. Although the federal government has lifted its ban on the hiring of gays and lesbians, the situation of gays in the military has remained controversial. The Clinton administration's policy of "Don't ask, don't tell," which allowed gays to stay in the military as long as they did not admit their sexual preference, has led some gays who have been discharged from the armed services to pursue their rights in court. Although there was resistance within the military to allowing gay Americans to serve openly, public opinion shifted dramatically; by 2010, 70% of respondents polled by Gallup favored allowing openly gay men and lesbian women to serve in the military. In 2011, President Barack Obama proposed and Congress approved the end to that policy.

Public opinion toward gays has changed rapidly over the past four decades with regard to these basic rights. As shown in Table 10.5, in 1977, 56% of the public believed that homosexuals should have equal rights in job opportunities. By 2008, 89% of those polled by Gallup supported equal rights in employment. However, if polls ask about specific occupations (the public has doubts about some jobs being held by homosexuals), holding jobs such as salesperson, doctor, or member of the military,

Table 10.5. Equal Job Opportunities for Homosexuals (percent)[a]

	1977	1982	1989	1992	1993	1999	2001	2003	2005	2008
Should have equal opportunities	56	59	71	74	80	83	85	88	87	89
Should not have equal opportunities	33	28	18	18	14	13	11	9	11	8

[a]Question wording: "In general, do you think homosexuals should or should not have equal rights in terms of job opportunities?"

Source: The Gallup Poll.

it is approved by more than 70% of Americans; however, only about half of those polled approved of homosexuals being elementary school teachers or members of the clergy.

Gay and lesbian Americans have long sought legal recognition for their long-term personal relationships. The legal recognition of a partnership confers numerous rights and benefits, ranging from the ability to share health information to access to insurance and inheritance and the ability to adopt children. The question of whether gays and lesbians can "marry" in the traditional sense of the term is very controversial. At the federal level, Congress has passed the Defense of Marriage Act, which forbids federal agencies from recognizing marriages other than those between a man and a woman. The situation in the states is very different. Although 42 states explicitly reserve the practice of marriage to heterosexual couples, in 2012 six states and the District of Columbia permit same-sex marriages and another five allow legal domestic partnerships or civil unions. As you can see from Table 10.6, American opinion strongly opposed recognizing such relations as valid marriages as recently as 1996. In 2011, the Gallup Poll found, for the first time, a slight majority in favor of recognizing gay marriages as valid.

Wilcox and Norrander (2002: 144–145) examined the demographic basis for such change in opinion and found increasingly liberal views on gay and lesbian issues in each successive generation of Americans. Older Americans still hold conservative views on gay and lesbian issues, but the youngest voters are much more willing to grant full rights to this group. However, as the change in opinion on gay marriages demonstrates, there appears to be a cultural shift in favor of more tolerance toward gays and lesbians that goes beyond generational changes.

AMERICAN VIEWS ON GUN CONTROL

Gun control is, without doubt, another one of the controversial issues that Americans debate in their local communities and in the halls of Congress. Like the issues of abortion and the right to die, legislative action is fairly constant. Gun control as an issue differs from abortion and other issues dealing with life and death in that there is only one intense minority at work: those Americans who oppose any increase in government restrictions on their right to purchase, keep, and use firearms. As we will see, those who oppose gun control do so on constitutional grounds and as a matter of libertarian philosophy rather than for religious reasons. The proponents of gun control are usually arguing from the side of increased safety and the reduction of violent crime.

Table 10.6 Opinions on the Validity of Gay Marriage (percent)

	1996	1999	2000[b]	2003	**2004**	2004	2005	2006	2007	2008	2009	2010	2011
Should be recognized as valid	27	35	34	35	32	42	37	39	46	40	40	44	53
Should not be recognized as valid	68	62	62	60	55	62	62	57	53	56	57	53	47

[a]Question wording: "Do you think marriages between homosexuals should or should not be recognized by the law as valid, with the same rights as traditional marriages?"
[b]The years in bold are those in which Gallup asked a series of questions about homosexual rights and relations before the questions about marriage. When the respondent's beliefs about homosexuality were articulated first, approval for marriage declined. Gallup tested these results with split/half samples.

Source: The Gallup Poll.

The Ownership of Guns

Surveys of the American people have indicated fairly consistently that about 50% of Americans own guns. About 70% of those who own guns have more than one in their possession. For the most part, polls have found that half of all gun owners say the purpose of having a gun is for sport, while about 20% say they own a gun for self-protection (Adams, 1996: 110–111). When we look at the characteristics of gun ownership, the most important determinants are living in a rural area or small town, having a higher income, being male, and being white. Although gun ownership is often associated with being Southern, higher proportions of people who live in the mountain states and in the Midwest own guns than those who live in the South or on either coast.

THINKING ABOUT WEAPONS AND GOVERNMENT CONTROLS

To those who study public opinion on gun control, it seems quite clear that Americans are able to differentiate the types of guns they believe are appropriate for people to own. According to Page and Shapiro (1992: 94), Americans are quite able to distinguish "fairly sharply among types of weapons (long guns, handguns, cheap "Saturday night special" handguns, assault rifles, automatic weapons), among different types of policies, and among different types of possible gun owners." Polls have consistently shown levels of support for the banning of assault weapons and automatic weapons at 70% or higher, although the details of such weaponry are not well understood (Roberts and Stalans, 1997: 285). The majority of Americans support the keeping of cheap, easily available handguns out of the hands of criminals but do not approve banning guns used for sport or hunting. In terms of who should be prohibited from owning weapons, most polls show that strong majorities support banning the sale of guns to juveniles and to persons who would pose a risk to society, including convicted felons, mentally disturbed people, and convicted drug dealers. Up until very recently, Americans were very supportive of laws that require people to obtain permits before they can buy a gun. By 2002, almost 80% of those surveyed supported requiring permits. Americans also were very supportive of the Brady Bill, which required a five-day waiting period to buy a gun.

However, even though several tragic mass murders have occurred in recent years—the Tucson shooting of congresswoman Gabrielle Giffords, the Virginia Tech and Columbine High School mass murders—Americans have become more supportive of gun rights over the past few years than in many decades. People are more opposed to the banning of the possession of handguns than at any time in the past 50 years (69% oppose such a ban) and, as shown on Table 10.7, the percentage of people who think that gun

Table 10.7. Public Opinion on Stricter Gun Laws (percent)[a]

	1990	1991	1993	1995	1999	2001	2003	2005	2007	2009	2010
Laws made more strict	78	68	67	62	64	53	55	57	51	44	44
Keep as now	2	5	7	12	7	8	9	7	8	12	12
Laws made less strict	17	25	25	24	28	38	36	35	39	43	42

[a]Question wording: "In general, do you think that the laws covering the sale of firearms should be made more strict, less strict, or kept as they are now?"

Source: The Gallup Poll.

laws should be more strict has fallen from 78% in 1990 to 44%. What accounts for such a strong shift in opinion regarding the possession of guns?
Although there is little firm evidence on this issue, there is also an increase
in the distrust of government and a perception that government has too
much power. Recent Supreme Court rulings have also tended to weaken the
power of local and state governments to regulate the possession of guns by
law-abiding individuals.

In recent years, the movement to uphold gun rights has embraced "concealed carry" laws in the states. These laws permit individuals who have
completed a set of classes and been licensed by the respective state to carry a
weapon on their persons in a concealed fashion. At present, all states except
Illinois permit the concealed carrying of guns with appropriate licensure.
States can, however, regulate where and under what conditions concealed
carry is legal. Proponents of this right advocate for the broadest possible
interpretation of where guns can be carried on the premise that there would
be less crime and fewer assaults in schools and public places if individuals
could defend themselves.

Why has there been an increase in objection to gun laws and a real
decline in attempts to increase regulations federally? This is one of those
issues in which the power of a national interest group that holds strong
views on the subject and has enough vocal members to influence members
of Congress makes a difference. A very interesting study by Adams (1996:
120–122) looked at the difference in activism and opinions between gun
owners and nonowners. Adams found that gun owners were much more
likely to promote their opinions on gun issues (25%) versus nonowners
(12%). Of those who owned guns for sport and protection, 37% reported
that they had voiced their opinions about gun control issues. As one might
expect, gun owners were more likely to want less strict laws or to keep laws
the same rather than to enact stricter laws. They were also much more likely
to see guns as a defense against government abuse (22%) and for personal
protection against criminals (50%). Although this study did not report
whether gun owners were members of an interest group like the National
Rifle Association, their high level of activism is certainly one reason that
gun control remains a controversial issue in the American mind.

IMMIGRATION: A MIND DIVIDED

Most Americans are descended from immigrants to North America or
are immigrants themselves. The only exceptions are the Native American
populations who are indigenous to the continent. The Statue of Liberty
symbolizes the welcoming of immigrant populations to the United States
over the past two centuries. In recent decades, however, the subject of immigration has become extremely controversial, particularly in regard to un-

documented immigrants who have entered the country illegally. The question of which policies to pursue with regard to the tremendous number of undocumented immigrants has engendered fiery debate on the campaign trail and huge rallies in support of immigrants, especially in California with its large Hispanic population.

Public opinion on immigration appears to be very inconsistent: Americans are generally supportive of the idea that immigration is a net benefit to the nation and, at the same time, are very supportive of strict measures to close the border and deny benefits to undocumented immigrants and their children. Proposals for immigration reform and for creating a path to legal citizenship for immigrants who are already in the United States find more or less support depending on how the survey question is worded. Such inconsistent and hard-to-decipher opinion has dissuaded the nation's leaders from proposing any new immigration legislation for some years.

Historically, American opinion has supported the idea that immigration at the current level is good for the United States. For the past ten years, Gallup has also asked whether immigration is "a good thing or a bad thing for the country today." The trend on this question is clear; over ten years more than 50% of all respondents said that it was a good thing and, in some years, the level of positive responses is over 65%. The Gallup Poll also has tracked opinion on the question "Should immigration be kept at the present level, increased or decreased?" for about 25 years. As shown in Figure 10.4, the general trend has been to either support keeping the present level or decreasing immigration throughout that time period.

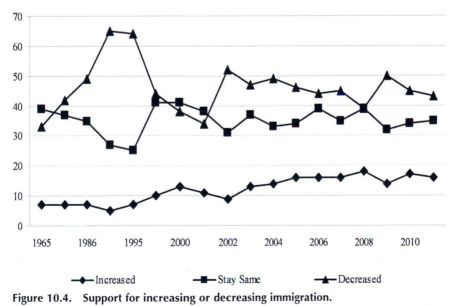

Figure 10.4. Support for increasing or decreasing immigration.

Source: The Gallup Poll.

The controversy over undocumented immigrants began to heat up in the late 1990s with an increasing number of Mexican workers finding their way into the United States through the border states of the Southwest. Many immigrants perished during the journey from heat exhaustion or dehydration. Others were brought north by "coyotes," criminals who extorted large sums of money to guide them north or bring them in large trucks. Complaints arose about the number of jobs that were given to immigrant workers, particularly in the agricultural and food processing industries. The complaints ranged from the view that immigrant workers took jobs from Americans to concerns about the working conditions and pay of these workers. Concerns have also been raised in numerous states about the types and extent of benefits extended to undocumented immigrants. In most states their children attend public school and benefit from public health programs and, in some states, get in-state tuition for college. Workers need and use health services, especially in the emergency room. Some workers pay into Social Security through fraudulent numbers while remaining ineligible for any benefits. In the past ten years, there has been increasing concern over whether the lawlessness of drug cartels in northern Mexico is spilling into the southwestern United States.

The question of which policies should be instituted to deal with illegal immigration is multifaceted. One set of issues surrounds border security: Should the border be secured by a physical barrier or through the increased use of troops and the border patrol? In regard to the undocumented immigrants themselves, most people admit that it is impossible to locate and deport more than 8 to 10 million people. At the same time, under what conditions should they be allowed to stay and work in the United States? And, in the long run, what process if any should be in place for undocumented immigrants to pay some penalty and become legal residents or even American citizens?

When polled on these issues, Americans are divided on the solutions and their answers are clearly swayed by the wording of the question. The most recent Pew Research Center survey on immigration (2011b) found that 42% of those polled said that the top priority in dealing with immigration should be to tighten border security and strictly enforce laws on immigration but also find a way for illegals to become legal. In that same survey, 35% of those polled put the priority on border security and law enforcement, while only 21% saw the priority as finding a way for illegal residents to become citizens. Generally, these responses were very consistent with a Pew poll in 2010.

However, if respondents are asked forced-choice questions about individual issues, the responses are starker. In a CNN/Opinion Research Corporation poll conducted in 2010, respondents were asked whether the main focus of government action should be to deport as many illegals as possible or work on a system for legal residency. Fifty-seven percent said to increase deportations, while 42% chose working on a system for residency. In the same poll, respondents were split almost 50-50 (over three different occasions) on support for building a 700-mile fence along the border. When asked whether there should be more border patrol agents and federal officers on the border, 81% agreed and only 18% disagreed. However, even with all this support for strong enforcement, when the poll asked whether they supported allowing illegal residents to stay and become legal residents if they had a job and paid all back taxes, 81% supported that idea and 19% opposed such a process.

Recently two additional immigration issues have been in the news. The state of Arizona passed a law that allowed police officers to ask for proof of legal residency when someone is stopped on suspicion of a crime. The federal government sued Arizona to stop enforcement of the law, and some parts of the law are currently on hold until all appeals are completed. Generally, polls have shown that a majority of the American people support the Arizona law. The other issue that has seen considerable discussion is the question of whether children of illegal immigrants who are born here should not be considered "natural born citizens" as is now the law. Polling on this question has generally shown low support for changing the Constitution in this regard. After reviewing the range of opinions on immigration, it seems that Americans want to support legal immigration but also want to secure their borders. However, there is considerable fluidity in opinions about undocumented immigrants who are already in the United States.

SUMMARY

American opinions on these controversial issues show both stability and polarization. On the issues surrounding crime and criminal justice, it is clear that the American mind has moved from a more liberal approach to criminals in the 1950s to a philosophy that supports punishment for the convicted criminal with support for rehabilitative services in prisons for those who benefit from them. The return to a more conservative view is most obvious on the death penalty: the Supreme Court opinion that effectively outlawed the death penalty in 1972 was, in part, an outgrowth of more liberal sentiments in the society, but it also forced states to redraw their death penalty statutes in a more rigorous fashion. Public opinion has supported the application of the death penalty in appropriate cases since that time.

Public opinion on the abortion issue, when observed over almost 50 years, is quite stable. However, it differs from opinion on the death penalty because there remain intense and vocal minorities who contest the majority's view. As we have seen, most Americans believe that a woman has a right to an abortion under certain situations, although the American mind certainly has not reached consensus on exactly which situations. The strong minorities who hold extreme views rarely gain any more adherents but continue to apply political pressure at all levels of government. Similarly, the status of gays and lesbians in American society is likely to remain controversial for some time, although the controversy will play out at the state level. Younger Americans are definitely more approving of equal rights and opportunities for gays, while older citizens are less supportive, although ideas seem to be changing across a broad spectrum of Americans.

Another issue that remains controversial is that of gun control. With the increase in school shootings by children and gun accidents involving children, there is public discussion about increasing the regulation of guns and gun owners. Although our examination of public opinion shows that most Americans support some regulation of guns and the banning of some types of weapons, the debate over who should be a legitimate gun owner and how the society makes that decision is likely to continue at all levels of government.

American opinion on illegal immigration is divided and fluid. Although Americans are generally positive about immigration and believe that the level of immigration should remain stable or decrease, they have widely varying ideas about what to do about illegal immigrants. Support for enhanced border security is high, although there is no clear agreement on how that can be achieved. Support for a process by which undocumented immigrants can become legal residents appears to have majority support, but the details of the process will be controversial. Most Americans do not want to discriminate against immigrants, but there is also support for the Arizona law that does look for proof of legal residency from suspected criminals. Policies in this area are likely to generate controversy as the public seeks to find workable and acceptable solutions to the issues.

Other issues, such as funding for stem cell research, the debate over teaching evolution versus creationism, and limits for cloning are also highly controversial topics. The division of opinions on these and other topics and how these divisions evolve over time will be extremely interesting to investigate in the future.

POLLS, POLLING, AND THE INTERNET

The commercial survey organization with the longest history of polling is, of course, the Gallup Organization. If you are interested in seeing the Gallup Reports (monthly) on current topics and on some of this chapter's controversial issues, point your browser to their very well-organized website at: www.gallup.com.

If you are interested in more data on criminal justice issues, you can search the biennial *Sourcebook of Criminal Justice Statistics*. It is available online at: www.albany.edu/sourcebook.

For an analysis of many public issues and a sampling of relevant public opinion on the issues, look at the website maintained by the Public Agenda Organization: www.publicagenda.org.

11

How Americans View Foreign and Defense Policies

The place of the United States in the world community has shifted so rapidly over the past two generations that it is hard to comprehend. On September 11, 2001, the United States suffered attacks on its home soil, attacks that were as shocking and devastating as the attack on Pearl Harbor in 1941. Since that day, the American people have been trying to understand the nation's place in the world: Should the United States continue to lead as a global superpower if this leads to terrorist attacks, or should the nation take a more restrained role in world affairs?

America's rise to world leadership was not, to a considerable extent, supported by public opinion. Although the United States did enter World War I in its last years and helped win the peace, the U.S. Senate rejected the treaty that formed the League of Nations, even though the world organization was the creation of President Woodrow Wilson. The United States retreated once again into its historical pose of isolationism. During the rise of fascism in Europe in the 1930s, most Americans believed that this nation should stay out of Europe's difficulties.

President Franklin Roosevelt extended various forms of aid from the United States to Great Britain in its fight against Hitler's Germany and persuaded the American people to support such forms of involvement. As documented by Page and Shapiro (1992: 184–185), less than 11% of the public thought that the United States should enter the war in late 1940, but by April 1941, more than 70% thought that the United States should do everything to help England and 60% thought it important to defeat Germany. Not until the Japanese attack on Pearl Harbor did Americans support the entry of the United States into the war. By the end of World War II, the United States was the most powerful military nation in the world, with control of nuclear weapons and a strong industrial sector and workforce. It was the United States that reached out to rebuild for its allies and defeated enemies in Europe after the war and that founded the United Nations. Those GIs who entered the war to defend an isolated nation came home to be citizens of the nation with more global responsibilities than any other on earth.

AMERICAN OPINION IN THE POST-9/11 WORLD

The terrorist attacks of 9/11 opened a new chapter in American foreign and defense policy. The George W. Bush administration's reaction to the attacks of 9/11 was twofold: first, to severely limit the degree to which terrorists can function in the world through cooperative relationships with other nations and heightened security measures, and second, to pursue a policy of rooting out governments in the Middle East that support terrorism or use terrorist tactics. The United States' attacks on the Taliban government in Afghanistan and, later, the Saddam Hussein government in Iraq were mandated by the Bush policy. Going further than pure defense, President Bush also declared that American policy would be to take "preemptive action when necessary to defend our liberty and our lives."[1]

The degree to which the United States will become involved or entangled with the affairs of other nations is a question that has challenged the nation since its founding. In his farewell address to the nation, President George Washington warned that it should be wary of forming ties to the nations of Europe. As he put it, "The great rule of conduct for us in regard to foreign nations is, in extending our commercial relations to have with them as little political connection as possible" (1796). This is probably the first articulation of the isolationist stance that the United States took as much for self-protection as for any other reason. As James McCormick points out, the Monroe Doctrine, issued by President James Monroe in 1823, carried this advice further by effectively separating the affairs of the Old World from those of the New World (1998: 14). The United States was to be interested only in affairs within its own hemisphere and, as the doctrine warned, European nations should stay out of that sphere. The degree to which the United States adhered to a policy of nonattachment to European affairs is revealed in McCormick's analysis of international agreements (1998: 16). Even though the United States did enter into more than 600 agreements with other nations up to 1899, the vast majority were for commerce or the settlement of claims. Only one treaty of alliance was signed. In contrast, the period from 1947 to 1960 saw the United States enter almost 5,000 international agreements, with more than 1,000 being military or other alliances with other nations.

Given this strong history of isolationism, it is not surprising that the measurement of public opinion most often taken on foreign affairs issues is whether the United States should take an active role in the world or stay out of world affairs. The Gallup Poll began asking a variation of this question in its surveys in 1943, and the question has been repeated by Gallup, Roper, or the National Opinion Research Center (NORC) many times since then. As you will note from Table 11.1, more than two-thirds of those surveyed in 1947 said that the United States should take an active part in world affairs. Although many commentators felt that the disillusionment of the Vietnam era would influence Americans to become more isolationist, the table shows that the lowest proportion of respondents supporting an active role was 54% in 1982. The proportion stayed in the low 60% range until 2002, when it rebounded to 71%. It is also important to note that the largest

Table 11.1.   Support for an Active Role in the World, 1947–2011 (percent)[a]

Year	Take an Active Role	Stay Out	Don't Know/ Unsure
1947	68	25	7
1948	70	24	6
1949	68	25	9
1950	66	25	9
1953	71	21	8
1954	69	25	6
1955	72	21	7
1956	71	25	4
1973	66	31	3
1974	66	24	10
1978	59	29	12
1982	54	35	11
1986	64	27	9
1990	62	28	10
1994	65	29	6
1998	61	28	11
2002[b]	71	25	4
2004	67	30	4
2006	69	28	3
2008	63	36	1
2010	63	36	1

[a]Question wording: "Do you think it will be best for the future of the country if we take an active part in world affairs or if we stay out of world affairs?"
[b]Beginning in 2002, the data are derived from the Chicago Council on Foreign Relations survey, utilizing a telephone survey in 2002 and Internet surveys in 2004–2010.

Source: The Gallup Poll; Chicago Council on Global Affairs, *Global Views 2010: Topline Data from U.S. Public Survey*, 2.

percentage saying that the United States should stay out of world affairs has been 36%, just over one-third of the public. Beginning in 2001, the Gallup organization began using another question, "Do you think the U.S. should take a leading role in world affairs, take a major role but not a leading role, take a minor role, or take no role at all in world affairs?" Gallup generally adds the categories together and reports the percentage who say leading and major role and those respondents who say minor or no role. This question regularly produces more than 70% who say the United States should play a leading or major role in world affairs.

Like some other standard questions in the development of survey research, this one has developed a life of its own. If only one question is asked on foreign policy, this is likely to be the one chosen by survey organizations. In part because of the nation's isolationist years and because this question seemed to capture the postwar change so well, many scholars who study the American mind have suggested that all Americans could be divided into those who are isolationists and those who are internationalists. As we will see in this chapter, American opinions on foreign policy and national security issues are much more complex than that typology would suggest.

PUBLIC OPINION AND FOREIGN POLICY: WHICH OPINIONS?

Some analysts have been content to ask only whether Americans support an isolationist role, while others have cast doubt on whether Americans actually have attitudes toward more specific foreign policy issues and, if they do, whether those views have much political impact. The constitutional framework of the United States and the decisions of the Supreme Court clearly vest the power to conduct foreign affairs with the president; the Congress does retain the power to declare war and to pass the budget, and the Senate to approve ambassadors, and, of course, to approve any treaties. Historically, the Congress and the people have looked to the president and other agencies of the executive branch to define and conduct the nation's foreign policy. This historical fact, combined with the general isolationist history of the nation, led to the idea of a bipartisan approach to foreign policy. Both political parties supported Roosevelt's leadership during World War II. At the end of that conflict, seeing the disarray of the global community, Republican and Democratic leaders of Congress called for bipartisan support for American foreign policy, particularly in the case of military force. As Senator Arthur H. Vandenberg often reminded his colleagues, "Partisanship ends at the water's edge" (quoted in Shafritz, 1988: 86).

During the 1950s and 1960s, the Cold War reinforced the need for a united, bipartisan approach to foreign policy among America's leaders.

Divisive elite opinions on foreign policy issues were not in evidence until the Vietnam conflict, when some members of both parties opposed the war while their colleagues supported it. The result of these years of bipartisanship is that few foreign policy issues have been or are defined in terms of ideological or partisan terms for the public. This, in turn, may make it more difficult for ordinary citizens to shape their own opinions on international issues, since there are few cues given by party leaders.

In addition, most members of the American public are not very interested in international affairs over the long term. Studies have shown Americans are not very knowledgeable about world geography or about the political systems of other nations. From time to time, polls ask questions about current international issues that demonstrate this low level of knowledge: For example, in a poll conducted by the Gallup organization in 2004, Americans were asked whether they knew much about the European Union (EU). Only 22% said that they knew a great deal or a fair amount about that organization. Thirty-seven percent admitted to knowing very little, and 40% said they knew nothing at all about it. However, although only 22% admitted some knowledge of the EU, all were willing to answer further questions about the size of the EU (65% were incorrect) and its impact on world problems. There have been numerous other studies that found similar low levels of knowledge about specific foreign policy issues (Delli Carpini and Keeter, 1996: 82–83). Critics suggest that the opinions expressed by most Americans on foreign policy issues should be given little weight because of the low levels of information and interest they demonstrate on these questions.

This concern for the ability of average Americans to formulate opinions on international issues has its roots in an elitist view of foreign policy decision making. Perhaps the foremost proponent of that view was Walter Lippmann (1922), who believed that Americans were too deeply involved in their own affairs and too easily swayed by emotional appeals to be able to make reasoned judgments on foreign policy questions. Lippmann and others such as Hans Morgenthau (1978) viewed foreign and defense policy as needing quick decisions based on information gathered by intelligence forces. Depending on the public to make judgments on such complicated issues would handicap the president in times of crises. Like Lippmann, Robert Dahl (1950) saw a need for the public to be educated by elites and policy makers on international issues so that they would support the decisions and actions taken by the nation. In Dahl's view, the media and local elites would act as a conduit to inform the public about international issues. This "distrust" of the public's ability to formulate and express opinions on foreign and military issues has led to a considerable scholarly interest in the degree to which the opinions of the public match or differ from those held by elites. As we will see in our investigation of public views on specific issues, there are a number of datasets available that compare elite and mass opinions; almost no such comparable datasets are available for examining opinions on domestic issues.

FOREIGN POLICY GOALS AND PRIORITIES

Another way to look at the public's views on foreign policy issues is to ask about the issues that confront the United States in the international arena. In a number of studies, this line of inquiry takes the form of asking respondents to indicate the importance of various goals for the United States. In this way, it is possible to rank the priority of foreign and defense policy goals for the American people. Looking at the priorities expressed by the American public lends considerably more detail to our understanding of public opinion than simply asking whether the United States should play an undefined internationalist role.

The longest ongoing study of public opinion on foreign policy has been conducted by the Chicago Council on Foreign Relations,[2] which has sponsored national surveys of mass opinion on foreign and defense policy. For many of those studies, the council also included an elite survey on the same issues. Many of the original questions about the foreign policy goals that should be pursued by the United States have been repeated throughout the series. Others have been dropped as they seemed less relevant, and new questions, addressing topics such as stopping drugs at the border and changing immigration policy, have been added in recent years.

The mass public's responses to the Chicago Council surveys from 1974 to the present on the foreign policy goals questions are displayed in Table 11.2. This presentation includes only those questions that have been asked at least five times over the course of the surveys. There appears to be considerable consistency within the public's responses over this 30-year period. The two items that have remained continuously at the top of the mass public's priorities are both concerned with protecting the well-being of the nation itself: Americans place a very high priority on maintaining adequate energy supplies and protecting the jobs of American workers. Two goals added in the 1990s—preventing the spread of nuclear weapons and combating terrorism—have also garnered strong, consistent levels of support. Americans also have steadfastly expressed a desire to reduce hunger in the world, a sentiment that may account for public support for humanitarian efforts such as the sending of troops to Haiti after the earthquake in 2009.

In the middle of this list of goals are the responses to the goal of "strengthening the United Nations." Clearly this goal usually garners

Table 11.2. Most Important Goals for U.S. Foreign Policy, 1974–2010 (percentage saying it should be a very important goal)

Goal Statement	1974	1978	1982	1986	1990	1994	1998	2002[a]	2006	2010
Secure adequate energy supplies	75	78	70	69	61	62	64	75	72	68
Protect jobs of American workers	74	78	77	77	84	83	80	85	76	79
Combat international terrorism	—	—	—	—	—	—	79	91	72	69
Prevent spread of nuclear weapons	—	—	—	—	84	82	82	90	74	73
Combat communism	58	64	62	60	58	—	—	—	—	—
Combat world hunger	62	62	61	64	—	56	62	54	—	—
Strengthen the United Nations	46	47	48	46	52	51	45	57	40	37
Help bring democratic government to other nations	26	29	30	28	25	29	34	34	17	19
Protect weaker nations from aggression	28	34	34	32	32	24	32	41	22	24

[a]Surveys conducted from 2002 to the present have been either telephone or Internet or both. In-person surveys ended with the 1998 study.

Source: Chicago Council on Foreign Relations now named the Chicago Council on Global Affairs, 1975–2011.

support from about half of the respondents, and the percentage is almost flat over the 13 surveys reported here. Below the UN item are listed two questions that show generally low levels of support over the three decades. The levels of response for "protect weaker nations from aggression" and "bring democracy to other nations" suggest that the American people are not very interested in making intervention into the domestic affairs of other nations a high priority.

Over the years, the priorities of the elites surveyed by the Chicago Council and, most recently, by the Pew Research Center[3] have often been different from those expressed by the general public. For example, the goal of improving the standard of living for other nations has generally ranked higher for the elites, and the goal of protecting the jobs of American workers has ranked much lower than it does for the general public. If we look at the ranking of selected goals by elites and the general public in the 2009 study, elites and the general public are in agreement on a number of issues, including the importance of preventing the spread of weapons of mass destruction (WMD) and combating international terrorism. The data in Table 11.3 show that one of the public's top concerns is "protecting the jobs of American workers," with 85% support as compared to elites who rank this goal near the bottom of their priorities at 21% support. The public is also more supportive of "combating drug trafficking" than the elites. Support by the public for strengthening the United Nation remains just under 40%, while elites have almost no concern for the United Nations (18% support).

Table 11.3   Comparing Elite and Public Views on American Foreign Policy Goals, 2009

Goal	*Percentage Saying the Goal Is Very Important*	
	Public	*Leaders*
Protect against terrorist attacks	85	81
Protect jobs of Am. workers	85	21
Stop spread of WMD	74	88
Reduce dependence on imported energy	64	65
Combat international drug trafficking	56	22
Reduce illegal immigration	45	11
Deal with global climate change	40	57
Strengthen the UN	37	18
Promote human rights abroad	29	21
Improve living standards in poor nations	26	35
Promote democracy abroad	21	10

Source: Pew Research Center for the People and the Press in association with the Council on Foreign Relations, "America's Place in the World 2009," New York, 2009: 27–29.

ISSUES OF WAR AND PEACE

Given the history of isolationism in U.S. foreign policy, it is not surprising that political leaders and commentators are intensely interested in the public's views on issues of peace and war. There is, in fact, a fair amount of controversy over the basic stance that Americans take toward any military involvement by U.S. troops. If one sees the support and involvement of U.S. citizens in World War II as an aberration in our history, then the public is regarded as basically suspicious of all military ventures overseas. This perception is heightened by the disillusionment suffered by the American public over the involvement in the Vietnam conflict. Alternatively, some commentators see the American public as dedicated to certain foreign policy goals and principles and, with appropriate leadership, willing to support the use of troops to achieve those goals. In some ways, this is a "Is the glass half empty or half full?" debate, but to policy makers who are trying to achieve foreign policy goals for the nation, the public's view is very important. They remember the degree to which public disapproval of Lyndon Johnson's leadership during the Vietnam era convinced a sitting president to leave office after one elected term.

The Vietnam Conflict

The Vietnam conflict tested the American public's resolve for military action overseas and, after many years of armed intervention, demonstrated that Americans have a limited tolerance for a war with no apparent strategy or likely outcome. If we look, however, at the early years of involvement in the Vietnam conflict, the American public strongly supported taking military action to defend American forces after the Gulf of Tonkin incident. In April 1965, after President Lyndon Johnson spoke to the public about the incident and his plans, 42% of the American public supported an increased escalation in the use of American military force, with 19% of the public favoring the combination of military force and negotiation (Page and Shapiro, 1992: 229). The support for use of military force increased steadily throughout 1965, rising to a high of 75% by the end of that year, as reported by Gallup.

Americans continued to support the use of military force in Vietnam through 1966 and into 1967, although protests against the war had begun and some media were reporting dissension within the executive branch about the military action. But public opinion stayed supportive of the U.S. troops while simultaneously seeking a way out until after the Tet offensive in January 1968. At first, Americans responded to the offensive by North Vietnam by becoming more aggressive in their outlooks, but within a few months disillusionment with the war began to increase and support for American involvement declined.

After the secret bombings of Laos were revealed in early 1970, large majorities of Americans began to favor immediate withdrawal from the war. In May 1970, when President Richard Nixon ordered U.S. troops into Cambodia, the nation's campuses exploded with protests, resulting in the shooting of students by National Guard troops at Jackson State University in Mississippi and at Kent State University in Ohio. To quote Page and Shapiro (1992: 235), "The proportion of Americans that favored continuing U.S. withdrawal, even if the South Vietnamese government collapsed, rose 13% (to a full 67%) between October 1969 and April 1970, and continued rising to 70% by April 1971 and to 76% by July 1971."

The Vietnam conflict presents several very interesting issues for the study of American public opinion. First, it is important to remember that the public was extremely supportive of the military action in the beginning of the conflict and that support for U.S. troops stayed strong throughout. Additionally, a majority of Americans would *not* call the military action a mistake until six months after the Tet offensive. This long and extremely difficult military action became much more of a mistake for most American citizens and for their political leaders in hindsight rather than during the war itself. The view of the Vietnam conflict as a mistake continued into the 1990s, with a 1992 survey taken by the Roper organization showing that 47% of Americans believed the war in Vietnam was the "wrong thing" for the United States to do and only 21% saying it was the right thing (*Public Perspective*, 1993: 101).

The retrospective disapproval of the U.S. role in the Vietnam conflict has shaped the way scholars and policy makers view American opinion toward the use of force in the past two decades. It is thought that the American public turned isolationist or at least much more cautious about committing troops after the Vietnam experience. Holsti and Rosenau (1984: 78) investigated the degree to which a "post-Vietnam syndrome" has influenced the way American elites evaluate American foreign policy goals and actions. They found that even though the post–World War II consensus about the role that the United States should play in the world had, in their terms, "shattered," it was not at all clear that a new consensus had emerged to replace it. They reported that there were clear disagreements within American elites about the future role of the United States in the world. To some extent these disagreements were rooted in the positions that individuals had taken toward the Vietnam conflict, but the views held by elites years after the war were not explained totally by their stance toward the Vietnam experience.

The change in American support for the U.S. involvement in the Vietnam conflict led to another interesting insight into the American public's mind. Mueller (1973) compared the trends in support for American involvement in the conflict with the reports of casualties in both the Vietnam conflict and the Korean conflict 15 years earlier and reported that disapproval for involvement in the war increased in a fairly regular pattern as the number of American casualties rose. This particular finding, based on data from two different conflicts, has become an important factor in the calculations of political leaders when they send American troops overseas. President Ronald Reagan, for example, quickly withdrew troops and ships from Lebanon in 1984 after several hundred U.S. marines were killed in an attack on their barracks in Beirut.

The studies of public opinion during the Vietnam conflict were among the first to highlight the importance of race and gender in influencing attitudes toward the use of military force. Although Shapiro and Mahajan (1986) reported gender differences toward the use of force in earlier decades, the analysis of Verba and his colleagues (1967: 325) was among the first to note the differences between men and women in support of escalation of the military effort in 1967. In analyzing a fairly intensive national study of attitudes toward the war, Verba and his colleagues were somewhat surprised to find that even though the mass public had fairly structured attitudes toward the involvement of the United States, the division between those who supported escalation and those who favored de-escalation was not related to standard demographic factors such as economic status, education, or region, nor were the divisions strongly related to political party identification or other political positions. However, in the case of gender, women were less informed about the war than were male respondents and were considerably less likely to support escalation of the effort. Race was an even stronger predictor of views on escalation, with African Americans significantly differing from white Americans in their preference for increased de-escalation of the war effort. This study, which was based on a survey completed in 1967, was among the first to identify these gender and race differences on foreign policy issues.

The Persian Gulf War

Public support for the American-led military attack on Iraq after that nation's invasion of Kuwait provides a direct contrast to the pattern of public support in the Vietnam era. Iraq's army invaded Kuwait on August 2, 1990. That action was condemned by the United Nations the following day. In the weeks that followed the invasion, U.S. troops were sent to bases in Saudi Arabia by the tens of thousands, and the United Nations imposed an economic and financial boycott on Iraq. By mid-November, the coalition military forces in the region totaled about half a million. In early January 1991, after talks with Iraq stalled, President George H. W. Bush asked Congress for a resolution approving the use of military force if Iraq did not withdraw from Kuwait by January 15. After heated debate, Congress approved the resolution on January 13. On January 17, during the evening news broadcast, American jets attacked Baghdad and the event was televised on CNN. Following intensive bombing and missile attacks by the United States and other coalition allies, the ground attack began on February 21 and ended on February 28 with the liberation of Kuwait and the defeat of the Iraqi army. Although there was talk of trying to capture Saddam Hussein, the Bush administration ended the war without toppling the Iraqi government. In contrast to the "retrospective" view of the Vietnam situation in which Americans now voice suspicion of foreign involvements, about two-thirds of the public agreed that the United States should take all action necessary, including the use of military force, to ensure the withdrawal of Iraq from Kuwait within one week of Iraq's incursion into Kuwait. Support for such a strategy stayed above 60% all the way up to the passage of the congressional resolution. The morning after the bombing began, support for the attack rose among the public and stayed high throughout the military campaign.

There were differences within the public over support for the Persian Gulf campaign, especially between men and women. In almost every survey from August through the campaign itself, women were less supportive than were men by 10% to 15%. However, since the overall level of support was so high, even the female respondents expressed support at levels of 50% to 70%.

Public opinion during the Persian Gulf War was remarkable for the strength of support given to the U.S. military, both before and during the actual use of force. It was also remarkable as a demonstration of the **rally-round-the-flag effect**. First noted by John Mueller (1973) in his studies of public support for the president during the Korean and Vietnam conflicts, this phenomenon is best described as a rapid improvement of presidential approval rating that occurs when the United States faces a foreign policy crisis or sends U.S. troops into military action. It has been suggested that the rally effect is caused by the public's identification of the good of the nation with that of the president and with the public's desire for cohesion in the face of an enemy. The rally effect is another manifestation of the bipartisanship that has characterized political debate on foreign policy for most of the nation's history.

The Persian Gulf War provided astounding evidence of the rally effect. Parker, who defines the rally effect as invoking "feelings of allegiance toward national political institutions and policies" (1995: 526), tracked public opinion toward the elder President Bush, toward the other institutions of government, toward family finances, and toward trust in government before, during, and after the military action in the Persian Gulf. She found that the rally effect, while spectacular in the case of Bush's approval ratings (which increased as much as 30% during the crisis), carried over to the public's attitudes toward other politicians, toward their view of economic conditions, and toward other institutions of government. The rally effect even increased the proportions of people who trusted the government. Even more interesting are the data collected after the crisis ended. Parker showed clearly that the rally effect is temporary, since, in the case of every survey question, responses dropped to the levels reported before the Gulf War. The public went from 57% saying Bush's job rating was good or excellent to 78% saying so during the crisis. The rating then returned to 59% after the Gulf War ended. Given these swings in public perceptions within one year, Parker concluded that "rally forces appear to be prototypical period forces—they arise in response to particular events and have the potential of moving large segments of the population in the same direction during the same time period. For most attitudes, such boosts are relatively short-lived" (1995: 541).

TERRORISM AND THE WARS IN AFGHANISTAN AND IRAQ

In the months following the 9/11 attacks on the Pentagon and the World Trade Center, public support for the Bush administration's "war on terrorism" was extremely strong and long lasting. In a series of questions asked within a few days of the attacks, the American public showed how strongly it supported military action. When asked whether the United States should take military action in retaliation for the attacks, 88% agreed that it should. When asked if military action would mean getting into a war, 86% supported the action; if it meant innocent civilians might be harmed overseas, 77% supported military action; and if it meant a long war with U.S. troops harmed or killed, 69% of those polled still supported military action (*Public Perspective*, 2001: 24). The public support for military action was stronger than it had been in the Persian Gulf War, and, as events unfolded, it stayed close to the September level for months.

As discussed previously, the first reaction could be described as a rally effect similar to those seen at other points in the nation's history. As in the case of the Persian Gulf War, support for military action translated immediately into higher approval ratings for the president. President George W. Bush's job approval ratings soared to close to 90% by the time he addressed Congress and announced the war on terrorism. The approval ratings stayed at that high level through his State of the Union speech in late January 2002.

At the same time, President Bush was confronted by an economic recession made worse by the economic impact of the 9/11 attacks. Public perceptions of the nation's economy declined throughout 2001, from a high of 77% in December 2000 to 46% at the end of September 2001 (*Public Perspective*, 2001: 52). The loss of public confidence in the economy had no impact on the ratings of the president's performance in wartime. As in the Persian Gulf War, people's trust in government increased following the 9/11 attacks.

The war on terrorism had a much greater impact on American life than did any military conflict since World War II. As laws were passed and plans were implemented to fight terrorism, Americans adapted to changes in daily life in the United States: airport security was greatly tightened; new regulations took effect for mail, shipping, and banking; and new laws were passed that constrained some privacy rights. In the years that followed the 9/11 attacks, there were many debates over the extent to which American liberties might be curtailed by antiterrorism measures. Indeed, Americans were shocked at the scandals revealed at the Abu Ghraib prison and at other actions taken by U.S. troops. However, continued terrorist attacks in Bali, Spain, and Great Britain kept the level of concern about terrorist attacks in the United States very high. The early levels of support for military action in Afghanistan and for other initiatives reflected both a rally effect and the shock of the attack on American soil.

As soon as the Al Qaeda organization was identified as the perpetrator of the 9/11 attacks, the United States began to build support for dislodging that terrorist organization from its base in Afghanistan and, at the same time, toppling the regime of the Taliban in that nation. With United Nations support, the first bombing attacks in Afghanistan began on October 7, 2001, and by December 2001 the Taliban government had been deposed and an interim government installed. Although the troops were at that time unable to capture Osama bin Laden, the leader of Al Qaeda, many members of the organization were killed in the military assault on Afghanistan. Public support for the attack was strong throughout the operation and continued for many months while the Afghans attempted to create a democratic government for themselves. U.S. troops remained in Afghanistan during the Bush administration, but with mixed results. Attempts to create a new national government were met with corruption and tribal enmities.

Early in 2002, President George W. Bush identified Iraq, Iran, and North Korea as an "axis of evil" in the world. Soon after, the United States began to pressure the United Nations to enforce its own resolutions against Iraq for not complying with the directive to end its development and mainte-nance of weapons of mass destruction. Although the nations of Europe and the United Nations continued to support dialogue and negotiation with Iraq over the weapons program, the Bush administration pushed for a military solution to the Iraq problem. On March 19, 2003, with support from Great Britain and more than a dozen other nations, the United States launched a military attack against Iraq. Baghdad fell on April 9, and major combat operations ceased by May 1. As the United States and its partner nations worked to rebuild Iraq and establish a democratic government over the next two years, insurgent attacks against the troops and against Iraqi civilians continued, with more Americans being killed after the combat ended than during the attack itself. After Bush's reelection in 2004, antiwar movements began to grow, and support for the president's handling of the war in Iraq declined steadily.

In the summer of 2007, the Bush administration recalibrated its strategy in Iraq and increased the troops on the ground in the so-called surge. Although support for the war itself did not increase, Americans were more likely to say that the military effort was doing better.

In 2008, candidate Barack Obama campaigned on the promise to pull troops out of Iraq over a stated period of months and end U.S. military involvement in that country. In his view, the Iraq war was a mistake, but the Afghanistan conflict was a necessary war because that nation was the home of the Taliban and the headquarters of Al Qaeda. After his inauguration, President Barack Obama began the planned troop drawdown in Iraq and, after deliberation, increased the U.S. troop levels in Afghanistan to defeat the Taliban and stabilize that nation. It is interesting to compare the levels of public support for the Iraq and Afghanistan wars as shown in Tables 11.4 and 11.5. The Gallup Poll has asked the question, "Do you think the United States made a mistake in sending troops to Iraq or not?" since 2003. The same question has been asked about the U.S. military invasion of Afghanistan. Approval of the decision to send troops to Afghanistan has

Table 11.4.   Public Views on the Iraq War as a Mistake, 2003–2010 (percent)[a]

	2003	2004	2005	2006	2007	2008	2009	2010
Yes, a mistake	32	46	51	54	58	59	56	54
No	67	51	49	45	40	38	41	43
Don't know	1	3	0	1	2	1	3	3

[a]Question wording: "In view of developments since we first sent our troops to Iraq, do you think the United States made a mistake in sending troops to Iraq, or not?"

Source: Gallup Poll.

Table 11.5.   Public Views on the Afghan War as a Mistake, 2001–2010 (percent)[a]

	2001	2002	2004	2007	2008	2009	2010
Yes, a mistake	9	6	25	25	31	35	41
No	89	93	72	70	66	60	55
Don't know	2	1	3	5	4	3	4

[a]Question wording: "In view of developments since we first sent our troops to Afghanistan, do you think the United States made a mistake in sending troops to Afghanistan, or not?"

Source: Gallup Poll.

always been stronger and has never shown a majority thinking that it was a mistake, even though casualties have been mounting and the likelihood of establishing a stable Afghan nation may be no better than it was a decade ago. However, the Gallup Poll (2011) also shows that a majority of Americans support setting a time table for withdrawing troops from Afghanistan whether the situation gets better or not. This pattern of public support for the war supports the view of John Mueller, who first investigated the impact of casualties on public opinion. He believes that the "public applies a fairly reasonable cost-benefit analysis when evaluating foreign affairs, but it values the lives of Americans very highly and tends to undervalue the lives of foreigners" (2002: 156). Mueller sees the public as accepting "some number" of casualties as the price of the mission but that the public's tolerance for losses is limited.

PEACEKEEPING, RESCUE, AND OTHER USES OF MILITARY FORCE

Since World War II, U.S. presidents have used military force for many types of missions: peacekeeping, rescue of American hostages or soldiers, humanitarian delivery of food supplies, and quick military strikes. Although Congress passed the War Powers Resolution presumably to require the president to consult with Congress before sending U.S. troops into military situations, no president has abided by the letter of that law and most have simply announced that they believe the act is unconstitutional in light of their powers as commander-in-chief. Presidents who contemplate the use of force often consult with a few key leaders of Congress about the possibility of using the troops or inform them after the troops have been ordered into action. To date, Congress has not attempted to force any president to meet the actual terms of the law by ordering troop withdrawals or cutting funding for the troops.

What do Americans think about these various uses of force? The lessons of Vietnam and the Persian Gulf War seem to hold for the most part: If the use of force is quick and successful, incurring few or no American casualties, most members of the public tend to approve of that use. However, if there is any possibility of Americans becoming mired in a complicated situation that will threaten their safety and require a long-term commitment, Americans are less eager to support involvement. The American public was generally supportive of the use of force in some instances, such as the air attack on Libya in 1986, the invasion of Grenada in 1983, and the use of force in the Persian Gulf War. Generally, the American people also supported the use of troops in Somalia in 1992 to assist in a humanitarian effort. However, after American Rangers were attacked by Somalia clans, support for the use of troops there dropped precipitously. Finally, the use of troops in what might be called "peacekeeping" or "democratizing situations" is usually a risky venture in terms of public opinion (Mueller, 2002: 165–168). Americans needed to be convinced that the proposed use of troops is likely to be mostly for peaceful purposes, that few troops will become casualties, and that no Americans will be taken hostage. Generally speaking, the group differences already discussed hold in most of the situations. Women are likely to be less supportive than men in almost any hypothetical situation requiring the use of troops. African Americans are also likely to be less supportive than white Americans. The use of troops in Somalia produced a different type of public response, in that women were not less supportive than men nor were African Americans less supportive than whites. One might hypothesize that because the mission was cast as humanitarian rather than military and targeted an African nation, the usual divisions within mass opinion did not develop. Neither women nor African Americans saw the usual dangers of military force associated with this use of U.S. troops. Later, when American Rangers were attacked and brutally killed, opinion on the Somalia operation changed rapidly.

FOREIGN AID AND OTHER INTERNATIONAL ISSUES

In the years since the end of World War II, the United States became the leader of the free world in terms of alliance-building, economic stability, and the formation of an international organization. In contrast to its refusal to join the League of Nations after World War I, the United States provided the leadership to create and, through its support, to sustain the United Nations. As part of the postwar leadership role, President Harry Truman put forth the Marshall Plan, which provided massive economic assistance to rebuild the shattered economies of Western Europe. The major goal of that assistance was to prevent some of those nations from moving toward the communist bloc, but in fact the Marshall Plan was foreign economic aid delivered at a scale never seen again since. Responding to the leadership of President Harry Truman and bipartisan support in Congress, the American public gave strong approval of the Marshall Plan, with 57% supporting this initiative in 1947 and 72% approving of the sending of economic aid to Western Europe in 1948 (*Public Perspective*, 1993: 97).

Another legacy of World War II was the development of military and peacekeeping alliances led by the United States. As previously mentioned, the United States helped create the United Nations and the Security Council system as a way to keep peace in the world. Then, as enmity developed between the United States and the Soviet Union, particularly in regard to the Eastern European states that became part of the Soviet bloc, the United

States created the North Atlantic Treaty Organization (NATO) as a mutual defense pact with the European nations. American public opinion supported that alliance as well as many others created by the United States in the years of the Cold War. However, much has changed in the world situation since the late 1940s, and even though Americans still support a global role for the United States, there have been important changes in the public's support for some of the nation's postwar initiatives.

Foreign Aid

When asked what government programs should be cut to balance the budget, foreign aid is often high on the priority savings list for many citizens. When asked how much the United States spends on foreign aid in comparison to other nations, few citizens know that other nations outspend the United States as a proportion of their GNP. This is quite a change from the climate of opinion in the postwar years, when the Marshall Plan to rebuild European economies was proposed. In 1947, 57% of Americans approved of the Marshall Plan; in 1948, 72% favored "continuing to send economic aid to Western Europe under the Marshall Plan." That level of support stayed above 60% for the next four years (*Public Perspective*, 1993: 97).

American support for foreign assistance efforts has declined precipitously since the postwar period among the mass public, although elites generally favor foreign assistance, particularly to specific regions of the world. If we look at the historic series of data from the Chicago Council on Foreign Relations, shown in Table 11.6, the contrast between mass and elite support for the general policy of sending economic assistance is very clear, with elites' support at more than 85% for the 25-year period and mass support averaging less than 50%. Why is there such disparity among elites and masses on the question of foreign economic assistance? More detailed survey questions have been asked at various points about the implications of foreign assistance for the United States. To some, American foreign economic assistance is simply a waste of public funds, especially compared to the use

Table 11.6. Elite and Public Support for Economic Aid, 1974–1998

Year	Percentage in Favor of Giving Economic Aid		Year	Percentage in Favor of Giving Economic Aid	
	Public	*Leaders*		*Public*	*Leaders*
1974	52	—	1990	45	90
1978	46	90	1994	45	86
1982	50	94	1998	47	88
1986	53	91			

Source: Chicago Council on Foreign Relations.

of such funds to solve domestic problems. To others, foreign economic assistance and its cousin, foreign military assistance, are the forerunners of involvement in another nation's problems, including the use of U.S. troops. Elites are much more conscious of the degree to which the American and world economy rests on the stability of individual nations, and they support foreign economic assistance as a way to bring stable conditions to other nations.

The United Nations

From time to time Americans have been less than enthusiastic about the United Nations as an organization. Although the United States led the world's nations in the formation of the United Nations, many Americans have questioned the United Nations' efficacy over the years and, indeed, the economic support that the United States has given to the United Nations. However, the data from the Chicago Council show that there is a consistent pattern of support for the United Nations: When asked whether strengthening the United Nations" was a very important goal, 46% of the respondents agreed in 1974. That percentage varied no more than two percentage points until 1994, when it increased to 51%. The most recent Chicago Council on Foreign Relations survey found a decline in that sentiment to 37%. Compared to other foreign policy goals embraced by Americans, strengthening the United Nations is in the second tier of preferences but, nevertheless, has consistent support.

American opinions about the United Nations are complicated by the changes in the world situation. During the Cold War, civil wars in less-developed nations such as Somalia or Vietnam frequently became surrogate conflicts between the United States and the Soviet Union, with each of the major powers backing one party to the conflict. The United States and the Soviet Union avoided direct confrontation but, through their rivalry, policed many of the lesser conflicts in the world. Neither of the powers nor their allies would allow the United Nations to become involved in these disputes. Since the end of the Cold War, this role has been given to the United Nations, with an ever-expanding peacekeeping function. In 2011, the United Nations mounted peacekeeping efforts in 16 nations involving more than 121,000 personnel and costing more than $7 billion. As the United Nations role has become greater in the peacekeeping arena, Americans have raised questions over the degree to which U.S. troops should take part in these efforts. Numerous surveys have asked whether Americans approve of U.S. troops participating in United Nations peacekeeping efforts around the world. An ABC News/*Washington Post* poll conducted in November 1993 found that 60% of Americans approved of sending U.S. troops, while 35% disapproved. The 2004 Chicago Council survey found

78% of their respondents agreeing that "the U.S. should be part of a U.N. peacekeeping force in a troubled part of the world when asked" with 19% opposed. Such a high level of support may be due, in part, to the nonspecific nature of the question. Asking about "a troubled part of the world" does not raise the same kinds of concerns as, for example, asking about stopping a civil war or ending genocide in a specific nation.

The issue of sending U.S. troops to be part of a United Nations peacekeeping force is sometimes complicated by the question of command structure. Although it appears that a majority of Americans supports U.S. involvement in these efforts, there is considerable disagreement over who should command those troops. A 1993 survey sponsored by the *Los Angeles Times* Mirror Corp. found that 69% of those questioned believed that U.S. troops should always remain under the command of an American officer and 25% approved of placing troops under UN command. The 1994 Chicago Council survey showed a more evenly divided public, with 44% saying the United States should insist on American command for U.S. troops and an equal number (44%) agreeing to the idea of UN command. These 1993 and 1994 surveys were conducted during the debate over whether to send U.S. troops to the former Yugoslavia to enforce peacekeeping in the Balkan states.

HOW DO AMERICANS THINK ABOUT FOREIGN POLICY?

Times have changed since Walter Lippmann expressed his doubts about the wisdom of having the American people express opinions about foreign policy. With the advent of widespread media coverage of events worldwide and the ability of the president to reach all Americans using that same media, the opinions that Americans express about foreign policy decisions have become much more important in the political process. It appears, given the research cited earlier in this chapter, that the American mass public is not, on the whole, well informed about international affairs, nor do most Americans follow international news on a frequent basis. This is not to say, however, that the mass public does not have opinions about the role played by the United States in world affairs or about specific policy questions. The longitudinal data on the role to be played by the United States in world affairs and the goals that the public thinks are most important show consistency and stability over more than 20 years. In the case of the global-role questions, the responses are stable for more than 40 years.

Americans are not only capable of holding stable opinions about these "big picture" questions but are also quite capable of formulating opinions about crises and foreign policy decisions when the information is made available to them. Although the elites may see issues such as the use of troops in Bosnia or support for foreign aid in more global strategic terms, the mass public, when asked, expresses opinions quite clearly on these matters. Not only does the public formulate opinions about questions like using troops overseas for peacekeeping or in an emergency, but members of the general public follow the news enough to change their views over time. Tracking opinion about the American assistance to the Libyan rebels in 2011 shows that the public, while supportive of a new democratic regime, had strong doubts about the use of U.S. armed forces in the conflict.

Given this evidence of stability and change, students of public opinion continue to investigate the mechanisms by which members of the public come to hold either stable or changing opinions. We do know that political partisanship and ideology have limited influence on these views; generational experience, gender, and race seem to have special effects; and educational achievement is associated with a more internationalist perspective. What forces, then, in the absence of partisanship and ideology, lead people to adopt opinions and attitudes in the international arena?

The Prudent Use of Force

Perhaps there has been more attention to the public's views on the use of military force than on any other aspect of foreign and security policy. Since the Vietnam War and its political effects on President Lyndon Johnson, politicians have been highly sensitive to the need to have public support for any use of troops that might risk the lives of Americans. One view of how Americans arrive at opinions about the proposed use of force is put forward by Jentleson (1992), who characterizes the citizenry as the "pretty prudent public." Jentleson hypothesizes that Americans view the use of force in the post-Vietnam period as falling into one of two general categories, depending on the policy objective of the administration. One of the categories is "foreign policy restraint," meaning, in Jentleson's view, using force to restrain an adversary that is an active threat to the United States, to U.S. citizens, or to our clear interests. He categorizes the American air strike against Libya in 1986 and, of course, the Persian Gulf War, as these kinds of actions. In each case, it appears that public support for the use of force was strong both before and after the military effort.

The other category of policy objective cited by Jentleson is "internal political change," meaning the use of force to change the political structure within another nation. To some extent, the Vietnam conflict fits this objective. In addition, American use of force in Nicaragua, Panama, El Salvador, and more recently in Afghanistan and Iraq fit this category. Americans are much less likely, according to this view, to support the use of troops in a situation where the United States is attempting to change the balance of power within another nation.

To summarize the view of Americans as a "prudent public," Jentleson believes that "the post post-Vietnam American public agrees that the world is a dangerous place . . . the American public is prepared to support the use of force to restrain [an] aggressor" (1992: 72). However, any administration that considers using force to get involved in the internal affairs of another nation must be quite cautious, because the public will be quite skeptical of such policy objectives.

Working from Types

Another way to understand how Americans come to hold specific opinions about international issues and decisions is to identify certain basic types or positions that may anchor individual opinions. A number of scholars have analyzed surveys of foreign policy issues and suggested that Americans hold opinions that can be aligned along two dimensions. Many of the opinions that Americans have expressed in the Chicago Council surveys, for example, can be grouped along a dimension that measures their propensity to use force, that is, a militarism dimension. Americans at one end of this dimension eschew the use of force. In contrast, Americans at the other end would always choose to use force to achieve foreign policy goals. Another dimension expresses Americans' willingness to participate in the international arena, with opinions ranging from "go it alone" views to multilateralist positions. By categorizing Americans according to their views on these two dimensions, scholars have suggested that there may be four basic "core positions" or types that influence the actual opinions that people give to pollsters (Hinckley, 1988; Holsti, 1996; Schneider, 1997a; Wittkopf, 1990).

The four basic *anchor* or pure types have been defined as follows: isolationists, who prefer no involvement with global affairs for the nation; hardliners, who prefer unilateral, military solutions to most international situations; cooperative internationalists, who believe in multilateral policy solutions but are less supportive of the use of force; and militaristic internationalists, who also support multination alliances but also support the use of force. The interpretation of the dimensions and resulting core types varies somewhat from scholar to scholar, but the basic premise is the same: Individual Americans have basic predispositions on these issues of use of military force and cooperation with other nations and, when queried about their opinions on a specific policy or crisis situation, are likely to respond from this basic set of dispositions. Generally, scholars find that the majority of Americans fall into either the cooperative internationalist or militarist internationalist sectors, with many fewer being identified as hardliners or true isolationists.

Using Cues or Schemas

The use of types or core predispositions is quite a strong predictor of opinions toward certain types of foreign policy issues such as the use of force or support for NATO. However, as the work by Jentleson suggests, many foreign policy issues are much more complicated politically: The decision to send U.S. troops to Haiti to support the return of President Jean-Bertrand Aristide was one such foreign policy decision that involved no real threat to the United States but, because of the constant immigration of Haitians to the United States, had serious domestic implications for the president and Congress. The typology discussed previously is quite limited in its ability to predict American views on issues such as Haiti or the more strictly economic issues such as joining the North American Free Trade Agreement. Still other questions of foreign and national security policy, such as promoting democracy in the Middle East or extending membership in NATO to Poland, are quite tangential to the fourfold system already outlined.

Opinions and attitudes toward specific policies or actions may be rooted in cognitive structures known as *schemas*. Each individual carries certain sets of information and prior opinion that are sorted into mental files called schemas. The schema provides information that has been learned in the past, past attitudes or preferences expressed by the individual, and emotions or affective positions toward the topic. For example, an 80-year-old American may carry a schema about Japan that includes not only what we know about Japanese technology and the economy today but also memories of Japan as an enemy in World War II. If this citizen is a veteran of that conflict, he may have strong emotions about the Japanese that date back six decades. When confronted by a foreign policy issue that involves U.S. relations with Japan, the individual responds to the cue (Japan) and then utilizes the information and emotional attachments in that schema to respond to the issue. It is very likely that the 9/11 attacks and the war on terrorism will create a schema for a large proportion of the American population. Public policy issues that involve security issues, homeland security, or Arab states are likely to evoke an emotional response similar to that felt by Americans in the days after the attack. A number of scholars have investigated this view of how Americans respond and attempted to outline the structure of such schemas (Hurwitz and Peffley, 1987).

Because of the range of issues in the international field and the complexity of these issues, it is unlikely there is a definite outside limit on the number of dimensions or schemas that may structure attitudes and opinions (Bardes and Oldendick, 1978; Oldendick and Bardes, 1981). Most scholars who have analyzed the Chicago Council datasets and other such surveys agree that clearly attitudes toward militarism form a specific dimension or position for most Americans. Attitudes toward international activity in general are also likely to be widespread across the general population. Other dimensions include international organizations, foreign assistance, economic relations, terrorism, and American domestic interests. As the world situation changes and the United States faces quite different challenges to its interests and sovereignty, we would expect the dimensions of foreign policy to change within the American public. New information and new international contacts will shape both the informational content and the emotional content of schemas and, as generations succeed, new points of view will be generated.

SUMMARY

Jentleson pointed out that the world is a "dangerous place," a fact that was confirmed for the American public by the events of September 11, 2001. Americans were reminded on that date that they must be aware of foreign policy issues more than they have been. For the most part, the data reviewed in this chapter suggest that Americans are more consistent and more responsive to world affairs than was believed by scholars, commentators, and elites before 1950. Of course, there are many more sources of information for the ordinary citizen today, and international contacts are much greater for many than in previous eras. And given the global role played by the United States since World War II, many more Americans have had experience with the military and peaceful initiatives taken by the nation in recent decades. All of this leads us to view the American public as aware of international affairs, if not always attentive to the details; as competent to make judgments about foreign and military policies if given the information; and as showing remarkably consistent support for the role played by the United States in world affairs.

POLLS, POLLING, AND THE INTERNET

As news stories break on foreign policy issues, you might look for polling data on the websites maintained by the major media, including:

- ABC News: www.abc.com
- CNN: www.cnn.com
- *USA Today*: www.usatoday.com
- *New York Times*: www.nytimes.com
- *Washington Post*: www.washingtonpost.com

To look more closely at the 13 surveys conducted by the Chicago Council on Foreign Relations, go to the website for the (newly named) Chicago Council on Global Affairs: www.thechicagocouncil.org.

For information about the two latest public and elite surveys and a comprehensive database on global public opinion, go to the website of the Council on Foreign Relations: www.cfr.org.

In addition, the Program on International Policy Attitudes (PIPA) project at the University of Maryland regularly releases their findings on the website: www.pipa.org.

Part IV

PUBLIC OPINION:
A CRITICAL PERSPECTIVE

12

Challenges Facing Public Opinion Research: Issues of Reliability and Trust

In the seven preceding chapters, we have used the results of survey research to describe the origins of opinions on political issues and what the public knows about them, to discuss the public's orientation toward the political system, and to examine public opinion on social-welfare, racial, cultural, and foreign policy issues in an attempt to describe the American mind. This chapter explores some of the challenges that survey researchers face and identifies a number of factors that should be considered in deciding how much confidence to place in the findings reported in a public opinion survey.

As part of its special 50th issue, the editors of *The Public Perspective* (1998b: 86–94) asked nine senior survey practitioners to write about "the greatest challenges, or problems, now confronting public opinion research in the U.S." Although each of these researchers cited a different aspect of the survey profession, the theme running throughout these articles concerned the reliability and trustworthiness of polls. Although the specific challenges identified included the quality of data collection, response rates, interpreting results appropriately, and reporting them better, they all touched on the need to produce valid data. As Newport (1998: 87) noted, "The reliance on survey results to guide the ship of state necessitates that polls be trustworthy and reliable when they are first published." Although there have been significant changes in the way public opinion research is conducted since *The Public Perspective* issue was published, many of the themes identified remain relevant today. In order for public opinion data to be trustworthy, they must be **reliable**, producing consistent results, and **valid**, measuring what they intend to measure.

Though it is somewhat ironic to attempt to measure the public's opinion about polls using data from a public opinion poll, previous research has shown that although Americans have some reservations about poll results, they generally view surveys in a positive light (Dran and Hildreth, 1995; Goyder, 1986; Kohut, 1986; Roper, 1986).

Prior investigations of this topic have shown that the public generally believes that polls interview typical, representative people; are honest and accurate; work for the interests of the general public; and are an enjoyable and satisfactory experience (Roper, 1986: 10–13). Later research, such as that of Dran and Hildreth (1995, 1997), found a more mixed view of public opinion on the polls, with less than half of the public expressing confidence in their accuracy. A 1996 survey by the Gallup Organization found an increase in the number of people who pay attention to poll results. It also found that two-thirds of the public has faith in the accuracy of surveys. In addition, almost three-fourths of their respondents said that the country would be better off if the nation's leaders followed public opinion polls more closely, 87% felt polls are a "good thing" for the country, and 68% believed that polls work for the best interests of the general public (Gallup and Moore, 1996: 51–52). By 1999, however, only 38% of respondents said they had a good deal or fair amount of trust in what they saw or heard in public opinion polls, 52% felt that the country would be better off if less attention were paid to polls, and 54% believed that political officeholders and public officials paid too much attention to polls (Gallup Report, 1999).

Studies conducted by the Council for Marketing and Opinion Research (CMOR) have also found a mix of positives and negatives in citizen attitudes about public opinion polls. On the positive side, CMOR's studies have shown the public to believe that the survey research industry serves a useful purpose, that responding to surveys is in their best interest, and that polls and surveys are useful in providing government officials with an understanding of how the public feels about important issues. On the negative side, the public believes that there are too many polls on subjects of little value, is skeptical of results reported in surveys, and does not understand how the small number of people interviewed in the typical survey can represent the entire population. The CMOR studies have also shown that positive perceptions of surveys are declining, while negative perceptions are increasing. Although the public generally feels that participating in a poll is a pleasant experience and finds the subject matter of polls interesting, there has been a marked increase in public concern over the issue of privacy. A higher percentage of the public now feels that polls are an invasion of privacy, and a large majority does not believe that organizations that conduct polls and surveys can be trusted to protect their privacy rights. Even though survey researchers diligently protect the confidentiality of respondents, the industry rules related to privacy issues are not being communicated clearly or are not being understood by the public.[1]

A September 2011 Gallup Poll did not directly assess the public's views on polls, but did provide an indirect indication of the public's belief in their results. Gallup asked, "If the leaders of our nation followed the views of public polls more closely, do you think the nation would be better off or worse off than it is today?" A clear majority—68%—believes that the nation would be better off if leaders paid closer attention to polls. Gallup has asked this question four times since 1996, and "in all instances a substantial majority has said that the nation would be better off" (Newport, 2011). Americans want their leaders to pay more attention to the views of the people. As Newport notes, "In a country with more than 300 million people, the most efficient and practical way for leaders to assess the public's views is through polls."

Overall, there is some skepticism in the American mind about how survey data are collected and how such information is used and reported. In recent years, increasing concern over the confidentiality of information provided has contributed to a decline in the public's view of surveys. Despite the general confidence that the public has in polls as a mechanism for expressing their views, a number of factors can lead to errors in the way survey data are collected, interpreted, or reported that might cause the public to lose more faith in the polling process. In the remainder of the chapter we examine several of these elements, including pseudo-polls, technological developments, and respondent factors.

PSEUDO-POLLS

Pseudo-polls involve contacts with individuals and have some elements of a legitimate survey but are not attempts to collect information from a representative sample of the public. Chapter 3 described one type of pseudo-poll, the "call-in" poll to an 800 or 900 telephone number, and we reiterate the point that such "polls" do not legitimately represent the views of any population. Such polls can be especially troubling or cause confusion among the American public when they are used by major news organizations, which also conduct scientific surveys and report results based on representative samples. In describing the results of one of the first such polls that was done in conjunction with an on-air broadcast, in which the distinction between the results of a call-in poll and a companion survey with a representative sample were not always clear, Kathy Frankovic, director of surveys for CBS News, noted: "We never wanted to say the 'poll' in referring to the callers. There were slipups in the course of the live broadcast, where the conclusion was drawn that the call-ins represented change" (1992: 19). In commenting on this poll, Albert Cantril (1992: 23) declared, "The credibility of all public polls was set back when CBS News conducted its call-in 'poll.' . . . The broadcast was especially hazardous to polling credibility because of the stature of CBS as a source of news"[2] (Moore, 1992: 288). Whether reported by a major media source or your local radio station, the results of a call-in poll cannot be treated as representing the views of some larger population.

Another type of pseudo-poll, previously described in Chapter 3, is the push poll. There is no research component to a push poll; this is telemarketing under the guise of survey research. Such polls damage the electoral process in that "they injure candidates, often without revealing the source of the information" and "represent the worst kind of imposition on respondents" (Gawiser, 1995: 1). Push polling is condemned by survey research professional associations such as the American Association for Public Opinion Research (AAPOR) and Council for Marketing and Opinion Research. Push polls violate the AAPOR code of ethics by intentionally lying to or misleading respondents. They corrupt the electoral process by disseminating false and misleading attacks on candidates. And because so-called push polls can easily be confused with real polls, they damage the reputation of legitimate polling, thereby discouraging the public from participating in legitimate survey research. Despite these reservations, many campaign professionals regard push polling as a valuable tool for winning elections. Because these push polls foster cynicism about the use of polling in the political process, they remain a continuing concern for survey research practitioners.[3]

Mail "surveys" of constituents conducted by elected officials, typically members of Congress, represent another type of pseudo-poll. Such devices often contain questions that are worded in a way to make the results support the officeholder's position or are designed to provide information about the candidate (for example, "During the last session of Congress, Senator X voted for a bill that brought over $800 million in new federal highway funds to this state. Do you support this position?"). When the results of such totally nonscientific mail surveys are reported, they can lead to confusion among the public as to what the "public" actually thinks.

TECHNOLOGICAL DEVELOPMENTS

As described in Chapter 4, in recent years there has been an enormous rise in electronic data collection and the use of the Internet for gathering information on "public opinion." Although significant strides have been made in using electronic data collection to gather reliable and valid information on both targeted groups and general populations, the Internet provides considerable opportunities for information collection that can best be described as pseudo-polls. The development of web-based surveys means that large-scale data collection is no longer restricted to organizations with extensive resources. As Couper (2000: 465) has noted, "The relatively low cost of conducting Web surveys essentially puts the tool in the hands of almost every person with access to the Internet." But such widespread access makes it more difficult to distinguish the good from the bad. In the earlier description of electronic data collection it was noted that one of the most difficult aspects of conducting such surveys—particularly of a general population—is identifying and contacting a representative sample of the population. When respondents are recruited by e-mail, by visiting various websites, by participating in sweepstakes, or there is some other type of uncontrolled instrument distribution, it is extremely difficult to judge not only the representativeness of the results but also what population the respondents represent. Some websites that solicit respondents by e-mail promise payment for people's opinions. One such e-mail read, in part, "Your opinions have value. Are you getting paid for them? Start now! Take surveys at home and get paid $15–$125/hr for your opinions. There are over 1500 surveys everyday for you to participate in GUARANTEED!" To the extent that the results of web surveys are the expression of the views of professional survey takers or are otherwise unrepresentative, they are of questionable utility in understanding the American mind. The development of the Internet has been a positive development in that, when used properly, it provides another means for collecting information about the views of some population of interest. But it also has its drawbacks in that the relative ease of posting a "survey" increases the likelihood of information being produced that represents the views of no identifiable group except the respondents themselves.

As noted in Chapter 4, groups such as Knowledge Networks and Harris Online have made considerable advances in developing methods for selecting a sample for web surveys. Although the approaches used by these two groups in recruiting panel members from which these samples are selected are quite different, they are both complex and require considerable resources to develop and maintain. Despite the significant advances that have been made in the use of the Internet for survey data collection, this mode still faces substantial challenges in collecting information from a representative sample of the population. Although there has been a rise in the proportion of households with access, Internet users continue to be younger, have more education, and to be more affluent. In addition, Internet surveys face issues related to privacy and confidentiality as well as methodological issues related to the presentation of items on the screen in order to collect the most reliable information and avoid context effects. None of these obstacles are insurmountable. Although much additional research needs to be done in this area, there seems little question that the use of the Internet to collect survey information will continue to increase and will be significant in the survey research of the 21st century (Goidel, 2011).

Over the past 45 years, there have been a number of other technological developments that have had an impact on the polling profession, some of which have been very positive and others quite negative. Among the positive examples, the development of computer-assisted telephone interviewing, audio-assisted **computer-assisted self-interviewing**, and voice recognition technology have each improved the quality and efficiency of survey data collection. Other developments, such as the increased use of telephone answering machines and caller-ID services and the vast change in the public's use of cellular telephones, have made the business of collecting information from a representative sample of the population more difficult.

As noted by Tuckel and O'Neill (1996: 34), the problem that the technologies such as answering machine devices, privacy managers, and caller ID pose for survey researchers is that "they may make it more difficult for telephone surveyors to establish contact with respondents and therefore compromise the representativeness of the samples selected for interviewing." Households with telephone answering machines can use the device to screen unwanted calls and, if a message is left by a survey organization, choose not to return the call. Similarly, users of caller ID or call-blocking devices are unlikely to recognize the phone numbers of most survey research organizations when these numbers are displayed on their units. If they are unwilling to answer calls from an unrecognized number, then the opportunity for public opinion researchers to contact them and determine their views on "matters of public interest" is diminished. As potential survey respondents systematically exclude themselves from participation through the use of these devices, the threat increases that the results of the survey will not accurately represent "what the public thinks."

When random-digit dialing (RDD) was being developed (Cooper, 1964), telephone answering machines for residential households were virtually nonexistent. By 1990, an estimated 43% of U.S. households were equipped with such devices (Electronic Industries Association, 1991). By 1995, two-thirds of households reported answering machine ownership, and this figure reached more than 80%, though this percentage has declined in recent years as more households have abandoned their landlines and have no need for an answering machine device in the home. Caller-ID services became available later than answering machines but made the same rapid penetration into the U.S. market. In 1993, only 3% of households subscribed to caller-ID services, a percentage that increased to 10% in 1995. Since then, there has been a phenomenal growth in caller-ID users, with the percentage of households subscribing to this service reaching 45% in 2000 (Tuckel and O'Neill, 2001: 3) and continuing to grow in acceptance since then, especially among those with unlisted telephone numbers. When the approximately 20% of the population that has other types of privacy manager services such as call blocking, "do not disturb" service, or a distinctive ringing feature on their phone is added to this mix, it becomes apparent that a substantial portion of the population has the ability to screen calls from survey researchers.

As these devices have become more pervasive, they have made it more difficult for survey researchers to reach those selected to be interviewed (Herrmann, 2001; Link and Oldendick, 1998). Early research on the impact of these call-screening devices on the representativeness of telephone surveys demonstrated that only a small percentage of households used these devices on a consistent basis to screen unwanted calls and that a substantial proportion of households continued to be accessible to survey researchers (Oldendick and Link, 1994: 266; Tuckel and Feinberg, 1991: 206–207; Tuckel and O'Neill, 1996: 40).

Although the early studies of the impact of screening devices on telephone surveys concluded that such devices had only a limited impact on representativeness, the increasing percentage of households using such devices raised this threat considerably. In Tuckel and O'Neill's (2001) investigation, they found that the potential negative impact from caller-ID users rose dramatically. As they note, "Roughly two-thirds of caller-ID subscribers (whether or not they have an answering machine) now report screening either 'always' or 'most of the time'" (Tuckel and O'Neill, 2001: 4). When coupled with the significant rise in the number of households that have caller ID and a reported increase in the percentage of answering machine owners who screen calls, a substantial proportion of potential respondents now screens their calls on a frequent basis. Moreover, the likelihood that caller-ID users will answer the phone when an unrecognized number appears has declined significantly. The percentage of users who said they were "almost certain" or "very likely" to answer dropped over 20 percentage points between 1995 and 2000 and is likely to have continued this decline since then. These findings are consistent with those of Steeh and her colleagues (2001), who found that the decrease in response rates in telephone surveys was due to a substantial increase in noncontact rates, not to an increase in refusals to participate. In sum, the use of screening devices presents "major obstacles that now impede the ability of survey researchers to establish contact with potential respondents and to secure their cooperation" (Tuckel and O'Neill, 2001: 10). Public opinion researchers must commit increasing resources to overcoming these obstacles if they are to maintain the representativeness of telephone samples on which many survey researchers have come to rely.

Though the use of screening devices has had an impact on telephone surveys, this has not been nearly as dramatic as the effect of the increased use of cell phones. The way in which Americans use telephones has changed significantly in recent years. As noted in Chapter 4, the percentage of U.S. households that do not have landline telephones and have become "cell phone–only" was estimated to be 29.7% in 2011 (Blumberg and Luke, 2011). In 2011 the number of cellular telephone subscribers in the United States was approximately 327 million, and the percentage has been growing by about 10% each year. As an increasing percentage of households abandoned their landline phone and became cell phone–only households, residents of these households have not been reached by traditional random-digit dialing (RDD) survey methods, which were based on only landline exchanges. Moreover, not only were the people in cell phone–only households being excluded from telephone samples, they were also systematically different from the overall population, in that people living in cell phone–only households were more likely to be under the age of 25, renters, and those living in households with unrelated roommates.

One might think that an obvious solution to this problem would be to include cell phone exchanges in the sampling frame for telephone surveys. There are a number of reasons that such a solution is not as straightforward as it might seem. Lavrakas and Shuttles (2005: 347) describe these in their statement, "Accounting for Cell Phones in Telephone Survey Research in the U.S.," which was issued following the Cell Phone Sampling Summit II Conference:

> Cell phones have traditionally been excluded, whenever possible, from most RDD studies because they pose numerous challenges, such as: (a) determining sample design weights; (b) defining new response codes and response rate formulas; (c) defining new calling and interview protocols; (d) re-evaluating the necessity for compensation for respondents; (e) working with cell phone providers to obtain 800 numbers that are truly free for cell phone calls and can be used by survey companies when asking the respondents to call back; (f) complying with the Telephone Consumer Protection Act restrictions; and (g) foregoing the geographic precision of landline telephone numbers.

Given the scope and importance of the issue of cell phone–only households, a considerable amount of research has been done on this topic. In 2007, *Public Opinion Quarterly* devoted a special issue to the topic of cell phone numbers in telephone surveying. Similarly, the American Association for Public Opinion Research formed a taskforce to study this issue.

Research on this issue has consistently shown that surveys based on landline only samples were producing estimates that were not only biased in terms of the demographic characteristics of the respondents but also in the answers to substantive questions. As Christian et al. (2010) noted, "Non-coverage bias is now appearing regularly in landline telephone samples. For some estimates, even a small amount of bias may have important substantive consequences for the political or social implications of the research." Moreover, they noted that the differential decrease in landline coverage across groups means that "some key subgroups in surveys based only on landlines may be severely underrepresented, making reliable estimates of attitudes and behaviors among these groups difficult or impossible to obtain" (6).

The AAPOR task force on sampling cell phone numbers for telephone surveys addressed many of the concerns raised by Lavrakas and Shuttles. The recommendations of this task force represent a "best practices" for conducting research involving cell phones. Implementing these practices requires some challenging adjustments in the way traditional landline surveys have been done. Interviews with cell phone respondents require more time to locate an eligible respondent, are less efficient, and more expensive. Developing the appropriate weighting schemes to account for differential probabilities of selection due to the fact that landline telephones are household based while cell phones are more individual communication devices and adjusting for those people who can be reached on both landline and cell phones adds to the cost of processing and analyzing the data. But to this point, the perceived hurdles in conducting interviews with cell phone respondents have not been impossible to overcome. Many survey organizations including Gallup and the Pew Research Center now routinely use a dual-frame sampling approach, which includes both landline and cell phone exchanges, in conducting telephone surveys.[4]

As Lavrakas and his colleagues (2007: 853) concluded, "Surveying the U.S. cell phone population is possible, if at a higher cost than surveying their landline counterparts, and if with less precision than can currently be done surveying the landline population. The next five years should see a considerable growth in the methodological and statistical know-how. . . . There is a great deal that still must be learned."

A final technological change that has raised concerns about telephone surveys conducted with traditional RDD samples is that of number **portability**. One of the great advantages of an RDD sample has been that if the population of interest were in a particular geographic region, this area could be defined fairly well by area codes and telephone exchanges. Traditionally, area codes did not cross state boundaries, so that if you were conducting a statewide survey your sampling frame would include all the telephone exchanges in the area codes assigned to that state. Even for smaller geographic areas, such as counties or cities, the geographic boundaries could be fairly well defined by telephone exchanges, with only a minimum amount of screening needed to identify a respondent in the target area. The Telecommunications Act of 1996 mandated number "portability," meaning that consumers could keep their phone numbers when switching service providers, changing services, or moving locations. The portability provision of this act went into effect in 2003. If you live in Cincinnati, Ohio, and have a telephone number with an area code of 513, and then move to Columbia, South Carolina (which has an area code of 803), you can retain your Cincinnati telephone number, including the area code. The potential problem is not one of including respondents in a survey who should not be included, since most surveys contain screening questions to verify the respondent's eligibility, including the location of their residence. The potential problem is more in the other direction, in that a researcher who is conducting a survey in South Carolina would include numbers from the area codes assigned to the state (803, 843, and 864); in doing so, individuals who had moved from other locations and taken advantage of number portability would not be included. Number portability does not yet pose a significant problem for RDD samples, but over time, as more people move from one area to another and take their telephone numbers with them, the magnitude of this problem for survey researchers will increase.

RESPONDENT FACTORS

Abuse of survey research is one factor that can affect the public's confidence in its results. Another set of factors involves characteristics of the population; that is, aspects of the public that can affect the reliability and validity of poll findings. These characteristics, which we have labeled *respondent factors*, include locating respondents, gaining their cooperation, and getting them to provide candid answers to the questions asked of them.

More than 15 years ago, increasing public participation in the polls had been labeled "the greatest and most frustrating challenge" facing public opinion researchers (O'Neill, 1996: 54); since that time this challenge has gotten significantly greater. In Chapter 4, we described the importance of selecting a sample appropriately to produce results that are representative of the population in which you are interested. But the results of the most carefully drawn sample can be called into question if the people selected do not participate in the survey.

Response rates involve both locating the individuals selected and convincing them to participate. During the time when most surveys of the general population were done by face-to-face interviewing, response rates were generally high. Individuals selected to be interviewed were relatively easy to contact and usually agreed to cooperate.

Although certain studies, such as the Current Population Survey, have been able to maintain a relatively high response rate (Tuckel and O'Neill, 2001), "the prevailing view, both based on these trend data and from practitioners' knowledge of the situation, is that response rates are declining and have been doing so for some time" (Groves and Couper, 1998: 159). More than 15 years ago, Brehm (1994: 5) noted that "response rates for all surveys—academic, government, business, media—have been falling since the 1950s." In the National Election Studies (NES), for example, refusal rates rose from 6% in 1952 to 21% in 1992. Overall nonresponse[5] to the NES was 23% in 1952 and 26% in 1992, but has reached more than 30% several times since then. In 2008, the response rate for the NES was 64%. In their study of changes in nonresponse in the Survey of Consumer Attitudes, Curtin, Presser, and Singer (2005: 96) found that the response rate for this survey had "declined rapidly over the past quarter century, averaging roughly one percentage point a year. Moreover, the decline has accelerated in the last few years." They also reported that response rates for the General Social Survey (GSS) fell to their lowest levels after 1998 and have been about 70% in the surveys conducted since then.

We have already described how technological devices such as telephone answering machines and caller ID have led to increasing noncontacts with selected households and contributed significantly to this decline in response rates. Factors such as fear of crime, increased cynicism, and concerns over privacy issues have also contributed to the increase in refusal rates, and societal changes, such as the increasing participation of women in the workforce and the reduction in the number of adults per household, means that households are occupied a smaller percentage of the time than before, making contact more difficult. Although response rates are declining for both face-to-face and telephone surveys, the decline in response rate seems to be greater in telephone surveys, driven in part by "the proliferation of telemarketing [which] is threatening the use of this mode of data collection for representative surveys of the general population" (Couper, 2000: 465).[6] In their research on this issue of declining response rates, Tuckel and O'Neill (2001) describe the vanishing respondent in telephone surveys and note that the average response rate in commercial sector RDD telephone surveys was less than 15%, and in 2011 response rates for even well-designed and executed telephone surveys are below 20%. Although there is evidence that the decline in response rates in telephone surveys is due more to the increasing difficulty in contacting respondents than an increase in refusals (Steeh et al., 2001), the potential impact on the representativeness of the results is the same. As Daves (2000: 50) has noted, "No matter what the measure, response rates in telephone surveys have been declining. This is a potentially serious problem for a host of industries that depend on sample surveys."

Some survey practitioners have considered these various challenges facing survey research, particularly surveys done by telephone, and reached a rather bleak conclusion. For example, Mark Blumenthal (2009) describes a presentation by Jay Leve, president of Survey USA. Levy argued that all phone polling depends on a set of assumptions:

> You're at home; you have a [home] phone; your phone has a hard-coded area code and exchange which means I know where you are; . . . you're waiting for

your phone to ring; when it rings you'll answer it; it's OK for me to interrupt you; you're happy to talk to me; whatever you're doing is less important than talking to me; and I won't take no for an answer—I'm going to keep calling back until you talk to me. (quoted in Blumenthal, 2009)

But the reality, as we have described, is much different. An increasing percentage of households do not have a home phone. The number being called may have been ported and can ring anywhere in the world, not necessarily in the geographic area in which the population of interest resides. When the phone rings, it is not answered; the potential respondent does not recognize the number displayed on the caller ID and lets the call be picked up by the answering machine. Potential respondents are busy; they don't want to give an unknown pollster 15 to 20 minutes of their time to answer questions on a topic about which they may not be that familiar or in which they have little interest.

Given these considerations, Leve (quoted in Blumenthal, 2009), concluded that, for phone polling, "if you look at where we are here in 2009, it's over . . . this is the end." Research on this issue has reached a less alarming conclusion. Low and declining responses are certainly a great concern to survey researchers. In a special issue of *Public Opinion Quarterly* devoted to the issue of nonresponse bias in household surveys, Groves (2006: 646) noted that "nonresponse can, but need not, induce non-response bias in survey estimates." An extensive investigation by Keeter and his colleagues (2006) compared the results from a survey using the Pew Research Center's "standard" 5-day survey methodology with those from a more "rigorous" survey conducted over a much longer field period and with a much higher response rate. They found "few significant differences in estimates produced by its Standard survey and by one employing more rigorous techniques aimed at obtaining a high rate of response. In terms of objective measures such as demographic characteristics and certain personal behaviors, the findings are generally reassuring. When compared with government benchmarks, the demographic and social composition of the sample in the Standard survey was quite representative on most measures" (778).

Survey researchers also point to the accuracy of preelection polls as evidence that falling response rates are not necessarily having a negative effect on polls' ability to reflect accurately the American mind. An analysis by the National Council on Public Polls (2010) following the 2010 midterm elections found that the average accuracy of statewide polls done in conjunction with state and national elections had remained stable. The methods that researchers have employed to address the issue of declining response rates have been relatively effective. As summarized by Mark Blumenthal (2011), "despite some high-profile misfires, doubts expressed by pollsters themselves and an eroding ability to reach and interview willing respondents, the overall accuracy of campaign polling remains surprisingly strong."

Another respondent characteristic affecting the reliability and validity of polls involves the information that individuals provide as part of the interview. In Chapter 4 we detailed many of the factors to be considered in designing survey questions properly. Even with the most well-designed questions, however, we find that many respondents exhibit **nonattitudes**; that is, there is a significant proportion of the public who, for lack of information about a particular issue, offer meaningless opinions that vary randomly in direction during repeated trials over time (Converse, 1964, 1970). Similarly, about one-third of the public will give opinions on fictitious or largely obscure items (Bishop et al., 1980; Schuman and Presser, 1981).[7]

Such "errors" in surveys, we believe, are not the product of people deliberately lying to pollsters, as at least one noted columnist once encouraged them to do (Royko, 1992). Instead, these responses reflect the interview situation, for a survey interview is a social interaction between the interviewer and respondent. In this situation the interviewer asks questions and the expectation is that the person being interviewed will respond. Faced with an issue with which they are unfamiliar, respondents can either answer "don't know" or quickly develop a response based on the information available to them in the question and the context in which the question is asked. The respondents' desire to present themselves in a favorable light (for example, as knowledgeable or agreeable) leads them to honor the interviewer's request for an answer (Martin, 1984). The interview, as a social interaction, represents more than a respondent providing answers to questions.

Similarly, research has shown that respondents will provide different answers to interviewers of their own race than to an interviewer of a different race. Such results are particularly evident when the question has racial overtones. Over the past 25 years, some of the largest discrepancies between the results of election polls and electoral outcomes have involved contests in which one of the candidates was a racial minority (Oldendick and Link, 1998). In these situations respondents are more likely to give answers that "defer" to the race of the interviewer (for example, whites are more likely to voice support for a black candidate to black interviewers than to whites; conversely, black respondents are more likely to indicate support for a white candidate to white interviewers). In cases where race is salient, respondents have a tendency to give "socially desirable" answers and are reluctant to be interpreted as racist (Davis, 1997; Finkel, Guterbock, and Borg, 1991; Hatchett and Schuman, 1975). Such race-of-interviewer effects again do not represent widespread "lying" on the part of respondents, but rather a recognition of the social nature of the interview and a desire to maintain "a polite conversation between the respondent and the interviewer" (Anderson, Silver, and Abramson, 1988: 319). Failure to account for such effects, however, can lead to inaccurate reporting of public attitudes and, over time, erode public trust and confidence in survey research.

With Barack Obama's candidacy in 2008, there was some concern among pollsters that a **Bradley effect**—the tendency for minority candidates to fare worse on election day than in preelection polls—might surface. In Blumenthal's (2008) view, "The unambiguous answer is that there was no Bradley effect." Similarly, Krosnick argued that "there's no point in continuing that discussion anymore. If there had been a discrepancy, there's every reason to believe it could have been explained by many other aspects of methodology" (quoted in Zernike and Sussman, 2008).

THE COST OF SURVEY ERRORS

A final challenge facing public opinion research involves survey errors. Although the *"Literary Digest* fiasco" of 1936 helped the scientific study of public opinion to gain acceptance, similar incorrect "forecasts" on the basis of scientific surveys have raised questions about the methods used to determine the state of the American mind. Following the 1948 headline, based largely on poll results, that "Dewey Defeats Truman," the Social Science Research Council conducted an extensive investigation of the factors that led to this "perceived failure" of the polls (Mosteller et al., 1949), and similar though less extensive, concerns were raised following the 1980 and 1996 U.S. elections (Ladd, 1996a; Ladd and Ferree, 1981).

In the 2000 and 2004 presidential elections, the perceived failure of the polls has centered on the results of exit polls. In Chapter 3 we described the role of the exit polls, combined with results from sample precincts, in the networks' call of the presidential race in Florida for Al Gore in 2000. As more vote tallies came in, the networks reversed the call and marked Florida as "too close to call." Then, in the middle of the night, basing their projection on reports of precinct vote counts, the networks called the vote for George W. Bush (Mitofsky and Edelman, 2002). Although this may have been a rare case in which "a designed and tested sample yield[ed] an estimate that [was] wide of the mark" (Mitofsky, 2001), the perception was that the exit polls had been in error.

In 2004, the exit polls again experienced problems, and in this year they significantly overstated the support for John Kerry. Following this election, the Social Science Research Council again conducted an investigation of the events surrounding these "errors" and misreporting of exit poll results (Traugott, Highton, and Brady, 2005). As this report notes, "The early exit poll data were incorrect in that they suggested that John Kerry was ahead in the national poll and leading in several key states that would have been sufficient to give him an electoral college majority. Furthermore, even the final data had a Kerry bias in their estimate of the outcome." These results led to "sufficient public discussion and consternation that a committee of the U.S. House headed by Rep. John Conyers (D-MI) held open sessions about election administration and the exit polls" (2).

The organizations responsible for collecting the exit poll data, Edison Media Research and Mitofsky International (2005), also conducted an extensive evaluation of their procedures. As the Social Science Research Council report (Taugott, Highton, and Brady, 2005: 8) noted, "This is unusual in that the same people who conducted the exit polls and the projection apparatus also did the evaluation." The Edison and Mitofsky evaluation report provides an extensive analysis of how the exit poll interviews were used to estimate the actual support for George W. Bush and John Kerry, discusses survey weighting issues, and describes the technical problems with the computer system that disrupted operations. Although this report acknowledged that the estimates produced by the exit poll were not as accurate as those in previous years, the evaluation did not find any systematic problems with the way in which the exit poll data were collected and processed. They concluded that the most likely source of errors was the differential response patterns by Kerry and Bush voters leaving the polls; that is, Kerry voters were more likely to agree to be interviewed while Bush voters were less likely. Although this report makes available "an unprecedented amount of information," it has not silenced the critics of the National Election Pool and its data (Traugott, Highton, and Brady, 2005: 9).

The preelection polls for the 2008 Democratic primary in New Hampshire all indicated that Barack Obama would defeat Hillary Rodham Clinton. The average poll difference was about 7%, with some polls indicating an advantage of more than 10% for Obama. When Clinton defeated Obama, 39% to 36%, it again caused survey researchers to reflect on "what went wrong?" AAPOR convened a special committee to investigate these results (AAPOR, 2009). Such highly visible and well-publicized "failures" of polls potentially damage the credibility of all survey-based results. The AAPOR report on this election identified a number of potential sources of error in the preelection polls, which serve as a reminder to survey practitioners not only of the difficulties in conducting preelection polling but also of the many factors that must be considered in designing and reporting on such races. Despite the many advances that have been made in the methods for conducting surveys, these principles must be carefully applied to avoid these types of "errors in forecasting." As users of poll data, you should recognize and appreciate "the deep 'validity problems' that can inhere to even the best research" and be aware that ensuring quality survey data is difficult and requires continuing effort (Ladd, 1998b: 86).

THE CONTINUING CASE FOR POLLING

This chapter has described many of the obstacles faced and problems associated with collecting information to describe the American mind accurately. Although these factors have made it difficult and more expensive to conduct surveys that provide a true picture of what the public thinks on a variety of issues, research has shown that surveys remain a viable means for collecting public opinion data. Studies such as those done by Keeter and his colleagues (2000, 2006), Curtin, Presser, and Singer (2005), and Blumberg, Luke, and Cynamon (2006) have found that factors such as lower response rates and the substitution of wireless for landline telephones have not led to significant differences in survey results or produced bias in reports of the topics of interest. As Blumberg and his colleagues (2006: 931) conclude, "Noncoverage bias is not presently a reason to reject the continued use of general population telephone surveys to help guide . . . decisions."

Moreover, polls continue to play an important role in the political process. In his book, *Polling Matters*, the Gallup Organization's Frank Newport (2004) makes the case that polling is an invaluable source of information that gives us a unique and consistently accurate window into issues as diverse as voting preferences, gender differences, race relations, child-rearing, consumer habits, health care, and education.

In a similar vein, in Shapiro's (2004: 2) case for why people should respond to opinion polls, he argues that polls "can be strikingly democratic and, especially, *egalitarian*, because they attempt to find out the opinion of a sample of everyone, not just those who have the opportunity and economic or other interest in being engaged actively in politics." Despite the problems with conducting polls that we have described, the results of such polls provide us with the means "to understand better and reflect upon our history, our society, and our nation . . . we have learned much about change and stability in American opinion since 1935, when George Gallup and others began and continued to do surveys" (Shapiro, 2004).

CONCLUSION

Given these concerns about the science of public opinion polling, what are we to conclude about the state of the American mind? Survey research has provided a great deal of information that feeds into this debate, some of which has been discussed in this book. One of the most surprising findings of the early survey researchers (Lazarsfeld, for example) was that Americans do not think about political parties and candidates in nearly as sophisticated a way as do citizens of nations with more ideological parties. Using the National Election Studies, Converse and others documented the relatively informal way that Americans come to make voting decisions and the relative lack of connections between that vote choice and their preferences on issues. Additionally, it became clear through these and many subsequent studies that most Americans do not find it important to maintain consistency in their political beliefs; that is, they do not necessarily respond to survey questions about issues and candidates in a way that would indicate a clear philosophical or ideological viewpoint.

Further undermining the portrait of an "ideal citizen" were data gathered by polls about the lack of knowledge held by Americans. Not only could survey researchers ask about totally fictitious policy issues and legislation and get answers from respondents, but other surveys found that only a dismally small proportion of Americans could answer such "easy" questions as the name of their representative or senator, or give basic information about the Constitution or Bill of Rights. In their analysis of Americans' political information, Delli Carpini and Keeter (1996) conclude that there are many reasons for the relative lack of political knowledge displayed by Americans, including low economic and social status, lack of education, and less than adequate sources of information. They also believe that most Americans are information "generalists" who have broad knowledge about the system and preferences about issues and politics but are not likely to have detailed knowledge about an issue unless it is very relevant to their own lives.

Although individual-level opinions may be volatile, the aggregate of the American mind is generally quite stable and changes slowly in predictable ways. As Page and Shapiro (1982: 39–40) note, "Our examination of the data indicates that there has been considerable stability in Americans' policy preferences . . . when changes did occur, they were not random or inexplicable; they were usually related to important changes in citizens' lives and in their social and economic environments." On many issues, ranging from gun control to the impact of slavery, the American mind has expressed stable and sensible preferences about what the government should or should not do.

Moreover, public opinion has been shown to have an impact on policy. Researchers such as Monroe (1979) have shown that not only does the public follow politics and express opinions but that over time government policy often follows public preferences. In examining the relationship between public opinion and policy change, Page and Shapiro (1983: 189) conclude that "opinion changes are important causes of policy change. When Americans' policy preferences shift, it is likely that congruent changes in policy will follow."

Monroe (1979, 1998, 2001) has also studied the relationship between public opinion on individual policy issues and the changes that may occur in response to those opinions in later years. His original study looked at policy change and public preferences between 1960 and 1979: Monroe found that policy changes or maintenance of the status quo corresponded to the public's expressed opinions in 63% of the cases. His later work (1998: 12) reported a decline in the percentage of times that policy was consistent with opinion to 55%. Furthermore, the most consistency was found on foreign policy and defense issues, presumably due to the president's ability to take decisive action in this area. The policies that were most likely to be inconsistent with public views were in the areas of political reform, including campaign finance and other electoral reforms. Monroe notes that resistance to policy change has been higher since 1980 and suggests that strongly divided government (with a president from one party and Congress controlled by the other) might contribute to a stalemate in making policy changes. He also suggests, however, that the increasing complexity of issues, combined with increased partisanship in the Congress, may have prevented policy changes consistent with public views.

The work of Monroe, Page and Shapiro, and many others on the linkages between policy and public opinion, is extremely interesting because it suggests that the public does have the power to direct the outcomes of the government. However, this research only hints at the complexity of the forces at work in a democracy: the media, interest groups, political manipulation of the public agenda, campaign strategies, presidential initiatives, congressional needs, and the public, to name only a few. Understanding that dynamic is work for scholars and researchers in the future.

Faced with this interplay of political forces is the American public, which, as we have seen, has a modest attachment to political ideologies and a rather broad, pragmatic approach to partisanship. Yet it is quite clear that Americans understand their political environment: Conservatives and liberals, as well as Republicans and Democrats, hold issue preferences that make sense in relation to their philosophic positions or party platforms. Even more striking is the congruity between group interests—especially for blacks, for blue-collar workers, for the wealthy, and for members of religious groups—and their perceptions of parties and issue positions.

The American mind—loyal to the nation, aware of national issues, involved in the varied and ongoing concerns of contemporary life in the United States—generally shows stability in its outlook on the policy issues facing the country. It does not shy away from tough decisions or from adapting to a new viewpoint if the needs of the nation require it.

Appendix A

Sources of Public Opinion Data

Throughout this book we have described how to collect and evaluate public opinion data and have presented a wide range of results from surveys of the American public. Although you may never have the need to conduct your own survey, this material has, hopefully, sparked your interest in "what the public thinks." If so, there are a number of available sources of public opinion data to which you can turn.

One of the largest collections of data—not just on public opinion, but for a variety of studies—is maintained by the Inter-University Consortium for Political and Social Research (ICPSR). The ICPSR is a membership-based organization of colleges and universities that provides access to the world's largest archive of computer-based research and instructional data for the social sciences. Information about the data available through the ICPSR is described in its *Guide to Resources and Services*, which can be obtained by contacting:

ICPSR
University of Michigan
Institute for Social Research
P.O. Box 1248
Ann Arbor, MI 48106
(734) 647-5000

Much of this data is also available through the ICPSR website (available at: www. icpsr.umich.edu). This website also contains information on the two series from which much of the data in this book were obtained, the American National Election Studies and the General Social Survey (NES: www.electionstudies.org and GSS: www.icpsr.umich.edu/icpsrweb/ICPSR/series/28/studies?archive=ICPSR&sortBy=7).

Also available at the ICPSR site are data from the series of surveys on American foreign policy opinion conducted in 1975, 1979, 1982, 1986, 1990, 1994, 1998, 2002, 2004, and 2008 for the Chicago Council on Foreign Relations (available at www.icpsr.umich.edu/icpsrweb/ICPSR/ series/4/studies?archive=ICPSR&sortBy=7). Other examples of the type of data archived at the ICPSR site are the polls conducted by news organizations, such as ABC News, CBS News, the *New York Times,* and the *Washington Post.* To locate data from these sources, go to the website www.icpsr. umich.edu and click the "Find and Analyze Data Tab" link. Then click "Find ICPSR data" and enter the term for the desired source using either "ABC News," "CBS News," "New York Times," or "Washington Post."

Another valuable archive that contains a wealth of information on public opinion is maintained by the Odom Institute for Research in Social Science (IRSS) at the University of North Carolina. The Odom Institute maintains one of the oldest and largest archives of machine-readable data in the United States, including a computer-searchable catalog of the more than 3,000 studies and series. Two unique aspects of the IRSS archives are, first, that it is the exclusive national repository for Louis Harris public opinion data—containing information on over 1,200 surveys going back to 1958—and contains over 160,000 questions asked of more than 1.2 million respondents. Many questions have been repeated over time, allowing researchers to track changes in opinions and attitudes. Second, it includes data from the National Network of State Polls (NNSP). The NNSP data provide researchers with access to over 580 state-level studies consisting of more than 70,000 questions from more than 660 studies, contributed from 44 survey organizations in 25 states. More than 600,000 respondents contributed to the surveys. You can contact the IRSS for more information at:

Howard W. Odom Institute for Research in Social Science
Manning Hall CB #3355
University of North Carolina
Chapel Hill, NC 27599
(919) 962-3061

A similar extensive collection of data is archived at the Roper Center for Public Opinion Research, which can be contacted at:

Roper Center for Public Opinion Research
University of Connecticut
Homer Babbidge Library
369 Fairfield Way, Unit 2164
Storrs, CT 06269-2164
(860) 486-4440
E-mail: rcweb@ropercenter.uconn.edu

The Roper Center maintains what is by far the most complete collection of public opinion information. Its online database, iPOLL, is "the most comprehensive source for U.S. nationwide public opinion available," and contains nearly a half million questions covering the period from 1935 to the present. Although a subscription is required to gain access to much of the data, some information, such as cross-time trends on presidential approval as measured by a number of organizations or opinions on selected current topics, is freely available. iPOLL includes survey results from academic, commercial, and media survey organizations such as the Gallup Organization, Harris Interactive, Pew Research Associates, and many more. The data come from all the surveys in the Roper Center archive that have U.S. national adult samples or samples of registered voters, women, African Americans, or any subpopulation that constitutes a large segment of the national adult population (available at: www.ropercenter.uconn.edu).

If you are concerned about issues related to the press and public policy, then information available from the Pew Research Center may be of particular interest. This center is an independent research group that studies attitudes toward the press, politics, and public policy issues and is best known for regular national surveys that measure public attentiveness to major news stories and for polling that charts trends in values and fundamental political and social attitudes (available at: www.people-press.org). Those interested in the media will also find some useful information at the Public Agenda Online (available at: www.publicagenda.org). Public Agenda is a nonpartisan, nonprofit opinion research and citizen education organization whose mission is to help leaders better understand the public's point of view on major policy issues and to help citizens better understand critical policy issues so they can make their own more informed and thoughtful decisions.

Although media polls from previous years are accessible through various archives, news releases and information on surveys conducted more recently are often available on the websites of these news organizations. To locate polling data, access the organization's website, then do a search of the site using the word "poll." Following are the website locations for some of the major news organizations:

ABC News: http://abcnews.go.com/blogs/politics/polls
CNN: www.cnn.com/POLITICS/pollingcenter/
CBS News: www.cbsnews.com/sections/opinion/polls/main500160.shtml
Los Angeles Times: www.latimes.com
New York Times: http://topics.nytimes.com/top/reference/timestopics/
   subjects/n/newyorktimes-poll-watch/index.html
USA Today: www.usatoday.com
Washington Post: www.washingtonpost.com/politics/polling

A number of academic survey research organizations have established websites that provide information on polls they conduct, many of which are statewide or local polls. Among these are:

Eagleton Poll (Rutgers University): http://eagletonpoll.rutgers.edu
Keystone Poll (Franklin and Marshall College): www.fandm.edu/fandm poll
Quinnipiac College Polling Institute: www.quinnipiac.edu/x271.xml
Marist Institute for Public Opinion: www.maristpoll.marist.edu
Ohio Poll (University of Cincinnati): www.ipr.uc.edu/OhioPoll/Ohio Poll.html

Commercial polling firms, such as the Gallup Organization, Louis Harris and Associates, and the Roper Organization, conduct both proprietary studies, the results of which are generally not available to other users, as well as studies for which you can access the data. As noted earlier, data from many of the publicly released studies of these organizations are available through different data archives. Information from more recent Harris polls is available through the IRSS website, and results from current surveys of the Roper Organization are available at the Roper Center website (access to findings and press releases from recent Gallup Polls is available at: www.gallup.com).

Data from recent public opinion surveys as well as historical trends are also available through published sources. *The Polling Report*, for example, is "an independent survey of trends affecting elections, government, and business" that provides data on a variety of issues, with a particular emphasis on campaigns and elections. More information on this publication is available from:

The Polling Report, Inc.
P.O. Box 42580
Washington, DC 20015-2580
(202) 237-2000

Some information from *The Polling Report* is also available on its website (available at: www.pollingreport.com).

Appendix B

Questions from the American National Election Studies and General Social Surveys

Much of the data presented in this book comes from two extensive series of surveys of the American public: the American National Election Studies (NES) and the General Social Survey (GSS). The following provides the question wording for the items from these two data series.

AMERICAN NATIONAL ELECTION STUDIES

Political Ideology

We hear a lot of talk these days about liberals and conservatives. Here is a seven-point scale (extremely liberal; liberal; slightly liberal; moderate, middle-of-the-road; slightly conservative; conservative; extremely conservative) on which the political views that people hold are arranged from extremely liberal to extremely conservative. Where would you place yourself on this scale, or haven't you thought much about this?

Party Identification

Generally speaking, do you think of yourself as a Republican, a Democrat, an Independent, or what?

(If Republican): Would you call yourself a strong Republican or a not very strong Republican?

(If Democrat): Would you call yourself a strong Democrat or a not very strong Democrat?

(If Independent, Minor Party, or other): Do you think of yourself as closer to the Republican or Democratic Party?

Trust in Government

How much of the time do you think you can trust the government in Washington to do what is right—just about always, most of the time, or only some of the time?

Would you say the government is pretty much run by a few big interests looking out for themselves or that it is run for the benefit of all the people?

Do you think that people in the government waste a lot of the money we pay in taxes, waste some of it, or don't waste very much of it?

Do you feel that almost all of the people running the government are smart people who usually know what they are doing, or do you think that quite a few of them don't seem to know what they are doing?

Do you think that quite a few of the people running the government are a little crooked, not very many are, or do you think hardly any of them are crooked at all?

Political Efficacy

Do you agree or disagree with the following statements:

People like me don't have any say about what the government does.

Voting is the only way that people like me can have any say about how the government runs things.

Sometimes politics and government seem so complicated that a person like me can't really understand what's going on.

I don't think public officials care much about what people like me think.

Generally speaking, those we elect to Congress in Washington lose touch with the people pretty quickly.

Parties are only interested in people's votes, but not in their opinions.

Power of the Federal Government

Some people are afraid the government in Washington is getting too powerful for the good of the country and the individual person. Others feel the government has not gotten too strong for the good of the country. Have you been interested enough in this to favor one side over the other? (2000: Do you have an opinion on this or not) (If yes): What is your feeling, do you think the government is getting too strong or the government has not gotten too strong?

Government Services

Some people think the government should provide fewer services, even in areas such as health and education, in order to reduce spending. Other people feel it is important for the government to provide many more services even if it means an increase in spending. Where would you place yourself on this scale or haven't you thought much about this issue? (Seven-point scale shown to respondents, with point 1 labeled "government should provide fewer services, reduce spending a lot"; point 7 labeled "government should provide many more services, increase government spending a lot"; and points 2 through 6 not labeled.)

Education

(1956, 1958, 1960; 1962—slight variation in wording)

If cities and towns around the country need help to build more schools, the government in Washington ought to give them the money they need. Do you have an opinion on this or not? (If yes): Do you think the government should do this? (Five response categories: agree strongly; agree, but not very strongly; not sure, it depends; disagree, but not very strongly; disagree strongly.)

(1984, 1988, 1990, 1992, 1996, 2000, 2002, 2004, 2008)

Should federal spending on public schools be increased, decreased, or kept about the same?

Medical Care

(1956, 1960)

The government in Washington ought to help people get doctors and hospital care at low cost. Do you have an opinion on this or not? (If yes): Do you think the government should do this? (Five response categories: agree strongly; agree, but not very strongly; not sure, it depends; disagree, but not very strongly; disagree strongly).

(1964, 1968)

Some people say the government in Washington ought to help people get doctors and hospital care at low cost; others say the government should not get into this. Have you been interested enough in this to favor one side over the other? (If yes): What is your position? Should the government in Washington help people get doctors and hospital care at low cost or stay out of this? (Forced-choice item, with an "other, depends" middle category.)

(1970, 1972, 1976, 1978, 1984, 1988, 1992, 1994, 1996, 2000, 2004, 2008)

There is much concern about the rapid rise in medical and hospital costs. Some people feel there should be a government insurance plan which would cover all medical and hospital expenses (2000: for everyone). Others feel that medical expenses should be paid by individuals and through private insurance like Blue Cross (2000: or other company paid plans). Where would you place yourself on this scale or haven't you thought much about this? (Seven-point scale shown to respondents, with point 1 labeled "government insurance plan"; point 7 labeled "individuals/private insurance"; and points 2 through 6 not labeled.) In 2000, the order of the alternatives was reversed for half of the sample.

Jobs and Living Standards

(1956, 1958, 1960)

The government in Washington ought to see to it that everybody who wants to work can find a job. Do you have an opinion on this or not? (If yes): Do you think the government should do this? (Five response categories: agree strongly; agree, but not very strongly; not sure, it depends; disagree, but not very strongly; disagree strongly.)

(1964, 1968)

In general, some people feel that the government in Washington should see to it that every person has a job and a good standard of living. Others think the government should just let each person get ahead on his own. Have you been interested enough in this to favor one side over the other? (If yes): Do you think that the government should see to it that every person has a job and a good standard of living or should it let each person get ahead on his own? (Forced-choice item, with an "other, depends" middle category.)

(1972, 1974, 1976, 1978, 1980, 1982, 1984, 1986, 1988, 1990, 1992, 1994, 1996, 1998, 2000, 2004, 2008)

Some people feel that the government in Washington should see to it that every person has a job and a good standard of living. Others think the government should just let each person get ahead on his (their) own. (1972–78: And, of course, other people have opinions somewhere in between.)/(1998–2000: And, of course, other people have opinions somewhere in between, at points 2, 3, 4, 5, or 6). Where would you place yourself on this scale, or haven't you thought much about this? (Seven-point scale shown to respondents, with point 1 labeled "government see to jobs"; point 7 labeled "let each person get ahead on own"; and points 2 through 6 not labeled.)

(2002)

Some people feel the government in Washington should see to it that every person has a job and a good standard of living. Others think the government should just let each person get ahead on their own. Which is closer to the way you feel or haven't you thought much about this? (Forced-choice item, with an "other, depends" middle category.)

School Integration

(1956, 1958, 1960)
The government in Washington should stay out of the question of whether white and colored children go to the same school. Do you have an opinion on this or not? (If yes): Do you think the government should stay out of this question? (Five response categories: agree strongly; agree, but not very strongly; not sure, it depends; disagree, but not very strongly; disagree strongly.)

(1962)
The government in Washington should see to it that white and colored children are allowed to go to the same schools. Do you have an opinion on this or not? (If yes): Do you agree that the government should do this or do you think the government should not do it? (Five response choices: (1) yes; (2) yes, qualified, (3) yes, but no force; (4) no, qualified; (5) no.)

(1964, 1966, 1968, 1970, 1972, 1976, 1978, 1986, 1990, 1992, 1994)
Some people say that the government in Washington should see to it that white and Negro (colored/black) children are allowed to go to the same schools. Others claim that this is not the government's business. Have you been concerned enough about this to favor one side over the other? (If yes): Do you think the government in Washington should see to it that white and Negro (colored/black) children go to the same schools or stay out of this area as it is none of its business? (Forced-choice item, with an "other, depends" middle category.)

(2000)
Some people say that the government in Washington should see to it that white and black children go to the same schools. Others claim that this is not the government's business. Have you been interested enough in this question to favor one side over the other? (If yes): Do you think the government in Washington should see to it that white and black children go to the same schools or stay out of this area as it is not the government's business?

Busing

(1972, 1974, 1976, 1980, 1984)
There is much discussion about the best way to deal with racial problems. Some people think that achieving integration of public schools is so important that it justifies busing children to schools out of their own

neighborhood. Others think letting children go to their neighborhood schools is so important that they oppose busing. Where would you place yourself on this scale, or haven't you thought much about this? (Seven-point scale shown to respondents, with point 1 labeled "bus to achieve integration"; point 7 labeled "keep in neighborhood schools"; and points 2 through 6 not labeled.)

Neighborhood Integration

(1964, 1968, 1970, 1972, 1976)

Which of these statements would you agree with: White people have a right to keep black people out of their neighborhood if they want to; or, black people have a right to live wherever they can afford to, just like anybody else? (Forced-choice item.)

Minority Employment

(1956, 1958, 1960)

If Negroes are not getting fair treatment in jobs and housing, the government should see to it that they do. Do you have an opinion on this or not? (If yes): Do you think the government should do this? (Five response categories: agree strongly; agree, but not very strongly; not sure, it depends; disagree, but not very strongly; disagree strongly.)

(1964, 1968, 1972)

Some people think that if Negroes (colored people/black people) are not getting fair treatment in jobs the government in Washington ought to see to it that they do. Others feel that this is not the federal government's business. Have you had enough interest in this question to favor one side over the other? (If yes): How do you feel? Should the government in Washington see to it that Negroes (colored people/black people) get fair treatment in jobs or leave these matters to the states and local communities? (Forced-choice item, with an "other, depends" middle category.)

(1986, 1988, 1992, 1996, 2000, 2004, 2008)

Some people think that if black people are not getting fair treatment in jobs, the government in Washington ought to see to it that they do. Others feel that this is not the federal government's business. Have you had enough interest in this question to favor one side over the other? (If yes): How do you feel? Should the government in Washington see to it that black people get fair treatment in jobs or is this not the government's business? (Forced-choice item, with an "other, depends" middle category.)

Affirmative Action

(1978)

Some people say that women and minority group members should be given preferential treatment in getting jobs or being admitted to colleges or professional schools. Other people say that the individual's ability or experience should be the only consideration in hiring people or admitting them to school. Where would you place yourself on this scale or haven't you thought much about this question? (Seven-point scale shown to respondents, with point 1 labeled "give preferential treatment to a woman or minority member"; point 7 labeled "the individual's ability or experience should be the only consideration"; and points 2 through 6 not labeled.)

(1986, 1988 (alternate wording), 1990, 1992, 1994, 1996, 1998, 2000, 2004, 2008)

Some people say that because of past discrimination blacks should be given preference in hiring and promotion. Others say that such preference in hiring and promotion of blacks is wrong because it gives blacks advantages they haven't earned. What about your opinion—are you for or against preferential hiring and promotion of blacks? (Respondents answer "for" or "against" and are then asked whether they "favor preference in hiring and promotion strongly or not strongly" or "oppose preference in hiring and promotion strongly or not strongly.")

Aid Minority Groups

(1970, 1972, 1974, 1976, 1978, 1980, 1982, 1984, 1986, 1988, 1990, 1992, 1994, 1996)

Some people feel that the government in Washington should make every possible effort to improve the social and economic position of Negroes (blacks) and other minority groups. Others feel that the government should not make any special effort to help minority peoples but they should be expected to help themselves. Where would you place yourself on this scale, or haven't you thought much about this? (Seven-point scale shown to respondents, with point 1 labeled "government help minority groups"; point 7 labeled "minority groups help themselves"; and points 2 through 6 not labeled.)

(1998, 2000, 2004, 2008)

Some people feel that the government in Washington should make every effort to improve the social and economic position of blacks. Others feel that the government should not make any special effort to help blacks because they should help themselves. And, of course, some other people have opinions somewhere in between. Where would you place yourself on this scale, or haven't you thought much about this? (Seven-point scale with point 1 labeled "government should help blacks"; point 7 labeled "blacks should help themselves"; and points 2 through 6 not labeled.)

Speed of the Civil Rights Movement

(1964, 1966 (variation in response categories), 1968, 1970, 1972, 1976, 1980, 1984, 1986, 1988, 1990, 1992)

Do you think that civil rights leaders are trying to push too fast, are going too slowly, or are moving at about the right speed? (Forced-choice item.)

Impact of Slavery

(1972, 1986, 1988, 1990, 1992, 1994)

Please tell me whether you agree or disagree with each reason as to why white people seem to get more of the good things in life. Generations of slavery and discrimination have created conditions that make it difficult for blacks to work their way up. Do you strongly agree, agree somewhat, neither agree nor disagree, disagree somewhat, or disagree strongly?

(2000, 2008)

Generations of slavery and discrimination have created conditions that make it difficult for blacks to work their way out of the lower class. Do you agree strongly, agree somewhat, neither agree nor disagree, disagree somewhat, or disagree strongly with this statement?

GENERAL SOCIAL SURVEY

Confidence in Institutions

I'm going to name institutions in this country. As far as the people running these institutions are concerned, would you say you have a great deal of confidence, only some confidence, or hardly any confidence at all in them?

Military
Major companies
Organized religion
Education
Executive branch of government
Banks and financial institutions
Supreme Court

Organized labor
Congress
Medicine
Press
Scientific community
Television

Government Services

Some people think that the government in Washington is trying to do too many things that should be left to individuals and private businesses. Others disagree and think that the government should do even more to solve our country's problems. Still others have opinions somewhere in between. Where would you place yourself on this scale, or haven't you made up your mind on this?

Government Spending

We are faced with many problems in this country, none of which can be solved easily or inexpensively. I'm going to name some of these problems, and for each one I'd like you to tell me whether you think we're spending too much money on it, too little money, or about the right amount. Are we spending too much money, too little money, or about the right amount on . . .

Social security
Improving the nation's education system
Improving and protecting the nation's health
Improving and protecting the environment
Improving the conditions of blacks
Assistance to blacks
Welfare

Medical Care

In general, some people think that it is the responsibility of the government in Washington to see to it that people have help in paying for doctors and hospital bills. Others think that these matters are not the responsibility of the federal government and that people should take care of these things themselves. Where do you put yourself on this scale or haven't you made up your mind on this? (Five-point response scale with point 1 labeled "government responsibility"; point 3 labeled "agree with both"; point 5 labeled "people care for themselves"; and points 2 and 4 not labeled.)

Jobs and Living Standards

(1975, 1983, 1984, 1986, 1987, 1988, 1989, 1990, 1991, 1993, 1994, 1996, 1998, 2000, 2002, 2004, 2006, 2008, 2010)

Some people think that the government in Washington should do everything possible to improve the standard of living of all poor Americans; they are at Point 1 on this card. Other people think it is not the government's responsibility, and that each person should take care of himself; they are at Point 5. Where would you place yourself on this scale, or haven't you made up your mind on this? (Five-point response scale with point 1 labeled "government responsibility"; point 3 labeled "agree with both"; point 5 labeled "people help themselves"; and points 2 and 4 not labeled.)

(1985, 1989, 1990, 1991, 1996, 1998)

On the whole, do you think it should or should not be the government's responsibility to provide a job for everyone who wants one? (Four-point response scale: (1) definitely should be; (2) probably should be; (3) probably should not be; (4) definitely should not be.)

Environment

(1993, 1994, 2000, 2010)

If you had to choose, which one of the following comes closest to your views? Government should let businesses decide for themselves how to protect the environment, even if it means they don't always do the right thing, or government should pass laws to make businesses protect the environment, even if it interferes with business' right to make their own decisions. (Forced-choice item.)

(1993, 1994, 2000, 2010)

If you had to choose, which one of the following comes closest to your views? Government should let ordinary people decide for themselves how to protect the environment, even if it means they don't always do the right thing, or government should pass laws to make ordinary people protect the environment, even if it interferes with people's right to make their own decisions. (Forced-choice item.)

(1993, 1994, 2000, 2010)

How much do you agree or disagree with the following statement? In order to protect the environment, America needs economic growth. (Five-point scale: (1) strongly agree; (2) agree; (3) neither agree nor disagree; (4) disagree; (5) strongly disagree.)

(1993, 1994, 2000, 2010)

How much do you agree or disagree with the following statement? Economic growth always harms the environment. (Five-point scale: (1) strongly agree; (2) agree; (3) neither agree nor disagree; (4) disagree; (5) strongly disagree.)

(1993, 1994, 2000, 2010)

How much do you agree or disagree with the following statement? People worry too much about human progress harming the environment. (Five-point scale: (1) strongly agree; (2) agree; (3) neither agree nor disagree; (4) disagree; (5) strongly disagree.)

(1993, 1994, 2000, 2010)

How much do you agree or disagree with the following statement? We worry too much about the future of the environment, and not enough about prices and jobs today. (Five-point scale: (1) strongly agree; (2) agree; (3) neither agree nor disagree; (4) disagree; (5) strongly disagree.)

(1993, 1994, 2000, 2010)

How willing would you be to pay much higher prices in order to protect the environment? (Five response choices: (1) very willing; (2) fairly willing; (3) neither willing nor unwilling; (4) not very willing; or (5) not at all willing.)

(1993, 1994, 2000, 2010)

How willing would you be to pay much higher taxes in order to protect the environment? (Five response choices: (1) very willing; (2) fairly willing; (3) neither willing nor unwilling; (4) not very willing; or (5) not at all willing.)

(1993, 1994, 2000, 2010)

How willing would you be to accept cuts in your standard of living in order to protect the environment? (Five response choices: (1) very willing; (2) fairly willing; (3) neither willing nor unwilling; (4) not very willing; or (5) not at all willing.)

School Integration

(1972, 1976, 1977, 1980, 1982, 1984, 1985)

Do you think white students and (Negro/Black) students should go to the same schools or to separate schools? (Forced-choice item.)

Busing

(1972, 1974, 1975, 1976, 1977, 1978, 1982, 1983, 1985, 1986, 1988, 1989, 1990, 1991, 1993, 1994, 1996)

In general, do you favor or oppose the busing of (Negro/Black/African-American) and white school children from one school district to another? (Forced-choice item.)

Neighborhood Integration

(1980, 1982, 1984, 1985, 1987, 1988, 1989, 1990, 1991, 1993, 1994, 1996)

White people have a right to keep (Negroes/Blacks/African-Americans) out of their neighborhoods if they want to, and (Negroes/Blacks/African-Americans) should respect that right. (Four response choices: (1) agree strongly; (2) agree slightly; (3) disagree slightly; (4) disagree strongly.)

Affirmative Action

(1994, 1996, 1998, 2000, 2002, 2004, 2006, 2008, 2010)

Some people say that because of past discrimination, blacks should be given preference in hiring and promotion. Others say that such preference in hiring and promotion of blacks is wrong because it discriminates against whites. What is your opinion—are you for or against preferential hiring and promotion of blacks? (Four response categories: (1) strongly support preferences; (2) support preferences; (3) oppose preferences; (4) strongly oppose preferences.)

Aid Minority Groups

(1975, 1983, 1984, 1986, 1987, 1988, 1989, 1990, 1991, 1993, 1994, 1996, 1998, 2000, 2002, 2004, 2006, 2008, 2010)

Some people think that (Blacks/Negroes) have been discriminated against for so long that the government has a special obligation to help improve their living standards. Others believe that the government should not be giving special treatment to (Blacks/Negroes). Where would you place yourself on this scale, or haven't you made up your mind?

Voting for a Black Candidate for President

(1972, 1974, 1975, 1977, 1978, 1982, 1983, 1985, 1986, 1988, 1989, 1990, 1991, 1992, 1994, 1996, 2008, 2010)

If your party nominated a (Negro/Black/African-American) for president, would you vote for him if he were qualified for the job?

Racial Intermarriage

(1972, 1973, 1974, 1975, 1976, 1977, 1980, 1982, 1984, 1985, 1987, 1988, 1989, 1990, 1991, 1993, 1994, 1996, 1998, 2000, 2002)

Do you think there should be a law against marriages between (Negroes/Blacks/African-Americans) and whites?

Death Penalty

Do you favor or oppose the death penalty for persons convicted of murder?

Abortion

Please tell me whether or not you think it should be possible for a pregnant woman to obtain a legal abortion:

(a) if there is a strong chance of serious defect in the baby?
(b) if she is married and does not want any more children?
(c) if the woman's own health is seriously endangered by the pregnancy?
(d) if the family has a very low income and cannot afford any more children?
(e) if she became pregnant as a result of rape?
(f) if she is not married and does not want to marry the man?

Gun Permits

Would you favor or oppose a law which would require a person to obtain a police permit before he or she could buy a gun?

Glossary

acquiescence response set: The tendency of some respondents to agree with a statement regardless of its content.

affirmative action: A policy that gives special consideration or compensatory treatment to traditionally disadvantaged groups in an effort to overcome the effect of past discrimination.

agenda setting: The media's role in identifying the most important issues and concerns facing the electorate.

agree-disagree format: A way of presenting questions in which respondents are read a statement and asked whether they agree or disagree with its content.

archive: A collection of documents, reports, statistics, data, and other material that are accessible to researchers and other interested individuals.

attitude: A relatively enduring orientation toward objects that provides individuals with a mental framework for making economical sense of the world.

belief: The inclination to accept something as true.

benchmark poll: A poll taken before a political campaign that begins to identify the candidate's image and issue positions with the electorate.

biased sample: A sample that systematically produces results that are different from those in the population of interest.

bivariate analysis: Examining the relationship between two variables, generally by constructing some type of table or correlation.

Bradley effect: In preelection polling, the tendency for the support for a minority candidate to be overrepresented.

busing: The transportation of public school students from areas where they live to schools in other areas to eliminate school segregation based on residential patterns.

census block: The smallest entity for which the Census Bureau collects and tabulates decennial census information; bounded on all sides by visible and nonvisible features.

census tract: A small, relatively permanent statistical subdivision of a county in a metropolitan area or a selected nonmetropolitan county used for presenting decennial census data. Census tract boundaries normally follow visible features but may follow governmental unit boundaries and other nonvisible features in some instances; they always rest within counties. Census tracts usually contain between 2,500 and 8,000 inhabitants.

closed-ended question: A question in which respondents select their answer from a list of choices provided for them.

cluster sample: A sample in which the population is divided into groups (clusters), often on the basis of geography. Cluster samples generally involve several stages of sampling after the initial groups have been selected.

computer-assisted self interview (CASI): Use of a laptop computer by respondents to complete a self-administered questionnaire. In audio-CASI, an audio component is added, in which respondents can listen to the questions through a headset at the same time they appear on the screen.

computer-assisted telephone interviewing (CATI): The use of interactive computing systems to assist interviewers and their supervisors in performing the basic data collection tasks of telephone surveys.

confidence level: The estimated probability that a characteristic of a population lies within a given range of values based on the value of the characteristic in a sample.

consensus: General agreement among the population on an issue.

constraint: Consistency among idea elements.

context effect: A condition in which responses to a survey question are influenced by the items preceding it in a questionnaire.

convenience sample: The collection of data from individuals who are easy to locate and gather information from; a convenience sample is a nonprobability sample and the information cannot be used to generalize about the characteristics of some larger population.

cross-time analysis: Comparing results on the same survey question asked at different points in time.

cugging: Campaigning under the guise of research.

deliberative opinion poll: A technique that combines deliberation in small-group discussions with scientific random sampling to provide public consultation for public policy and for electoral issues.

electronic data collection: Gathering survey information through electronic means such as over the Internet, via e-mail, or with a touchtone telephone.

errors in forecasting: Errors in predicting some event, frequently an election outcome. When based on survey information, such errors can result from factors such as a biased sample, poor questionnaire design, nonresponse, poor data collection, or flawed analysis of the data.

establishment bias: A theory that sees the media as exhibiting bias toward the government and other established institutions of society.

exit poll: A poll taken outside the election polling place that asks a random sample of voters to answer questions about the election immediately after they have voted.

feeling thermometer: A type of question based on the concept of a thermometer, generally ranging from 0 degrees to 100 degrees, often used to measure reactions to political figures, countries, or groups.

filter question: A question that is frequently included as part of opinion items in order to limit responses to some subset of the sample, such as those who have an interest in an issue.

forced-choice format: Presenting respondents with two sides of an issue and asking them which comes closer to their point of view.

framing: Defining how a story should be understood by the citizens through the way the media attributes responsibility for the problem or issue.

frugging: Fundraising under the guise of research.

gender gap: Differences in the political views of men and women.

generational effects: Political beliefs or attitudes attributable to events that impact a particular generation.

horse-race journalism: A view of the coverage of campaigns and elections by the various news media that perceives coverage as overly concerned with the polls and considerations of which candidate is leading.

hostilization: The process by which some children learn and internalize attitudes of hostility toward politics and political authority.

idealization: Children's view of political figures or institutions as benevolent and trustworthy.

institutionalization: Children's development of the concept of political institutions as apart from the individuals who hold public positions.

intensity of opinion: The strength of an individual's views on an issue.

issue publics: A group of people who are knowledgeable and have meaningful beliefs about an issue and who are more likely to write letters to the editor, contact public officials, or change their vote on the basis of this issue.

liberal-conservative continuum: The primary dimension underlying political thinking in the United States.

life cycle effects: Changes in political opinions and attitudes that are attributable to aging or other changes in the life cycle.

Likert-type item: A type of question that uses responses such as strongly agree, agree, disagree, and strongly disagree—often with a neutral or middle alternative—to measure an individual's attitude.

middle alternative: A logical position between two extremes that some respondents might prefer to either of the contrasting alternatives in a survey question.

modified area sample: A form of sampling in which geographic areas such as census tracts or blocks serve as sampling units.

multiple publics: The variety of groups or sets of individuals that a policy maker considers in deciding how to act on some issue. The general population, interest groups, members of a particular union, or clients of a program are examples of possible publics.

multivariate analysis: Examining relationships among three or more variables.

nonattitudes: Meaningless opinions that vary randomly in direction in repeated trials over time.

nonprobability sample: A sample that is based on human judgment or self-selection. The characteristics of a nonprobability sample do not represent those of some larger population.

nonresponse bias: The difference between the characteristics of the population and the estimates of these characteristics in a sample resulting from the fact that individuals from whom data are not collected (because they are not in the sampling frame, cannot be located, refuse to participate, etc.) may differ in significant ways from those who do participate.

open-ended question: A question to which respondents supply their own answer in their own words and are not limited to a set of choices provided for them by the researcher.

opinion: The verbal expression of an attitude.

panel: A study in which data are collected from individuals at several points in time.

paper-and-pencil interviewing (PAPI): Survey data collection in which interviewers ask respondents questions and record their answers on a paper questionnaire.

party identification: A "standing decision" to support one party or the other. It is generally a psychological identification, which can persist without legal recognition or evidence of formal membership and even without a consistent record of party support.

personalization: The view of a young child that perceives individuals such as a policeman or the mayor as being the government.

pilot investigation: A small-scale trial of a study for the purpose of checking all aspects of the study design.

political authority: The concept of the government, its institutions, and officials as having power over the individuals and the society.

political cynicism: The belief that the government is not producing results in accord with individual expectations.

political efficacy: The belief that individual political action does have, or can have, an impact on the political process.

political ideology: A closely linked set of beliefs about the proper order of society and how it can be achieved.

political socialization: The process by which children and adults learn political attitudes, beliefs, and behaviors that are accepted by their culture.

politicization: The process by which children become aware of political authorities beyond their families and immediate experience.

population coverage: The extent to which the group that a researcher is interested in can be reached by the mode of data collection.

population of interest: An identifiable group of individuals whose opinion on some issue or set of issues is important to a policy maker.

portability: A feature of the Telecommunications Act of 1996 that requires telephone service providers to give consumers the choice of keeping their telephone number when they switch local service providers.

presidential approval: A measure included in many polls that asks whether the respondent approves or disapproves of the job being done by the president.

primacy effect: A condition in which the alternative that is given to the respondent first is selected more often, simply because it is presented first.

priming: How the media's choice of issues and stories prepares citizens to form opinions about political issues.

probability sample: A sample in which each individual or combination of individuals in the population has some known chance of being selected.

pseudo-polls: Contacts with individuals that have some elements of a legitimate survey but are not true attempts to collect information from a representative sample of some population.

public judgment: A state of highly developed public opinion that exists once people have engaged an issue, considered it from all sides, understood the choices it leads to, and accepted the consequences of the choices they make.

public opinion: The aggregate of the views of individual adults on matters of public interest.

purposive study: A study in which elements are selected based on the researcher's judgment as to their usefulness. Purposive studies use nonprobability samples, and the results are not representative of some larger population.

push poll: An insidious form of negative campaigning disguised as a political poll that is designed to change opinions, not measure them.

push question: A question asked in a poll to test potential arguments against a candidate that might be used in a political campaign or in advertising.

quota sampling: A type of nonprobability sample in which units are selected into the sample on the basis of prespecified characteristics.

rally-round-the-flag effect: The tendency for public support for the president to increase when American troops are sent into conflict or harm's way.

random-digit dialing (RDD): Telephone interviewing coupled with the use of a sample of telephone numbers generated completely at random.

ranking scale: A type of question in which respondents are presented with a list of items and asked to order them along some dimension, such as importance, desirability, or preference.

rating scale: A type of question in which respondents are asked to make judgments along a continuum varying between two extremes, such as from excellent to poor or from extremely satisfied to extremely dissatisfied.

recency effect: A condition in which the alternative that is given to the respondent last is selected more often, simply because it is presented last.

reliability: The extent to which measurements are repeatable by different researchers or by the same researcher at different points in time.

religiosity: The measure of how often a respondent attends religious services or takes part in religious observances, including daily prayer.

representative sample: A subset of a population selected in a way that its characteristics represent those of the larger population from which it is drawn.

response format: The way in which choices in survey questions are presented to respondents. Examples of response formats include agree–disagree format, forced-choice format, Likert-type scales, rating scales, ranking scales, and feeling thermometers.

response rate: The extent to which those selected for a sample actually participate. The response rate is calculated by dividing the number of complete interviews with reporting units by the number of eligible reporting units in the sample.

sample: A subset of the population that, when selected using probability methods, is designed to represent the characteristics of the population.

sample size: The number of elements for which data are collected.

sampling error: The potential difference between the results from a sample and the actual value in the population, resulting from the fact that data are not obtained from all members of the population.

sampling frame: The list of units composing a population from which a sample is selected.

secondary analysis: Analysis of data by researchers other than those who originally collected the data.

seven-point forced-choice scale: A form of a forced-choice format in which the alternatives are placed at points "1" and "7" of the scale and the remaining points are left for respondents who have opinions that fall between the two extremes.

simple random sample (SRS): A sample in which each element in a population has a known and equal probability of being selected. In the typical simple random sample, each element in the population is listed and assigned a number and a sample is drawn using a computer program or a random number table to generate the selected elements.

stratified sample: A sample in which the elements of the population are divided into groups (strata), and independent samples (either random or systematic) are selected within each stratum.

straw poll: A form of gathering public opinion information, particularly about voting intentions, that has been used in the United States since the early 1800s.

sugging: Selling under the guise of research.

systematic random sample: A sample typically drawn from a list of elements that involves randomly selecting a single number, then taking every *n*th number in the list until the desired number of elements has been selected.

tone of wording: The language used in framing survey questions.

touchtone data entry (TDE): Data collection in which the respondent calls a computer and responds to questions using the telephone keypad.

tracking poll: Daily polls using a very small sample, usually less than 200 respondents, which are aggregated to give an indication of changing voter opinions.

trial heats: Polls that attempt to determine which candidate is leading in an election campaign.

trust in government: Evaluation of the government in which citizens are either satisfied with the procedures and products of government (trust) or believe that it is not producing policies according to expectations (cynicism).

univariate analysis: The analysis of a single variable for purposes of description.

valence issue: Those issues on which there is uniform agreement or disagreement.

validity: The extent to which measurement taps what it intends to measure.

voice recognition entry (VRE): Data collection in which the respondent calls a computer and responds to questions by saying the appropriate numbers.

Notes

CHAPTER 1

1. The question of multiple publics is distinct from the question of issue publics as discussed by Converse (1964) and others (e.g., Hennessy, 1981; Weissberg, 1976). An **issue public** is a group of people who are knowledgeable and have meaningful beliefs about an issue and who are more likely to write letters to the editor, contact public officials, or change their vote on the basis of this issue. Concerns about the effects of differences in interest and awareness among such publics parallel those in our previous discussion of the effect of such differences on public opinion more generally. As noted earlier, identifying the size, correlates, and consequences of such issue publics is an important consideration in the analysis of public opinion.

2. Paul Burstein's 2001 study reviewed virtually all of the prior research on the impact of public opinion on public policy. He concluded that the studies all show that the impact is substantial and that the impact is likely to be greater if the issue has high salience. Although Monroe finds some decrease in policy responsiveness to public opinion over time, Burstein does not find the same. In a later work, Burstein (2006) argues that research showing that public opinion has an impact on policy overstates this influence by focusing on issues that are especially important to the public. It is on such issues that opinion is most likely to affect policy, and taking less salient issues into account would lower the estimates of this impact.

3. For information on another use of information from a deliberative opinion poll see Sturgis, Roberts, and Allum (2005). The results of a deliberative poll on foreign policy are reported by Brady, Fishkin, and Luskin (2003).

CHAPTER 2

1. A 1971 *Science* magazine article ranked the contributions of Morris Hansen, a mathematical statistician at the U.S. Census Bureau, in extending formal sampling theory to large-scale survey research designs as one of the major advances in social science between 1900 and 1965 (Deutsch, Platt, and Senghass, 1971).

2. Differences in the way survey organizations identify likely voters and in how they allocate "undecided" voters are largely responsible for the variation that is often observed in preelection polls, and survey researchers involved in preelection polling continue to refine their methods in these areas (Kiley and Dimock, 2009; Pew Center for People and the Press, 2004; Traugott, 2001). In the 2004 election, for example, the "incumbent rule," which held that voters who are undecided in the late stages of an election break overwhelmingly against the incumbent, was found not to hold, with John Kerry having only a modest advantage over George W. Bush among the late deciders.

3. This is not to imply, however, that such preelection polls have been perfect or without their critics. For an example of some of the controversies that surrounded the 1980 election, see Ladd and Ferree (1981); for those associated with the 1996 outcome, see Ladd (1996a) and Moore (1996b). A careful assessment of the accuracy of polling in the 2000 presidential election has been provided by Traugott (2001), and a discussion of the 2004 preelection polls, which were found to be largely accurate, can be found at the Pew Center for People and the Press (2004).

4. Since the 2000 Census there has been a shift in the pattern of telephone usage among Americans. The dramatic increase in the use of wireless telephones has led to an increasing percentage of households abandoning their land line telephones. By 2005, the percentage of households without a land line phone was estimated to be about 7%; this percentage increased rapidly, and by 2010 it had reached almost 30% (Blumberg and Luke, 2011). This shift in the pattern of telephone use has posed increasing challenges for surveys conducted with a sample selected by RDD, which are also discussed in more detail in Chapter 4 and in Chapter 12.

5. *Survey Research*, the newsletter of these academic organizations, regularly publishes brief reports of research done by these units. In 2010–2011, it reported 80 projects; of these, 20% were sponsored by the federal government, 24% by state governments, and 17% by local governments. The remaining 19% were university supported or sponsored by not-for-profit groups, media organizations, or foundations. It should be noted that these reports do not represent all the research conducted by these organizations, because not all groups provide information on each of their studies and all reported studies are not printed in the newsletter.

CHAPTER 3

1. Frequently the results from the last two or three days of interviewing are combined to form a "moving average" based on a larger number of cases, which is less likely to be influenced by day-to-day fluctuations that may be the product of sampling error.

2. Much of the polling done for candidates is done by commercial organizations, some of which only do political polling, while others do political polling plus market and product research.

3. The New Hampshire statute prohibiting unidentified push polling can be found online at: www.gencourt.state.nh.us/rsa/html/LXIII/664/664-16-a.htm.

4. Jacobs and Shapiro (1995: 164) argue that the full maturation of a "public opinion apparatus" in the White House occurred during the Nixon administration. The central point of their analysis, and ours, is that the White House's sensitivity to public opinion has become "an enduring institutional characteristic of the modern presidency; it no longer mirror(s) the personal inclination of the sitting President."

5. For a quick overview of the Obama polling operation, see Ben Smith, "Meet Obama's Pollsters," as reported at Politico: www.politico.com.

6. For an excellent discussion of the political struggle that culminated in the passage of the Patient Protection and Affordable Care Act, see the book by Lawrence R. Jacobs and Theda Skocpol, *Health Care Reform and American Politics: What Everyone Needs to Know*.

7. More than 10 years ago, Brehm (1993: 9) reported that in one year a single federal department—the Department of Health and Human Services—conducted interviews with 1,437,102 respondents that required over 1.2 million hours to complete.

8. The information in this section is derived from the U.S. Department of Commerce, Bureau of the Census website. A very complete list of government survey efforts with quick links is given at: www.census.gov/econ/overview.

9. State governments use survey research for many of the same purposes as the federal government. Though states do not have as many large-scale or ongoing survey projects as the federal government, state agencies use surveys for monitoring quality of life, program evaluation, needs assessment, and determining the public's views on policy issues. Local governments have similar needs for survey data as the states and the federal government. Although the use of surveys by local governments varies considerably, such data collection efforts have been shown to be valuable in monitoring citizen satisfaction with services, determining voters' budget priorities, and evaluating programs.

10. The federal government has a history of resistance to the collection of attitudinal or opinion data. For example, despite the Census Bureau's long-term efforts in gathering data on population characteristics, not until 1967 did it agree to collect data on the subjective indicator of asking women how many children they expected to have, even though such measurements were thought to be useful in making population projections (DeMaio, Marsh, and Turner, 1984: 31).

11. As an indicator of the extent to which media resources are devoted to survey data, it is estimated that combining their exit polling operations saved the three major networks $9 million each over a four-year period (Moore, 1992: 265).

12. It should be noted that the conclusions of Edison Media Research and Mitofsky International have not been universally accepted, with groups such as US Count Votes contending that the differences between the exit polls and the election results may be due to errors in the election tally and that the voters' intent was not accurately recorded or counted. For additional information, see the US Count Votes

report, "Study of the 2004 Presidential Election Exit Poll Discrepancies" (2005) at: http://electionarchive.org/ucvAnalysis/US/Exit_Polls_2004_Mitofsky-Edison.pdf.

For another analysis of the controversies surrounding the 2004 exit polls, see Traugott, Highton, and Brady (2005).

13. The question that Gallup first used in the 1930s, "Do you approve or disapprove of the job (name of President) is doing as president?" is generally considered the standard method for measuring presidential approval and is used by a number of other organizations, including the CBS News/*New York Times* poll and the ABC News/*Washington Post* poll. Other organizations, such as the Harris poll, use ratings of the president, that is, "How would you rate the overall job President [name of president] is doing as president . . . excellent, pretty good, only fair, or poor?" rather than "approval" in measuring presidential performance. In addition, many Gallup Polls, as well as other surveys, contain additional questions that measure how the American public feels about the president, such as whether the public has a favorable or unfavorable opinion of him and whether or not a number of different characteristics (for example, "can get things done," "honest and trustworthy") apply to the president. Though these data are used in describing the public's overall perceptions of the president, it is the question "Do you approve or disapprove of the job [name of president] is doing as president?" that is generally referred to in describing presidential approval.

CHAPTER 4

1. With the fairly rapid changes in communication that have taken place in recent years, including blogs, Facebook, Twitter, and YouTube, some scholars are questioning the portrayal of public opinion based on statistics produced from a survey and believe that an accurate description of public opinion needs to take into account "textured talk, dialogue, exchange, and conversation." However, even those who see limitations in the "counting" aspect of surveys recognize that "democracy needs credible public opinion polling" (Goidel, Kirzinger, and Xenos, 2011; Herbst, 2011).

2. For a more complete discussion of RDD, see Tuchfarber and Klecka, *Random Digit Dialing: Lowering the Cost of Victimization Surveys* and Groves and Kahn, *Surveys by Telephone: A National Comparison with Personal Interviews.*

3. Historically, this process was fairly straightforward when the population of interest was the country or a state, but it became more difficult when a smaller area such as a county, city, or local community was the target area. Since telephone exchanges do not coincide with political boundaries, decisions must be made as to which exchanges to include in the sampling frame. For example, if 90% of the numbers in an exchange lie outside the target area, should the exchange be excluded (meaning some residents of the area will be systematically excluded from the sample) or included (leading to more screening and higher survey costs)? In any survey in which the boundaries of the area of interest and the telephone exchanges are not coterminous, a screening question must be included to identify those households or individuals who are in the target area and eligible to be included in the sample. More recently, the Telephone Consumer Protection Act (1991) gave U.S. consumers

the option to keep their existing telephone number, or "port" their number, when changing from one service provider to another. Together with the increasing use of cell phones, there is much less certainty that a number dialed within a given area code will reach a respondent living in a particular geographic location. As a result, it is now common to include a geographic screening question in telephone surveys.

4. The description of telephone surveys provided to this point is based on an interview that is conducted by a human interviewer. You should recognize, however, that there is another type of telephone interviewing—interactive voice response (IVR)—in which a computer automatically dials a sample of telephone numbers (typically generated by RDD) and, when the call is answered, questions are read with a recorded voice. The respondent then answers by pressing the appropriate numbers on the telephone keypad or having their responses recorded by voice recognition technology (Rasmussen, 2000). In Traugott's (2000: 36) assessment of this method, he noted that "until there is more information about their methods and a longer track record to evaluate their results, we shouldn't confuse the work they do with scientific surveys, and it shouldn't be called polling." Although IVR has a number of limitations, it frequently produces results that are similar to those found with other methods.

5. A discussion of probability theory underlying the concept of sampling error is beyond the scope of the current text, but it can be found in most social statistics or survey methods texts (see, for example, Babbie, 1990; Kalton, 1983). You should be aware, however, that the sampling error is based on the standard error, which is calculated by the formula:

Where S = the standard error;
P = the percentage of the population having a given characteristic;
$Q = 1 - P$; and
N = the number of cases in the sample.

Probability theory demonstrates that certain proportions of the sample estimates will fall within specified increments of standard errors from the population value. Approximately 95% of the samples fall within two standard errors of the population value. While increasing the sample size will reduce sampling error, the relationship is not a straight-line one. For example, to cut your sampling error in half, you would need to collect data on four times as many individuals.

6. Almost 25 years ago this survey was called the "best United States Survey" (Bradburn and Sudman, 1988: 130), and its high level of precision has been maintained over time. The high degree of precision of this survey, however, comes at a price: the current annual cost of the Current Population Survey is close to $50 million.

7. For an extensive discussion of attitudes and non-attitudes, see P. Converse (1970).

8. J. Converse and Presser (1986: 37) suggest another alternative for dealing with the question of whether to offer an explicit middle alternative. In their view, the solution is to "not explicitly provide the middle category and thereby avoid losing information about the direction in which people lean, but follow the question with an intensity item, thus separating those who definitely occupy a position from those who only lean toward it."

9. One of the most significant controversies in American electoral behavior—the extent to which the mass public exhibits consistent attitudes—centers on changes in question wording and format. Briefly, this controversy involves whether changes in the American electorate, which were noted in the 1960s, were a result of "true" changes in mass behavior or were a result of changes in the format used for measuring opinions. For more on this controversy, see Bishop, Tuchfarber, and Oldendick (1978); Bishop et al. (1978); Converse (1964); and Nie, Verba, and Petrocik (1976).

10. The wording of this question was, "Do you think it should be possible for a pregnant woman to obtain a legal abortion if she is married and does not want any more children?"

11. The wording of this question was, "Do you think it should be possible for a pregnant woman to obtain a legal abortion if there is a strong chance of a serious defect in the baby?"

12. Although this order of costs is generally true for the traditional modes of survey data collection, determining where electronic data collection falls is more difficult given the tremendous variability in methods for implementing such data collection. An electronic survey of a closed population with a list of e-mail addresses available could be done very inexpensively, with the cost even less than that of a comparable mail survey. On the other hand, an electronic survey of a general population in which the initial sample was selected by address-based sampling is likely to be more expensive than a comparable mail survey and, depending on the technology provided to selected households, could approach the cost of face-to-face interviewing. Although this ranking reflects the relative costs of a "typical" survey, the cost of data collection, by mode, for any survey depends on factors such as the population of interest and the method of sample selection.

13. In one of the most comprehensive comparisons of face-to-face and telephone interviews, Groves and Kahn (1979: 188) reported that the cost of conducting a face-to-face survey was approximately 2.5 times greater than carrying out the same data collection effort by telephone, while Tuchfarber and Klecka (1976: 19) estimated that the cost of personal interviews was 3.4 times that of those done by telephone. Although these studies were conducted more than 30 years ago, they remain among the few large-scale studies in which extensive comparisons were made between these modes. More recent experience with cost comparisons of face-to-face and telephone surveys indicates that the magnitude of these differences remains similar today.

14. The initial demonstration of these procedures conducted by Knowledge Networks in 1999 was done at a cost of $6 million (Brady, Fiorina, and Iyengar, 2003).

15. Although these visual images provide some interesting possibilities for conducting surveys, researchers will need to consider the impact that such images will have on the context in which the questions are answered. More generally, Internet surveys face some unique concerns related to the appearance of the questions on a computer screen (e.g., how questions are handled by different browsers or how they appear on a desktop computer as opposed to a laptop or a cell phone), having clear instructions for respondents, and the confidentiality of data transmitted electronically (Dillman, 2000).

16. In addition to the election results, comparisons of the findings from surveys conducted by Knowledge Networks to those from the Behavioral Risk Factor Sur-

veillance System, the Current Population Survey, and the 2000 U.S. Census have shown results that are quite comparable (Huggins and Eyerman, 2001).

CHAPTER 5

1. The Kids Voting USA organization is based in Topeka, Kansas, and is sponsored at the present time by the Kansas Press Association, the Gannett Foundation, and the Scripps Howard Foundation. The national organization prepares curricula and outlines that are adopted and implemented at the state or regional level within a state.

2. Some studies suggest that there may also be a phenomenon known as *period effects*, which means that historical events influence citizens of all age groups. It is possible that the Watergate scandal increased political cynicism throughout the electorate, not just in the generation that came of age during that period, or that the events of September 11, 2001, may have had an impact on the feelings of security of all Americans.

3. There is some controversy within the scholarly community over the degree to which the media actually influences opinions. Though many scholars, like Graber and others, find that people do learn from the media and pay attention to media stories that interest them, research on how people decide between candidates and how they formulate political opinions has shown limited media impact. This body of research is sometimes called the minimal effects model.

CHAPTER 6

1. As Bennett (1989: 424) has noted, one of the challenges in studying political knowledge is the availability of identical questions over any appreciable length of time. For this research, "It would be best if additional identically worded items were available over a wider range of topics and over a longer time span, these are about the best available."

2. A more complete description of the extensive process that these researchers used in identifying these items can be found in Delli Carpini and Keeter (1996: 66–67).

3. Delli Carpini and Keeter also reported that 16% in 1987 could define sampling error. Those of you who remember this information from Chapter 4 are among a small group of the knowledgeable population on this topic.

4. In Chapter 3 we cautioned consumers of polls to be wary of results provided by interest groups. Though the sponsor of this survey, the Intercollegiate Studies Institute, is not a typical interest group, its purpose is "to further in successive generations of college students a better understanding of the values and institutions that sustain a free and humane society." The largely "negative" results reported in this survey could serve to draw attention to the need for and importance of this group's mission.

5. Events such as those of September 11, 2001, may have had an effect on Americans' willingness to trade off civil liberties for greater personal safety and security. An example of research on this aspect of civil liberties is provided in Davis (2004).

CHAPTER 7

1. Although much of the research involving these two variables has focused on their roles as independent variables (Jacoby, 1991: 202), there is also a line of research that demonstrates that they can be influenced by positions on policy issues (e.g., Franklin and Jackson, 1983; Rice and Hilton, 1996).

2. Although a large majority of the American public is able to place themselves along this continuum, it should be noted that a significant minority—generally around 25%—is not able or willing to place itself on this scale. For this subset of the population, ideological identifications make little, if any, difference in their policy positions (Jacoby, 1991: 196).

3. The data presented in Table 7.1, as well as much of the data to be presented in the following chapters, are from the American National Election Studies (NES). As described in Chapter 3, the NES was first conducted in 1948 and was conducted in every presidential or off-year congressional election year between 1958 and 2004. No NES was done in 2006, and while data were collected in 2010, the mode used was the Internet and respondents had previously participated in the Election Studies' 2008–2009 panel. Given concerns about potential mode effects and changes in question wording, the NES data from 2010 are not included in the tables that provide cross-time comparisons.

4. Although the questions used in other surveys differ somewhat from those used in the NES, the basic pattern of ideological identification is the same, with conservatives outnumbering liberals and the percentage of conservatives increasing slightly during this period. For the period 1973–2010, the percentage of liberals reported in the General Social Survey ranges between 23% and 30%, while the percentage of conservatives reached highs of 37% in 1994 and 38% in 2004. The CBS/*New York Times* surveys (which ask, "How would you describe your views on most political matters? Generally do you think of yourself as liberal, moderate, or conservative?") consistently demonstrate that a higher percentage of the American public identifies themselves as conservative rather than as liberal.

5. As the Hispanic population has grown in the United States, the political views of this group have received increasing attention. As Suro, Fry, and Passel (2005: 6) note, "Between the 2000 and 2004 elections the Hispanic population grew by 5.7 million persons accounting for half of the increase in the U.S. population of 11.5 million. . . . Hispanics are indeed a fast growing population and a fast growing political presence at a time when other major segments of the U.S. population are growing slowly, if at all." In the 2004 National Election Study, Hispanics were much more likely than either whites or blacks to classify themselves as liberal; 41.4% of Hispanics classified themselves as liberal, 32.9% were middle-of-the-road, and 25.7% viewed themselves as conservatives. Although this gap narrowed in 2008, Hispanics were still more likely to identify themselves as liberal—35.6%—with 33.0% classifying themselves as middle-of-the-road and 31.4% as conservative.

6. In grouping these data into three categories, the responses to the root question, "Generally speaking, do you usually think of yourself as a Republican, a Democrat, an Independent, or what?" have been used, as suggested by Warren Miller (1991). That is, those who identify themselves as "strong" or "weak" partisans are considered to be

aligned with that party, while those who "lean" toward a party are treated as Independents. Although there is some evidence that "leaners" behave more like partisans than true Independents (Smith et al., 1995; Weisberg, 1980), using the distributions from the root question provides a more accurate measure of the stability and meaningfulness of an individual's identification with a party (Miller, 1991: 558).

7. Researchers such as Keith and his colleagues (1992) have made the argument that the rise of independent voters is a myth. They contend that most of the electorate will admit that they are closer to one party or the other when given the opportunity to do so (i.e., the "leaners" in this question), and that over time there is a core of only about 10% of the public that is truly "independent." Moreover, they argue that these leaners resemble partisans in their vote, other political behavior, and attitudes. As Miller (1991: 558) has noted, however, "The question is not whether 'independent leaners' may, from time to time, be more partisan in their voting behavior or issue preferences than are weak identifiers. . . . The question is the stability (and the meaningfulness) of one's self-identification as a Democrat, a Republican, or as something else." Over the past 60 years, the percentage of the public identifying with one of the two major parties has declined significantly.

8. Data aggregated from 21 Gallup Polls conducted in 2010 found that 31% of Americans identified themselves as Democrats, 29% as Republicans, and 38% as Independents. Data on party identification from other sources such as the General Social Survey show similar patterns of decline in the number of Democrats and the rise of Independents in the past 25 years. In the 1972 GSS data, for example, almost 50% of those responding identified themselves as Democrats, 28% were Independents, and 22% were Republicans. More recent GSS data have shown a fairly equal division among Democrats, Independents, and Republicans. Despite the consistent increase in Independents identified by various polling organizations, the data do not seem to indicate that Americans are "so strongly dissatisfied with the two major parties that they are actively seeking a third party to save them" (Moore, 1996a: 1).

9. In 2008, the identification of Hispanics with the two major parties fell between those of blacks and whites. In this year, 44% of Hispanics identified themselves as Democrats, 17% said they were Republicans, and 39% were Independents.

10. The five items are: (1) How much of the time do you think you can trust the government to do what is right—just about always, most of the time, or only some of the time? (2) Would you say that the government is pretty much run by a few big interests looking out for themselves or that it is run for the benefit of all the people? (3) Do you think that people in the government waste a lot of the money we pay in taxes, waste some of it, or don't waste very much of it? (4) Do you think that quite a few of the people running the government are a little crooked, not very many are, or do you think hardly any of them are crooked at all? and (5) Do you feel that almost all of the people running the government are smart people who usually know what they are doing, or do you think that quite a few of them don't seem to know what they are doing? The item involving whether "the people running the government know what they are doing" was dropped from the NES series after 1980 because some respondents offered the cynical response that "the people running the government know exactly what they are doing," implying deception and abuse of power rather than competence (Lipset and Schneider, 1983: 18).

11. It should be noted that Caddell's assessment was not universally shared. For a contrary view of the public's attitudes toward government during this period, see Warren Miller (1979).

12. Another aspect of the responses to this item involves the percentage of respondents who give "don't know" or "it depends" answers to this question. As Bennett and Bennett (1990: 28) caution, a fairly significant portion of the public does not have an opinion on this issue, and "failure to determine who those without opinion are, or why one-quarter to two-fifths of the public take no position on the question, may lead to misinterpretation of public opinion on this issue." Although this is important to an overall understanding of this issue, our interest is more in the division of "powerful" versus "not too powerful" responses among those with an opinion. Bennett and Bennett provide an excellent extensive discussion of the various dimensions of this issue.

13. Unfortunately, the trend on this issue cannot presently be extended past 2000, since this question was not included in the 2002, 2004, or 2008 election studies. The 2002, 2004, and 2008 studies did contain the following three common items related to the power of the federal government:

(percentages for the years 2002, 2004, 2008)

Next, I'm going to ask you to choose which of the two statements I read comes closer to your own opinion:

(A) One, the less government, the better; OR 41 43 41

Two, there are more things that government should be doing; 59 57 59

(B) One, we need a strong government to handle today's complex economic problems; OR 63 67 69

Two, the free market can handle these problems without the government being involved; 37 33 31

(C) One, the main reason the government has become bigger over the years is because it has gotten involved in things that people should do for themselves; OR 43 43 44

Two, government has become bigger because the problems we face have become bigger; 57 57 56

These results paint an image of the public's views about the power of the federal government that is quite different from that provided on the basis of the question used from 1964 to 2000, and again demonstrate the importance of the questions used in measuring the American mind.

CHAPTER 8

1. As in the previous chapter, much of the data reported here is taken from the National Election Studies (NES) and General Social Surveys. The examination of social-welfare issues is complicated by the cross-time changes in question wording and format that occur in the NES series. In sum, before 1964 the usual question form used in the NES was a five-point strongly agree–strongly disagree format. From 1964 to 1970, this was changed to a forced-choice alternative, which was expanded to a seven-point format in 1972. These variations in format were accompanied by changes in question wording, which make cross-year comparisons hazardous.

We have strived to make these data as comparable as possible, while noting those instances where question wording makes trend comparisons impossible (Bishop, Oldendick, Tuchfarber, and Bennett, 1978; Bishop, Tuchfarber, and Oldendick, 1978; Sullivan, Piereson, and Marcus, 1978).

2. The issue of Social Security is one that clearly demonstrates some of the dynamics of public opinion in the United States that have been described in previous chapters. The use of polls by interest groups, for example, is demonstrated by the surveys conducted for the American Association of Retired Persons, which has used these results to lobby against some of the proposals for changing Social Security, particularly private accounts (AARP, 2010). This issue is one on which there are clear partisan differences. For example, a June 2011 survey done by the Pew Center for the People and the Press found that 47% of Republicans thought it was more important to keep Social Security benefits as they are rather than to take steps to reduce the deficit, compared to 71% of Democrats. Republicans were also more likely than Democrats or Independents to approve reducing Social Security benefits for seniors with higher incomes and gradually raising the age at which people can begin receiving Social Security, and less likely to favor making more of high-earners income subject to the Social Security payroll tax.

3. The issue of support of public schools is one where the change in question wording in the NES limits the extent of the time-series data on this question. The 1964 and 1968 NES included a question on whether "the government in Washington should help towns and cities provide education for grade and high school children" or whether this "should be handled by states and local communities." As Page and Shapiro (1992: 133) note, the public expresses skepticism about the role in education of "the government in Washington" as opposed to "states and local communities." As they point out, "local 'handling' does not preclude federal aid."

4. That Gallup Poll question on this topic asks, "Do you think it is the responsibility of the federal government to make sure that all Americans have health care coverage, or is that not the responsibility of the federal government?" Each time this question was asked between 2000 and 2008, approximately 60% of respondents said this is the government's responsibility. In both 2009 and 2010, 50% chose the "government responsibility" option, 47% thought this was not the federal government's responsibility, and 3% had no opinion.

5. During this period the GSS has also included a question on spending "on the environment." Trends on this question parallel those for the item on improving and protecting the environment.

6. A related Gallup Poll question on this issue asks, "Do you think the U.S. government is doing too much, too little, or about the right amount in terms of protecting the environment?" The results for this item lead to a similar conclusion. In March 2011, 49% said the government was doing too little, 33% thought it was doing the right amount, 16% said too much, and 2% had no opinion. Since 1992, the percentage that gave the "too little" response to this item has far exceeded the percentage who thought the government was doing too much.

7. Additional evidence from the Gallup Poll indicates that the public's support of the environment relative to the economy may be waning. The Gallup Poll asks, "With which of these statements about the environment and the economy do you most agree—protection of the environment should be given priority even at the

risk of curbing economic growth or economic growth should be given priority, even if the environment suffers to some extent?" In each of the 19 surveys in which this question was asked between September 1984 and March 2006, the percentage selecting protecting the environment was higher than that for economic growth, with the largest difference in 2000, when 70% chose the environment and 23% the economy. This majority flipped in March 2009, when 51% gave priority to economic growth and 42% selected the environment. In March 2011, 54% said economic growth should be given priority, 36% chose protection of the environment, 6% said they should be of equal priority, and 4% had no opinion.

8. The Pew Center (2010b) research on this topic also indicates the great divide in opinion on this issue along party lines. As noted in its report, "Views about climate change continue to be sharply divided along party lines. A substantial majority of Democrats (79%) say there is solid evidence that the average temperature on earth has been increasing over the past few decades, and 53% think the earth is warming mostly because of human activity. Among Republicans only 38% agree the earth is warming and just 16% say warming is caused by humans. . . . Republicans who agree with the Tea Party movement are much more likely than other Republicans to say that there is no solid evidence that the earth's temperature has been rising."

CHAPTER 9

1. By 1999, the distribution of opinion on school desegregation issues reached such a level of consensus that it might be considered a *valence issue*, as discussed in Chapter 1.

2. The question asked by NORC and later in the GSS was, "White people have a right to keep (Negroes/Blacks/African-Americans) out of their neighborhoods if they want to, and (Negroes/Blacks/African-Americans) should respect that right."

3. This is another good example of how question wording can affect results. Both the NES and GSS questions on this topic begin with the phrase, "Some people say that because of past discrimination blacks should be given preference in hiring and promotion. Others say that such preference in hiring and promotion of blacks is wrong . . ." The completion of this statement in the NES is "because it gives blacks advantages they haven't earned," contrasted with the GSS question, which concludes, "because it discriminates against whites." See Appendix B for more details on these questions.

4. Data from a June 2003 Gallup Poll tap the diversity in college admissions aspect of this issue. Respondents in this survey were asked, "Which comes closer to your view about evaluating students for admission into a college or university—Applicants should be admitted solely on the basis of merit, even if that results in few minority students being admitted; or an applicant's racial and ethnic background should be considered to help promote diversity on college campuses, even if that means admitting some minority students who otherwise would not be admitted?" The percentage choosing the "basis of merit" alternative option was greater than that for the "promote diversity" option, 63.2% to 36.8%.

5. This conclusion that the public feels that about the right amount is being spent on assistance to blacks is reinforced by the results from the NES, which asked a similar question in 2000 and 2002. The question posed was "whether spending

on aid to blacks should be increased, decreased, or kept about the same," and a solid majority selected the "kept about the same" alternative. The balance between the percentage choosing the "increase" and "decrease" options switches between the two years, with a slightly higher percentage saying that such spending should be decreased in 2000 (24% to 18%) and a higher percentage saying it should be increased in 2002 (22% to 17%).

6. This question was not asked of black respondents in 1972, 1975, and 1977. As a result, the data for "whites" and for the "total sample" is the same in these years.

7. Note that the 1972 distribution is not strictly comparable to those of later years, since the 1972 item did not include a "neither agree nor disagree" middle category.

8. With the available data, it is not possible to disentangle how much of this change was due to the change in question wording and how much to a longer-term trend in the decline in the percentage of the public disagreeing about the harmful effect of slavery—another example of the importance of question wording in attempting to monitor cross-time changes in the American mind.

9. The exception to the general pattern in 1966 is likely due to different response categories that were used for this question in this year.

10. One of the more extensive surveys of Latinos can be found in the Pew Hispanic Center's report *The National Survey of Latinos 2010*. Additional information on the views of Hispanics and about the Pew Hispanic Center can be found at http://pewhispanic.org.

CHAPTER 10

1. After using the question, "Is there any area around here—that is, within a mile—where you would be afraid to walk alone at night?" for many years, the polling organizations came to believe that the question conflated an individual's fear of personal crime with their perceptions of the neighborhood. This question is often supplemented by one that asks, "Overall, how would you describe the problem of crime in the United States/in the area where you live (rotated)—is it extremely serious, moderately serious, not too serious, or not serious at all?"

2. The Innocence Project was founded in 1992 at the Benjamin N. Cardozo School of Law at Yeshiva University. It has since evolved into a national organization that coordinates the efforts of state-level or regional organizations to free individuals who have been wrongfully convicted. It is well known for using DNA and other forms of evidence to appeal the convictions of murders. By 2011, more than 250 individuals have been exonerated due, in some measure, to the work of the Innocence Project.

CHAPTER 11

1. President George W. Bush, speech at West Point, New York, June 2, 2002.

2. The Chicago Council on Foreign Relations, now named the Chicago Council on Global Affairs, has sponsored 13 national surveys (1974, 1978, 1982, 1986, 1990, 1994, 1998, 2002, 2004, 2005, 2006, 2008, and 2010), interviewing both mass and elite samples. Each survey has been comprehensive in regard to foreign

and defense policy questions. It is important to note that the surveys included an Internet component in 2002 and both Internet and telephone samples in 2004. Since that time, surveys have been conducted via Internet. The effects of changing survey methods for these surveys has been examined and found to have little effect. The surveys have been supported at various times by the Ford Foundation and the MacArthur Foundation. Data are available for analysis through the Inter-University Consortium for Political and Social Research (ICPSR) at the University of Michigan.

3. The Chicago Council stopped including the elite sample after 2004. The Council of Foreign Relations in New York has sponsored two parallel surveys of the public and elites since that time. The Pew Research Center has conducted and analyzed the surveys.

CHAPTER 12

1. One of the more extensive studies of public opinion on polling was conducted in 2001, when the Henry J. Kaiser Family Foundation commissioned a large-scale study "to explore Americans' opinions about public opinion polling, to see whether polls are regarded as an effective instrument for expressing the people's will to leaders in government" (Brodie et al., 2001). The results of this study were also a mix of good and bad news for survey researchers. Americans overwhelmingly believed that the will of the majority should influence the decisions of government officials and felt that public opinion polls are a good way for public policy makers to learn what people think. Moreover, three-fourths of the public thought that decision makers should pay a great deal or fair amount of attention to public opinion polls in considering important issues. On the negative side, "Majorities of the public think that polls are inaccurate, have inherent limitations that prevent them from communicating the public's views, and are subject to manipulation. While half believe that they are based on sound scientific practices, half disagree or are not sure about the polling process" (Brodie et al., 2001: 13). These results are now more than ten years old, and factors such as the increased difficulty in gaining respondent cooperation in all surveys would lead one to suspect that this "mix of good and bad news" would be tilted more in the negative direction if this study were repeated today.

2. Other media outlets have had similar experiences and have been subject to similar criticisms. During the 1980 election campaign, ABC News conducted a call-in poll following a televised debate between Ronald Reagan and Jimmy Carter. In addition to the self-selection and unrepresentativeness that attend to all call-ins, there were several additional sources of potential bias in this case. As noted by Moore (1992: 288): "The debate ended late in the evening on the East Coast, thus favoring respondents from the Western parts of the country, which were more heavily for Reagan than Carter. The cost of 50 cents would deter some of the less affluent from participating, yet they were proportionately more likely to support Carter. And an electronic glitch made it more difficult for urban areas than rural areas to complete their calls, again a bias against Carter's political support."

In reporting the results of call-in polls, ABC would include a disclaimer that the results were "unscientific," but during programs, the results "would be discussed as though they reflected the general opinion of the American public" (Moore, 1992: 288).

3. Other types of pseudo-polls that can cause the public to lose faith in surveys include **sugging** (selling under the guise of research), **frugging** (fundraising under the guise of research), and **cugging** (campaigning under the guise of research). These practices "trade on the prestige of science and . . . exploit the willingness of people to reveal information about themselves in the public interest" (Research Industry Coalition, 1996). These practices were made illegal by the Telemarketing Consumer Fraud and Abuse Prevention Act (1994), which requires telemarketers to disclose promptly their name and that the purpose of the call is sales related, including the nature and price of the product the caller is attempting to sell. Part of the intent of this law was to differentiate legitimate survey research calls from sales calls, and while there is some evidence that this law has been effective in reducing such practices, it has not eliminated them entirely.

4. The Pew Research Center for the People and the Press began routinely including a cell phone sample in nearly all of its surveys in 2008. (For a more complete description of the methodology used in conducting its telephone surveys, see www.people-press.org/methodology/sampling/cell-phones/.) Gallup has been including cell phone–only households in all national telephone Gallup Polls since January 2008. Further, cell phone–only households are now as likely to fall into national Gallup Poll samples as those living in traditional landline households. (See www.gallup.com/poll/110383/Does-Gallup-call-cell-phones.aspx.)

5. Although refusals are the largest contributor to nonresponse in surveys, overall nonresponse includes other factors, such as being unable to locate respondents or to collect information from them during the study's fielding period, or failures to complete the interview due to illness or a language barrier. Telephone surveys also suffer from nonresponse due to consistent nonanswered telephone numbers or repeated attempts to contact a household that reach an answering machine.

6. Public annoyance over the rapid increase in telemarketing calls and growing concern about privacy were among the factors that led to the establishment of the federal "Do Not Call" list. The Telemarketing and Consumer Fraud and Abuse Protection Act of 1994 included a provision that enabled consumers to stop most unwanted telemarketing calls through a single registration of their telephone number on the national "Do Not Call" list. Enforcement of this provision went into effect on October 1, 2003. On the day the registry was launched more than 7 million numbers were logged into the system, and by August 11, 2005, the Federal Trade Commission (2005) announced that the national Do Not Call registry had topped *100 million* numbers. Although research, such as the polls and surveys reported on in previous chapters, is exempt from the Do Not Call list provisions, the enactment of such legislation and the reaction to it is an indication of the public's wariness regarding unsolicited calls. This is a matter of concern to survey researchers and a factor that they must take into consideration in designing telephone surveys.

7. Given factors such as the public's lack of information on many topics and its willingness to provide a response to survey questions, which can vary significantly over a short period of time or depending on the context in which it is asked, data from polls and surveys have been characterized as providing the "illusion of public opinion" (Bishop, 2005).

References

Abramowitz, Alan I., and Kyle L. Saunders. 1998. "Ideological Realignment in the U.S. Electorate." *Journal of Politics* 60 (August): 634–652.

———. 2008. "Is Polarization a Myth?" *Journal of Politics* (April): 542–555.

Achen, Christopher H. 1975. "Mass Political Attitudes and the Survey Response." *American Political Science Review* 69 (December): 1218–1231.

Adams, Kenneth. 1996. "Guns and Gun Control." In *Americans View Crime and Justice: A National Public Opinion Survey.* Eds. Timothy J. Flanagan and Dennis R. Longmire. Thousand Oaks, CA: Sage.

Adams, William C., and Paul H. Ferber. 1980. "Measuring Legislator-Constituency Congruence: Liquor, Legislators and Linkage." *Journal of Politics* 42 (February): 202–208.

Allport, Gordon W. 1935. "Attitudes." In *Handbook of Social Psychology.* Ed. Carl Murchison. Worcester, MA: Clark University Press.

Alpert, Harry. 1952. "Opinion and Attitude Surveys in the U.S. Government." *Public Opinion Quarterly* 16 (Spring): 33–41.

American Association for Public Opinion Research. 2003. "Push Polls." www.aapor.org/pdfs/2003/2003pushpollstatement.pdf.

———. 2009. *An Evaluation of the Methodology of the 2008 Pre-Election Primary Polls.* www.aapor.org/Content/aapor/AdvocacyandInitiatives/Reports/AAPOR_Rept_FINAL-Rev-4-13-09.pdf.

———. 2010a. "AAPOR Report on Online Panels." *Public Opinion Quarterly* 74 (Winter): 711–781.

———. 2010b. *New Considerations for Survey Researchers when Planning and Conducting RDD Telephone Surveys in the U.S. with Respondents Reached via Cell Phone Numbers.* www.aapor.org/Content/aapor/AdvocacyandInitiatives/Reports/CellPhoneTaskForceReport/2010AAPORCellPhoneTFReport.pdf.

American Association of Retired Persons. 2010. *Social Security 75th Anniversary Survey Report: Public Opinion Trends*. Washington: AARP.

American National Elections Studies, 1952–2010. Ann Arbor, MI: Inter-University Consortium for Political and Social Research.

Anderegg, William R. L., James W. Prall, Jacob Harold, and Stephen H. Schneider. 2010. "Expert Credibility in Climate Change." *Proceedings of the National Academy of Sciences* 107 (27): 12107–12109.

Anderson, Barbara A., Brian D. Silver, and Paul R. Abramson. 1988. "The Effects of the Race of the Interviewer on Race-Related Attitudes of Black Respondents in SRC/CPS National Election Studies." *Public Opinion Quarterly* 52 (Fall): 289–324.

Arterton, F. Christopher. 1974. "The Impact of Watergate on Children's Attitudes toward Political Authority." *Political Science Quarterly* 89 (June): 269–288.

Austin, Erica Weintraub, and C. Leigh Nelson. 1993. "Influences of Ethnicity, Family Communication, and Media on Adolescents' Socialization to U.S. Politics." *Journal of Broadcasting and Electronic Media* (Fall): 419–435.

Babbie, Earl. 1990. *Survey Research Methods*. 2nd ed. Belmont, CA: Wadsworth.

Baker, Peter, and Dan Balz. 2005. "Bush Words Reflect Public Opinion Strategy." www.washingtonpost.com/wp-dyn/content/article/2005/06/29/.

Bardes, Barbara A. 1997. "Public Opinion and Foreign Policy: How Does the Public Think about America's Role in the World." In *Understanding Public Opinion*. Eds. Barbara Norrander and Clyde Wilcox. Washington, DC: Congressional Quarterly Press.

Bardes, Barbara A., and Robert W. Oldendick. 1978. "Beyond Internationalism: The Case for Multiple Dimensions in the Structure of Foreign Policy Attitudes." *Social Science Quarterly* 59 (December): 496–508.

Bartels, Larry M. 2000. "Partisanship and Voting Behavior: 1952–1996." *American Journal of Political Science* 44 (January): 35–50.

Beck, Paul Allen. 1977. "The Role of Agents in Political Socialization." In *Handbook of Political Socialization*. Ed. Stanley A. Renshon. New York: Free Press.

Bennett, Linda L. M., and Stephen Earl Bennett. 1990. *Living with Leviathan: Americans Coming to Terms with Big Government*. Lawrence, KS: University of Kansas Press.

Bennett, Stephen E. 1988. "Know-Nothings Revisited: The Meaning of Political Ignorance Today." *Social Science Quarterly* 69: 476–490.

———. 1989. "Trends in Americans' Political Information, 1967–1987." *American Politics Quarterly* 17 (October): 422–435.

———. 1995a. "Americans' Knowledge of Ideology, 1980–1992." *American Politics Quarterly* 23 (July): 259–278.

———. 1995b. "Americans' Political Information in 1988 and 1992." *Journal of Politics* 7 (May): 521–542.

———. 1996. "'Know-Nothings' Revisited Again." *Political Behavior* 18 (September): 219–223.

Bennett, Stephen E., and Robert W. Oldendick. 1977. "The Power of the Federal Government." Paper presented at the annual meeting of the Midwest Political Science Association, Chicago.

Bennett, Stephen E., and David Resnick. 1990. "The Implications of Nonvoting for Democracy in the United States." *American Journal of Political Science* 34 (August): 771–802.

Bennett, W. Lance. 1996. *News: The Politics of Illusion*. 3rd ed. New York: Longman.

Berelson, Bernard R., Paul F. Lazarsfeld, and William N. McPhee. 1954. *Voting: A Study of Opinion Formation in a Presidential Campaign.* Chicago: University of Chicago Press.

Bishop, Bill. 2008. *The Big Sort: Why the Clustering of Like-Minded America Is Tearing Us Apart.* New York: Mariner Books.

Bishop, George F. 2005. *The Illusion of Public Opinion.* Lanham, MD: Rowman & Littlefield.

Bishop, George F., Robert W. Oldendick, and Alfred J. Tuchfarber. 1983. "Effects of Filter Questions in Public Opinion Surveys." *Public Opinion Quarterly* 47 (Winter): 528–546.

———. 1984. "What Must My Interest in Politics Be if I Just Told You 'I Don't Know'?" *Public Opinion Quarterly* 48 (Winter): 510–519.

Bishop, George F., Robert W. Oldendick, Alfred J. Tuchfarber, and Stephen E. Bennett. 1978. "The Changing Structure of Mass Belief Systems: Fact or Artifact?" *Journal of Politics* 40 (August): 781–787.

———. 1980. "'Pseudo-Opinions' on Public Affairs." *Public Opinion Quarterly* 44 (Summer): 198–209.

Bishop, George, and Andrew Smith. 2001. "Response-Order Effects and the Early Gallup Split-Ballots." *Public Opinion Quarterly* 65 (Winter): 479–505.

Bishop, George F., Alfred J. Tuchfarber, and Robert W. Oldendick. 1978. "Change in the Structure of American Political Attitudes: The Nagging Question of Question Wording." *American Journal of Political Science* 22 (May): 250–269.

Blendon, Robert J., Drew E. Altman, John M. Benson, Humphrey Taylor, Matt James, and Mark Smith. 1992a. "The Implications of the 1992 Presidential Election for Health Care Reform." *Journal of the American Medical Association* 268 (December): 3371–3375.

Blendon, Robert J., and John M. Benson. 2010. "Public Opinion at the Time of the Vote on Health Care Reform." *New England Journal of Medicine* 362 (April 22): www.nejm.org/doi/full/10.1056/NEJMp1003844.

Blendon, Robert J., John M. Benson, Mollyann Brodie, Drew E. Altman, and Mario Brossard. 1998. "The Public and the President's Commission on Race." *Public Perspective* 9 (February/March): 66–69.

Blendon, Robert J., John M. Benson, Mollyann Brodie, Drew E. Altman, and Matt James. 2000. "Risky Business: Reforming Social Security and Medicare." *Public Perspective* 11 (January/February): 40–43.

Blendon, Robert J., and Karen Donelan. 1991. "The Public and the Future of U.S. Health Care System Reform." In *System in Crisis: The Case for Health Care Reform.* Eds. Robert J. Blendon and Jennifer N. Edwards. New York: Faulkner and Gray.

Blendon, Robert J., and Jennifer N. Edwards, eds. 1991. *System in Crisis: The Case for Health Care Reform.* New York: Faulkner and Gray.

Blendon, Robert J., Ulrike S. Szalay, Drew E. Altman, and Gerald Chervinsky. 1992b. "New Hampshire, Health Care, and the 1992 Election." *Journal of American Health Policy* 2 (May/June): 16–22.

Blumberg, Stephen J., and Julian V. Luke. 2011. *Wireless Substitution: Early Release of Estimates from the National Health Interview Survey, July–December, 2010.* National Center for Health Statistics. www.cdc.gov/nchs/data/nhis/earlyrelease/wireless201106.pdf.

Blumberg, Stephen J., Julian V. Luke, and Marcie L. Cynamon. 2006. "Telephone Coverage and Health Survey Estimates: Is Concern about Wireless Substitution Warranted?" *American Journal of Public Health* 96: 926–931.

Blumenthal, Mark. 2008. "Is Polling as We Know It Doomed?" *National Journal.* www .nationaljournal.com/njonline/is-polling-as-we-know-it-doomed--20090810.

———. 2009. "Pollster Accuracy and the National Polls." www.pollster.com/blogs/ pollster_accuracy_and_the_nati.php?nr=1.

———. 2011. "Poll Accuracy Held Steady in 2010." February 14. www.huffington-post.com/2011/02/14/poll-accuracy-held-steady-in-2010_n_823181.html.

Blumer, Herbert. 1948. "Public Opinion and Public Opinion Polling." *American Sociological Review* 13 (October): 542–554.

Bradburn, Norman M., and Seymour Sudman. 1988. *Polls and Surveys: Understanding What They Tell Us.* San Francisco: Jossey-Bass.

Brady, David, Morris Fiorina, and Shanto Iyengar. 2003. "A New Frontier in Polling." *Hoover Digest* (November).

Brady, Henry E., James S. Fishkin, and Robert C. Luskin. 2003. "Informed Public Opinion about Foreign Policy: The Uses of Deliberative Polling." *Brookings Review* 21 (Summer): 16–19.

Brehm, John. 1993. *The Phantom Respondents: Opinion Surveys and Political Representation.* Ann Arbor: University of Michigan Press.

———. 1994. "Stubbing Our Toes for a Foot in the Door? Prior Contact, Incentives, and Survey Response." *International Journal of Public Opinion Research* 6 (Spring): 45–63.

Brodie, Mollyann, Lisa Ferraro Parmalee, April Brackett, and Drew E. Altman. 2001. "Polling and Democracy." *Public Perspective* 12 (July/August): 10–14.

Brown, Ethan, and Timothy P. Johnson. 2011. "Diffusion of Web Survey Methodology, 1995–2009." *Survey Research* 42 (1): 1–3.

Burstein, Paul. 2001. "The Impact of Public Opinion on Public Policy: A Review and an Agenda." Paper presented at the annual meeting of the American Sociological Association, Anaheim, CA.

———. 2006. "Why Estimates of the Impact of Public Opinion on Public Policy Are Too High: Empirical and Theoretical Implications." *Social Forces* 84 (June): 2273–2289.

Caddell, Patrick H. 1979. "Crisis of Confidence—I: Trapped in a Downward Spiral." *Public Opinion* 2 (October/November): 2–8.

Campbell, Angus, Philip E. Converse, Warren E. Miller, and Donald E. Stokes. 1960. In *American Voter.* New York: John Wiley and Sons.

Campbell, Angus, Gerald Gurin, and Warren E. Miller. 1954. *The Voter Decides.* New York: Harper and Row.

Campbell, David A. 2008. "Voice in the Classroom: How an Open Classroom Climate Foster Political Engagement among Adolescents." *Political Behavior* 30: 437–454.

Cantril, Albert H. 1992. "The CBS Call-In: A Setback for All Public Polls." *The Public Perspective* 3 (March/April): 23–24.

Cantrell, Paul. 1992. "Opinion Polling and American Democratic Culture." *International Journal of Politics, Culture, and Society* 5: 405–432.

Cantril, Albert, ed. 1980. *Polling on the Issues.* Cabin John, MD: Seven Locks Press.

Cantril, Hadley. 1967. *The Human Dimension: Experiences in Policy Research*. New Brunswick, NJ: Rutgers University Press.

Carmines, Edward G., and James A. Stimson. 1980. "The Two Faces of Issue Voting." *American Political Science Review* 74 (March): 78–91.

———. 1989. *Issue Evolution: Race and the Transformation of American Politics*. Princeton, NJ: Princeton University Press.

Carroll, Joseph. 2005. "American Public Opinion about Immigration." Gallup Report, July 26.

Christian, Leah, Scott Keeter, Kristen Purcell, and Aaron Smith. 2010. "Assessing the Cell Phone Challenge." Pew Center for the People and the Press. http://pewresearch.org/pubs/1601/assessing-cell-phone-challenge-in-public-opinion-surveys.

Citrin, Jack. 1996. "Affirmative Action in the People's Court." *Public Interest* 122 (Winter): 39–48.

Clark, Nina. 1997. *The Politics of Physician Assisted Suicide*. New York: Garland Publishing.

CNN. 2010. "Should illegal immigrants be allowed to stay?" http://politicalticker.blogs.cnn.com/2010/07/29.

CNN/ORC. 2011. "Presidential Job Approval Rating," www.pollingreport.com/obama_job.htm.

Cohen, Steven M., and Charles S. Liebman. 1997. "American Jewish Liberalism: Unraveling the Strands." *Public Opinion Quarterly* 61 (Fall): 405–430.

Conover, Pamela Johnston. 1984. "The Influence of Group Identifications on Political Perceptions and Evaluation." *Journal of Politics* 46 (August): 760–784.

Converse, Jean M. 1987. *Survey Research in the United States: Roots and Emergence 1890–1960*. Berkeley, CA: University of California Press.

Converse, Jean M., and Stanley Presser. 1986. *Survey Questions: Handcrafting the Standardized Questionnaire*. Newbury Park, CA: Sage.

Converse, Philip E. 1964. "The Nature of Belief Systems in Mass Publics." In *Ideology and Discontent*. Ed. David E. Apter. New York: Free Press.

———. 1970. "Attitudes and Non-Attitudes: Continuation of a Dialogue." In *The Quantitative Analysis of Social Problems*. Ed. Edward R. Tufte. Reading, MA: Addison-Wesley Publishing.

———. 1972. "Change in the American Electorate." In *The Human Meaning of Social Change*. Eds. Angus Campbell and Philip E. Converse. New York: Russell Sage Foundation.

———. 1975. "Public Opinion and Voting Behavior." In *Handbook of Political Science*. Eds. Fred I. Greenstein and Nelson W. Polsby. Reading, MA: Addison-Wesley.

———. 1976. *The Dynamics of Party Support: Cohort-Analyzing Party Identification*. Beverly Hills, CA: Sage.

———. 1980. *American Social Attitudes Data Sourcebook, 1947–1978*. Cambridge, MA: Harvard University Press.

———. 1987. "Changing Conceptions of Public Opinion in the Political Process." *Public Opinion Quarterly* 51 (Winter): S12–S24.

———. 1990. "Popular Representation and the Distribution of Information." In *Information and Democratic Processes*. Eds. John A. Ferejohn and James H. Kuklinski. Urbana, IL: University of Illinois Press.

Converse, Philip E., and Gregory B. Markus. 1979. "Plus ça change . . . The New CPS Election Study Panel." *American Political Science Review* 85 (March): 32–49.

Converse, Philip E., Warren E. Miller, Jerrold G. Rusk, and Arthur C. Wolfe. 1969. "Continuity and Change in American Politics: Parties and Issues in the 1968 Election." *American Political Science Review* 63 (December): 1083–1105.

Cook, Corey. 2002. "The Contemporary Presidency: The Permanence of the 'Permanent Campaign': George W. Bush's Public Presidency." *Presidential Studies Quarterly* 32 (December): 753–764.

Cook, Elizabeth Adell, Ted G. Jelen, and Clyde Wilcox. 1992. *Between Two Absolutes: Public Opinion and the Politics of Abortion.* Boulder, CO: Westview Press.

Cooper, Sanford L. 1964. "Random Sampling by Telephone—An Improved Method." *Journal of Marketing Research* 1 (November): 45–48.

Cornyn, John. 2009. "Remarks by Senator John Cornyn on the Public Option." *Congressional Record 111th Congress* (October 26).

Council for Marketing and Opinion Research. 1995. *CMOR Refusal Rates and Industry Image Survey.* New York: Council for Marketing and Opinion Research.

———. 2003. *2003 Respondent Cooperation and Industry Image Study.* New York: Council for Marketing and Opinion Research.

Couper, Mick P. 2000. "Web Surveys: A Review of Issues and Approaches." *Public Opinion Quarterly* 64 (Winter): 230–253.

Couper, Mick P., Johnny Blair, and Timothy Triplett. 1999. "A Comparison of Mail and E-Mail for a Survey of Employees in Federal Statistical Agencies." *Public Opinion Quarterly* 65 (Summer): 464–494.

Couper, Mick P., Frederick G. Conrad, and Roger Tourangeau. 2007. "Visual Context Effects in Web Surveys." *Public Opinion Quarterly* 71 (Winter): 623–634.

Couper, Mick P., and Peter V. Miller. 2008. "Web Survey Methods: Introduction." *Public Opinion Quarterly* 72 (Special Issue): 831–835.

Craig, Barbara Hinkson, and David M. O'Brien. 1993. *Abortion and American Politics.* Chatham, NJ: Chatham House Publishers.

Cribb, T. Kenneth, Jr. 2008. *Our Fading Heritage: Americans Fail a Basic Test on Their History and Institutions.* Wilmington, DE: American Civic Literacy Program.

Crigler, Ann N., ed. 1996. *The Psychology of Political Communication.* Ann Arbor, MI: University of Michigan Press.

Crossen, Cynthia. 1991. "Studies Galore Support Products and Positions, but Are They Reliable?" *Wall Street Journal,* November 14: A-1.

Cummings, Milton C., Jr., and David Wise. 1974. *Democracy under Pressure.* 2nd ed. New York: Harcourt, Brace, Jovanovich.

Curtin, Richard, Stanley Presser, and Eleanor Singer. 2005. "Changes in Telephone Survey Nonresponse over the Past Quarter Century." *Public Opinion Quarterly* 69 (Spring): 87–98.

Dahl, Robert A. 1950. *Congress and Foreign Policy.* New York: Harcourt, Brace.

Daves, Robert P. 2000. "Talk to Me: Understanding Noncontracts, Refusals, and Response Rates." *Public Perspective* 11 (May/June): 50–51.

Davis, Darren W. 1997. "Nonrandom Measurement Error and Race of Interviewer Effects among African Americans." *Public Opinion Quarterly* 61 (Spring): 183–207.

Davis, Darren W., and Brian D. Silver. 2004. "Civil Liberties vs. Security: Public Opinion in the Context of the Terrorist Attacks on America." *American Journal of Political Science* 48 (January): 28–46.

Davis, James A. 1975. "Communism, Conformity, Cohorts, and Categories: American Tolerance in 1954 and 1972–73." *American Journal of Sociology* 81 (3): 491–513.

———. 2004. "Did Growing Up in the 1960s Leave a Permanent Mark on Attitudes and Values? Evidence from the General Social Survey." *Public Opinion Quarterly* 68 (Spring): 161–183.

Davis, Richard. 1996. *The Press and American Politics: The New Mediator.* 2nd ed. New York: Prentice-Hall.

Dawson, Richard E., Kenneth Prewitt, and Karen S. Dawson. 1977. *Political Socialization.* 2nd ed. Boston: Little, Brown.

Delli Carpini, Michael X. 1999. "In Search of the Informed Citizen: What Americans Know about Politics and Why It Matters." Presented at the conference on the Transformation of Civic Life, Murfreesboro, TN, November 12–13.

Delli Carpini, Michael X., and Scott Keeter. 1991. "Stability and Change in the U.S. Public's Knowledge of Politics." *Public Opinion Quarterly* 55 (Winter): 583–612.

———. 1992. "The Public's Knowledge of Politics." In *Public Opinion, the Press, and Public Policy.* Ed. J. David Kannamer. Westport, CT: Praeger

———. 1993. "Measuring Political Knowledge: Putting First Things First." *American Journal of Political Science* 37 (November): 1179–1206.

———. 1996. *What Americans Know about Politics and Why It Matters.* New Haven, CT: Yale University Press.

DeMaio, Theresa J., Catherine Marsh, and Charles F. Turner. 1984. "The Development and Contemporary Use of Subjective Surveys." In *Surveying Subjective Phenomena.* Eds. Charles F. Turner and Elizabeth Martin. New York: Russell Sage Foundation.

Dennis, Jack. 1969. *Political Learning in Childhood and Adolescence.* Madison, WI: University of Wisconsin.

Dennis, Jack, and Carol Webster. 1975. "Children's Images of the President and of Government in 1962 and 1974." *American Politics Quarterly* 3 (October): 386–405.

Deutsch, Karl W., John Platt, and Dieter Senghaas. 1971. "Conditions Favoring Major Advances in Science." *Science* 171 (February): 450–459.

Dillman, Don A. 1978. *Mail and Telephone Surveys: The Total Design Method.* New York: John Wiley and Sons.

———. 2000. *Mail and Internet Surveys: The Tailored Design Method.* New York: John Wiley and Sons.

Donelan, Karen, Robert J. Blendon, Cathy Schoen, Karen Davis, and Katherine Binns. 1999. "The Cost of Health System Change: Public Discontent in Five Nations." *Health Affairs* 18 (May): 206–216.

Dran, Ellen M., and Anne Hildreth. 1995. "What the Public Thinks about How We Know What It Is Thinking." *International Journal of Public Opinion Research* 7 (Summer): 129–144.

——. 1997. "Studying Public Opinion about Public Opinion: To Poll or Not to Poll." Paper presented at the annual meeting of the American Association for Public Opinion Research, Norfolk, VA.

Easton, David, and Jack Dennis. 1969. *Children in the Political System: Origins of Political Legitimacy.* New York: McGraw-Hill.

Edison Media Research and Mitofsky International. 2005. *Evaluation of Edison/Mitofsky Election System 2004.* Somerville, NJ: Edison Media Research and Mitofsky International.

Electronic Industries Association. 1991. *Consumer Electronics U.S. Sales.* Washington, DC: Electronic Industries Association.

Entman, Robert. 1989. *Democracy without Citizens: Media and the Decay of American Politics.* New York: Oxford University Press.

Erbring, Lutz, Edie N. Goldenberg, and Arthur H. Miller. 1980. "Front Page News and Real-World Cues: A New Look at Agenda-Setting by the Media." *American Journal of Political Science* 24 (February): 16–49.

Erikson, Robert S. 1979. "The SRC Panel Data and Mass Attitudes." *British Journal of Political Science* 9 (January): 89–114.

Erikson, Robert S., Norman R. Luttbeg, and Kent L. Tedin. 1980. *American Public Opinion: Its Origins, Content, and Impact.* 2nd ed. New York: John Wiley and Sons.

Erikson, Robert S., and Laura Stoker. 2011. "Caught in the Draft: the Effects of the Vietnam Draft Lottery Status on Political Attitudes." *American Political Science Review* 105 (May): 221–237.

Erikson, Robert S., and Kent L. Tedin. 2011. *American Public Opinion: Its Origin, Contents, and Impact.* 8th ed. New York: Longman.

Erskine, Hazel Gaudet. 1962. "The Polls: The Informed Public." *Public Opinion Quarterly* 26 (Winter): 669–677.

——. 1963a. "The Polls: Textbook Knowledge." *Public Opinion Quarterly* 27 (Spring): 133–141.

——. 1963b. "The Polls: Exposure to Domestic Information." *Public Opinion Quarterly* 27 (Fall): 491–500.

——. 1963c. "The Polls: Exposure to International Information." *Public Opinion Quarterly* 27 (Winter): 658–662.

Evans, Marilyn. 1996. "The Next Generation and American Democracy: Encouraging Political Participation in the Next Generation: Kids Voting USA." *Public Perspective* 7 (June/July): 47.

Exoo, Calvin F. 1994. *The Politics of the Mass Media.* Minneapolis: West.

The Federalist. No. 10, No. 63. New York: Mentor Books, 1961.

Federal Trade Commission. 2005. "Statement of Federal Trade Commission Chairman Deborah Platt Majores on the 100 Millionth Number on the National Do Not Call Registry." http://www.ftc.gov/opa/2005/08/dncstatment.shtm.

Feld, Karl G. 2001. "When Push Comes to Shove: A Polling Industry Call to Arms." *Public Perspective* 12 (September/October): 37–39.

Field, John O., and Ronald Anderson. 1969. "Ideology in the Public's Conceptualization of the 1964 Election." *Public Opinion Quarterly* 33 (Fall): 380–398.

Finkel, Steven E., Thomas M. Guterbock, and Marian J. Borg. 1991. "Race-of-Interviewer Effects in a Presidential Poll: Virginia 1989." *Public Opinion Quarterly* 55 (Fall): 313–330.

Fiorina, Morris, Samuel J. Abrams, and Jeremy C. Pope. 2004. *Culture War? The Myth of a Polarized America.* New York: Pearson Longman.

———. 2008. "Polarization in the American Public: Misconceptions and Misreadings." *Journal of Politics* 70 (April): 556–560.

———. 2010. *Culture War? The Myth of a Polarized America.* 3rd ed. New York: Longman.

Fisher, Bonnie S., and Steven P. Lab. 2010. *Encyclopedia of Victimology and Crime Prevention.* New York: Sage.

Fishkin, James S. 1996. "The 'Deliberative Opinion Poll' Comes to Texas—and to Campaign '96." *Public Perspective* 7 (December/January): 1–4.

Fishkin, James S., and Robert C. Luskin. 1996. "The Deliberative Poll: A Reply to Our Critics." *Public Perspective* 7 (December/January): 45–49.

Flanagan, Timothy J. 1996. "Public Opinion on Crime and Justice: History, Development, and Trends." In *Americans View Crime and Justice: A National Public Opinion Survey.* Eds. Timothy J. Flanagan and Dennis R. Longmire. Thousand Oaks, CA: Sage.

Flanagan, Timothy J., and Dennis R. Longmire, eds. 1996. *Americans View Crime and Justice: A National Public Opinion Survey.* Thousand Oaks, CA: Sage.

Frankenberg, Erica, and Rebecca Jacobsen. 2011. "The Polls—Trends School Integration Polls." *Public Opinion Quarterly* 75 (Winter): 788–811.

Franklin, Charles H., and John E. Jackson. 1983. "The Dynamics of Party Identification." *American Political Science Review* 77 (December): 957–973.

Frankovic, Kathleen. 1982. "Sex and Politics—New Alignments, Old Issues." *PS* 15 (Summer): 439–448.

———. 1992. Interview. "The CBS News Call-In: Slipups in the Broadcast." *Public Perspective* 3 (March/April): 19–21.

Free, Lloyd A., and Hadley Cantril. 1968. *The Political Beliefs of Americans: A Study of Public Opinion.* New York: Simon and Schuster.

Frey, James H. 1989. *Survey Research by Telephone.* 2nd ed. Newbury Park, CA: Sage.

Funk, Tim, and Jim Wrinn. 1992. "President Tells Large N.C. Crowds He Can Still Win." *Charlotte Observer,* October 22: 1A.

Gallup, Alec, and David W. Moore. 1996. "Younger People Today Are More Positive about Polls Than Their Elders." *Public Perspective* 7 (August/September): 50–53.

Gallup, George. 1947. "The Quintamensional Plan of Question Design." *Public Opinion Quarterly* 11 (Fall): 385–393.

Gallup, George, and Saul Forbes Rae. 1940. *The Pulse of Democracy.* New York: Simon and Schuster.

Gallup Poll. 2005. "Death Penalty," October 13–16.

Gallup Report. 1999. April 18. www.gallup.com/poll/content/default.aspx?ci=1684.

———. 2011a. "Government." www.gallup.com/poll/27286/Government.aspx.

———. 2011b. "Trust in Government." www.gallup.com/poll/5392/Trust-Government.aspx.

———. 2011c. "Environment." www.gallup.com/poll/1615/Environment.aspx#3.

Gawiser, Sheldon. 1995. "Push Polls: Next Wave of Dangerous Pseudo Polls." *AAPOR News* 23 (Fall): 1.

Gawiser, Sheldon R., and G. Evans Witt. 2005. *20 Questions a Journalist Should Ask about Poll Results.* 3rd ed. Poughkeepsie, NY: National Council of Public Polls.

Geer, John. 1996. *From Tea Leaves to Opinion Polls: A Theory of Democratic Leadership.* New York: Columbia University Press.

Gelman, Andrew. 2008. *Red State, Blue State, Rich State, Poor State: Why Americans Vote the Way They Do.* Princeton, NJ: Princeton University Press.

General Social Survey. 1972–2010. www3.norc.org/GSS+Website/.

Gibson, James L. 2006. "Enigmas of Intolerance: Fifty Years after *Stouffer's Communism, Conformity, and Civil Liberties.*" *Perspectives on Politics* 4 (March): 21–34.

Gilroy, John M., and Robert Y. Shapiro. 1986. "The Polls: Environmental Protection." *Public Opinion Quarterly* 50 (Summer): 270–279.

Goidel, Kirby. 2011. "Public Opinion Polling in a Digital Age: Meaning and Measurement." In *Public Opinion Polling in a Digital Age: The Challenge of Measuring and Understanding Public Opinion.* Ed. Kirby Goidel. Baton Rouge: Louisiana State University Press.

Goidel, Kirby, Ashley Kirzinger, and Michael Xenos. 2011. "Too Much Talk, Not Enough Action? Political Expression in a Digital Age." In *Public Opinion Polling in a Digital Age: The Challenge of Measuring and Understanding Public Opinion.* Ed. Kirby Goidel. Baton Rouge: Louisiana State University Press.

Goldwater, Barry. 1960. *The Conscience of a Conservative.* Shephardsville, KY: Victor Publishing Company.

Gordon, Cynthia. 2004. "'Al Gore's Our Guy': Linguistically Constructing a Family Political Identity." *Discourse and Society* 15 (5): 607–631.

Goyder, John. 1986. "Surveys on Surveys: Limitations and Potentialities." *Public Opinion Quarterly* 50 (Spring): 27–41.

Graber, Doris A. 1976. "Press and TV as Opinion Resources in Presidential Campaigns." *Public Opinion Quarterly* 40 (Fall): 285–303.

———. 1984. *Processing the News: How People Tame the Information Tide.* New York: Longman.

———. 1997. *Mass Media and American Politics.* 5th ed. Washington, DC: Congressional Quarterly Press.

Green, Joshua. 2002. "The Other War Room." *Washington Monthly Online.* February. www.washingtonmonthly.com/features/2001/0204.green.html.

Greenberg, Anna, and Douglas Rivers. 2001. "Pioneer Days: The Promise of Online Polling." *Public Perspective* 12 (March/April): 40–41.

Greenberg, Edward. 1970. "Black Children and the Political System." *Public Opinion Quarterly* 34 (Fall): 335–348.

Greenstein, Fred I. 1965. *Children and Politics.* New Haven, CT: Yale University Press.

———. 1969. *Personality and Politics.* Chicago: Markham Publishing.

———. 1973. "Sex-Related Political Differences in Childhood." In *Socialization to Politics: A Reader.* Ed. Jack Dennis. New York: John Wiley and Sons.

———. 1975. "The Benevolent Leader Revisited: Children's Images of Political Leaders in Three Democracies." *American Political Science Review* 69 (December): 1371–1398.

Groves, Robert M. 2006. "Nonresponse Rates and Nonresponse Bias in Household Surveys." *Public Opinion Quarterly* 70 (Special Issue): 646–675.

Groves, Robert M., and Mick P. Couper. 1998. *Nonresponse in Household Interview Surveys.* New York: John Wiley and Sons.

Groves, Robert M., and Robert M. Kahn. 1979. *Surveys by Telephone: A National Comparison with Personal Interviews.* New York: Academic Press.

Groves, Robert M., Stanley Presser, and Sarah Dipko. 2004. "The Role of Topic Interest in Survey Participation Decisions." *Public Opinion Quarterly* 68 (Spring): 2–31.

Haghighi, Bahram, and Jon Sorenson. 1996. "America's Fear of Crime." In *Americans View Crime and Justice: A National Public Opinion Survey.* Eds. Timothy J. Flanagan and Dennis R. Longmire. Thousand Oaks, CA: Sage.

Harris Interactive. 2009. "ESOMAR 26: Questions and Answers." www.harrisinteractive.com/vault/HI_Corp_ESOMAR26_QandA.pdf.

Harris Poll Online. 2002. http://harrrispollonline.com/.

Hatchett, Shirley, and Howard Schuman. 1975. "White Respondents and Race-of-Interviewer Effects." *Public Opinion Quarterly* 39 (Winter): 523–528.

Hennessy, Bernard H. 1981. *Public Opinion.* 4th ed. Monterey, CA: Brooks/Cole Publishing.

Herbst, Susan. 2011. "(Un)Numbered Voices? Reconsidering the Meaning of Public Opinion in a Digital Age." In *Public Opinion Polling in a Digital Age: The Challenge of Measuring and Understanding Public Opinion.* Ed. Kirby Goidel. Baton Rouge: Louisiana State University Press.

Herrmann, Melissa J. 2001. "Managing Privacy Managers." *Public Perspective* 12 (November/December): 49–50.

Hess, Robert D., and Judith V. Torney. 1967. *The Development of Political Attitudes in Children.* Chicago: Aldine.

Hetherington, Marc J. 1998. "The Political Relevance of Political Trust." *American Political Science Review* 92 (December): 791–808.

Hinckley, Ronald H. 1988. "Public Attitudes toward Key Foreign Policy Events." *Journal of Conflict Resolution* 32 (June): 295–318.

Holbrook, Allyson L., Jon A. Krosnick, David Moore, and Roger Tourangeau. 2007. "Response Order Effects in Dichotomous Categorical Questions Presented Orally: The Impact of Question and Respondent Attributes." *Public Opinion Quarterly* 71 (Fall): 325–348.

Holsti, Ole R. 1996. *Public Opinion and American Foreign Policy.* Ann Arbor, MI: University of Michigan Press.

Holsti, Ole, and James N. Rosenau. 1984. *American Leadership in World Affairs and the Breakdown of Consensus.* Boston: Allen and Unwin.

Hubert, David A. 1992. "Publics, Polls, and Public Opinion." *Public Perspective* 3 (January/February): 30–31.

Huggins, Vicki, and Joe Eyerman. 2001. "Probability Based Internet Surveys: A Synopsis of Early Methods and Survey Research Results." Paper presented at the research conference of the Federal Committee on Statistical Methodology, Arlington, VA.

Hurwitz, Jon, and Mark Peffley. 1987. "How Are Foreign Policy Attitudes Structured: A Hierarchical Model." *American Political Science Review* 81 (December): 1099–1120.

Hyman, Herbert H. 1959. *Political Socialization: A Study in the Psychology of Political Behavior.* Glencoe, IL: Free Press.

Hyman, Herbert H., and Paul B. Sheatsley. 1947. "Some Reasons Why Information Campaigns Fail." *Public Opinion Quarterly* 11 (Fall): 412–423.

Inhofe, James. 2009. "Remarks by Senator James Inhofe on Global Warming." *Congressional Record 111th Congress* (March 12).

Intercollegiate Studies Institute. 2008. Enlightened Citizenship. "Civic Literacy Report." www.americancivicliteracy.org/.

Inter-University Consortium for Political and Social Research. 2005. *Guide to Resources and Services*. Ann Arbor, MI: ICPSR.

Iyengar, Shanto, and Donald Kinder. 1987. *News That Matters*. Chicago: University of Chicago Press.

Iyengar, Shanto, and Jennifer A. McGrady. 2007. *Media Politics: A Citizen's Guide*. New York: Norton.

Jacobs, Lawrence R., and Robert Y. Shapiro. 1995. "The Rise of Presidential Polling: The Nixon White House in Historical Perspective." *Public Opinion Quarterly* 59 (Summer): 163–195.

——. 1997. "Debunking the Pandering Politician Myth." *Public Perspective* 8 (April/May): 3–5.

Jacobs, Lawrence R., and Theda Skocpol. 2010. *Health Care Reform and American Politics: What Everyone Needs to Know*. New York: Oxford University Press.

Jacoby, William G. 1988. "The Impact of Party Identification on Issue Attitudes." *American Journal of Political Science* 32 (August): 643–661.

——. 1991. "Ideological Identification and Issue Attitudes." *American Journal of Political Science* 35 (February): 178–205.

Jajich-Toth, Cindy, and Burns W. Roper. 1990. "Americans' Views on Health Care: A Study in Contradictions." *Health Affairs* 9 (Winter): 149–157.

Jaros, Dean. 1973. *Socialization to Politics*. New York: Praeger.

Jaros, Dean, and Lawrence V. Grant. 1974. *Political Behavior: Choices and Perspectives*. New York: St. Martin's Press.

Jaros, Dean, Herbert Hirsch, and Frederic J. Fleron, Jr. 1968. "The Malevolent Leader: Political Socialization in an American Sub-Culture." *American Political Science Review* 62 (June): 564–575.

Jelen, Ted G. 1989. "Biblical Literalism and Inerrancy: Does the Difference Make a Difference?" *Sociological Analysis* 49 (Winter): 421–429.

——. 1992. "Political Christianity: A Contextual Analysis." *American Journal of Political Science* 36 (August): 662–692.

Jennings, M. Kent. 1996. "Political Knowledge across Time and Generations." *Public Opinion Quarterly* 60 (Summer): 228–252.

Jennings, M. Kent, Kenneth P. Langton, and Richard G. Niemi. 1974. "Effects of the high school civics curriculum." In M. Kent Jennings and Richard G. Niemi (eds), *The Political Character of Adolescence: The Influence of Fammilies and Schools*. Princeton, NJ: Princeton University Press.

Jennings, M. Kent, Lee H. Ehrman, and Richard G. Niemi. 1974. "Social Studies Teachers and Their Students." In *The Political Character of Adolescence*. Eds. M. Kent Jennings and Richard G. Niemi. Princeton, NJ: Princeton University Press.

Jennings, M. Kent, and Gregory B. Markus. 1984. "Partisan Orientations over the Long Haul: Results from the Three-Wave Political Socialization Panel Study." *American Political Science Review* 78 (December): 1000–1018.

Jennings, M. Kent, and Richard Niemi. 1968. "The Transmission of Political Values from Parent to Child." *American Political Science Review* 62 (March): 169–184.

——. 1974. *The Political Character of Adolescence: The Influence of Families and Schools*. Princeton, NJ: Princeton University Press.

——. 1975. "Continuity and Change in Political Orientations: A Longitudinal Study of Two Generations." *American Political Science Review* 69 (December): 1316–1335.

Jensen, Richard. 1980. "Democracy by the Numbers." *Public Opinion* 3 (February/March): 53–59.

Jentleson, Bruce. 1992. "The Pretty Prudent Public: Post Post-Vietnam American Opinion on the Use of Military Force." *International Studies Quarterly* 36 (March): 49–74.

Kaiser Family Foundation. 2011. "Kaiser Health Tracking Poll." August. www.kff.org/kaiserpolls/trackingpoll.cfm.

Kalton, Graham. 1983. *Introduction to Survey Sampling*. Beverly Hills, CA: Sage.

Karpowitz, Christopher F., J. Quin Monson, Kelly D. Patterson, and Jeremy C. Pope. 2011. "Tea Time in America? The Impact of the Tea Party Movement on the 2010 Midterm Elections." *PS* 44 (April): 303–315.

Katz, Daniel. 1960. "The Functional Approach to the Study of Attitudes." *Public Opinion Quarterly* 24 (Summer): 163–177.

Keeter, Scott, Courtney Kennedy, Michael Dimock, Jonathan Best, and Peyton Craighill. 2006. "Gauging the Impact of Growing Nonresponse on Estimates from a National RDD Telephone Survey." *Public Opinion Quarterly* 70 (Special Issue). 759–779.

Keeter, Scott, Carolyn Miller, Andrew Kohut, Robert M. Groves, and Stanley Presser. 2000. "Consequences of Reducing Nonresponse in a Large National Telephone Survey." *Public Opinion Quarterly* 64 (Summer): 125–148.

Kegeles, S. Stephen, Clinton F. Fink, and John P. Kirscht. 1969. "Interviewing a National Sample by Long-Distance Telephone." *Public Opinion Quarterly* 33 (Fall): 412–419.

Keith, Bruce E., David B. Magleby, Candice J. Nelson, Elizabeth Orr, Mark C. Westlye, and Raymond E. Wolfinger. 1992. *The Myth of the Independent Voter*. Berkeley: University of California Press.

Kerber, Linda K. 1980. *Women of the Republic: Intellect and Ideology in Revolutionary America*. Chapel Hill: University of North Carolina Press.

Key, V. O., Jr. 1967. *Public Opinion and American Democracy*. New York: Knopf.

Kiefer, Francine. 2001. "How the White House Uses (Gasp!) Polls." *Christian Science Monitor*, June 15.

Kiley, Jocelyn, and Michael Dimock. 2009. "Understanding Likely Voters." http://people-press.org/files/2011/03/UnderstandingLikelyVoters.pdf.

Kinder, Donald R., and D. Roderick Kiewiet. 1979. "Economic Grievance and Political Behavior: The Role of Personal Discontents and Collective Judgments in Congressional Voting." *American Journal of Political Science* 23 (August): 495–527.

Kirkpatrick, Samuel A., and Melvin E. Jones. 1974. "Issue Publics and the Electoral System: The Role of Issues in Electoral Change." In *Public Opinion and Political Attitudes*. Ed. Allen R. Wilcox. New York: John Wiley and Sons.

Klas, Mary Ellen. 2011. "Polls Show Strong Local Support for Casinos in Miami-Dade, but Statewide Reluctance." *Miami Herald*, October 18.

Knowledge Networks. 2011. "Knowledge Panel Design Summary." www.knowledgenetworks.com/knpanel/docs/KnowledgePanel%28R%29-Design-Summary-Description.pdf.

Kohut, Andrew. 1986. "Rating the Polls: The Views of Media Elites and the General Public." *Public Opinion Quarterly* 50 (Spring): 1–9.

———. 2008. "Getting It Wrong." *New York Times*, January 10. www.nytimes.com/2008/01/10/opinion/10kohut.html.

Kohut, Andrew, and Carroll Doherty. 2005. "Cross-Currents in Opinion about Private Accounts." Pew Center for the People and the Press. January 27.

Kohut, Andrew, Richard Morin, and Scott Keeter. 2007. "What Americans Know: 1987–2007." Pew Center for the People and the Press. April 15. www.people-press.org/files/legacy-pdf/319.pdf.

Krisberg, Barry, and Susan Marchionna. 2006. "Attitudes of US Voters toward Prisoner Rehabilitation and Reentry Policies." *Focus* (April) published by National Council on Crime and Delinquency, Washington, DC.

Krysan, Maria, Howard Schuman, Lesli Jo Scott, and Paul Beatty. 1994. "Response Rates and Response Content in Mail versus Face-to-Face Surveys." *Public Opinion Quarterly* 58 (Fall): 381–399.

Ladd, Everett Carll. 1990. "What Do Americans Really Think about the Environment?" *Public Perspective* 1 (May/June): 11–13.

———. 1992. "The Trials of Election Polling: Election Polls—1948 and Today." *Public Perspective* 3 (May/June): 24–28.

———. 1995. "Americans on Public Education." *Public Perspective* 6 (October/November): 22–37.

———. 1996a. "The Election Polls: An American Waterloo." *Chronicle of Higher Education* 43 (November): A52.

———. 1996b. "Election 1996: A Roper Center Data Review." *Public Perspective* 7 (October/November): 15–54.

———. 1998a. "The American Ethnic Experience as It Stands in the Nineties." *Public Perspective* 9 (February/March): 50–65.

———. 1998b. "What's the Biggest Hurdle for the Polls?" *Public Perspective* 9 (February/March): 86.

Ladd, Everett C., and Karlyn H. Bowman. 1997. *Public Opinion about Abortion: Twenty-Five Years after Roe v. Wade.* Washington, DC: American Enterprise Institute.

Ladd, Everett C., and G. Donald Ferree. 1981. "Were the Pollsters Really Wrong?" *Public Opinion* 3 (December/January): 13–20.

Lamare, James W. 1974. "Language Environment and Political Socialization of Mexican-American Children." In *The Politics of Future Citizens.* Eds. Richard G. Niemi and Associates. San Francisco: Jossey-Bass.

Langer, Gary. 2011. "Health Care Reform: An Opinion Summary." March 23. http://abcnews.go.com/blogs/politics/2010/03/health-care-reform-an-opinion-summary/.

Langton, Kenneth P. 1969. *Political Socialization.* New York: Oxford University Press.

Langton, Kenneth, and M. Kent Jennings. 1968. "Political Socialization and the High School Civics Curriculum in the United States." *American Political Science Review* 62 (September): 852–867.

Langton, Kenneth, and D. Karns. 1969. "A Cross National Study of the Relative Influence of School Education: A Causal Analysis." ERIC, ED034320.

Larson, Jessica, Stephen Menendian, John A. Powell, and Andrew Grant-Thomas. 2008. *Anti-Affirmative Action Ballot Initiatives*. Columbus, OH: Kirwan Institute for the Study of Race and Ethnicity.

Lau, Richard R., and Ralph Erber. 1987. "Political Sophistication: An Information-Processing Perspective." In *Mass Media and Political Thought: An Information Processing Approach*. Eds. Sidney Kraus and Richard M. Perloff. New York: Sage.

Lavrakas, Paul J., and Charles D. Shuttles. 2005. "Accounting for Cell Phones in Telephone Survey Research in the U.S." Cell Phone Sampling Summit II Conference, New York.

Lavrakas, Paul J., Charles D. Shuttles, Charlotte Steeh, and Howard Fienberg. 2007. "The State of Surveying Cell Phone Numbers in the United States: 2007 and Beyond." *Public Opinion Quarterly* 71 (Special Issue): 840–854.

Lazarsfeld, Paul, Bernard Berelson, and Hazel Gaudet. 1944. *The People's Choice*. New York: Columbia University Press.

Leege, David C., and Michael R. Welch. 1989. "Religious Roots of Political Orientations: Variations among American Catholic Parishioners." *Journal of Politics* 51 (February): 137–162.

Levondusky, Matthew. 2009. *The Partisan Sort: How Liberals Became Democrats and Conservatives Became Republicans*. Chicago: University of Chicago Press.

Levy, Mark R. 1983. "The Methodology and Performance of Election Day Polls." *Public Opinion Quarterly* 47 (Spring): 54–67.

Lewis-Beck, Michael S., William G. Jacoby, Helmut Norpoth, and Herbert F. Weisberg. 2008. *The American Voter Revisited*. Ann Arbor: University of Michigan Press.

Link, Michael W., Michael P. Battaglia, Martin R. Frankel, Larry Osborne, and Ali H. Mokdad. 2006. "Address-Based versus Random-Digit Dialed Surveys: Comparisons of Key Health and Risk Indicators." *American Journal of Epidemiology* 164 (10): 1019–1025.

———. 2008. "A Comparison of Address-Based Sampling (ABS) versus Random-Digit Dialing (RDD) for General Population Surveys." *Public Opinion Quarterly* 72 (Spring): 6–27.

Link, Michael W., and Robert W. Oldendick. 1996. "Social Construction and White Attitudes toward Equal Opportunity and Multiculturalism." *Journal of Politics* 58 (February): 149–168.

———. 1998. "Caller-ID: Does It Help or Hinder Survey Research?" Paper presented at the annual meeting of the American Association for Public Opinion Research, St. Louis.

Lippmann, Walter. 1922. *Public Opinion*. New York: Harcourt, Brace.

———. 1956. *The Public Philosophy*. New York: Mentor.

Lipset, Seymour Martin, and William Schneider. 1978. "The Bakke Case: How Would It Be Decided at the Bar of Public Opinion?" *Public Opinion* 1 (March/April): 38–44.

———. 1983. *The Confidence Gap: Business, Labor, and Government in the Public Mind*. New York: Free Press.

————. 1987. "The Confidence Gap during the Reagan Years, 1981–1987." *Political Science Quarterly* 102 (Spring): 1–23.

Litt, Edgar. 1963. "Civic Education, Community Norms, and Political Indoctrination." *American Sociological Review* 28 (February): 69–75.

Lopez, Mark Hugo. 2010. *Latinos and the 2010 Elections: Strong Support for Democrats; Weak Voter Motivation.* Washington, DC: Pew Hispanic Center.

Luevano, Patricia. 1994. "Response Rates in the National Election Studies, 1948–1992." NES Technical Report 44. Ann Arbor: Center for Political Studies.

MacKuen, Michael Bruce. 1981. "Social Communication and the Mass Policy Agenda." In *More Than News: Media Power in Public Affairs.* Eds. Michael Bruce MacKuen and Steven Coombs. Beverly Hills, CA: Sage.

MacKuen, Michael B., Robert S. Erikson, and James A. Stimson. 1992. "Peasants or Bankers? The American Electorate and the U.S. Economy." *American Political Science Review* 86 (September): 1125–1142.

Manza, Jeff, and Faye Lomax Cook. 2002. "The Impact of Public Opinion on Public Policy: The State of the Debate." In *Navigating Public Opinion: Polls, Policy, and the Future of American Democracy.* Eds. Jeff Manza, Faye Lomax Cook, and Benjamin I. Page. Oxford: Oxford University Press.

Marquette, Heather, and Dale Mineshima. 2002. "Civic Education in the United States: Lessons for the UK." *Parliamentary Affairs* 55 (5): 539–555.

Martin, Elizabeth. 1984. "The Role of the Respondent." In *Surveying Subjective Phenomena.* Eds. Charles F. Turner and Elizabeth Martin. New York: Russell Sage Foundation.

Massey, James T. 1988. "An Overview of Telephone Coverage." In *Telephone Survey Methodology.* Eds. Robert M. Groves, Paul P. Biemer, Lars E. Lyberg, James T. Massey, William L. Nicholls II, and Joseph Waksberg. New York: John Wiley and Sons.

Mayer, William G. 1992. *The Changing American Mind: How and Why American Public Opinion Changed between 1960 and 1988.* Ann Arbor, MI: University of Michigan Press.

McClosky, Herbert. 1964. "Consensus and Ideology in American Politics." *American Political Science Review* 58 (June): 361–382.

McClosky, Herbert, Paul Hoffman, and Rosemary O'Hara. 1960. "Issue Conflict and Consensus among Party Leaders and Followers." *American Political Science Review* 54 (June): 406–427.

McClure, Robert D., and Thomas E. Patterson. 1976. *The Unseeing Eye: The Myth of Television Power in National Elections.* New York: Putnam.

McCormick, James M. 1998. *American Foreign Policy and Process.* 3rd. ed. Itasca, IL: F. E. Peacock.

McSweeney, Dean, and John Zvesper. 1991. *American Political Parties: The Formation, Decline, and Reform of the American Party System.* New York: Routledge.

Memmott, Mark. 2004a. "Predictions Burn Pollsters, Pundits—Again." *USA Today,* November 13: A1.

————. 2004b. "Exit Poll Data Will Be Delayed." *USA Today,* November 17: A1.

Merelman, Richard M. 1971. *Political Socialization and Educational Climates: A Study of Two School Districts.* New York: Holt, Rinehart and Winston.

Milbrath, Lester W. 1965. *Political Participation.* Chicago: Rand McNally.

Miller, Arthur H. 1974. "Political Issues and Trust in Government, 1964–1970." *American Political Science Review* 68 (September): 951–972.

Miller, Warren E. 1979. "Crisis of Confidence—II: Misreading the Public Pulse." *Public Opinion* 2 (October/November): 9–17.

———. 1991. "Party Identification, Realignment, and Party Voting: Back to Basics." *American Political Science Review* 85 (June): 557–568.

Miller, Warren E., and Donald E. Stokes. 1963. "Constituency Influence in Congress." *American Political Science Review* 57 (March): 45–56.

Miller, Warren E., and Santa Traugott. 1989. *American National Election Studies Data Sourcebook, 1952–1986*. Cambridge, MA: Harvard University Press.

Minow, Newton N., John Bartlow Martin, and Lee M. Mitchell. 1973. *Presidential Television*. New York: Basic Books.

Mitofsky, Warren J. 1989. Review of *Polling and the Public*, by Herbert Asher. *Public Opinion Quarterly* 53 (Winter): 617–619.

———. 1996. "It's Not Deliberative, and It's Not a Poll." *Public Perspective* 7 (December/January): 4–6.

———. 1999. "Pollster.com." *Public Perspective* 10 (June/July): 24–26.

———. 2001. "Fool Me Twice: An Election Nightmare." *Public Perspective* 12 (May/June 2001): 35–38.

Mitofsky, Warren J., and Murray Edelman. 2002. "Election Night Estimation." *Journal of Official Statistics* 18 (June): 165–179.

Monroe, Alan D. 1975. *Public Opinion in America*. New York: Dodd, Mead.

———. 1979. "Consistency between Public Preferences and National Policy Decisions." *American Politics Quarterly* 7 (January): 3–20.

———. 1998. "Public Opinion and Public Policy, 1980–1993." *Public Opinion Quarterly* 62 (Spring): 6–28.

———. 2001. "Public Opinion and Public Policy, 1960–1999." Paper presented at the annual meeting of the American Political Science Association, San Francisco, CA.

Montgomery, Lori and Amy Goldstein. 2009. "Health Care Tops Fiscal Need List." *Washington Post.* www.washingtonpost.com/wp-dyn/content/story/2009/02/23/ST2009022301480.html.

Moore, David W. 1992. *The Superpollsters: How They Measure and Manipulate Public Opinion in America*. New York: Four Walls Eight Windows.

———. 1996a. "The Party Really Isn't Over." *Public Perspective* 7 (October/November): 1–3.

———. 1996b. "Perils of Polling '96: Myth and Fallacy." *Polling Report* 12 (December): 1–8.

———. 2003. "Trust in Government Falls to Pre-9/11 Levels." *Gallup Report*, October 6.

Moore, David W., and Frank Newport. 1994. "Misreading the Public: The Case of the Holocaust Poll." *Public Perspective* 5 (March–April): 28–29.

———. 1996. "Public Policy Questions and Response Order: Prevalence of the Recency Effect." Paper presented at the annual meeting of the American Association for Public Opinion Research, Salt Lake City.

Morgenthau, Hans J. 1978. *Politics among Nations*. 5th ed. New York: Knopf.

Mosteller, Frederick, Herbert Hyman, Philip J. McCarthy, Eli S. Marks, and David B. Truman. 1949. *The Pre-election Polls of 1948: Report to the Committee on Analysis of Pre-election Polls and Forecasts*. New York: Social Science Research Council.

Mueller, John. 1971. "Trends in Popular Support for the Wars in Korea and Vietnam." *American Political Science Review* 65 (June): 358–375.

———. 1973. *Wars, Presidents, and Public Opinion.* New York: John Wiley and Sons.

———. 1988. "Trends in Political Tolerance." *Public Opinion Quarterly* 52 (Spring): 1–32.

———. 1994. *Policy and Opinion in the Gulf War.* Chicago: University of Chicago Press.

———. 2002. "American Foreign Policy and Public Opinion in a New Era: Eleven Propositions." In *Understanding Public Opinion.* 2nd ed. Eds. Barbara Norrander and Clyde Wilcox. Washington, DC: CQ Press.

Murray, Shoon Kathleen, and Peter Howard. 2002. "Variation in White House Polling Operations: Carter to Clinton." *Public Opinion Quarterly* 66 (Winter): 527–558.

Natchez, Peter B., and Irvin C. Bupp. 1968. "Candidates, Issues, and Voters." *Public Policy* 17 (Summer): 409–437.

National Council on Public Polls. 2010. "NCPP Analysis of Final Statewide Election Polls in 2010." www.ncpp.org/files/NCPP%20Election%20Poll%20Analysis%20 2010%20-%20Final-%200202.pdf.

Neuman, W. Russell. 1986. *The Paradox of American Politics: Knowledge and Opinion in the American Electorate.* Cambridge, MA: Harvard University Press.

Neuman, W. Russell, Marion R. Just, and Ann N. Crigler. 1992. *Common Knowledge: News and the Construction of Political Meaning.* Chicago: University of Chicago Press.

Newcomb, Theodore M. et al. 1958. "Attitude Development as a Function of Reference Groups: The Bennington Study." In *Readings in Social Psychology.* Eds. Eleanor E. Maccoby et al. New York: Holt, Rinehart and Winston.

"New Poll Shows 70% Oppose Stem Cell Research That Kills Unborn Children." 2001. Washington, DC: National Conference of Catholic Bishops.

Newport, Frank. 1998. "Reporting Poll Results Better." *Public Perspective* 9 (February/ March): 87.

———. 2001. "Trust in Government Increases Sharply in Wake of Terrorist Attacks." *Gallup Report,* October 12.

———. 2004. *Polling Matters: Why Leaders Must Listen to the Wisdom of the People.* Princeton, NJ: Gallup Organization.

———. 2009a. "Little 'Obama Effect' on Views about Race Relations." Gallup Poll. October 29. www.gallup.com/poll/123944/little-obama-effect-views-race-relations.aspx.

———. 2009b. "In U.S., Two-Thirds Continue to Support Death Penalty." *The Gallup Poll,* October 13.

———. 2011. "Americans Want Leaders to Follow Public's Views More Closely." Gallup Poll. www.gallup.com/poll/149636/American-Leaders-Follow-Publics-Views-Closely.aspx.

New York Times. 1936. "Dr. Gallup Chided by *Digest* Editor." *New York Times,* July 19: 21.

Nickelsburg, Michael, and Helmet Norpoth. 2000. "Commander-in-Chief or Chief Economist? The President in the Eye of the Public." *Electoral Studies* 19: 313–332.

Nie, Norman H., with Kristi Anderson. 1974. "Mass Belief Systems Revisited: Political Change and Attitude Structure." *Journal of Politics* 36 (August): 541–591.

Nie, Norman H., Sidney Verba, and John R. Petrocik. 1976. *The Changing American Voter*. Cambridge, MA: Harvard University Press.

Niemi, Richard, and M. Kent Jennings. 1974. *The Political Character of Adolescence*. Princeton NJ: Princeton University Press.

Nisbet, Matthew C. "The Polls—Trends Public Opinion about Stem Cell Research and Human Cloning." *Public Opinion Quarterly* 68 (1): 131–54.

Noelle-Neumann, Elisabeth. 1984. *The Spiral of Silence*. Chicago: University of Chicago Press.

Nunn, Clyde A., Harry J. Crockett, and J. Allen Williams. 1978. *Tolerance for Nonconformity*. San Francisco: Jossey-Bass.

Oldendick, Robert, and Barbara Bardes. 1981. "The Continuing Case for Multiple Dimensions in the Structure of Foreign Policy Attitudes." *Social Science Quarterly* 62 (March): 124–126.

Oldendick, Robert W., and Michael W. Link. 1994. "The Answering Machine Generation: Who Are They and What Problem Do They Pose for Survey Research?" *Public Opinion Quarterly* 58 (Summer): 264–273.

———. 1998. "Race-of-Interviewer and the Study of Public Opinion." Paper presented at the annual meeting of the American Association for Public Opinion Research, St. Louis.

Oldendick, Robert W., and Alfred J, Tuchfarber. 1984. *Evaluation of Queen City Metro's Weekend Fare Experiment*. Cincinnati, OH. Institute for Policy Research.

O'Neill, Harry W. 1996. "Our Greatest and Most Frustrating Challenge Is How to Increase the Rate of Public Participation in Polls." *Public Perspective* 7 (August/September): 54–56.

O'Rourke, Diane, Seymour Sudman, and Marya Ryan. 1996. "The Growth of Academic and Not-for-Profit Survey Research Organizations." *Survey Research* 27 (Winter-Spring): 2–5.

O'Sullivan, Jim. 2011. "Perry Tells N.H. Audience He's a Global-Warming Skeptic." *National Journal*. August 17. www.nationaljournal.com/politics/perry-tells-n-h -audience-he-s-a-global-warming-skeptic-with-video-20110817.

Page, Benjamin I., and Robert Y. Shapiro. 1982. "Changes in Americans' Policy Preferences, 1935–1979." *Public Opinion Quarterly* 46 (Spring): 24–42.

———. 1983. "Effects of Public Opinion on Policy." *American Political Science Review* 77 (March): 175–190.

———. 1992. *The Rational Public: Fifty Years of Trends in Americans' Policy Preferences*. Chicago: University of Chicago Press.

Palmer, Paul A. 1936. "The Concept of Public Opinion in Political Theory." In *Essays in History and Political Theory*. Ed. Carl Wittke. Cambridge, MA: Harvard University Press.

Parker, Suzanne. 1995. "Toward an Understanding of 'Rally' Effects: Public Opinion in the Persian Gulf War." *Public Opinion Quarterly* 59 (Winter): 526–546.

Parsons, Talcott. 1959. "The School Class as a School System: Some of its Functions in American Society." *Harvard Educational Review* 29 (4): 297–318.

Pasek, Josh, and Jon A. Krosnick. 2010. *Measuring Intent to Participate and Participation in the 2010 Census and Their Correlates and Trends: Comparisons of RDD Telephone and Non-probability Sample Internet Survey Data*. Washington, DC: U.S. Census Bureau.

Patterson, Kelly D., and David B. Magelby. 1992. "The Polls—Poll Trends: Public Support for Congress." *Public Opinion Quarterly* 56 (Winter): 539–551.

Patterson, Thomas E. 1980. *The Mass Media Election*. New York: Praeger.

Payne, Stanley L. 1951. *The Art of Asking Questions*. Princeton, NJ: Princeton University Press.

Penner, Rudolph. 1982. "Spooking the Public: The Social Security Specter." *Public Opinion* 5 (October/November): 16–18.

Perry, James M. 1994. "Clinton Relies Heavily on White House Pollster to Take Words Right Out of Public's Mouth." *Wall Street Journal*, March 23: A16.

Pew Center for People and the Press. 2004. "Pre-Election Polls Largely Accurate: Lessons from Campaign '04." www.people-press.org/2004/11/23/pre-election-polls-largely-accurate/.

———. 2005. "Bush Failing in Social Security Push." www.people-press.org/2005/03/02/bush-failing-in-social-security-push/.

———. 2010. "Americans Spending More Time Following the News." www.people-press.org/2010/09/12/americans-spending-more-time-following-the-news/.

———. 2011. "GOP Divided Over Benefit Reductions Public Wants Changes in Entitlements, Not Changes in Benefits." June. http://people-press.org/files/legacy-pdf/7-7-11%20Entitlements%20Release.pdf.

Pew Hispanic Center/Kaiser Family Foundation. 2004. "The 2004 National Survey."

Pew Research Center. 2010. "Public's Top Stories of the Decade—9/11 and Katrina." www.pewresearch.org/pubs/1841/publics-top-news-stories-2001-2010-september-11-katrina.

Pew Research Center for the People and the Press. 2003. "Evenly Divided and Increasingly Polarized: 2004 Political Landscape." http://people-press.org/files/legacy-pdf/196.pdf.

———. 2006. "The American Journalist Politics and Party Affiliation." www.journalism.org/node/2304.

———. 2010a. "Distrust, Discontent, Anger, and Partisan Rancor: The People and Their Government." http://people-press.org/2010/04/18/distrust-discontent-anger-and-partisan-rancor/.

———. 2010b. "Little Change in Opinions about Global Warming." http://people-press.org/2010/10/27/little-change-in-opinions-about-global-warming/.

———. 2011a. "Fewer Want Spending to Grow, but Most Cuts Remain Unpopular: Changing Views of Federal Spending." http://people-press.org/2011/02/10/fewer-want-spending-to-grow-but-most-cuts-remain-unpopular/.

———. 2011b. "Public Favors Tougher Border Controls and Path to Citizenship." www.people-press.org/files/legacy-pdf/707.pdf.

———. 2011c. "Well-Known: Clinton and Gadhafi; Little Known: Who Controls Congress." March. www.people-press.org/2011/03/31/well-known-clinton-and-gadhafi-little-known-who-controls-congress/.

Pierce, John C., and Paul R. Hagner. 1980. "Changes in the Public's Political Thinking: The Watershed Years, 1956–1968." In *The Electorate Reconsidered*. Eds. John C. Pierce and John L. Sullivan. Beverly Hills, CA: Sage.

Pildes, Richard. 2010. "Why the Center Does Not Hold: The Causes of Hyperpolarized Democracy in America." *New York University Public Law and Legal Theory Working Papers*, Paper 207. http://lsr.nellco.org/nyu_plltwp/207.

Pineau, Vicki, and Daniel Slotwiner. 2003. *Probability Samples vs. Volunteer Respondents in Internet Research: Defining Potential Effects on Data and Decision-Making in Marketing Applications.* Menlo Park, CA: Knowledge Networks.

Polling Report. 1986. "Campaign '00 Update." *Polling Report* 12 (November): 4.

Prothro, James W., and Charles M. Grigg. 1960. "Fundamental Principles of Democracy: Bases of Agreement and Disagreement." *Journal of Politics* 22 (May): 276–294.

Public Perspective. 1993. "Sensible Internationalism." *Public Perspective* 4 (March/April): 95–104.

———. 1994. "The Public Decides on Health Care Reform: A Polling Review of a Great Debate." *Public Perspective* 5 (September/October): 23–28.

———. 1997. "Crime in America." *Public Perspective* 8 (June/July): 9–33.

———. 1998a. "Thinking about Government: Health Care Reform, 1993–94." *Public Perspective* 9 (February/March): 36–39.

———. 1998b. "Thinking about Polls and Polling." *Public Perspective* 9 (February/March): 86–94.

———. 2001. "September 11, 2001: First Shock." *Public Perspective* 12 (November/December): 23–29.

Rademacher, Eric W. 2003. *The Greater Cincinnati Survey, Spring 2003: Project Report for the Cincinnati Police Department.* Cincinnati, OH: Institute for Policy Research.

Ragsdale, Lyn. 1997. "Disconnected Publics: Public Opinion and Presidents." In *Understanding Public Opinion.* Eds. Barbara Norrander and Clyde Wilcox. Washington: Congressional Quarterly Press.

Rasmussen, Scott W. 2000. "For 'Yes,' Press 1: Automated Polling at Rasmussen Research." *Public Perspective* 11 (September/October): 41–43.

Reilly, John E. 1995. "The Public Mood at Mid-Decade." *Foreign Policy* 98 (Spring): 76–93.

———, ed. 1999. *American Public Opinion and Foreign Policy 1999.* Chicago: Chicago Council on Foreign Relations.

Research Industry Coalition. 1996. *Integrity and Good Practice in Marketing and Opinion Research.* Port Jefferson, NY: Research Industry Coalition.

Rice, Tom W., and Tracey A. Hilton. 1996. "Partisanship over Time: A Comparison of United States Panel Data." *Political Research Quarterly* 49 (March): 191–201.

Richardson, Laura. 2010. "Extension of Remarks: Don't Ask, Don't Tell Repeal Act of 2010." *Congressional Record 111th Congress* (December 21).

Richman, Alvin. 1996. "Trends: American Support for International Involvement, General and Specific Components of Post–Cold War Changes." *Public Opinion Quarterly* 60 (Summer): 305–321.

Rivers, Doug. 2009. "Second Thoughts about Internet Surveys." www.pollster.com/blogs/doug_rivers.php?nr=1.

Roberts, Julian V., and Loretta J. Stalans. 1997. *Public Opinion, Crime and Criminal Justice.* Boulder, CO: Westview Press.

Robinson, Claude E. 1932. *Straw Votes: A Study of Political Prediction.* New York: Columbia University Press.

Rodgers, Harrell R., and George Taylor. 1971. "The Policeman as an Agent of Regime Legitimation." *Midwest Journal of Political Science* 15 (February): 72–86.

Rogoff, B., R. Paradise, R. M. Auauz, M. Correa-Chavez, and C. Angelillo. 2003. "Firsthand Learning through Intent Participation." *Annual Review of Psychology* 54: 175–203.

Roll, Charles W., and Albert H. Cantril. 1980. *Polls: Their Use and Misuse in Surveys.* Cabin John, MD: Seven Locks Press.

Roper, Burns W. 1986. "Evaluating the Polls with Poll Data." *Public Opinion Quarterly* 50 (Spring): 10–16.

Roscho, Bernard. 1999. "The Devil's Tunes and the Sirens' Song: 'Privatizing' Social Security." *Public Perspective* 10 (October/November): 25–28.

Rosenberg, Milton J., Sidney Verba, and Philip E. Converse. 1970. *Vietnam and the Silent Majority: The Dove's Guide.* New York: Harper & Row.

Royko, Mike. 1992. "Annoy Pollster—Resort to Lying." *Chicago Tribune*, October 28: 3.

Saad, Lydia K. 1998. "After 25 Years, Abortion Attitudes Register a Slight Conservative Shift." *Public Perspective* 9 (February/March): 7–8.

———. 2001. "Fear of Conventional Crime at Record Lows." Gallup Poll, October 22.

———. 2008. "Americans Rate National and Personal Healthcare Differently." Gallup Poll, December 4. www.gallup.com/poll/112813/Americans-Rate-National Personal-Healthcare-Differently.aspx

———. 2009. "Two in Three Americans Worry About Identity Theft." *The Gallup Poll*, October 16.

———. 2010. "Nearly 4 in 10 Americans Still Fear Walking Alone at Night." *The Gallup Poll*, November 5.

Saletan, William. 2000. "Push Me, Poll You." *Slate.* February 15. http://www.uvm .edu/~dguber/POLS234/articles/saletan.htm.

Sapiro, Virginia. 2004. "Not Your Parents' Political Socialization: Introduction for a New Generation." *Annual Review of Political Science* 7: 1–23.

Scammon, Richard M., and Ben J. Wattenberg. 1970. *The Real Majority: An Extraordinary Examination of the American Electorate.* New York: Coward, McCann and Geoghegan.

Schmidt, Steffen W., Mack C. Shelley, II, and Barbara A. Bardes. 2005. *American Government and Politics Today, 2005–2006 Edition.* Belmont, CA: Wadsworth.

Schneider, William. 1997a. "The New Isolationism." In *Eagle Adrift: American Foreign Policy at the End of the Century.* Ed. R. J. Lieber. New York: Longman.

———. 1997b. "The Pollster General: A Brief History of Polling for the President." *Polling Report* 13 (May): 7.

Schonlau, Matthias, Ronald D. Fricker, Jr., and Marc N. Elliott. 2001. *Conducting Research Surveys via E-Mail and the Web.* Santa Monica, CA: Rand.

Schuman, Howard. 2009. "Context Effects and Social Change." *Public Opinion Quarterly* 73 (Spring): 172–179.

Schuman, Howard, and Stanley Presser. 1981. *Questions and Answers in Attitude Surveys.* New York: Academic Press.

Schuman, Howard, Charlotte Steeh, Lawrence Bobo, and Maria Krysan. 1997. *Racial Attitudes in America: Trends and Interpretations.* Rev. ed. Cambridge, MA: Harvard University Press.

Sears, David O. 1990. "Whither Political Socialization Research? The Question of Persistence." In *Political Socialization, Citizenship Education. and Democracy.* Ed. Orit Ichilov. New York: Columbia University Press.

Sears, David O., Carl P. Hensler, and Leslie K. Speer. 1979. "Whites' Opposition to 'Busing': Self-Interest or Symbolic Politics?" *American Political Science Review* 73 (June): 369–384.

Sears, David O., Collette van Laar, Mary Carillo, and Rick Kosterman. 1997. "Is It Really Racism? The Origins of White Americans' Opposition to Race-Targeted Policies." *Public Opinion Quarterly* 61 (Spring): 16–53.

Seelye, Katharine Q., and Marjorie Connelly. 2004. "New York: The Convention-eers; Delegates Leaning to Right of G.O.P. and the Nation." *New York Times*, August 29: 15-1.

Selltiz, Claire, Marie Jahoda, Morton Deutsch, and Stuart W. Cook. 1959. *Research Methods in Social Relations*. New York: Holt, Rinehart and Winston.

Settle, Jaime E., Robert Bond, and Justin Levitt. 2011. "The Social Origins of Adult Political Behavior." *American Politics Research* 39 (2): 239–263.

Shafritz, Jay. 1988. *The Dorsey Dictionary of American Government and Politics*. New York: Dorsey Press.

Shapiro, Robert. 2004. "Why Respond to Polls: Public Opinion Polling and De-mocracy." *Public Opinion PROS*. November. www.publicopinionpros.norc.org/features/2004/nov/shapiro.htm.

Shapiro, Robert, and Harpreet Mahajan. 1986. "Gender Differences in Policy Prefer-ences: A Summary of Trends from the 1960s to the 1980s." *Public Opinion Quarterly* 50 (Spring): 42–61.

Shapiro, Robert, and Benjamin I. Page. 1988. "Foreign Policy and the Rational Pub-lic." *Journal of Conflict Resolution* 32 (June): 211–247.

Shapiro, Robert Y., Kelly D. Patterson, Judith Russell, and John T. Young. 1987a. "The Polls: Public Assistance." *Public Opinion Quarterly* 51 (Spring): 120–130.

———. 1987b. "The Polls: Employment and Social Welfare." *Public Opinion Quarterly* 51 (Summer): 268–281.

Shapiro, Robert Y., and Tom W. Smith. 1985. "The Polls: Social Security." *Public Opinion Quarterly* 49 (Winter): 561–572.

Sharp, Laure M. 1984. "Researchers and Respondents in the 1980s." *Public Opinion Quarterly* 48 (Fall): 680–685.

Shaw, Greg M., and Sarah Mysiewicz. 2004. "The Polls–Trends: Social Security and Medicare." *Public Opinion Quarterly* 68 (Fall): 394–423.

Sheatsley, Paul B. 1966. "White Attitudes toward the Negro." *Daedalus* 95 (Winter): 217–238.

Sigel, Roberta S., ed. 1970. *Learning about Politics: A Reader in Political Socialization*. New York: Random House.

Sigelman, Lee, and Susan Welch. 1991. *Black Americans View of Racial Inequality—Dream Deferred*. Cambridge, UK: Cambridge University Press.

Simon, Rita James. 1974. *Public Opinion in America: 1936–1970*. Chicago: Rand McNally.

Smith, Andrew E., Alfred J. Tuchfarber, Eric W. Rademacher, and Stephen E. Ben-nett. 1995. "Partisan Leaners Are *Not* Independents." *Public Perspective* 6 (October/November): 9–12.

Smith, Ben. 2009. "Meet Obama's Pollsters." Politico.com, April 3. www.politico.com/news/stories/0409/20852.html.

Smith, Eric R. A. N. 1989. *The Unchanging American Voter*. Berkeley, CA: University of California Press.

Smith, Tom W. 1987. "That Which We Call Welfare by Any Other Name Would Smell Sweeter: An Analysis of the Impact of Question Wording on Response Patterns." *Public Opinion Quarterly* 51 (Spring): 75–83.

———. 1990. "The First Straw: A Study of the Origins of Election Polls." *Public Opinion Quarterly* 54 (Spring): 21–36.

———. 1997. "Tall Oaks from Little Acorns Grow: The General Social Surveys, 1971–1996." *Public Perspective* 8 (February/March): 28–30.

Smith, Tom W., Seokho Kim, Kyle Tateyama, and Conor Looney. 2004. *An Analysis of GSS Research Research, 1972–2003.* Chicago: NORC.

Smith, Tom W., and Frederick D. Weil. 1990. "The Polls—A Report. Finding Public Opinion Data: A Guide to Sources." *Public Opinion Quarterly* 54 (Winter): 609–626.

Sniderman, Paul M., Thomas Piazza, Philip E. Tetlock, and Ann Kendrick. 1991. "The New Racism." *American Journal of Political Science* 35 (May): 423–447.

Snowe, Olympia. 2011. "Remarks by Senator Olympia Snowe on Biennial Budgeting." *Congressional Record 112th Congress* (March 7).

Sorenson, Theodore C. 1965. *Kennedy.* New York: Harper and Row.

Sourcebook of Criminal Justice Statistics Online. http://www.albany.edu/sourcebook/.

Squire, Peverill. 1988. "Why the 1936 *Literary Digest* Poll Failed." *Public Opinion Quarterly* 52 (Spring): 125–133.

Stanley, Harold W., and Richard G. Niemi. 1995. *Vital Statistics on American Politics.* Washington, DC: Congressional Quarterly Press.

Steeh, Charlotte, Nicole Kirgis, Brian Cannon, and Jeff DeWitt. 2001. "Are They Really as Bad as They Seem? Nonresponse Rates at the End of the Twentieth Century." *Journal of Officials Statistics* 17 (2): 227–248.

Stein, Lana. 1996. "American Jews and Their Liberal Political Behavior." In *The Politics of Minority Coalitions: Race, Ethnicity and Shared Uncertainties.* Ed. Wilbur C. Rich. Westport, CT: Praeger.

Stimson, James A. 1991. *Public Opinion in America: Moods, Cycles and Swings.* Boulder, CO: Westview Press.

Stokes, Donald E. 1966. "Some Dynamic Elements of Contests for the Presidency." *American Political Science Review* 60 (March): 19–28.

Stouffer, Samuel A. 1955. *Communism, Conformity, and Civil Liberties: A Cross-section of the Nation Speaks Its Mind.* Garden City, NY: Doubleday.

Sturgis, Patrick, Caroline Roberts, and Nick Allum. 2005. "A Different Take on the Deliberative Poll." *Public Opinion Quarterly* 69 (Spring): 30–65.

Sudman, Seymour, and Norman H. Bradburn. 1987. "The Organizational Growth of Public Opinion Research in the United States." *Public Opinion Quarterly* 51 (Winter): S67–S78.

Sullivan, John L., James E. Piereson, and George E. Marcus. 1978. "Ideological Constraint in the Mass Public." *American Journal of Political Science* 22 (May): 233–249.

———. 1979. "An Alternative Conceptualization of Political Tolerance: Illusory Increases 1950s–1970s." *American Political Science Review* 73 (September): 781–794.

Suro, Roberto, Richard Fry, and Jeffrey Passel. 2005. *Hispanics and the 2004 Election: Population, Electorate and Voters.* Washington, DC: Pew Hispanic Center.

Taylor, Humphrey, John Brenner, Cary Overmeyer, Jonathon W. Siegel, and George Terhanian. 2001. "Touchdown! Online Polling Scores Big in November 2000." *Public Perspective* 12 (March/April): 38–39.

Taylor, Humphrey, and George Terhanian. 1999. "Heady Days Are Here Again: On-line Polling Is Rapidly Coming of Age." *Public Perspective* 10 (June/July): 20–23.

Time/CNN Poll. 1997. "Kids and Race," *Time*, November 24.

Toepoel, Vera, and Mick P. Couper. 2011. "Can Verbal Instructions Counteract Visual Context Effects in Web Surveys?" *Public Opinion Quarterly* 75 (Spring): 1–18.

Traugott, Michael W. 2000. "Auto-Dialing for Data: A Reply to Scott Rasmussen." *Public Perspective* 11 (November/December): 34–36.

———. 2001. "Assessing Poll Performance in the 2000 Campaign." *Public Opinion Quarterly* 65 (Fall): 389–419.

Traugott, Michael, Benjamin Highton, and Henry E. Brady. 2005. *A Review of Recent Controversies Concerning the 2004 Presidential Election Exit Polls*. New York: Social Science Research Council.

Tringali, Brian C. 1996. "Experimenting with Artificial Democracy." *Public Perspective* 7 (December/January): 19–20.

Tuchfarber, Alfred J., and William R. Klecka. 1976. *Random Digit Dialing: Lowering the Cost of Victimization Surveys*. Washington, DC: Police Foundation.

Tuchfarber, Alfred J., and Robert W. Oldendick. 1986. *Queen City Metro: Marketing Baseline Study*. Cincinnati, OH: Institute for Policy Research.

Tuchfarber, Alfred J., Robert W. Oldendick, and George F. Bishop. 1984. "Citizen Attitudes toward Taxation and Spending: Inconsistent Answers or the Wrong Questions?" Presented at the annual meeting of the American Political Science Association, Washington.

Tuchfarber, Alfred J., and Andrew E. Smith. 1995. *City of Cincinnati Citizen Attitude Survey*. Cincinnati, OH: Institute for Policy Research.

Tuchfarber, Alfred J., and R. Eric Weise. 1982. *Queen City Metro Public Financing Study Report*. Cincinnati, OH: Institute for Policy Research.

Tuckel, Peter, and Barry M. Feinberg. 1991. "The Answering Machine Poses Many Questions for Telephone Survey Researchers." *Public Opinion Quarterly* 55 (Summer): 200–217.

Tuckel, Peter, and Harry W. O'Neill. 1996. "Screened Out." *Marketing Research* 8 (Fall): 34–43.

———. 2001. "The Vanishing Respondent in Telephone Surveys." Paper presented at the annual meeting of the American Association for Public Opinion Research, Montreal. November 14.

US Count Votes. 2005. "Study of the 2004 Presidential Election Exit Poll Discrepancies." http://electionarchive.org/ucvAnalysis/US/Exit_Polls_2004_Mitofsky -Edison.pdf.

U.S. Department of Commerce. Bureau of the Census. 2000, *Historical Census of Housing Tables*. Washington, DC: Government Printing Office.

U.S. Department of Commerce. Bureau of the Census. 2004–05. *Statistical Abstract of the United States 2004–05*. Washington, DC: Government Printing Office.

U.S. Department of Defense. 2010. *Report of the Comprehensive Review of the Issues Associated with a Repeal of "Don't Ask, Don't Tell."* www.defense.gov/ home/features/2010/0610_gatesdadt/DADTReport_FINAL_20101130%28secure -hires%29.pdf.

U.S. Department of Education, Institute of Education Sciences, National Center for Education Statistics. 2010. *The Nation's Report Card Civics 2010*. Washington, DC.

U.S. Department of Labor, Bureau of Labor Statistics. 2001. *Current Population Survey*. Washington, DC: Government Printing Office.

Valentino, Nicholas A., and Ted Brader. 2011. "The Sword's Other Edge: Perceptions of Discrimination and Racial Policy Opinion after Obama." *Public Opinion Quarterly* 75 (Summer): 201–222.

Verba, Sidney, Richard A. Brody, Edwin B. Parker, Norman H. Nie, Nelson W. Polsby, Paul Ekman, and Gordon S. Black. 1967. "Public Opinion and the War in Vietnam." *American Political Science Review* 61 (June): 317–333.

Verba, Sidney, Nancy Burns, and Kay Lehman Schlozman. 1997. "Knowing and Caring about Politics: Gender and Political Engagement." *Journal of Politics* 59 (November): 1051–1072.

Waksberg, Joseph. 1978. "Sampling Methods for Random Digit Dialing." *Journal of the American Statistical Association* 73 (March): 40–46.

Washington, George. 1796. "Farewell Address," The Avalon Project, Yale University Law. www.avalon.law.yale.edu.

Weaver, Carolyn L., and Derrick A. Max. 1995. "The Economics of an Aging Social Security Program." *The Public Perspective* 6 (February/March): 16–18.

Weisberg, Herbert E. 1980. "A Multidimensional Conceptualization of Party Identification." *Political Behavior* 2 (1): 33–60.

Weissberg, Robert. 1974. *Political Learning, Political Choice, and Democratic Citizenship*. Englewood Cliffs, NJ: Prentice-Hall.

———. 1976. *Public Opinion and Popular Government*. Englewood Cliffs, NJ: Prentice-Hall.

Wheeler, Michael. 1980. "Reining in Horserace Journalism." *Public Opinion* 3 (February/March): 41–45.

Wilcox, Clyde, J. Ferrara, and Dee Alsop. 1991. "Before the Rally: The Dynamics of Attitudes toward the Gulf Crisis before the War." Paper presented at the annual meeting of the American Political Science Association, Washington, DC.

Wilcox, Clyde, and Barbara Norrander. 2002. "Of Moods and Morals: The Dynamics of Opinion on Abortion and Gay Rights." In *Understanding Public Opinion*. 2nd ed. Eds. Barbara Norrander and Clyde Wilcox. Washington, DC: Congressional Quarterly Press.

Wittkopf, Eugene R. 1990. *Public Faces of Internationalism Opinion and American Foreign Policy*. Durham, NC: Duke University Press.

Wittkopf, Eugene R., and Michael Maggiotto. 1983. "The Two Faces of Internationalism: Public Attitudes toward American Foreign Policy and Beyond?" *Social Science Quarterly* 64 (June): 288–304.

Wolak, Jennifer. 2009. "Explaining Change in Party Identification in Adolescence." *Electoral Studies* 28: 573–583.

Yankelovich, Daniel. 1991. *Coming to Public Judgment*. Syracuse, NY: Syracuse University Press.

Zaller, John. 1992. *The Nature and Origins of Mass Opinions*. Cambridge, UK: Cambridge University Press.

Zernike, Kate, and Dalia Sussman. 2008. "For Pollsters, the Racial Effect that Wasn't." *New York Times*. November 5. www.nytimes.com/2008/11/06/us/politics/06poll.html.

LEGAL CASES

Adarand Constructors, Inc. v. Pena, 115 S. Ct. 2097 (1995).
Adarand Constructors, Inc. v. Mineta, 534 U.S. 730 (2001).
Brown v. Board of Education of Topeka, 347 U.S. 483 (1954).
Dred Scott v. Sanford, 19 Howard 393 (1857).
Furman v. Georgia, 408 U.S. 238 (1972).
Gibbons v. Ogden, 9 Wheaton 1 (1824).
Gregg v. Georgia, 428 U.S. 153 (1976).
Griswold v. Connecticut, 381 U.S. 479 (1965).
Grutter v. Bollinger et al., 02-241 U.S. 539 (2003).
Plessy v. Ferguson, 163 U.S. 537 (1896).
Regents of the University of California v. Bakke, 438 U.S. 265 (1978).
Ricci v. DeStefano, 557 U.S. 129 (2009).
Roe v. Wade, 410 U.S. 113 (1973).
Swann v. Charlotte-Mecklenburg Board of Education, 402 U.S. 1 (1971).
Trop v. Dulles, 356 U.S. 86 (1958).

Index

AAPOR. *See* American Association for Public Opinion Research

abc.com, 268

ABC News/*Washington Post*, 46

abortion issues, 100–101, 217; Bush, G. W., and, 231–32; Clinton, B., and, 231; public opinion on, 78, 226–32, *228, 229, 230,* 322n11; traumatic *v.* elective, 227

ABS. *See* address-based sampling

Abu Ghraib prison, 258

academic surveys, 24–25, 31

"Accounting for Cell Phones in Telephone Survey Research in the U.S." (Lavrakas and Shuttles), 280–81

acculturation, 93

Achen, Christopher H., 3

acquiescence response set, 73

ACS. *See* American Community Survey

activism, 96, 139, 238, 317n1

Adams, Kenneth, 238

Adams, William C., 9

Adarand Constructors, Inc. v. Mineta, 195

Adarand Constructors, Inc. v. Pena, 195

address-based sampling (ABS), 62, *63,* 65, 80

adolescents and children, political learning of, 89–93

advertisements, 64, 111; by candidates, 23nb, 115; television, 33, 65; in trade magazines, 46

affirmative action, 194–98, *197, 198;* Hispanic Americans and, 195, 197

Afghan War, 246, 257–60, *259,* 265

African Americans, 94, 100–101; black candidate for president, public opinion on, 206, *206;* interracial marriage and, 209–10, *210;* loyalty in, 94; party identification of, 109; slavery and, 100, *207,* 207–8, *208;* social security and, 183. *See also* affirmative action; racial issues

age groups, 105, 108–9, 137, 142, 185

agenda setting, 111

agree-disagree format, 73, 74

Agricultural Adjustment Administration, 159

airport security, 258

Alcohol and Other Drug Abuse Treatment Needs Assessment, 43

Alderman, Jeff, 51

Allum, Nick, 317n3

alternatives: middle, 71–73, *73;* order of, 76–77

American Association for Public Opinion Research (AAPOR), 24, 27, 33, 83, 276, 280–81; ethical code of, 276

American Association of Retired Persons, 38

americancivicliteracy.org, 130

American Civic Literacy Program, 122–23

American Community Survey (ACS), 43

American Medical Association, 38

American National Election Studies (NES), 52–53, 55, 61, *63*, 67, 135, 139, 149, 152, 324n3, 326n1

American public opinion: abortion issues, 78, 226–32, *228, 229, 230*, 322n11; affirmative action, 194–98, *197, 198*; assisting needy, 173–77, *174, 175, 176*; black candidate for president, 206, *206*; capital punishment, 12, 217, 223–25, *224, 225*; civil rights movement, 189, 205, 208–9, *209*; communism, 70, *70*, 124–25; crime, and criminal justice, 218–25, *219, 222, 224, 225*; defense policy, 253–61, *259*; desegregation, 190–93, 328n2; education, 165–67, *166, 167*; environment, 177–82, *178, 179–81*; fair employment practices, *193*, 193–94, *194*; foreign policy, U.S., 245–53, *247, 251, 252*, 261–68, *262*; global warming, 182–83; government aid to minority groups, 198–202, *199, 200, 201*; government spending on racial issues, 202–5, *203, 204, 205*; gun control, 234–38, *235, 237*; health care, 167–73, *168, 169, 170, 172*, 327n4; homosexuality, 232–34, *233, 235*; immigration issues, 211, 238–41, *239*; individual rights, 225; influence of Hispanic Americans, 211–13, *212*; interracial marriage, 209–10, *210*; news reporting, 77, 111–13; polls, 274–75; slavery, 100, *207*, 207–8, *208*; social security,

161–65, *162, 164–65*, 168, 176, 185, 327n2; stem cell research, 44–45, 242; tax system, 76–77, 100; war, and peace, 253–57

American Rangers, 260, 261

American Statistical Association, 84

The American Voter (Campbell, A., et al.), 53, 118, 131, 133–34

answering machines, telephone, 278–79, 283–84, 331n5

anti-Federalists, 132, 151, 159

antiwar movements, 259

apportionment, 42

area codes, 63, 281–83, 320n3

Aristide, Jean-Bertrand, 267

Aristotle, 3

Arizona residency law, 211–12, 241–42

Arterton, F. Christopher, 91

Asian Americans, 101–2

assisting needy, 173–77, *174, 175, 176*

attitudes, 14, 285

Austin, Warren, 119

Axelrod, David, 38

axis of evil, 258

Baby Boomers, 109

Bakke, Alan, 195

Balkan states, 264

Beck, Paul Allen, 89

Behavioral Risk Factor Surveillance System (BRFSS), 41, 43, 322n16

beliefs, 14–15, 53

benchmark polls, 32

Benenson, Joel, 38

Bennett, Linda L. M., 151–52, 326n12

Bennett, Stephen E., 112, 120–21, 128, 131, 151–52, 154, 323n1, 326n12

Berelson, Bernard R., 118

bias: establishment, 112; non-coverage, 280; nonresponse, 19, 284, 331n5

Bill of Rights, 119–21, 123, 289

bin Laden, Osama, 258

biological racism, 189–90

bipartisanship, 161, 248–49, 256, 261

bivariate analysis, 79

Black Power, 189

Blendon, Robert J., 170

Blumberg, Stephen J., 288
Blumenthal, Mark, 171, 283–84
Blumer, Herbert, 6, 7
Board of Governors of the Federal
    Reserve System, 40
Boehner, John, 122, 128
Bond, Robert, 107
Booth, Charles, 19
border security, 240, 242
Bosnia, 265
Boston Globe, 18, 46
Bowley, Arthur, 20
Bradburn, Norman M., 66
Bradley effect, 286
Brady, Henry E., 317n3, 319n12
Brady Bill, 236
Brehm, John, 46, 282, 319n7
BRFSS. *See* Behavioral Risk Factor
    Surveillance System
Brown, Ethan, 26
Brown v. Board of Education, 189
Bureau of Applied Social Research, 24,
    25
Bureau of Justice Statistics, U.S., 40
Bureau of the Census, U.S. *See* Census
    Bureau, U.S.
Burger, Warren, 121
burglary, fear of, 220–21
Burns, Nancy, 105
Burstein, Paul, 317
Bush, George H. W., 37, 44, 50, 255–57
Bush, George W.: abortion and, 231–
    32; approval ratings of, 50–51, 161;
    candidacy of, 34, 48–49, 286–87,
    318n2; No Child Left Behind
    legislation of, 122, 167; social
    security and, 161; terrorism and,
    246, 257–59; use of polls by, 38
busing, school, 191–92

Caddell, Pat, 36–37, 148, 326n11
California Civil Rights Initiative, 196
call-blocking, 278
caller ID, 278–79, 283–84
call-in polls, 51–52, 275
call screening, 62, 278–79
campaign cycle, 31

campaign issues, 32
Campbell, Angus, 53, 118, 131, 133–
    34, 139
Campbell, David A., 96
candidate poll, first, *21*
Cantril, Albert, 275
Cantril, Hadley, 14, 36
capital punishment, 12, 217, 223–25,
    224, 225
Carmines, Edward G., 207
Carter, Jimmy, 36–37, 148, 330n2
CASRO. *See* Council of American
    Survey Research Organizations
Castro, Fidel, 101
Catholicism, 101–2, 230–31
CATI. *See* computer-assisted telephone
    interviewing
CBS/*New York Times* polls, 46, 55,
    275–76, 324n4
cell phone-only (CPO) households, *63,
    81, 279–80*
cell phones, 62, 81–82, 280–81
Cell Phone Sampling Summit II
    Conference, 280
census blocks, 61
Census Bureau, U.S., 20, 39–40, 211;
    Census of 2000, 25, 42, 318n4;
    polls of, 42–43, 319n10; Supreme
    Court and, 42
census tracts, 61
Center for Deliberative Democracy, 16
Center for Substance Abuse Treatment
    State Demand and Needs
    Assessment Project, 41
Centers for Disease Control and
    Prevention, 41
cfr.org, 269
Chaffee, Steven, 87–88
The Changing American Voter (Nie et
    al.), 53
checks and balances, 17
Chicago Council on Foreign Relations,
    250, 266, 269, 329n2
Chicago Council on Global Affairs,
    269
Chicago Daily Tribune, 22
Chicago Examiner, 46

children: and adolescents, political learning of, 89–93; loyalty in, 95, 99
Christian, Leah, 280
church-state separation, 104, 159
Cincinnati Enquirer, 18, 46
Citrin, Jack, 196
civic norms, 107
civics knowledge, 98–99; of Hispanic Americans, 98
civil liberties, 54, 104, 323n5
civil literacy, 130
Civil Rights Act of 1964, 190, 194
civil rights movement, 189, 205, 208–9, *209*; California Civil Rights Initiative, 196
Civil War, 93, 100, 132, 159, 189
Clinton, Bill: abortion and, 231; candidacy of, 4, 23nb, 105, 137; Census of 2000 and, 42; "Don't Ask, Don't Tell" policy of, 11, 232; health care and, 169, 171; impeachment of, 4, 51; use of polls by, 37–38
Clinton, Hillary Rodham, 22–24, 287
cloning, 242
closed-ended questions, 67–68
cluster sampling, 61, *63*
CMOR. *See* Council for Marketing and Opinion Research
cnn.com, 268
CNN/*USA Today*, 6
Cohen, Steven M., 104
Cold War, 248, 262–63
Columbine High School shootings, 236
commercial polling firms, 294
communism, 70, *70*, 124–25
computer-assisted self-interviewing, 278
computer-assisted telephone interviewing (CATI), 26
confidence, in governmental institutions, 144–47, *145*; in leaders of, 1966–2010, *146*; in leaders of, trends in, *147*
confidentiality, 274–75, 277, 322n15
consensus, 191
conservatism, 131–39
Constitution, U.S., 17, 42, 121, 159, 289

constraint, 134
Consumer Product Safety Commission (CPSC), 10
context effects, 77–79, *78*
continuous monitoring surveys, 53
Converse, Jean M., 321n8
Converse, Philip, 4, 5, 6, 11, 118, 120, 133, 288–89, 321n7
Conyers, John, 286
Cook, Charlie, 34
Cook, Elizabeth Adell, 227–28, 231
Cook, Faye Lomax, 10
Cornyn, John, 11
corrections, purpose of, 221–23
Council for Marketing and Opinion Research (CMOR), 35, 274, 276
Council of American Survey Research Organizations (CASRO), 35
Country Life Movement surveys, 20
Couper, Mick P., 78, 277
CPO. *See* cell phone-only households
CPS. *See* Current Population Survey
CPSC. *See* Consumer Product Safety Commission
creationism *v.* evolution, 242
crime, and criminal justice, 218–25, *219*, *222*, *224*, *225*
Crockett, Harry J., 125
Crossley, Archibald, 20, 21, 46
cross-time analysis, 53
Cuban Americans, 101
cugging, 331n3
Cummings, Milton C., Jr., 5
current environment, of American electorate, 15
Current Population Survey (CPS), 40, 66, 282, 321n6, 322n16
curriculum, 94–95
Curtin, Richard, 81, 283
Cynamon, Marcie L., 288
cynicism, 91, 100, 102, 147–48, 276, 283, 323n2

Dahl, Robert, 249
data analysis, 79–83
data collection, 21–22, 24; electronic, 26, *64*, 64–65, 80, 322n12; by surveys, 58; by telephone, 25–26

Daves, Robert P., 283
Davis, Darren W., 323n5
Davis, James A., 109, 125, 129
Dawson, Karen S., 94
Dawson, Richard E., 94, 97
death penalty, 12, 217, 223–25, *224,* *225*
Defense of Marriage Act, 234
defense policy, U.S., 253–61, *259*
deliberative opinion polls, 13–14, 16, 317n3
delivery sequence file (DSF), 62
Delli Carpini, Michael X., 117–18, 121–23, 127–29, 289, 323nn2–3
democracy: applying principles of, 123–27, *125, 126*; paradox of, 118; in U.S., 3–16
Democratic National Committee, 38
Dennis, Jack, 89–90, 91
Department of Agriculture, U.S., 20–21, 40
Department of Commerce, U.S., 25, 43, 319n8
Department of Defense, U.S., 11
Department of Education, U.S., 39, 98
Department of Health and Human Services, U.S., 40, 319n7
deportation, 240–41
desegregation, 190–93, 328n2
deterrence, 222
Dewey, Thomas E., 21–22, 286
Dillman, Don A., 83
DNA testing, 13, 224, 329n2
Doerflinger, Richard, 45
"Do Not Call" list, 331n6
"Don't Ask, Don't Tell" policy, 11, 232
Dran, Ellen M., 274
Dred Scott v. Sanford, 189
DSF. *See* delivery sequence file

early election calls, 49
Easton, David, 89–90
economic issues, 50
Edison Media Research, 48–49, 287, 319n12
education: Department of, 39, 98; ideologies and, 137–39, 185; parental, 98–99; political knowledge

and, 128–29; public opinion on, 165–67, *166, 167*; as source of opinions, 93–99
Ehrman, Lee H., 95
Eisenhower, Dwight D., 36
election calls, early, 49
Election Science Institute, 55
elective versus traumatic abortions, 227
electoral process, 276
electronic data collection, 26, 64, 64–65, 80, 322n12
e-mail addresses, 64
e-mail surveys, 80
employment practices, fair: for African Americans, *193,* 193–94, *194*; for homosexuals, 232, *233*
Energy Information Administration, U.S., 41
English social survey, 19
Enlightenment movement, 3
environment, 177–82, *178, 179–81*; movement, of 1970s, *177*
Erikson, Robert S., 5, 109
Erskine, Hazel Gaudet, 118, 120–22, 128
establishment bias, 112
ethical code, of AAPOR, 276
ethnic identity: Hispanic Americans and, 99; as source of opinions, 99–102, 115
EU. *See* European Union
European Union (EU), 249
euthanasia, 218
Evangelicalism, 103
evolution *v.* creationism, 242
exit polls, 47–49, 286–87, 319n12
Exoo, Calvin F., 112

Facebook, 7, 320n1
face-to-face interviewing, 25, 58, *63,* 79, 81, 322n12
fair employment practices: for African Americans, *193,* 193–94, *194*; for homosexuals, 232, *233*
Farm Journal, 18
fascism, 245
Federal Election Commission, 34–35
The Federalist, 3, 17

Federalists, 132, 151, 159
Federal Trade Commission, 331n6
feeling thermometer, 76
Feld, Karl G., 34–35
feminism, 54, 231
Ferber, Paul H., 9
Ferree, G. Donald, 318n3
filter questions, 68–69, *69*
Fiorina, Morris, 15
Fisher, R. A., 20
Fishkin, James S., 13, 317n3
Fleron, Frederic J., 91
Florida 2000 vote, 48, 55, 286
focus groups, 37–38
forced-choice format, 73; seven-point,
    74, 75
Ford Foundation, 329n2
forecasting errors, 22
foreign aid, 262–63, *263*
foreign policy, U.S., 245–53, *247*, *251*,
    252, 261–68, *262*
Founding Fathers, 3, 17
framing, 111, 113
Frankovic, Kathy, 51, 275
Free, Lloyd A., 14
Frey, James H., 79
frugging, 331n3
Fry, Richard, 324n5
Funk, W. J., 20
Furman v. Georgia, 223

Gallup, George, 18, 20–21, 46, 288
Gallup preelection polls, *23*
gambling, 45
Gannett Foundation, 323n1
Gawiser, Sheldon R., 33
gay issues. *See* homosexuality
gender issues: "Don't Ask, Don't Tell"
    policy, 11, 232; gender gap, in
    presidential elections, 142; political
    interest and, *106*; as sources of
    opinions, 105–6
General Social Survey (GSS), 24, 53–
    55, 61, 80, 125–26, 160, 165, 168,
    283, 325n8, 326n1
generational effects, 92, 108–10
Gibbons v. Ogden, 132
Giffords, Gabrielle, 236

global warming, 182–83
Goldwater, Barry, 152
Gore, Al, 48, 286
government: aid to minority groups,
    198–202, *199*, *200*, *201*; confidence
    in institutions of, 144–47, *145*,
    146, *147*; insurance plans, 169–70,
    170, 297–98; local, polls of, 43–44;
    power of, 151–55, *153*; provide
    more or fewer services, 1975-2010,
    160; spending on racial issues, 202–
    5, *203*, *204*, *205*; state, polls of, 43;
    trust in, 147–51, *148*, *150*, 325n10;
    use of polls by agencies, 39
Graber, Doris A., 112–13, 115, 323n3
Great Depression, 109, 114
Great Society programs, 132
Greenberg, Stanley, 37, 90
Gregg v. Georgia, 224
Grenada invasion, 260
Grigg, Charles M., 124, 128
Griswold v. Connecticut, 226
group differences: in attitudes, on
    social-welfare, 183–86, *184*; in
    political knowledge, 127–29
Groves, Robert M., 284, 320n2, 322n13
Grutter v. Bollinger et al., 195
GSS. *See* General Social Survey
Gulf of Tonkin incident, 253
gun control, 234–38, *235*, *237*

handguns, 236
Hansen, Morris, 318n1
Harris Black International, 82
Harrisburg Pennsylvanian, 46
Harris Interactive, 83
Harris Poll Online, 64–65, 82, 277
Harris polls, 24
Harstad, Paul, 38
health care: Clinton, B., and, 169, 171;
    Obama plan, 15, 44, 132, 171–73;
    opinions on, 167–73, *168*, *169*, *170*,
    172, 327n4; reform of, 15, 38, 44,
    100, 132, 319n6
*Health Care Reform and American
    Politics: What Everyone Needs to Know*
    (Jacobs and Skocpol), 319n6
Hennessy, Bernard H., 5

Henry J. Kaiser Family Foundation, 173, 330n1
Hensler, Carl P., 192
Hess, Robert D., 90, 95
Highton, Benjamin, 319n12
Hildreth, Anne, 274
Hirsch, Herbert, 91
Hispanic Americans: affirmative action and, 195, 197; civics knowledge of, 98; Cuban Americans, 101; ethnic identity and, 99; immigration issues and, 239, 324n5; influence of, 211–13, *212*; Mexican Americans, 101
Hitler, Adolf, 245
Holocaust, 71
Holsti, Ole, 254
homosexuality: "Don't Ask, Don't Tell" policy, 11, 232; employment practices, fair, 232, *233*; marriage and, *234*, *235*; public opinions on, 232–34, *233*, *235*; rights of homosexuals, 218, 225; tolerance of, 126, *126*, 234
Hoover, J. Edgar, 121
horse-race journalism, 47
hostilization, 91
House of Representatives, U.S., 42, 119, 121, 128, 135, 154
Howard, Peter, 37
Huckabee, Mike, 47
Hume, David, 3
Hussein, Saddam, 246, 256
Hyman, Herbert H., 118, 120

ICPSR. *See* Interuniversity Consortium for Political and Social Research
idealization, 90
identity theft, 220
ideological identification, 1972-2008, *135*, *136*
ideologies: education and, 137–39, 185; political orientations and, 132–39, *135*, *136*, *138*
immigration issues: Hispanic Americans and, 239, 324n5; public opinions on, 211, 238–41, *239*
incumbent rule, 318n2
Independents, 141–42

Indiana Rural Health Association, 45
individual rights, 225
Information Agency, U.S., 24
information sources, 111–13
Inhofe, James, 11
Innocence Project, 329n2
Institute for Political and Social Research, 157
Institute for Public Service and Policy Research, 43
Institute for Research in Social Science, 215
Institute for Social Research, 84
institutionalization, 90
institutions, confidence in governmental, 144–47, *145*, *146*, *147*
insurance: government, 169–70, *170*, 297–98; private, 169–70, *170*, 298
interactive voice response (IVR), 321n4
Intercollegiate Studies Institute, 122–23, 323n4
interest groups, 44–45, 95, 115, 323n4
internationalism, 248, 250, 265–66
international issues, 249, 261–64, 268
Internet: news on, 110; party identification and, 157; polling industry on, 16, 26–27, 55, 58, 82–83; Web surveys, 277, 322n15
interracial marriage, 209–10, *210*
Interuniversity Consortium for Political and Social Research (ICPSR), 54
interviewing, 22; CATI, 26; computer-assisted self-interviewing, 278; costs of, 79; face-to-face, 25, 58, *63*, 79, 81, 322n12; paper-and-pencil, 59; as social interaction, 285; by telephone, 25–26, 58, 62–64, *63*, 79, 278–79
Iran-Contra hearings, 4
Iraq War, 47, 112, 257–60, *259*, 265
isolationism, 245–48, 253–54, 266
issue public, 317n1
IVR. *See* interactive voice response
Iyengar, Shanto, 113

Jackson State University shootings, 254
Jacobs, Lawrence R., 36, 319n6
Jacoby, William G., 131

Jaros, Dean, 91
JDRF. *See* Juvenile Diabetes Research Foundation
Jefferson, Thomas, 189
Jelen, Ted G., 227–28, 231
Jennings, M. Kent, 91–92, 94–96, 107
Jentleson, Bruce, 265–66, 267, 268
Jewish Americans, 104
Jindal, Bobby, 47
Johnson, Lyndon, 4, 36, 194, 253, 265
Johnson, Timothy P., 26
Joint Program in Survey Methodology, 84
Juvenile Diabetes Research Foundation (JDRF), 44

Kahn, Robert M., 320n2, 322n13
Kaiser Family Foundation, Henry J., 173, 330n1
Kansas Press Association, 323n1
Katz, Daniel, 14
Keeter, Scott, 117–18, 121–22, 127–29, 284, 289, 323nn2–3
Keith, Bruce E., 325n7
Kennedy, John F., 36
Kent State University shootings, 254
Kerry, John, 49, 286–87, 318n2
Key, V. O., 5
Kids Voting USA, 87–89, 323n1
Kinder, Donald, 113
King, Martin Luther, Jr., 90
Klecka, William R., 320n2, 322n13
Knowledge Networks (KN), 64–65, 82, 277, 322n14, 322n16
Kohut, Andrew, 122
Korean conflict, 255, 256
Krosnick, Jon A., 286

labor movement, 115
labor unions, 34, 44, 108
Ladd, Everett Carll, 167, 318n3
landline telephones, 25, 81–82, 278–81, 288, 318n4, 331n4
Landon, Alfred M., 19, 20
Langer, Gary, 171–72
Langton, Kenneth P., 94–95, 107
latimes.com/news/custom/timespoll, 268

Lavrakas, Paul J., 280–81
Lazarsfeld, Paul F., 118
League of Nations, 245, 261
Leege, David C., 103
Lemke, William, 19
Leve, Jay, 283–84
Levitt, Justin, 107
Lewis-Beck, Michael S., 92, 132, 134
liberalism, 131–39
libertarianism, 133, 234
Libya, 260, 265
Liebman, Charles S., 104
life cycle effects, 92, 109
Likert-type item, 73
Lincoln, Abraham, 3, 90, 94, 100
Lindner, Carl, 52
Lippmann, Walter, 249, 264
Lipset, Seymour Martin, 144, 147–48, 213
Literary Digest, 18–21, 46, 59, 82, 286, 290
Litt, Edgar, 94
local governments, polls of, 43–44
Louis Harris and Associates, 36, 46, 82, 222, 292, 294
loyalty, 290; in African Americans, 94; in children, 95, 99
Luke, Julian V., 288
Luskin, Robert C., 317n3
lying, 285

MacArthur, Douglas, 118
MacArthur Foundation, 329n2
MacKuen, Michael Bruce, 114
Madison, James, 17
Magelby, David B., 147
Mahajan, Harpreet, 255
mail surveys, *63*, 79, 83, 276, 322n12
Manza, Jeff, 10
Marcus, George E., 126–27
marriage: between homosexuals, 234, *234*; interracial, 209–10, *210*
Marshall Plan, 128, 261–62
Marxism, 133
Mayer, William G., 166, 189
McCain, John, 34, 83
McCarthy, Eugene, 121
McClosky, Herbert, 124

McClure, Robert D., 115
McCormick, James, 246
McGrady, Jennifer A., 113
McPhee, William N., 118
measuring public opinion, 57–84
media influences, 110–15
media use of polls, 46–47
Medicare, 122, 162, 171
Merelman, Richard M., 96
message spin, 114–15
Mexican Americans, 101
middle alternatives, 71–73, *73*
Miller, Arthur H., 132, 144, 147
Miller, Warren E., 9, 324n6, 325n7,
    326n11
minimal effects model, 323n3
minority employment, *193*, 193–94,
    194
Mitofsky, Warren, 48–49, 82
Mitofsky International, 287
modified area samples, 22
Monitoring the Future Study, *63*
Monroe, Alan D., 5, 10, 289–90, 317n2
Monroe, James, 246
Monroe Doctrine, 246
Moore, David W., 37, 71, 318n3,
    330n2
Morgenthau, Hans, 249
Morin, Richard, 122
Morrill Act of 1862, 93
MTV, 108
Mueller, John, 125, 254, 256, 260
mugging, 220–21
multilateralist policy, 266
multipart questions, *75*
multiple publics, 8–9
Murray, Shoon Kathleen, 37

name recognition, 32
National Center for Health Statistics,
    40
National Civics Assessment Test
    (2010), *98*
National Civics Awareness Test (1988),
    97
National Civics Test, 93, 99, 116
National Conference of Catholic
    Bishops (NCCB), 44–45

National Council on Public Polls
    (NCPP), 33, 35, 284
National Crime Survey, 83
National Crime Victimization Survey,
    40
National Election Pool (NEP), 48, 287
National Health and Nutrition
    Examination Survey, 40
National Health Interview Survey
    (NHIS), 40, 83
National Household Survey on Drug
    Use and Health, 40
National Institutes of Health, 42, 45
National Medical Expenditure Survey,
    40
National Network of State Polls
    (NNSP), 215
National Opinion Research Center
    (NORC), 24, 25, 53, 192, 220, 226
National Recovery Administration, 159
National Rifle Association (NRA), 8,
    238
National Science Foundation, 42
National Survey of Family Growth, 40
The National Survey of Latinos 2010,
    329n10
The Nation's Report Card, 98
Native Americans, 102, 238
NATO. *See* North Atlantic Treaty
    Organization
NBC/*Wall Street Journal*, 46
NCCB. *See* National Conference of
    Catholic Bishops
NCPP. *See* National Council on Public
    Polls
needy, assisting, 173–77, *174*, *175*, *176*
negative message testing, 34
NEP. *See* National Election Pool
NES. *See* American National Election
    Studies
Neuman, W. Russell, 131
New Deal, 100, 132, 152, 159, 190
Newport, Frank, 71, 149, 273, 275,
    288
news: on Internet, 110; reporting, 77,
    111–13
New York Herald, 18, 46
Neyman, Jerzy, 20

NHIS. *See* National Health Interview Survey
Nicaragua, 4, 265
Nickelodeon network, 87
Nie, Norman H., 53, 133
Niemi, Richard G., 91–92, 95, 107
900 number call-in polls, 51
Nixon, Richard, 4, 36, 254
NNSP. *See* National Network of State Polls
No Child Left Behind legislation, 122, 167
Noelle-Neumann, Elisabeth, 3, 5
nonattitudes, 285
non-coverage bias, 280
nonprobability sampling, 59, 61, 65, 83
nonresponse bias, 19, 284, 331n5
NORC. *See* National Opinion Research Center
norms, 88; civic, 107; social, 104, 107
Norrander, Barbara, 232, 234
North, Oliver, 4
North American Free Trade Agreement, 267
North Atlantic Treaty Organization (NATO), 262, 267
NRA. *See* National Rifle Association
nuclear weapons, 121–22, 246, 250
Nunn, Clyde A., 125
nytimes.com, 268

Obama, Barack: candidacy of, 22, 38, 47, 189, 206, 259, 286–87; health care plan of, 15, 44, 132, 171–73; polls on, 83, 154–55, 215, 319n5; presidency of, 51, 161–62, 232; social security and, 161–62
officeholders, use of polls by, 36–39
Ohio 2004 vote, 55
Oldendick, Robert W., 154
O'Neill, Harry W., 278–79
open-ended questions, 67–68
Operation Desert Storm, 47, 147
Opinion Research Corporation, 24

Page, Benjamin I., 9–10, 162, 173, 177, 190, 192, 218, 223, 226, 236, 245, 254, 289–90, 290

Palin, Sarah, 47
paper-and-pencil interviewing, 59
parental education, 98–99
parent *v.* student partisanship, 91–92, 92
Parker, Suzanne, 256–57
Parsons, Talcott, 97
partisanship, 91–92, 92
party identification, 139–44, 140, 141, 143, 212; of African Americans, 109; Internet and, 157
party polarization, 15
Passell, Jeffrey, 324n5
passivity, 95–97
Pathfinder, 18
Patient Protection and Affordable Care Act of 2010, 11, 15, 132, 154, 167–68, 171, 319n6
Patterson, Kelly D., 147
Patterson, Thomas E., 113–14, 115
peace, and war, 253–57
peacekeeping, 260–61, 263–65
Pearl Harbor, 245
peer influence, 97, 106–8
Penn and Schoen firm, 37
period effects, 323n2
Perot, Ross, 23nb
Perry, Rick, 182
Persian Gulf War, 44, 50, 53, 106, 255–57, 260, 265
personalization, 90
Personal Responsibility and Reconciliation Act of 1996, 176
Petri, Thomas E., 34
Pew Center for Excellence in Journalism, 111, 116
Pew Center for the People and the Press, 67, 110, 116, 122, 128, 211, 331n4
Pew Hispanic Center, 211, 329n10
Pew Research Center, 83, 112, 116, 122, 154–55, 281
Piereson, James, 126–27
pilot investigations, 61
PIPA. *See* Program on International Policy Attitudes
Pittsburgh Survey, 20
Plato, 3

Pledge of Allegiance, 94, 95
Plessy v. Ferguson, 189
Plouffe, David, 38
podcasts, 110
polarization, political, 15
political authority, 90
The Political Beliefs of Americans: A Study of Public Opinion (Free and Cantril, H.), 14
political campaigns, 31–35
political interest, and gender, *106*
political knowledge: consequences of, 129; early research on, 118–20, *119*; education and, 128–29; group differences in, 127–29; later research on, 120–23, *123*; Supreme Court and, 117, 121, 144, 146, 248
political learning, of children and adolescents, 89–93
political orientations, 131–32, 155–57; confidence in governmental institutions and, 144–47, *145*, *146*, *147*; ideologies and, 132–39, *135*, *136*, *138*; individual rights, 225; party identification and, 109, 139–44, *140*, *141*, *143*, 157, *212*; power of government and, 151–55, *153*; trust in government, 147–51, *148*, *150*, 325n10
political socialization, 105–8; schools and, 89–99
politicization, 89
polling industry, 5, 35; Internet and, 16, 26–27, 55, 58, 82–83; origins of, 17–19; technological developments in, 276–82
Polling Matters (Newport), 288
polls: benchmark, 32; Bush, G. W.'s, use of, 38; call-in, 51–52, 275; of Census Bureau, 42–43, 319n10; Clinton, B.'s, use of, 37–38; data from, 11–12; deliberative opinion, 13–14, *16*, 317n3; exit, 47–49, 286–87, 319n12; government agencies' use of, 39; of local governments, 43–44; media use of, 46–47; on Obama, 83, 154–55, 215, 319n5; officeholders' use of, 36–39; of

presidential approval ratings, 49–51, *50*, 320n13; by presidential incumbents, 36–38; pseudo-polls, 33–35, 275–76, 331n3; public opinions on, 274–75; push, 33–34, 276, 319n3; Reagan's use of, 12, 37; of state governments, 43; straw, 18, 27; tracking, 32–33
population coverage, 80
populations of interest, 58–59
portability, 281
Postal Service, U.S., 62, *63*
post-Vietnam syndrome, 254
Pregnancy Risk Assessment Monitoring System, 43
presidential approval ratings, polls of, 49–51, *50*, 320n13
presidential elections, 19–20; gender gap in, 142; of 1948, 21–24; after 1948, 24–25
presidential incumbents, polls by, 36–38
Presser, Stanley, 70, 78, 81, 283, 321n8
Prewitt, Kenneth, 94
primacy effect, 76
priming, 111, 113
print media, *21*
prisons, 221–23, *222*
privacy rights, 258, 274
private insurance, 169–70, *170*, 298
private sector, 7
probability sampling, 59, 61, 65, 83
probability theory, 321n5
pro-choice respondents, 227
Program on International Policy Attitudes (PIPA), 269
pro-life respondents, 227
Protestantism, 102, 231
protest movements, of 1960s, 109
Prothro, James W., 124, 128
pseudo-polls, 33–35, 275–76, 331n3
psychology, 14, 88–90, 109; social, 52
Public Agenda Organization, 243
public interest, 7
public opinion: defining, 4–9; importance of, 9–12; measuring, 57–84; public judgment *v.*, 12–14; research challenges of, 273–90;

scientific study of, 19–21. *See also* American public opinions
Public Opinion Quarterly, 26–27, 118, 280, 284
The Public Perspective, 273
public policy, 9, 45, 57
punishment, 221–23, *222*
purposive studies, 61
Push Poll Disclosure Act of 2007, 34
push polls, 33–34, 276, 319n3
push questions, 34

Al Qaeda, 258–59
questionnaires: design of, 21, 67–79; length of, 80–81; self-administered, 58, *63*
questions: closed-ended and open-ended, 67–68; filter, 68–69, *69*; multipart, *75*; push, 34

race relations, 54
racial issues: affirmative action, 194–98, *197, 198*; biological racism, 189–90; black candidate for president, 206, *206*; civil rights movement, 189, 205, 208–9, *209*; desegregation, 190–93, 328n2; fair employment practices, *193*, 193–94, *194*; government aid to minority groups, 198–202, *199, 200, 201*; government spending on, 202–5, *203, 204, 205*; influence of Hispanic Americans, 211–13, *212*; interracial marriage, 209–10, *210*; racism, 100, 125, 214; slavery, 100, *207*, 207–8, *208*
rally-round-the-flag effect, 256
random-digit dialing (RDD), 25–26, 62–65, 80–81, 278, 280–81, 318n4, 321n4
Random Digit Dialing: Lowering the Cost of Victimization Surveys (Tuchfarber and Klecka), 320n2
random samples, simple and systematic, 60
ranking format, *75*
ranking scales, 76
rating format, *75*

rating scales, 75–76
RDD. *See* random-digit dialing
Reagan, Ronald: candidacy of, 105, 109, 123n2, 135, 219, 330n2; presidency of, 148–49, 152, 255; use of polls by, 12, 37
recency effect, 76
Reconstruction, 132
refusal rates, 282–83, 331n5
Regents of the University of California v. Bakke, 195
rehabilitation, 222
reliability, 273
religion: as source of opinions, 102–4; trust in, 146
religiosity, 104
representative samples, 58
Republican National Committee, 37, 38
Residential Energy Consumption Survey, 41
respondent factors, 282–86
response formats, 73–76, *74–75*
response rates, 62, 80–83, 273, 282–84
Ricci v. DeStefano, 195
Richardson, Laura, 11
rights: civil rights movement, 189, 196, 205, 208–9, *209*, 225; of homosexuals, 218, 225; individual, 225; of privacy, 258, 274
ritual, 95
Roberts, Caroline, 317n3
Robinson, Claude E., 18, 46
"Rock the Vote" series, 108, 116
Roe v. Wade, 218, 226–27
Rogoff, B., 96
Romney, Mitt, 47
Roosevelt, Franklin D., 19, 20, 36, 100, 109, 114, 248
Roper, Elmo, 20, 24, 46
Roper Center, 55, 187, 254
Roscho, Bernard, 163
Rosenau, James N., 254
Rousseau, Jean-Jacques, 3
Rudman, Warren, 4

Saad, Lydia K., 231
Sabato, Larry, 48

St. Louis Republic, 18

samples: modified area, 22; random samples, simple and systematic, 60; representative, 58; size of, 66–67; stratified, 60, 62, *63*

sampling, 21, 64–65; address-based, 62, *63*, 65, 80; cluster, 61, *63*; errors in, 22, 61, 65–66, 278, 318n1, 321n5; frames, 19; methods of, 46; probability and nonprobability, 59, 61, 65, 83; simple random, 60

schemas, 267

Schlozman, Kay Lehman, 105

Schneider, William, 144, 147–48, 213

schools: behaviors, 97–99; busing, 191–92; political socialization and, 89–99

Schuman, Howard, 69, 78, 189, 213–14

Science (magazine), 318n1

Scripps Howard Foundation, 320n1

Sears, David O., 192

self-administered questionnaires, 58, *63*

self-interviewing, computer-assisted, 278

self-selection, 51, 64, 82, 108, 330n2

September 11, 2001, terrorist attacks, 50, 147, 149, 245–48, 268, 323n2, 323n5

Settle, Jaime E., 107

seven-point forced-choice format, *74*, *75*

sexual assault, 220–21

Shapiro, Robert Y., 9–10, 36, 162, 173, 176, 177, 190, 192, 218, 223, 226, 236, 245, 254, 255, 289–90

Sheatsley, Paul B., 118, 120, 190

Shuttles, Charles D., 280–81

Sigel, Roberta, 88

Sigelman, Lee, 100–101

Silver, Brian D., 323n5

Simon, Rita James, 5

simple random sampling (SRS), 60

Singer, Eleanor, 81, 283

SIPP. *See* Survey of Income and Program Participation

situationalists, 227

Skocpol, Theda, 319n6

slavery, 100, *207*, 207–8, *208*

Smith, Ben, 319n5

Smith, Tom W., 54, 70, 71

Snowe, Olympia, 11

social interaction, interviewing as, 285

socialization, 115; political, 89–99, 105–8

social norms, 104, 107

social psychology, 52

Social Science Research Council, 22, 286–87

social security: African Americans and, 183; Bush, G. W., and, 161; Obama and, 161–62; public opinions on, 161–65, *162*, *164–65*, 168, 176, 185, 327n2

Social Security Act of 1935, 162

social-welfare issues, public opinion on, 159–87; assisting needy, 173–77, *174*, *175*, *176*; education, 165–67, *166*, *167*; environment, 177–82, *178*, *179–81*; global warming, 182–83; group differences in attitudes, 183–86, *184*; health care, 167–73, *168*, *169*, *170*, *172*, 327n4; social security, 161–65, *162*, *164–65*, 168, 176, 185, 327n2

socioeconomic issues, 88, 90, 94, 96–99, 108

Somalia operation, 260–61, 263

Sourcebook of Criminal Justice Statistics, 243

sources of opinions: education, 93–99; ethnic identity, 99–102, 115; gender, 105–6; generational influences, 108–10; media influences, 110–15; peer influence, 97, 106–8; political learning, of children and adolescents, 89–93; religion, 102–4

South Carolina State Survey, 43, *63*

Spanish language usage, 99, 101

Speer, Leslie K., 192

spin control, 114–15

SRC. *See* Survey Research Center

SRS. *See* simple random sampling

state governments, polls of, 43

stem cell research, 44–45, 242
Stimson, James A., 207, 217–18
Stoker, Laura, 109
Stokes, Donald E., 9
Stonewall riots, 232
Stouffer, Samuel A., 124–25, 127, 129
stratified samples, 60, 62, *63*
straw polls, 18, 27
Sturgis, Patrick, 317n3
Substance Abuse and Mental Health
    Services Administration, 41
Sudman, Seymour, 66
suffrage, universal, for men, 93
Sullivan, John L., 126–27
superpower status, of U.S., 245–46
support for U.S. active role in world,
    247
Supreme Court, U.S.: Census Bureau
    and, 42; political knowledge and,
    117, 121, 144, 146, 248; rulings of,
    132, 189–91, 195, 223–26, 238, 241
Suro, Roberto, 324n5
Survey of Consumer Attitudes, 81, 283
Survey of Consumer Finances, 41
Survey of Income and Program
    Participation (SIPP), 40, 83
survey research, 19–21
Survey Research (newsletter), 318n5
Survey Research Center (SRC), 24, 25
surveys: academic, 24–25, 31;
    continuous monitoring, 53; data
    collection modes by, 58; by e-mail,
    80; on Internet, 277, 322n15; length
    of, 80–81; by mail, *63*, 79, 83,
    322n12. *See also specific surveys*
*Surveys by Telephone: A National
    Comparison with Personal Interviews*
    (Groves and Kahn), 320n2
Survey USA, 283
*Swann v. Charlotte-Mecklenburg School
    District*, 191
systematic random samples, 60

Taliban faction, 246, 258–59
tax system, 76–77, 100
Taylor, Humphrey, 82
TDE. *See* touchtone data entry

Teamsters Union, 115
Tea Party movement, 154, 328n8
technological developments, in polling
    industry, 276–82
Tedin, Kent L., 5
telemarketing, 33, 276, 283, 331n3,
    331n5
Telemarketing Consumer Fraud and
    Abuse Prevention Act of 1994,
    331n3, 331n6
Telephone Consumer Protection Act of
    1991, 320n3
telephones: answering machines
    for, 278–79, 283–84, 331n5; cell
    phones, 62, 81–82; computer-
    assisted interviewing by, 26; CPO
    households, *63*, 81, 279–80; data
    collection by, 25–26; interviewing
    by, 25–26, 58, 62–64, *63*, 79, 278–
    79; landline, 25, 81–82, 278–81,
    288, 318n4, 331n4
television advertisements, 33, 65
Terhanian, George, 82
terrorism: Bush, G. W., and, 246, 257–
    59; September 11, 2001, attacks,
    50, 147, 149, 245–48, 268, 323n2,
    323n5; wars in Afghanistan and Iraq
    and, 257–60
text banners, 65
thechicagocouncil.org, 269
Thornburgh, Richard, 170
Thurmond, Strom, 119
Times-Picayune, 22
tolerance, 124–28, *125*; of
    homosexuality, 126, *126*, 234
tone, of wording, 70–71, 322
Torney, Judith V., 90, 95
touchtone data entry (TDE), 26
tracking polls, 32–33
trade magazines, 46
Traugott, Michael W., 318n3, 319n12
traumatic *v.* elective abortions, 227
trial heats, 47
trickle up effect, 88
Trop v. Dulles, 223
Truman, Harry S, 21, 36, 118, 261, 286
Trump, Donald, 52

trust: in government, 147–51, *148, 150,* 325n10; in religion, 146
Tuchfarber, Alfred J., 320n2, 322n13
Tuckel, Peter, 278–79
Twitter, 110, 320n1

uncontrolled instrument distribution, 64
United Nations, 52, 119, 246, 250–52, 263–64
United States (U.S.): Bureau of Justice Statistics, 40; Census Bureau, 20, 25, 39–40, 42–43, 211, 318n4, 319n10; Constitution, 17, 42, 121, 159, 289; defense policy, 253–61, *259;* democracy in, 3–16; Department of Agriculture, 20–21, 40; Department of Commerce, 25, 43, 319n8; Department of Defense, 11; Department of Education, 39, 98; Department of Health and Human Services, 40, 319n7; Energy Information Administration, 41; foreign policy, 245–53, *247, 251, 252,* 261–68, *262;* House of Representatives, 42, 119, 121, 128, 135, 154; Information Agency, 24; Postal Service, 62, *63;* superpower status of, 245–46; support for active role in world, *247;* Supreme Court, 42, 117, 121, 132, 144, 146, 189–91, 195, 223–26, 238, 241, 248
univariate descriptions, 79
universal suffrage, for men, 93
U.S. *See* United States
USA Today, 6, 52, 268, 293
usatoday.com, 268
US Count Votes, 319n12

valence issues, 8, 328n1
validity, 273
Vandenberg, Arthur H., 248
Van Etten, Peter, 44
Verba, Sidney, 105, 255
verbal language, 79
Vietnam War, 4, 36, 100, 149, 218, 249, 253–55, 263, 265

Virginia Tech shootings, 236
visual cues, 81
visual images, 79
VNS. *See* Voter News Service
voice recognition entry (VRE), 26
The Voter Decides (Campbell, A., et al.), 53
voter groups, 32
Voter News Service (VNS), 48
Votewatch, 55
voting behavior, 87–89, 120–23
VRE. *See* voice recognition entry

war, and peace, 253–57
War Powers Resolution, 260
Washington, George, 93, 246
washingtonpost.com, 268
Watergate scandal, 91, 121, 148–49, 218, 323n2
weapons of mass destruction (WMD), 252, 258
Webster, Carol, 91
Web surveys, 277, 322n15
Weissberg, Robert, 5, 10
Welch, Michael R., 103
Welch, Susan, 100–101
welfare. *See* social-welfare issues
Wilcox, Clyde, 227–28, 231, 232, 234
Williams, J. Allen, 125
Wilmington Morning News, 22
Wilson, Woodrow, 245
Wirthlin, Richard, 12, 37
Wirthlin Group, 44
Wise, David, 5
Witt, G. Evans, 33
WMD. *See* weapons of mass destruction
Wofford, Harrison, 170
Wolak, Jennifer, 92
wording, tone of, 70–71, 322n9
Works Progress Administration, 20
World War I, 245, 261
World War II, 21, 24, 36, 39, 111

Yankelovich, Daniel, 12, 225
yes/no format, *74*
You-Gov/Polimetrix, 83
YouTube, 320n1

About the Authors

Barbara A. Bardes is professor *emeriti* of political science at the University of Cincinnati. She has served in faculty and decanal positions at Loyola University of Chicago and at the University of Cincinnati. She earned her PhD at the University of Cincinnati. Her published books include *American Government and Politics Today 2010–2011* (with Schmidt and Shelley), *Declarations of Independence: Women and Political Power in 19th Century American Novels* (with Gossett), and *Thinking about Public Policy* (with Dubnick). Her research interests center on public opinion and foreign policy and women and politics.

Robert W. Oldendick is professor of political science and the director of the Institute for Public Service and Policy Research at the University of South Carolina. He received his PhD from the University of Cincinnati, where he worked for fifteen years in the University's Institute for Policy Research before moving to South Carolina. He has more than thirty-five years experience in the field of survey research and public opinion and has served as principal investigator or project manager on more than two hundred and fifty survey-based projects. He is the author of numerous articles on survey research methodology, including procedures for sample selection in telephone surveys, methods of respondent selection within households, and the effects of question wording and format on responses to survey questions.